# RADICAL SCHOOL REFORM
*Critique and Alternatives*

3713
T 855

Library of Congress Catalog Card No. 72-13644

First Printing

Published simultaneously in Canada
by Little, Brown & Company (Canada) Limited

Printed in the United States of America

# RADICAL SCHOOL REFORM

## Critique and Alternatives

Edited by

### Cornelius J. Troost
University of California, Los Angeles

Foreword by Sidney Hook

Little, Brown and Company
Boston

*To my love, Martha*

# FOREWORD

No one in the field of medicine assumes that when recommended treatment is rejected as inadequate, or even exposed as quackery, the critic is denying the existence of the disease or claiming that he himself has the solution in hand. In the field of education, however, those who critically scrutinize proposals to reform our schools and conclude by rejecting their claims as unfounded, or as making a bad situation worse, are often taxed with being defenders of the status quo. Sometimes they are denounced as mere apologists of the existing educational order refusing to see any merit in the new ways or any defect in the old.

Directed to the contributors of this book, such rejoinders would be very wide of the mark. All are critics of one or another aspect of our school system from the primary to the postgraduate level. Some have been associated with the movement of progressive education virtually since its inception. All would accept John Dewey's dictum that the currents of change in modern education are so many and swift that there is no such thing as the status quo, that the basic issues arise from decisions concerning the direction in which to move. Move we must, but not every move, whether radical or not, is a move in the right direction.

Common to all these contributors is the belief that despite very serious shortcomings the educational system of the United States is not beyond redemption, but that these shortcomings are not being met by the movement currently characterizing itself as "radical school reform." They further agree that the deficiencies in learning and in attitude in American schools are what they are in light of present-day needs and possibilities, not in comparison with past achievements. Were we to compare our schools only with those of the past, we would have cause for congratulation. Without subscribing to the absurd view that the school at any level is a political community, the contributors accept the centrality of democratic values in education and the plurality of its institutional forms. They consequently reject the elitist position that liberal education is for a select few and the masses should receive an education primarily to help them perform their functions more efficiently and make their leisure time less tedious.

Underlying many criticisms of the radical school reformers is the judgment that they have systematically slighted the intellectual content of education. Learning can be fun but not all fun and fooling around result in learning. Fun and fooling around have a place in education both intrinsically and instrumentally, just as physical exercise, fresh air, and wholesome food have a place during the school day. But they cannot be permitted to crowd out learning in the classroom. Education, of course, is more than imparting knowledge. It is just as much, perhaps more, a matter of developing attitudes, encouraging habits of thought and evaluation, and broadening and deepening sensitivity to other human beings.

Surely, it may be objected, one can hardly fault the radical school reformers for neglecting the development of attitudes and the life of emotion. Do they not strongly stress affective experience? Do they not glorify the values of freedom, spontaneity, and self-expression? They do—but in a manner that raises grave doubts as to their educational validity. For without intellectual awareness of the ways in which our actions affect others, our emotions become self-centered. Everything is then measured by the yardsticks of what gives *us* pleasure or pain, of what eases *our* path or places hurdles in it. Without intellectual discipline and understanding of our society and its history, how can students learn that our freedom is always paid for by some restraints upon the freedom of others who might move to prevent us from enjoying our specific freedoms, and vice versa? How can they learn the relation between rights and responsibilities? "Freedom" has become a shibboleth among the radical school reformers. But do we want "freedom" without thoughtfulness, without measure, without concern or respect for the rights of others? How do we distinguish between the freedom of rational dissent, of courageous challenge to power, and the freedom of ruthless egoism, of unconcern with the desperate need of others?

It is not their failure to appreciate the importance of values that evokes criticism of the radical school reformers but their individualization of values to a point where the values of the democratic community are neglected, slighted, and sometimes violated. Intellectual sophistication for radical school reformers is manifested only by dissent and rejection of American culture. To assent to any basic institution of the society, to any of its traditional ideals, to its historic achievements, regardless of the grounds of assent, is to be "square," a victim of middle-class prejudice. Patriotism, the martial virtues that are not identical with military virtues, a sense of continuity with, and obligation toward, those who suffered in the past to ensure a happier and freer America in the present are scorned as masks of aggression or as empty of content as the concepts of "civic virtue" and the "public good."

But how can values, democratic values and the value of democracy both as a political form of government and a way of life, be taught without imposition and indoctrination? The proponents of radical school reform justify their practices of indoctrination on the ground that all teaching is indoctrination. They pride themselves on doing openly and consciously what all others, including their critics, allegedly do just as wholeheartedly, even if unconsciously.

If all teaching entails indoctrination, what would the opposite of indoctrination be? Nonteaching? Ordinary English usage requires a distinction between teaching that indoctrinates and teaching, however rare, that does not. Even if all teachers indoctrinated, it would still be necessary to differentiate conceptually between indoctrination and its absence. Otherwise we could not even identify indoctrination. Even if all men were dishonest, there would still be a conceptual difference in the meanings of "honesty" and "dishonesty."

To deny that teaching without indoctrination is possible is like denying that objectivity is possible. It would be like obliterating the distinction between truth and falsity, history and fiction. Indoctrination is the mode of teaching that induces the acceptance of beliefs by nonrational or irrational means or both. Teaching is free of indoctrination when it induces the acceptance of beliefs by rational means.

The crucial distinction here is the presence or absence of rational means or methods in teaching. Some have objected that teaching students to be rational—to make valid inferences, assess evidence, detect formal and material fallacies, uncover ambiguities—is itself an exercise in indoctrination, a form of imposition on them. It is hard to make sense of this position. Reason or intelligence is self-critical. At most one can say that we make a choice between teaching by indoctrination and not, just as we make a choice between lying and telling the truth. But to choose is not ipso facto to indoctrinate. Nonetheless democratic values are taught to children by nonrational means and methods, and so are being taught by indoctrination. Does this not confirm the radical school reformer's claim that *all* teaching is and should be by its very nature indoctrination?

Not at all. Examine first knowledge of fact and then knowledge of values. Children must be taught the multiplication tables when they are quite young and not yet able to read or understand *Principia Mathematica* by Russell and Whitehead, which offers a proof that

2 + 2 = 4. Learning the tables cannot be postponed until they understand the proof. They therefore acquire knowledge of these tables by rote memory, through song and verse, i.e., by nonrational methods. Children may be conditioned by nonrational methods to learn many other things. But this indoctrination is educationally permissible only, and only if, at the same time we are developing within the child his powers of intelligence to their fullest measure. When the child has reached his full maturity as a youth, he will then have the critical grasp, skills, and knowledge to test and check the validity of the multiplication tables himself. No reasonable objection can be made to nonrational methods (not irrational methods) of developing some beliefs about facts in some areas, provided the teacher recognizes his moral obligation to bring the student to critical logical maturity.

We turn now to values. Is it objectionable indoctrination to develop within students a positive attitude toward keeping one's promises, telling the truth, avoiding cruelty, helping the weak and those in distress, respecting the rights of others, learning to live with failure or defeat, courage and coolness under stress, good manners and cleanliness? Here, too, we cannot wait for the child to become a mature citizen and postpone moral education until his moral life becomes centered around this or another constellation of values. The child must learn to use a fork to spear his food and not to jab his siblings or friends long before he can understand why. The use of nonrational methods of inducing belief and concordant behavior with others at a tender age is perfectly legitimate. But, here too, and especially in this context, the teacher is morally obligated to develop among his students their rational gifts, imaginative powers, and capacities for empathetic identification to the utmost. The student will then be in a position to evaluate critically the moral ideals and social mores he has acquired as his cultural legacy. His social indoctrination will not have been blind. He will not have been molded into a conformist, conditioned forever afterward to accept the personal or social pattern of his early years. He will have acquired the capacity to think for himself and, when necessary, the courage to promulgate heresies and act on them.

This emphasis upon critical and creative intelligence differentiates those who believe in teaching the values of democracy from those radical school reformers who believe that the school must not inhibit the natural freedom of the child. It also differentiates them from those educators who espouse one or another variety of totalitarianism, for whom teaching moral values is oriented exclusively toward uncritical acceptance of the State, the Party, and the Leader.

We certainly can learn a great deal from some methods employed in rearing the young in countries like Spain, Yugoslavia, Soviet Russia, and China—learn what to avoid as well as what to adopt. Whatever the virtues of their socializing practices—using older pupils to instruct the younger, integrating students into community projects, setting models of desirable behavior—from a democratic point of view, they are far outweighed by their vices. These vices include excessive adult intervention, the politicization of the content of instruction, and, worst of all, the elimination of the critical spirit and the consequent intolerance of any deviant views on matters of concern to the present State, Party, Church, and Leader. For example, an excellent device in encouraging fluency in writing is the encouragement of students to keep diaries recording events in their homes, their circles of friends, and their community. But when these diaries are turned in for inspection and correction and then used as a means of ferreting out "antisocial" elements of the population—as has happened in totalitarian countries—their very pedagogical effectiveness becomes a threat to desirable educational experiences. Just as democracy is a middle way between despotism and anarchy, so democratic education, which stresses intelligence on behalf of compatible and cooperating freedoms, mediates between the indoctrinating techniques of totalitarianism and the undisciplined self-regarding expressions of anarchism.

Actually some desirable techniques of instruction in totalitarian countries, divorced from their political orientation, were used in American schools but gradually lost effectiveness as family and community bonds weakened. No school system can escape the dominant influence of the society in which formal education is given. However, the possibilities of redirecting and reconstructing society through education are greater in democratic societies than in any other. The schools can act for better or for worse. The confusions and fallacies of "radical school reform" are thus of great consequence, not only for the educational experience of individuals but for the political and cultural future of the community.

The follies of "radical school reform" in a few years will go the same way as the degenerate expressions of the progressive education movement in the thirties. Nonetheless the contributions of this book will retain their relevance. For in the pendular swings between the child-centered and curriculum-centered schools the tendencies here criticized will reassert themselves in new dress. Of special importance is the bearing of these tendencies on higher education. Their potential damage on the elementary and secondary levels of education is limited by the fact that the fruits of the "radical school reforms" are quickly observable wherever they are applied. Parents' concern about the educational development of their young offspring is still a brooding presence in the schools. It can explode into protest with all the greater fury for being deceived by the rhetoric and anecdotal tales of "radical school reform" writers.

On the college level, the academic fallout of radical school-reform ideology is expressed in the abolition of almost all curricular requirements. Scholastic requirements are regarded as an undemocratic imposition by an older, not necessarily wiser, generation upon the young. Here, too, the absurd is counterposed to the absurd. To reject Mr. Hutchin's prescribed program of studies and great books as the only legitimate curriculum that ensures a liberal education is one thing. To return to the cafeteria-style, all-elective curriculum system on the specious ground that each student is the best judge of his own educational needs is almost as bad. By the time the colleges work their way toward a new combination of required and elective programs based on the objective educational needs of individual students, an enormous amount of damage will have been done.

In the mansion of education, there are many rooms. Although some educational needs are common to all young men and women, others are personal and individual. Diversity of approaches and offerings based on some common requirements whose fulfillment is presupposed by any liberal education worthy of the name should be the order of the day. But we must be wary of underwriting any specific program or institutional feature as if it were a panacea for all our educational ills or the best for all students. For example, in coming years we shall hear a great deal about "universities without walls" and expanded "centers of continuing education" that will enable those who desire a certified degree to earn it by passing achievement examinations without attending any school or class of formal instruction.

This development should be welcomed not only in justice to those who were denied the opportunity of attending college or failed to exploit their opportunities when they did attend, but to meet the special needs of already highly motivated students who wish to make rapid professional progress. However, some alarming signs indicate that this excellent program for a small, special group of students is being recommended for many other groups of a quite different character. Important as they are, examinations and degrees are integral to certification but not necessarily to an education. An education acquired by self-study is feasible for those who are already highly motivated. But the arts of teaching are mainly directed toward those who are not already highly motivated. With respect to most disciplines, we can reasonably assume that most students are not sufficiently self-motivated to dispense with teachers and classrooms and the discourse of their fellows. There is a quality of great significance to the life of mind, inherent in the give and take of classroom teaching and learning and for which no surrogates can be found. Even the highly motivated student, who can learn enough by himself to pass examinations and earn a degree, can profit by rubbing his mind against the dialectic of an experienced practitioner of the Socratic method. No substitute can replace a good teacher in educating the young, and most of the young need good teachers.

Indeed, we can point to Socrates as the teacher of all reflective teachers, using a method Plato describes but does not himself exhibit in most of the wooden exchanges in his *Dialogues*. Socrates is the teacher of all reflective teachers because he defined the supreme moral virtue as intelligence, because he illustrated both in life and death that it is possible to combine a critical and ironical mind with unswerving fidelity to the ideals and necessities of our common life.

Sidney Hook
New York University

# ACKNOWLEDGMENTS

I acknowledge gratefully the benefits derived from many discussions with students in the teacher-training program at UCLA. Many of these students are very enthusiastic about free schools and open classrooms. Our exchanges of ideas, although always cordial, made me realize that an ideological gulf exists, one which involves far too much stereotyping, ignorance, and rigid adherence on all sides. Indeed, there is a blind belief in a false liberal-conservative dichotomy in education that is harmful.

I am thankful for the discussions with humanist colleagues, Thomas Robischon, Carl Weinberg, and Philip Reidford, all of whom are innocent of any errors and misinterpretations committed by me in presenting opposing viewpoints. Professor Robischon was especially helpful in clarifying theoretical features of the radical school-reform movement.

My gratitude must be extended to George Kneller, John McNeil, Evan Keislar, M. C. Wittrock, and Gary Fenstermacher, colleagues who generously discussed various aspects of humanistic education with me. On discipline problems I was very fortunate to have access to the wisdom of Lawrence Vredevoe. Bruce Joyce of Teachers College, Columbia University, was kind enough to review the initial manuscript and comment helpfully on it. I am grateful, too, for Professor Joyce's moral support.

To John Holt I am especially thankful. His visit to UCLA enabled me to argue some points with him and the unsatisfactory nature of his arguments inspired me to put forward my case. I was also the beneficiary of an invitation to the Center for the Study of Democratic Institutions, where the topic of radical school reform was discussed extensively with Robert Maynard Hutchins and Donald McDonald. To them I am exceedingly thankful.

It was my good fortune to be surrounded by many experimental schools and classrooms. I am indebted to the many school personnel who allowed me to visit and take notes. My own students who visited free schools and open classrooms provided a wealth of anecdotal reports that were extremely fruitful.

Finally, I am grateful to our Communications Processing Center. They did an excellent job of typing the manuscript and tolerated the changes I made along the way.

# CONTENTS

"IN SUCH A STATE OF SOCIETY (A STATE OF DEMOCRATIC ANARCHY) THE MASTER FEARS AND FLATTERS HIS STUDENTS, AND THE STUDENTS DE-SPISE THEIR MASTERS AND TUTORS; YOUNG AND OLD ARE ALIKE; AND THE YOUNG MAN IS ON A LEVEL WITH THE OLDER, AND THE OLDER MEN CONDESCEND TO THE YOUNG AND ARE FULL OF PLEASANTRY AND GAIETY; THEY ARE BOTH TO BE THOUGHT MOROSE AND AUTHORITATIVE, AND THEREFORE THEY ADOPT THE MANNERS OF THE YOUNG . . . "

PLATO

*THE REPUBLIC*, BOOK VIII

# INTRODUCTION

This book expresses several purposes of the editor. First, it contains an extensive critique of the radical school-reform movement. Second, it presents essays written by scholars whose values, beliefs, and arguments criticize the established order in education but provide a basis for intelligent reform. These scholars consider teacher authority, discipline, structured curricula, "subject matter," moral education, and reflective thinking essential to education in our American democracy. Third, several scholars make a case for universal moral principles and for the teacher as a "character educator," the need for teacher authority in the classroom, and the importance of reason in disputes about values. Finally, it provides several articles dealing with the problem of integrating humanistic values and techniques into curriculum models that retain a systematic, rational, and sometimes technological character.

There would be no need for this book were it not for the bandwagon atmosphere surrounding the free-school and open-classroom movement. As a fashion it has swept along, relatively untouched by scholarly criticism, leaving behind a graveyard of unsuccessful experiments. No rigorous studies of these experiments have been carried out to date, however, so enthusiasm for unstructured learning continues to spread. A critical analysis of the philosophy, policies, and methods of the radical reformers is needed with more rigorous evaluations to determine the nature and extent of the educational payoff in order to compare this payoff with that of other programs.

I have observed many open classrooms and seen extensive anecdotal reports from students studying at least twenty-five experimental schools and classrooms in Los Angeles and Santa Barbara. I have had lengthy discussions with radical educators, including vigorous talks with John Holt and Robert M. Hutchins. Distilled from these experiences is the belief that credulity and religiosity are very large elements in the movement. Most radical reformers are diligently antiintellectual, antiauthoritarian, and determined to set children free from what they characterize as "oppression." Furthermore, they oppose any rigorous assessment of what they are doing.

Free-school and open-classroom proponents call themselves facilitators and humanists. They are infatuated with John Dewey's idea of learning by doing and with the laissez-faire classroom. As we shall learn from Sidney Hook in Part 1, their version of learning by doing bears little resemblance to Dewey's educational philosophy. Indeed, I believe that Dewey would be repelled by the violence, obscenity, and exploitation common to many classrooms organized by those who invoke his name.

The noise, confusion, disrespect, and overt rebelliousness observed in free schools and open classrooms result in part from the adult-free school environment. The school environment simply reinforces certain negative features of American family life. The breakdown of the American family as socializing agent must be counterbalanced by more emphasis on socialization by the school. Free schools and open classrooms offer socialization in precisely the opposite direction: into a youth culture or counter-culture ethos with its inevitably disintegrating consequences for American democracy.

The eminent Cornell psychologist, Urie Bronfenbrenner, in his book *Two Worlds of Childhood: U.S. and U.S.S.R.*, discusses the substantial contrast between the childrearing practices of these two cultures. Russians are far more involved with their children, more demonstrative in affection, and much more concerned with discipline. American parents, since World War II, have relinquished responsibility for childrearing. They provide them with no adult models and with little of the love, physical contact, and discipline needed for developing a healthy personality and self-discipline. Years ago aunts, uncles, neighbors, older brothers and sisters, teachers, and especially parents cared about every aspect of a child's life—today there is little caring and an abyss of "freedom" in which to flounder.

Professor Bronfenbrenner found that character education in the United States disappeared in modern times. Today good citizenship, patriotism, orderliness, good manners, and cleanliness are ridiculed as old fashioned. The absence of adult values in the child's world is quickly filled by the peer group, of course. The desire to belong becomes a desperate search for many youths in a troubled, age-segregated culture. Along the way lies aggressive antisocial behavior, expressed by juvenile delinquency, drug abuses, sexual excesses, political extremism, and hippyism.

Isolated from adults, children are subjected to the powerful influence of television and tabloid sensationalism. The twin stimuli of sex and violence in our society are very great. The work of Albert Bandura on the effects of these media on antisocial behavior of children is worth careful consideration. Bronfenbrenner has found that only one country has youth who are as prone to antisocial behavior as those in America—England. England has somewhat less antisocial behavior than the United States, but it alone parallels the American phenomenon of parental disinvolvement and lack of affection.

In Part 4 of this book is a set of recommendations by Bronfenbrenner. The sociological background provided by his work surely bears very strongly upon our own theme. The free-school and open-classroom movement is designed precisely to remove adult models from the schools. Free-school advocates expressly desire to promote nonintervention in the lives of children, a policy directly conflicting with Bronfenbrenner's recommendations. This policy should cause deep concern, if Bronfenbrenner's thesis is correct.

The potential for developing age-segregated peer-group loyalties, anarchistic thinking, and involvement in thrill-seeking behavior related to drugs, sex, violence, and crime is greatly enhanced by the free-school and open-classroom movement. Bertrand Russell warned that progressive education in its extreme form will produce anarchists who are impatient of the restraints of social life. In a free society every right necessarily implies duties, for unless I carry out my duties, your rights are useless. Public standards of morality, some social consensus and constructive cooperation are essential to the functioning of our democracy. In a very complex technological-industrial order, Russell observes, individualism, although necessarily important, must be controlled more than it once was. We must not become a herd, but we must also avoid the extreme of "doing your own thing," a system that inevitably violates the rights and interests of others who get in the way of "the things to be done."

John Dewey's criticism of the old Progressive Education Movement, in his book *Experience and Education*, applies perfectly well to the contemporaneous neo-progressive, radical-school reform movement. Today's radical movement did not materialize as abruptly as it seems.

By the end of the nineteenth century the American system of public education was sharply criticized for its shortcomings. One of the earliest critics was a physician, Joseph Rice. As he traveled around visiting many schools, Rice found overcrowded classes, ineffective teachers, corrupt political influence, constant use of corporal punishment, poor facilities, and outdated curricula, materials, and texts. The dropout problem was very serious.[1]

Over the years critics like John Dewey, William Kilpatrick, and George Counts brought the undemocratic nature of the schools to the public attention. The classical curriculum and the concept of an intellectual elite came under heavy attack, and vocational education within a liberal perspective began making progress.

Early in this century there emerged a reform movement destined to give rise to continuing controversy—the Progressive Education Movement. It was a combination of a response to the austere, highly disciplined educational process of the previous century, and radical views of what the ends of education should be.

The progressives found their values and beliefs in the writings of Jean Jacques Rousseau, the French apostle of naturalism in education. Viewing the child as naturally good and adult authority as repressive and even evil, the progressives sought to free children from the institutional restraints causing so much unhappiness. Kilpatrick, Childs, Hullfish, Washburne, Rugg, and Counts were strong advocates of progressivism. Dewey's stress on learning by doing was the principle pedagogical theory of the movement. Life adjustment and vocational education were favored by some of the progressives. John Dewey, however, was extremely critical of the fatuous excesses of the movement, as Sidney Hook points out in Part 1 of this volume.

There were actually two factions among the old progressives: the naturalists and the Science of Education school. The former, symbolized by Kilpatrick, were very interested in allowing children to direct their own learning, as they saw their own needs, in a very natural manner. Not only should children determine *what* they will learn, they should determine *how* and *when* they will learn it.

If the naturalists emphasized student interests and self-direction, the Science of Education (Thorndike, et al.) faction stressed teacher authority (in terms of knowledge and experience), teacher-directed instruction, a structured curriculum, and correct responses. Obviously the orientation, methodology, and practical consequences of these two factions were in sharp opposition.

Despite their own house conflicts, these two schools of thought greatly influenced American education. The old progressive movement never succeeded in implementing its ideas and ideals on a wide scale. It received its obituary notice from Lawrence Cremin in his *The Transformation of the Schools.*[2] Cremin chose the year 1956 for its demise, and shortly afterward the Sputnik era began. Nonetheless it is clear today that the dominant ideas of the old progressivism are still alive in the neo-progressive open-classroom movement, but in a much debased form.

When the Great Depression of the early thirties created serious doubts about the capitalist philosophy, the Social Reconstructionists moved into the vacuum, offering theories for an education that involved indoctrination critical of our social institutions at every level in order to facilitate social and political change. They said that if capitalism and the protestant ethic are defective they must be discarded; a cooperative ethic, the principle of equality, scientific problem solving, and democratic living must become the dominant values in the classroom.

Boyd Bode, a colleague of John Dewey, judged these proposals to be an effort to indoctrinate children in liberal, left-wing philosophy. The American people were in no mood in the 1930s to adopt a left-wing philosophy, so the entire movement died away. Social Reconstructionism, however, never really died in intellectual circles—the schools (and schools of education) are still battlegrounds for these conflicting philosophies.

The years following World War II saw the development of the cold war, a global stalemate still in progress. American education responded to Sputnik with a tremendous stress on science, mathematics, and foreign languages. Art, music, and literature suffered de-emphasis as we attempted to "catch up" with the Russians.

The Science of Education movement has had an upward swing since World War II. It is still climbing. This rise is guaranteed by the growth of educational technology, educational research, and increasing specialization. In the curriculum, academic subjects and fierce competition for high grades have become the vogue, while a college education rapidly has become a necessity for upward mobility.

During the sixties the cultural bonds of American society weakened as a counter-culture emerged, Vietnam became a deeply divisive issue, religion decayed, and many symptoms of confusion and moral drift appeared. The time was ripe not only for "anti-imperialist" forces like Students for a Democratic Society (SDS), but for the rebirth of educational doctrines consonant with the antiauthoritarian drumbeat of the times.

So the radical school-reform movement arose, having as one of its chief inspirations the thoughts of utopian anarchists. The creation of a new social order is foremost in the minds of writers like John Holt, Paul Goodman, and Ivan Illich. They deplore the evils of capitalism and wish to promote egalitarian values that could eventually lead to the dismantling of many institutions in our society. The new progressives, in developing such a social philosophy, get much support from the Human Potential Movement and the New Left.

As one reads the works of Herbert Kohl, John Holt, Jonathan Kozol, Charles Silberman, Carl Rogers, and Ivan Illich, it is possible to derive the following main points:

1. American schools are moribund, repressive, authoritarian places.
2. Children are bored and unhappy with their educational experiences.
3. Education today is irrelevant and outmoded.
4. Children are naturally good—if left to their own devices, they will grow to be virtuous, self-actualizing beings.
5. The objectives of education should be derived from the needs of the learners.
6. Egalitarian values should permeate the curriculum.
7. Humanistic personal values should prevail: self-respect, self-reliance, personal freedom, self-fulfillment.
8. The teacher must be nondirective and nonjudgmental.
9. Honesty, fairness, moral rectitude (character), and high intellectual achievement are less important than private choice, gregariousness, and moral relativity.
10. Knowledge, especially factual knowledge, is undependable because it evolves at too fast a rate.
11. "Learning how to learn" must be the principal cognitive goal of education.
12. Classroom decisions should follow democratic procedures.
13. Feelings and emotions are more important than intellectual skills and knowledge.
14. Peer motivation is preferred to any other type.

Notice the pattern here—the radical neo-progressives take the relatively antiintellectual, egalitarian stand of their ideological ancestors of the twenties and thirties. They want a "relevant," practical education, and they do indeed favor criticism of the established social institutions. Today's progressives, however, are far more fanatical and influential than their forerunners. Large foundations provide funding and professional organizations pour forth the propaganda necessary for the growth and development of the movement.

To restore some intellectual balance to the arena of education, especially in the foundations courses, let us examine the conflicts that arise between radical values, assumptions, and beliefs and those implicit in the collected readings herein. A few points of opposition are:

1. Romantic views of nature and human freedom are inadequate foundations for teaching and learning in a complex modern society.
2. American education is not nearly as bad as is claimed by the radicals.

3. A higher, autonomous moral sense cannot develop without full participation by the teacher as a moral model, a developer of sound habits, and an encourager of rational analysis and justification of moral decisions.
4. Strong adult models are essential for the normal psychological and social development of every child.
5. The knowledge, skills, and values needed to sustain a technologically based culture require a structured curriculum and teachers who are authoritative compared to the learners, but not authoritarian.
6. Discovery learning, a *summum bonum* of most of the radicals, is by no means a panacea—its limitations demand careful consideration.
7. Informal experiences, by themselves, are blind alleys. Intellectual, moral, and aesthetic fulfillment are impossible goals if the route taken is random experience or even immediate experience.
8. Absolute freedom is impossible in a real world. Authority is an essential part of freedom. The society, through laws, rules, and other sanctions, protects the freedoms of each individual. A reasonable degree of benevolent authority is essential in the classroom.
9. While some extremists overemphasize law and order, others overemphasize individual freedom. Our society cannot be returned to primitiveness, so of necessity it requires moderate measures. Citizenship is not incompatible with intelligent individualism.
10. Excellence, efficiency, critical thinking, good character, and a sense of history are values preferred in the classroom to the existential, mental-health, and social-reconstruction values of the radicals.

The above list will help focus the discussion, but it is not exhaustive. As one proceeds through the book he will certainly find points of disagreement. Assuming one has read several of the radical books, one will be able to evaluate their worth more effectively once the scholarly but moderate viewpoints expressed in this book are considered.

In Part 1 there are critiques of the radical critics. Generally, the radical reformers have met little intellectual resistance in their exaggerated attacks on American education. This section very quickly remedies that state of affairs.

Part 2 includes discussions by scholars interested in the school curriculum—its content, the role of the teacher and learner, and the conditions of freedom that ought to prevail.

Because the development of a higher moral sense may well prove pivotal in our struggle for survival, Part 3 includes essays discussing the educational conditions essential for such moral development. The message is clear: informal, unstructured education will not achieve such an end.

Finally, in Part 4, we examine the elements in the free-school or open-classroom concept that may prove to have lasting value when integrated into other models of teaching and learning. The reader will realize that some humanistic values in the radical movement are indeed necessary for an education that serves the whole man, not simply the emotional, artistic man, social man, political man, or scientific man. Thus, we attempt to rescue those humanistic aspects of the radical movement that are valuable, while preserving the cognitive, structural, and efficient aspects of our more traditional models.

Rigid, formal, regimented schooling is not being defended here. The authoritarian extreme is both educationally unsound and almost impossible to sustain in an age of unprecedented permissiveness. The views of teaching and learning offered here are those of serious scholars who seem to be close to reconciling education and the existing technological society. At a minimum they pose a strong challenge to the radical reform movement. Through engagement in the debate and analysis stimulated by this controversy, one will develop his own philosophy of education.

# PART 1

# CRITIQUE OF THE NEW EDUCATION

The free-school and open-classroom fashions are not completely homogeneous, either in practice or in doctrine. The movement contains many who emphasize cognitive learning, carefully planned, individualized instruction, and even the use of performance objectives. A large number of more humanistically oriented persons favor an orthodox approach to Rousseauistic education. These, of course, are humanists of a specific stripe, disavowing the scientific philosophy of traditional humanists.

Although a spectrum of teachers and classroom methods indeed exists in the radical reform movement, the common points stressed in the general introduction are for the most part a reality, and the dangers flowing from this educational process remain very great.

Most of the articles in Part 1 do more than repudiate the radical reform position. The writers seem very much concerned about the need to preserve principles such as the authority of the teacher, high standards of excellence, the transmission of culture, and the structured curriculum. These positions seem implicit in their essays, and they serve as foci of conflict between the radicals and themselves.

The first writer, Samuel McCracken, unceremoniously assaults the radicals with sharp wit, sarcasm, and a sense of irony that nearly obscures his points of criticism. As diverting as his literary style is, the perceptive reader will gain new insights from Mc-Cracken.

Charles Silberman's *Crisis in the Classroom* is a radical book, impressively documented. Although its prescriptions for reform are vague, the documentary evidence demands careful analysis and evaluation. An expert on social policy, Amitai Etzioni, offers a critical examination of this popular work. One of his more disturbing assessments is the claim that Silberman's anecdotal reports are unscientific, because they do not represent an adequate sample of American classrooms.

Radical school-reform writers often refer to A. S. Neill's *Summerhill* as a reliable guide for the open-classroom approach to schooling. Neill's views are widely known, so it is important that they receive attention here. Fred Hechinger, the noted writer for the *New York Times*, points out assumptions in Neill's philosophy that appear to be incompatible with a highly structured, modern society.

The philosopher Sidney Hook critically examines several aspects of the radical reform movement. He is considered to be the foremost representative and continuator of the views of John Dewey in philosophy and education. His *Education for Modern Man* was enthusiastically endorsed by John Dewey. Professor Hook claims that the radicals misrepresent John Dewey's teachings vis-à-vis teacher authority, student freedom, the role of the intellect, the value of informal experience, and individual needs. If what he says is true, those who claim to be radicals today are purveying ideas which Dewey criticized as caricaturing the Progressive Education Movement.

Ivan Illich is a revolutionary priest whose proposal to "deschool society" has won serious discussion. Illich has a naked distaste for most of our institutions and processes. He proposes among other things that we adopt "learning webs" to further the transformation to an egalitarian society. Sidney Hook and Manfred Stanley subject both his criticisms and proposals to a rigorous criticism.

In the final article in Part 1 a prominent advocate of radical reform, Jonathan Kozol, repudiates aspects of his own free-school movement. He attacks those theorists and teachers who conceal their own competence while running free schools in ghetto areas. He decries their downgrading of traditional values like competence, efficiency, hard work, and complete commitment. Kozol calls this bohemian approach "The Cult of Incompletion."

SAMUEL McCRACKEN

# QUACKERY IN THE CLASSROOM

To begin on a note of solemn affirmation: I consider elementary and secondary education in this country to be a nightmare almost unrelieved, and were I king, all that would remain would be a few of the handsomer buildings, an occasional administrator, some of the teachers, and all of the students. Such views hardly set me apart these days, for we live in plague season. In such a time, the alchemists, geomancers, and sellers of mandrake root begin to sound as likely to heal as doctors of physics. A recent anthology of the new breed of romantic educational reformers, *Radical School Reform*, edited by Beatrice and Ronald Gross,[1] provides useful selections from just about every authority in that curious new school of educational theory where the bright, well-scrubbed, shiny faces on all the idealistic reformers almost make one forget the faint aroma of snake-oil about the halls.

I found myself pausing at the title: *Radical School Reform*? Why not *The Revolution in the Schools*? As it turns out, the editors have a special definition for what is educationally radical:

> Radical has many meanings, in fact. In politics, radical means revolutionary . . . in social relations, radical means libertarian . . . in a school situation, radical means unorthodox ways of promoting learning that fall outside the scope of conventional or even innovative school practice.

As opposed, no doubt, to *orthodox* ways of promoting learning that fall outside the scope, and so forth. Well, I suppose *Unorthodox School Reform* wouldn't quite have made it. . . .

If not the first of the prophets in time—Paul Goodman and Edgar Z. Friedenberg were notables when he was yet unknown—John Holt has attained an eminence and authority nearly papal, on the basis of his first two books[2] and a considerable spate of periodical literature, some of it recently collected in book form.[3]

*How Children Fail* is ultimately an infuriating book, infuriating because although it contains any number of exceptionally keen insights into the learning process, observations which would entitle their author to some importance in the history of education, it ends by finally marshaling these observations about the methodology of education into an exceptionally dogmatic and imperceptive theory of its content and end. Of that unfortunate marshaling more in time. The principal methodological insight of the work, carefully documented from Holt's experience as a teacher in "good" private schools, is that children respond to the strategies of their teachers by developing their own set of eventually self-defeating counters, and that by providing the inspiration for such, the most enlightened of teachers in the best of schools eventually end up by subverting learning. A principal part of the process is the ease with which students learn to regard *Yes* answers as preferable to *No*, quite without regard to the extrinsic value either may have. Thus, when playing "Twenty Questions," the object being to determine a number between 1 and 10,000, a standard gambit is to ask "Is it between 1 and 5,000?" Children in Holt's classes invariably applaud a *Yes* here, groan at a *No*. In the closing stages of such a game, children will repeatedly ask a question already answered *Yes*, apparently for the simple pleasure of hearing affirmation. Holt rightly believes that such irrational behavior grows out of an emphasis on getting right answers as opposed to defensible ones.

He observes that his students frequently know appallingly little about arithmetic, no matter what their assumed preparation, so little that the first task of the teacher is to plumb the depths of their ignorance, and to start from there: he provides several impressive anecdotes suggesting how such a technique can work to teach arithmetic to those apparently ineducable in it. Another notion, as provocative if less easily documented, is that students seek refuge in incompetence, knowing that they can sink to a level which convinces teachers that they are hopeless, at best not worth bothering anymore, at worst meriting praise for a pitiful level of performance.

Any reader who follows Holt through his observations of the learning process will be impressed by his ability to get inside his students, and the astuteness with which he handles what he sees there. As I shall make clear, I think Holt's short-run influence will be deleterious, but I think there can be no doubt that if the schools can make use of those nugget-like passages in which Holt talks about how children learn, and reject the surrounding fool's gold, Holt may yet be made to expedite that learning process which, even though he confuses it with education, is after all its basis.

An example of the detritus I have mentioned in the summary

chapter of *How Children Fail,* in which Holt makes the first of his assaults on the notion of curriculum, a notion which he seems to understand to mean only a body of knowledge judged all-sufficient in itself. Without for the moment arguing an alternative view, that curriculum may be seen rather as a body of knowledge perhaps useful in itself, but primarily important as a tool for developing certain habits of intellectual behavior quite apart from its intrinsic value, I want to sketch the lurid sort of argument Holt uses to discredit curriculum as he defines it.

Our information, he begins, is constantly subject to revision, and it is therefore difficult to be sure that any body of knowledge now taught will be *true* in twenty years, let alone relevant. He cites several examples from his own education:

> I studied physics at school from a fairly up-to-date text that proclaimed that the fundamental law of physics was the law of conservation of matter—matter is not created or destroyed. I had to scratch that out before I left school. . . . Not for many years after I left college did I learn that from Greeks, far from being a detached and judicious people surrounded by chaste white temples, were hot-tempered, noisy, quarrelsome, and liked to cover their temples with gold leaf and bright paint; or that most of the citizens of Imperial Rome, far from living in houses in which the rooms surrounded an atrium, or central court, lived in multi-storied apartment buildings, one of which was perhaps the largest building in the ancient world. The child who remembered everything he heard in school would live his life believing many things that were not so.

I am myself professionally incompetent to talk about conserving matter, but physicists tell me that the Law of the Conservation of Matter, no matter how badly clawed by Mr. Holt, is still around, and one of the most accepted of scientific propositions. It was last modified seriously in 1905, by something involving $E=MC^2$. If Holt was really taught the sort of nonsense he appears to have believed about the Greeks and the Romans, that is a sad commentary on the state of classical studies at Yale University in the last generation, and, at least with regard to the Greeks, upon Holt's ability to read such texts as the *Birds* or the *Apology.* In any event, the epiphanies vouchsafed Holt about the Greek psyche and Roman housing are far from representing a state of knowledge perfected after he took his B.A.: they represent improvements in his own understanding.

Note also the peculiar crudity of Holt's last sentence: what children hear in school equals what they believe all their lives (as long as they remember it); and the only way, given the imperfection of knowledge, to keep them from believing the false is to keep them from hearing anything at all. The problem with the argument is that eventually it is an argument against education. Now, if the schools were teaching the Ptolemaic cosmology as truth, and Holt could demonstrate that the Copernican cosmology were true, that would surely be compelling argument against requiring anyone to study Ptolemy. But although it would also be an argument against teaching Ptolemy at all, in the sense of teaching him as truth, it would hardly be an argument against teaching astronomy. No one should be forced to study the sort of nonsense about the Greeks to which Holt was apparently exposed. But that does not mean that no one should study the Greeks.

What Holt appears to demand of the curriculum, indeed of knowledge itself, is that it should be *perfected* before the young study it. This seems a curiously absolutist stand for one of Holt's general orientation, absolutist if not totalitarian: Holt's canon of perfection would be quite understandable to the curriculum consultants who must revise eighth-grade history texts in the Soviet Union.

Allied to Holt's view of curriculum is the claim that one piece of learning is as good as another, an assertion he supports by arguing that herpetology (which is rarely in the secondary curriculum) is as exciting to some students as chemistry (which usually is), and that science (whatever that is) may excite some more than Roman Britain. Without pointing out that herpetology is, after all, a branch of biology, which is in the curriculum, and that we live in a world threatened by the activities of scientists who were in effect allowed not to learn about Roman Britain, it can be said that these examples do not do a great deal to demonstrate the truth of the assertion that one piece of learning is as good as another, a statement, whatever its fatuity, which is beginning to be profoundly influential in contemporary educational theory. A group of my friends are starting an experimental college called, significantly, "The Learning Community." Their prospectus contains the remark, "We will not be concerned that certain things are being learned, but rather, that everyone in the Community is learning." The people who wrote that are cultivated and gifted scholar-teachers, and when I hear such people talk like that, I begin to wonder if education may indeed be obsolete. It ought to be patent that not all learning *is* equally desirable: the learning capacity includes at minimum the power to learn (a) truth, good habits, and sound values, as well as (b) falsehood, bad habits, and deplorable values. There is no evidence from history or behavioral science to indicate that man's capacity or disposition for learning (a) is greater than his capacity or disposition for learning (b).

Underlying Holt's argument here is a basic confusion common to most of the recent reformers, the confusion of education and learning. Historically the latter has been seen as a process by which the former may proceed. Holt and his school either fail to distinguish between the two, or, having made the distinction, prefer the part to the whole. Traditional education, warts and all, always assumed that something was needed to mobilize learning in the service of education, indeed to insure that the learning that went on was of the sort I have called (a) rather than of the sort I have called (b). One would not be excessively idealistic to suggest that education is learning of the (a) variety and that what goes on at (b) can best be called miseducation, a process no more a variety of education than National Socialism is a variety of Socialism. A principal device available to education to keep it from being miseducation is in fact a curriculum. No one in his right mind would argue that the curriculum as currently defined does much to prevent such degeneration; but to argue that the present misuse of a technique has led to nothing but failure does not lead to the conclusion that any other technique is necessarily better. "Nothing but failure" is an advised use of words: a prime article of faith for Holt and the others is that learning is simply impossible in a conventional setting. Holt himself begins *How Children Fail* by claiming that most children do fail. This belief is not unlike that dogma of the old education that no education ever took place before the birth of John Dewey, and that since his birth none has taken place outside the United States. Under Holt's assumption, it is difficult to understand how he learned to write and we to read.

This confusion of education and learning leads to a secondary one, that of methodology and content. *How Children Fail* often achieves brilliance as an analysis of methodology; as a treatment of content it is callow and unoriginal. While nowhere does it contain a persuasive argument that the adoption of a certain methodology makes a curriculum impossible, it does argue that *any* required learning is coercion and that coercion is always painful. The problem is that the Social Contract eventually coerces us all, and Holt thinks that education should be integrated with life. A school absolutely free would be a poor learning laboratory for even the most libertarian society: "Man is born free, and everywhere he is in chains." It is easy to forget that the chains of which Rousseau speaks are not the infamies of the Old Regime, but rather the minimal restraint necessary for a free society.

Holt's second book, *How Children Learn*, is at once less controversial and less original than his first. "Little children learn far more easily and effectively than we have realized." Such a statement accurately paraphrases any number of sentences in the work, and also its total content: the subset is the set. It is true enough, I suppose, if we imagine a *we* sufficiently ignorant, a nonparent, perhaps. Maria Montessori (1870–1952) knew all about the precocity of children, and used her knowledge to construct an educational system with rigors I presume Mr. Holt would deplore. I doubt that many observant parents would be surprised by Mr. Holt's descriptions of infant capacity to learn, but heaven knows the educational establishment might be.

Holt's lengthy discussions of learning to talk and read appear to be innocent of any knowledge of much of the relevant linguistic theory, particularly the work of Noam Chomsky. His major conclusion, that because we all teach ourselves to talk, admittedly a difficult task, we therefore have the capacity to learn every sort of difficult task, would seem to be challenged by Chomsky's notion of an innate linguistic competence, that man is predisposed to talk. He is not necessarily predisposed to play the 'cello, ski, or develop educational theory.

Oversimplification from inadequate knowledge runs throughout Holt's work (to a greater degree than it runs throughout everyone else's). He cultivates a simple style, and does not assume a great deal of knowledge on the part of his audience. ("Going south from London on a train, I found myself in a compartment—a small, closed-in section seating eight passengers.") Whether he really knows as little about linguistics as he appears to in the section on talking and reading, I cannot say: perhaps he simplifies for his presumed unsophisticated audience. Certainly to talk about talking and reading in 1967 without some knowledge of Chomsky would be as quaint as to talk about motion without some knowledge of Einstein.

Like *How Children Fail*, its successor, *How Children Learn*, follows a hundred pages or so of sensible observation with a section of weighty conclusion, and the conclusion is familiar:

> What we need to do, and all we need to do, is bring as much of the world as we can into the school and the classroom; give the children as much help and guidance as they need *and ask for*, listen respectfully when they feel like talking; and then get out of the way. We can trust them to do the rest. [Emphasis added.]

He again assaults the curriculum with the same knowledge-gets-out-of-date argument, trotting out the conservation of matter for a second appearance, sparing the Greeks and the Romans any embarrassment, and adding valence. ("I mentioned valence to a chemist the other day, and he laughed. When I asked what was so funny, he said, 'Nobody talks about valence any more; it's an outmoded concept.'" Holt's alchemical friends may be more *a la mode* than mine, several of whom assure me that while valence is not necessarily on the frontier of research, it is alive and well in one of the most widely used basic texts in physical chemistry, Coulson's *Valence.*)

What Holt grasps for—and does not reach—in these examples is some modern equivalent of one of the famous fossils of knowledge that everyone once knew and which have had to be unlearned, such as the Ptolemaic cosmology. Even had he succeeded, the search would have been pointless. Intellectual endeavor frequently proceeds by reacting against the vulnerable orthodoxies of the past: it is not at all certain that Newton would exist without Aristotle, or Einstein without Newton; Chomsky comes to his work in generative grammer from the training in structuralism which prepared him to overturn it. Although Holt may argue that the Einsteins and the Chomskys do not need an orthodoxy against which to kick, we have little evidence that this is so, and even less that lesser minds would challenge themselves without the spur of curriculum. Since Holt is fond of citing his miseducation, let me immodestly cite mine. One of my graduate schools coerced me into the study of linguistics, a subject which delighted me not. I still recall the classes as poisoned by the sort of coercive atmosphere Holt rightly detects in the required course. Yet I eventually became so interested in the discipline that it occupies a considerable amount of my intellectual life, and provides me with some of my most enjoyable teaching. My undergraduate college, on the other hand, allowed me to be a Bachelor of Arts without any exposure to mathematics, leaving me with no more than tenth-grade geometry, as dimly remembered as Holt's Hellas. My work in linguistics requires a knowledge of mathematics, however limited, in excess of what I have, and I am forced to go to my colleagues with questions they must at best regard as pitiful. In fact, it is precisely our inability to know at ten, fourteen, or twenty-three, exactly where we are headed intellectually that demonstrates the desirability of the liberal-arts curriculum, a chance to profit from the mistakes of others. . . .

I turn with some trepidation to one of Holt's most recent publications. While it is somehow fitting for our convolute and electronic culture to review in *Commentary* a review in the *New York Review of Books* of a book one plans to review in *Commentary*, it is nevertheless a considerable organizational challenge. But I shall try, since Holt's review of George Dennison's *The Lives of Children*[4] says as much about Holt as it does about Dennison.

With Holt's opening judgment of *The Lives of Children* as "by far the most perceptive, moving, and important book on education that I have ever read," I am in essential agreement, although not, as will be seen, for the same reasons. With another of Holt's judgments I am in some little disagreement:

> Our educational system, at least at its middle- and upper-class layers, likes to say and indeed believes that an important part of its task is transmitting to the young the heritage of the past, the great traditions of history and culture. The effort is an unqualified failure. The proof we see all around us. A few of the students in our schools, who get good marks and go to prestige colleges, exploit the high culture, which many of them do not really understand or love, by pursuing comfortable and well-paid careers as university Professors of English, History, and Philosophy, etc. Almost all the rest reject that culture wholly and utterly.

> The average Ivy League graduate is . . . estranged from the cultural tradition, certainly those parts of it that were shoved down his throat in school. . . . The entertainment highlight of the class dinner at my 25th college reunion, and the nearest thing to a cultural event during the whole weekend, was a low-comedy parody of grand opera. It seemed to be just what most of my classmates expected and wanted.

If this passage is a sample of the intellectual habits engendered by an Ivy League education, then I can only share Mr. Holt's contempt for it. There are two appalling statements here: first, that you can't even *exploit* the "high culture" except by way of a prestige college (a view suggestive of the sweeping snobbery which seems to characterize Holt's understanding of higher education, an impression reinforced by the assertion that *even* Ivy League graduates are estranged from that culture), and secondly, the imprudent claim that vast numbers of people whom Holt knows neither in person nor by reputation neither understand nor love that which they profess. The first claim is that of a snob, the second that of a bigoted dogmatist who has yet to show that he himself understands or loves any part of culture. (Now that I think of it, if Holt's classmates had what appears to have been his exposure to the Greeks, their estrangement is entirely understandable.) College teaching is, to be sure, now adequately paid, but the notion that the life of the mind is ever comfortable suggests that the holder has never experienced that life, and the view that the life of the mind on a college campus is *today* comfortable suggests further a surprising insensitivity to the world about us. Where can John Holt have been? The review's major failing, however, lies in its abstraction of Dennison's experience with seriously rebellious primary students into assertions about education in general. As will be seen, this is a fault of which Dennison himself is innocent.

Holt's latest word is a statement in a recent issue of *Look*, on the kind of schools he thinks we will need in the 70's. The compactness of the piece and the fact that it was intended for a mass audience combine to exaggerate two traits evident elsewhere in Holt's writing—a humble, retiring style masking a Johnsonian dogmatism:

> Abolish all compulsory testing and grading. If a student wants his teacher to test his knowledge or competence . . . fine. All other grading is destructive and inexcusable. . . . Students of any age should get academic credit, as some college students do now, for holding down a job. . . . Let people, of whatever age, go in and out of school when they see fit, using it when it seems most useful to them. Let the learner direct his own learning.

The self-effacing cast of these remarks conceals the essentially authoritarian nature of their content. Recast them, or add a prefatory statement such as, "Sir, the education of those in their nonage is best effectuated by . . ." and the disjunction will be marvellously reduced. Even though pomposity and dogma are often joined, he who eschews the first does not necessarily eschew the second. For proof of this dogma, see Holt, *passism.*

What to say in sum, then, about Holt, whose predominance in this essay accurately reflects his predominance in his movement, and his possible influence for evil or for good? He will still be read some years hence (unless some successor adapts his theories of learning without accepting his romantic excesses) because he really has a great deal to say about teaching. But he does not know a great deal about education, and his current development does not encourage the hope that he will begin to learn about it. One wishes that he had contented himself with doing what he is obviously very good at, looking at the ways children learn. Perhaps it is an inescapable artifact of a time desperately looking for easy solutions to difficult problems that a man who is good at one thing will eventually come to believe that that's all there is to the problem.

Unfortunately, his present eminence is likely to cause a good deal of trouble long before he has a place in history. I have already dealt with the consequences of his popularization of the hoary chestnut that learning equals education. But what is finally most dangerous in his doctrine, dangerous yet nonetheless popular, is his assault on the necessity of preserving and transmitting culture. Now, it is not clear to me that Holt believes that culture *ought* to be preserved and transmitted, but I am quite sure that if it is it will just as sure as he is that it is not being transmitted now. (In this connection, incidentally, it might be pointed out that the fact that Holt and his audience seem to know what he's talking about suggests that the failure is not quite so unqualified as he claims.)

Notwithstanding the forests heretofore consumed in arguing the desirability of liberal education on the grounds of cultural transmission, I will not take the transmission as obviously desirable, but content myself with two arguments in its favor, the hedonistic and the pragmatic.

The first is easily dealt with: "high culture" can be fun. It apparently is not fun for Mr. Holt, who does not exploit it with one of those well-paid and soft jobs in literature, philosophy, or history; it is clearly not fun for everyone; but it is fun for some of us. And unless one wishes to argue that some of us are somehow hereditarily competent to enjoy it while some are not—are you there, Mr. Holt?—it seems that what is needed is the improvement of transmission, not its suspension. The notion that the transmission is impossible for most ordinary blokes and provisionally possible for Yale graduates smacks of cultural snobbism, educational adventurism, high-culture elitism, and heaven knows what else.

Second, without wishing to argue for the sort of vulgar relevance now called for at every hand, I would suggest that "high culture" is in fact *useful*. It would be a dunderheaded reader of Thucydides' *Peloponnesian War* who did not find in its analysis of the downfall of the Athenian empire chilling omen for the American. Aristotle's treatment of rhetoric is still a cogent account of the art of persuasion. There is good stuff in Dante, Machiavelli, Hobbes, Kant, and so forth, and so forth. . . .

It is, I suppose, an indication of the desperation of the educational malady that a theorist of Holt's slender ability should be listened to. But, as I have remarked, it is plague season. Consider, for example, another work generously excerpted by the Grosses, *Teaching as a Subversive Activity*, by Neil Postman and Charles Weingartner.[5] This is the most jargon-ridden and pretentious of the current bibles, the most assiduous in setting forth vulgarizations of what competent teachers have always known, and dressing the result up in the sort of Choctaw currently in favor in the Regional Education Laboratories. This is not surprising, for the authors,

while lambasting the educational establishment, are in fact themselves professors of education, Postman at New York University
and Weingartner at Queens College. They are, it must be said, several orders of magnitude better than the authors who usually write
from schools of education, but the establishment against which they
rebel has left its dread mark on them, especially in terms of a weakness for the glorification of the routine and for the windily romantic
in terminology. (Sometimes you *can* tell a book by its cover: the
dust jacket is decorated with a red apple fitted with a burning fuse,
a device consonant with a general tone designed to blow the minds
of faculty malcontents smoking in the boiler-room at Kremlin High
School in Kremlin, Idaho.)

Thus well begun, the authors start with a discussion of the
need for the "built-in, shockproof crap detector," a concept the
sturdy elegance of which is doubtless explained by its derivation
from Hemingway, and which appears akin to *critical sense*, or perhaps to *skepticism*. The opening chapter, "Crap Detecting," proceeds
to an obligatory account to Marshall McLuhan, described as "one of
the most dangerous men around at the moment . . . because he
seems to be subverting traditional assumptions." Postman and
Weingartner are the only critics I know who treat McLuhan less critically than McLuhan.

Having defined education as crap-detecting, the authors proceed to develop one of the most original theses ever propounded in
a program of radical education:

> The Inquiry Method of teaching and learning is an attempt to
> redesign the structure of the classroom. It is a new medium, and
> messages are different than (sic) those usually communicated to
> students.

If the method is new, they tell us, the terms used by its critics
are not:

> In instances where someone wishes to dismiss the inquiry
> method, it is common to hear, "Oh, all you mean is the Socratic
> Method." That serves as terminal punctuation. No more need
> be said. In better circumstances, serious people search for a
> "real" name: the inductive method, inquiry training, the hypo-
> thetical mode of teaching, inferential learning, the deductive-
> inductive method, the inductive-deductive method, and so on.

It is not quite clear whether the authors regard "Socratic method" as a proper label, rightly understood, but they shortly suggest
that Socrates was in fact very close to developing the all-new In-

quiry Method, and suggest further a reason for the unhappy end of his promising career in the New Education: "All authorities get nervous when learning is conducted without a syllabus." This remark illumines the *Apology* in a light so intense as well-nigh to blind, and I can only retire blinkingly with the remark that if all the people in the world who use the term "Socratic method" were laid end to end, there would be a good deal less philosophical confusion among those left standing.

If the Inquiry Method is really anything new, then I guess I don't understand it, but let me quote the authors on the behavior characterizing the Inquiry Teacher:

> The teacher rarely tells students what he thinks they ought to know. His basic mode of discourse with students is questioning. Generally, he does not accept a single statement as an answer to a question. [Everyone knows there are two sides to every question—S.M.] He encourages student-student interaction as opposed to student-teacher interaction. And generally he avoids acting as a mediator or judge of the quality of ideas expressed. He rarely summarizes positions taken by students on the learnings that occur. His lessons develop from the responses and not from a previously determined logical structure. Generally, each of his lessons poses a problem for students. He measures his success in terms of behavioral changes in students.

Well, these are all reasonably harmless prescriptions, if administered with a reasonable dose of salt. A good teacher worries about the dangers of killing discussion by too hasty disagreement with ideas expressed; but an absolute commitment not to judge the quality of ideas presented in class is a commitment to irresponsibility. I presume the inquiry-centered doctor would not judge the somatic condition of his clients, but rather would try to get them to come to a self-diagnosis. As a matter of fact, there is almost nothing in these prescriptions to which any sound teacher would not give qualified assent. What is ludicrous about their appearance in *Teaching as a Subversive Activity* is the notion that somehow they characterize some sort of switched-on operative who becomes possible only after reading the relevant chapter in Postman and Weingartner.

From these truisms, the authors proceed to a discussion of the one issue it is my fervent hope to outlive: relevance. Speaking of doctors, as we were, they open the chapter with a witty playlet involving a group of doctors at a Blear General Hospital, including a

Dr. Gilluspie, a Dr. Killdear, a Dr. Fuddy, and a Dr. Carstairs, who, no one will be surprised to find out, is the Good Guy. The first three open the the scene with a good deal of discussion about gallstone removals *qua* gallstone removals, frontal lobotomies *qua* frontal lobotomies, and the like, leading into such snappy dialogue as:

> FUDDY: Frankly, I never cared much for appendectomies.
> GILLUSPIE: Appendectomies?
> FUDDY: Well, that seemed to be the trouble with the patient in 397.
> GILLUSPIE: But you stayed with the old pilonidalcyst excision, eh?
> FUDDY: Right, chief.

Although the playlet does not carry, well as it might, Artemus Ward's annotation, *N. B. This is wrote sarkastikul*, the authors do belabor the point: "Perhaps our playlet needs no further elaboration, but we want to underscore some of its points." The main point is that teachers who teach courses their students don't want are like doctors who perform operations their patients don't need. The shift from *want* to *need* or, rather, the confusion of these two, is a device absolutely essential to the contemporary ideology of relevance, even when comparatively sophisticated ideologues obfuscate the confusion further by talking about wants as *felt needs*. Implicit here is another confusion, that teaching = medicine, and hence student = patient. This confusion, heaven knows, is becoming epidemic, as education becomes more and more an essay at bootleg psychotherapy and less and less an attempt to deal with the healthy, but the educational theorists could take a leaf from the obstetricians, who are well aware that uncomplicated pregnancy and childbirth do not constitute a disease.

A good example of the unneeded operation, according to Postman and Weingartner, is grammar. Grammar, we are told, has its controversies, but

> . . . they are of such a sterile and generally pointless nature that only one who is widely removed from human concerns can derive much stimulation from them. Browning's line that grammarians are dead from the waist down captures the sense of what we are trying to say about them. (An emphatic exception to Browning's observation is Professor Noam Chomsky, who has recently distinguished himself as an invaluable "crap detector" of the language of political bureaucrats and "house intellectuals.") . . . You see, there simply aren't any children who

would have any possible reason—now or for the rest of their lives—to care about how a noun is defined, or what the transformational rules are for forming the passive voice, or how many allomorphs there are in the plural morpheme.

There is enough Yahooism in that passage to last your average educational romantic through several books, but here is God's plenty. One wonders whether Professor Chomsky is excluded from the authors' Browingesque strictures simply because he serves as a kind of latter-day Maury Maverick, or whether additionally they are making some special claims about his manliness. Of his profoundly original and influential contributions to our understanding of language, there is no mention. To say that there are no children who will *ever* have *any* reason at any time in life to care how many allomorphs there are in the plural morpheme says simply that no one should ever study linguistics. Such a position is perhaps comprehensible, but not in Messrs. Postman and Weingartner, who are, a jacket blurb informs us, co-authors of *Linguistics: A Revolution in Teaching.* I've already paid my debt to Postman and Weingartner and don't intend to read the book, but I have read the reviews, and they confirm one's inference from the title: the authors hold that (a) there is a science called linguistics; and (b) it can effect an educational revolution. What can one say of people who publish such a work in 1966, and who in 1969 argue that linguists are not only sterile but also impotent, practitioners of a discipline in any event of no use whatever to anyone? One can express admiration of their sense of the market, that's what one can do.

To intrude for a moment in my role as jackleg linguist, I should express my view that linguistics is irrelevant to learning to write, just as hydrocarbon chemistry is irrelevant to learning to drive, and that the current emphasis on "linguistic" high-school composition programs is 99.8 percent fraud, most of it impious. The proper place of linguistics in the secondary schools is next to chemistry, physics, and biology. Unfortunately, the schools are prone to gimmicky fads, and the teaching of composition so difficult, that the snake-oil salesmen do particularly well here. To say all of which is not to share in the sort of ignorant opportunism evident in Postman and Weingartner.

Lest I seem to select an isolated example of troglodyte argument, see next our antilinguists play at etymology:

> Advocates of "high standards" characteristically and unwittingly invoke other revealing metaphors. One of the most frequently used of these is "basic fundamentals." Indulging our propensity to inquire into the language of education, we find

that the essential portion of the word "fundamental" is the word "fundament." It strikes us as poetically appropriate that "fundament" also means the buttocks, and specifically the anus. We will resist the temptation to explore the unconscious motives of "fundamentalists."

Well, I'll resist the temptation to explore the intellectual qualifications of people who argue by means of such pitiful combinations of folk etymology and weak pun, but I cannot resist the temptation to quote them once again:

> The new education . . . enters into an entirely new "business": fundamentally[sic], the crap-detecting and relevance business.

My ability to resist temptation is even sufficient to keep me from speculating as to the unconscious motivations of those for whom "crap-detecting" is a basic metaphor for education. People with glass fundaments. . . .

Postman and Weingartner, to do them justice, do believe in the need for a curriculum, albeit a swinging one. Gracefully called a What's Worth Knowing Questions Curriculum, it consists, in one version, of such stuff:[6]

> What do you worry about most?
> What are the causes of your worries?
> Can any of your worries be eliminated? How?
> Which of them might you deal with first? How do you decide?
> Are there any other people with the same problem?
> How do you know? How do you find out?
>
> How can you tell "good guys" from "bad guys"?
> How can "good" be distinguished from "evil"?
>
> What do you think are some of man's most important ideas?
> Where do they come from? Why? How? Now what?
> What's a "good idea"?
>
> Which of man's ideas would we be better off forgetting?
> What is "progress"?
>
> If you wanted to stop one of the changes going on now (pick one), how would you go about it?
> What consequences would you have to consider?
>
> What's worth knowing? How do you decide?

We ought clearly to distinguish two questions about these questions: whether they are worth asking (they are), and whether they provide anything which could responsibly be called a curriculum (I think not). They are, first of all, distressingly inclined toward navel-watching, which may be a pleasant enough activity, but which is no substitute for education. A little experience with that fraction of the college generation which has ceased to worry about knowing anything except itself makes me suspect that we don't need to encourage such notions by institutionalization. One can accept Pope's advice to know first oneself, without forgetting that his next generalization was *not* "the proper study of mankind is you."

Other considerations militate against accepting these questions as a curriculum. The psychotherapeutic tone of the earlier ones suggest that the answers might well be sought from the answerers with some training in therapy. (If the craze for Sensitivity Training, T-Groups, and so forth continues we may well have a generation which thinks it is competent at the sort of therapy envisioned in this curriculum, but I prefer to take a more optimistic view.) It seems of dubious value for adolescents to undertake this sort of self-analysis under the quality of guidance likely to be available in most high schools. Moreover, answering questions like "What is change? What is progress?" is the sort of endeavor likely to be very difficult for anyone without considerable grounding in the methodologies and factual content of history and philosophy. There is, of course, no reason why the young should not ask these questions. The objection is to considering that asking such questions constitutes a curriculum.

And, finally, the later questions, for all of the authors' cautions against judging ideas in the classroom, have a distinct bias. There is a curious dearth of questions like "Is change a good thing?" and "What is stability?" Postman and Weingartner seem to be reasonably committed to the proposition that any change is a good thing, and their questions, in a world which agrees with them, are not likely to get students wondering whether an occasional *status quo ante* may not also be a good thing: the United States role in Vietnam prior to the Geneva conference, for example.

My objections so far have been to the way in which two theorists embody the principle of relevance. But the principle itself can also stand closer examination. *Relevant* has become such a term of praise—and its negative has been for so long a term of dispraise—that the proposition that learning ought to be relevant has become generally accepted, with the current battle fought largely on whether, say, Homer is as relevant as Cleaver. But there are at least two serious objections to imposing the test of relevance, however defined, on what is to constitute the curriculum, however defined: that the test of relevancy encourages an essentially destructive attitude toward knowledge, and that it can become the pretext for substituting emotional predispositions for serious thought.

Most thinking people would see the danger of requiring that the objects of learning be *National Socialist, Socialist, Capitalist, Christian, American, safe, clean,* or *courteous.* And the objection one could make to imposing such criteria is not that the implicit goals are necessarily evil, for who would object to *courtesy* as a goal? The trouble here is that each of these tests proscribes some large body of knowledge. The fact that the Inquisition required of Galileo that his teaching be *Christian* suggests clearly the danger here: *true,* like *pregnant,* cannot be qualified as *very,* or *slightly;* and further, it cannot be modified as *National Socialist, American,* or *relevant.* Such a statement as "All Americans desire to live in a suburb and have 2.3 children" might be said to have white middle-class truth, but that is a claim as false as the original statement. The term *All Americans* is not modified by talking about a species of truth derived from it, and the claim remains false. In the same way, *truth* cannot be properly modifed by *relevant,* and for reasons other than grammatical or logical: the truth is, truth can become relevant only after it is established. The calculus, for example, was not particularly useful when Newton devised it, at least not useful beyond making more efficient certain processes also operable with geometry, and the theories of relativity had at their birth little practical application. Had Newton and Einstein been successfully limited to the pursuit of the relevant, we would all know a good deal less than we do now. We do not know, often cannot know, as we pursue truth, whether we or anyone else will have any use for it, immediately or ultimately. What is relevant here, if you will, is that our inability to predict the relevancy of truth requires us to pursue it wherever it may be found. The life of the mind is as crippled when its objects are defined in terms of relevance as when they are defined in terms of any sort of orthodoxy. It is possible to make a case—as I have suggested earlier—that some objects of study are more relevant than may appear, but this should not obscure the fact that the very existence of a relevance test is more dangerous than any abuse which might be made of it by the unknowing.

It may be justly observed that the objections I raise here seem pertinent especially to higher education, and that since the high schools have not in the past been concerned with the pursuit of truth, one need not bother to attack conditions unfavorable to that pursuit. Well, that's just the problem with the high schools: they have concerned themselves largely with promulgating shoddy orthodoxies, and perhaps sending them on a relevancy kick will make the situation no worse. But I presume the authors are looking for ways to improve the situation. It will not matter how much truth is discovered at Behemoth State if the relevancy freaks at John Holt High suppress most of it as irrelevant.

And not all those who cry for relevance in the interest of the learner really know what they are doing. I recently came across a declaration issued by a teacher of "social studies" in a new and highly switched-on high school, wherein he tells his students that they ought to study only what is relevant, and that what is relevant is what will enable them to make more money or supply them with immediate enjoyment. They are not slaves any more, he informs them, and they are at long last free to do exactly as he tells them. That he has settled for them in advance two questions still being hotly debated outside his classroom—namely, whether there is a need for relevance, and what is relevant—does not seem to bother him. It appears that in the high schools, as elsewhere, it is possible to invoke the dictatorship of the proletariat in the service of the fascist ruling circles.

If the ideology of relevance is potentially dangerous because it provides a scheme for enforcing a new orthodoxy (which is, as Sydney Smith defined it, "my doxy; heterodoxy is another man's"), there is yet another danger. Relevant subjects are often defined as those subjects having immediate or prospective practical value, but this neo-Babbittry is in some ways less troubling than another definition—that relevant subjects are those subjects to which one can relate. Anyone who teaches, as I do, a required freshman course beginning with Homer and ending with Montaigne, spends a good deal of time debating the question of relevance with his students. And many of the bright and committed students with whom I deal, although they do their share of complaining about the irrelevancy of Montaigne on practical grounds—though they desperately wish to change their patently unsatisfactory environments, the last thing they want to do is learn about previous attempts at the same thing —often seem to regard the intellectual experience as essentially emotion, a sort of sweaty grappling with ideas. Now, while the life of the mind is frequently an emotional one—and there are few sights more noble than that of a man driven by passionate reason—the reason comes first, the passion second, and he who wrestles with ideas only because he is emotionally attracted to them is at least temporarily disabled as an intellectual. When one believes that only those ideas which are already somehow provisionally a part of one worthy of intellectual-emotional engagement, then the range of thought is seriously reduced. The sorts of ideas, moreover, which seem most amenable to the ecstatic embrace are often those which the intellect would, given its chance, reject, as witness the current fad for the irrational, from "serious" students who seek guidance in the *I-Ching* and the astrology manuals, to the activists who with a straight face denounce reason as a repressive device invented by the military-industrial complex. Why the *I-Ching* should be seen as relevant and Montaigne as not is beyond my comprehension, but it is not a time in general supportive of the belief that in reason lies salvation. I tend to believe that the doctrines being preached in the more turned-on high schools by the hierophants of Holt and Postman and Weingartner are not doing much to improve matters. Certainly, that some of the best of my students arrive from the high schools in a new sort of semicatatonic state, quite distinguishable from the apathy of the Eisenhower years, and seeming to result from corrupt education, rather than from the conversion of those literally our best hope into literal believers in witchcraft (itself a relevant discipline, considering its concern with altering the environment) is a dreadful situation, and I predict that the problem will become magnified as the new wisdom makes its way outward.

Late in *Teaching as a Subversive Activity* Postman and Weingartner suggest that teachers ask themselves the question, "Why am I a teacher, anyway?" and suggest some answers:[7]

> Some honest answers that this question has produced are as follows:
> I can control people.
> I can tyrannize people.
> I have captive audiences.
> I have my summers off.
> I love seventeenth century non-dramatic Elizabethan Literature [*sic*].
> I don't know.
> The pay is good, considering the amount of work I actually do.

That is the entire list. In these questions and answers we have a paradigm of what is right and what is wrong with the educational romantics. It is clear enough (was it not always clear?) that some teachers teach for each of the obscene motivations listed here, although I for one would regard a love for literature as a decent motivation for teaching it, even if the three-years' worth of nondramatic literature which is both seventeenth century and Elizabethan seems a narrow specialty, and I suspect that the workload in the public schools is such that the pay is not really all that good. The problem here, as elsewhere, is overkill. Some teachers teach for unworthy reasons, a conclusion extant at least since Plato began to belabor the Sophists. The authors take this time-honored conclusion, and by suggesting that all teachers teach for unworthy reasons (which is the only conclusion to be drawn from their apparent willingness to consider as honest only those answers confessing unworthiness), blow it up into the sort of dreadful revelation which our crisis mentality is presumed likely to take seriously. We all know about the Big Lie; what we need now is a realization of the dangers of the Big Truism.

Let us turn from so-called educational theory to educational science fiction, in the person of George Leonard. Leonard is represented in the Gross anthology by "Going to School in the Global Village," an article originally published in *Look* with Marshall McLuhan. The article is a sort of selective precis of Leonard's later *Education and Ecstasy*.[8]

The book itself is at once stimulating and irritating. Although one welcomes a theorist with some historical orientation, the history is the same sort of facile summary which has proved so useful to McLuhan and so fatal to truth. (It's a brilliant suggestion that the Renaissance was a result of the printing press, so long as you think that the printing press came first, which is a not unreasonable assumption if you limit yourself to looking at Northern Europe and are willing to forget that publishers in any event preceded printers.) The work appears athrob with many ideas, which at close inspection collapse into a handful: the human capacity for learning that we have imagined; education is overly devoted to something called the rational/verbal mode; civilization is a process from which we are just emerging; the education of the future must be tribal; much can be done toward this end with technology; man's brightest hope is the Esalen Institute (George Leonard, vice president); Ecstasy is a Good Thing, and there ought to be more of it, especially in education.

Leonard is easily the most switched-on of the present crop of writers, and his visions are the most apocalyptic: the schools as vast computer facilities, where under the kindly tuition of patient cybernons children can learn the present curriculum by the age of six, in an educational lifestyle reminiscent of the Fillmore Auditorium, and in the sort of huggingly conflictless world yearned for at Esalen. But Leonard is not really an educational reformer. Although he would probably reject the label of visionary, on the ground that the technology he wishes to marshal in the future is already visible just over the horizon, it seems exceedingly unlikely that school boards are going to be ready for it until 2001. Leonard's disciples, unlike

Holt's, can't very well set up a demonstration project in a store front. The book is—dare I say it?—irrelevant. Leonard appears to believe that his Kennedy School will just sort of grow as the experimental psychologists and neurologists tell us more about how we learn. Nothing, alas, in the history of American education suggests any special connection between what may be known by the best and brightest and what goes on in the schools. What is notably lacking in Leonard are instructions to get us from here to there. (Although there is one good suggestion in the book: that every parent ought to go and spend one day studying with his child as the child is forced to study. I can think of no event more likely to improve the schools than for this advice to be acted upon.)

But in sum, I am still having difficulty deciding whether the book is ingenious science fiction or dystopian satire. Satire is not something one can imagine coming out of so earnest and smooth a place as the Esalen Institute, but the similarities between the Kennedy School principal directing a guided tour and Huxley's Director of Hatcheries are tempting. One cannot help wondering who is going to do the programming, whether the same machines which will make students unable to read Thucydides without tears might as admirably administer the Four Hours' Hate. Well, as Mr. Nixon demonstrates, there are those capable of unconscious self-satire. Oh, what a brave new school is this, that hath such machinery in it!

It is a relief to turn from Holt, Postman and Weingartner, and Leonard to the work of George Dennison, whose article "The First Street School," in *Radical School Reform*, is an extract from his recent book, *The Lives of Children*.[9] If the first four authors suggest educational romanticism at its worst, Dennison is an example of it at its best. Moreover, what George Dennison has done is as important as what he has written. What he has done is to have been a guiding spirit of the First Street School, an institution of twenty-three students (most under ten) from the East Village and three and a half teachers. The students were for the most part children on whom the public schools had given up; during the school's brief existence most of them were put on the road to salvation; and the miracle was worked at a cost per pupil less than that of a public school. Dennison, then, writes with an authority not possessed by those I have been discussing: he writes from successful experience.

It is his claim that the miracle is simply attained: ". . . running a primary school—provided it be small—is an extremely simple thing." The essentials are this: a school which, by avoiding heavy capital expenditures, is able to put most of its budget into salaries, so as to achieve a student/faculty ratio of 8 to 1, and by staying small—under thirty students—is able to dispense with bureaucracy. From these master conditions flow secondary benefits: primarily, the ability to deploy teachers as students need them, thereby permitting individual attention for those unable to function in groups, and the ability to leave the design of the program in the hands of the teachers themselves. By simple, Dennison does not mean easy: "on the contrary, teachers find (work) in a free school taxing." While I am convinced that Dennison, whose authentic humility is one of the pleasantest traits in his book, may well be underestimating his personal contribution in the form of his extraordinary gifts, I find it indicative of the possibilities of such a school that by the end of its first year, the First Street School, far from having a dropout problem, was faced with the problem of a seriously disturbed student who refused to stay away. One is reminded that the capital penalty at Summerhill is suspension from its noncompulsory classes. There can be no better indication of what is wrong with the public schools than that an approach as tentatively fruitful as that of the First Street School is not being tried out on the widest possible scale.

Life at First Street was not much like life in an average elementary school: attendance was not compulsory, discipline was limited to that necessary for the protection of others from physical harm, there was great freedom of activity for the students, a good deal of time was spent exploring the city. The teachers were able to regard each student as a separate problem (one of the few irritations of the book is that it discusses fewer than half the students, without making clear whether these are a representative sample, the successes, the greatest challenges, or what), and to follow the oft-quoted injunction of Rousseau to lose time. Dennison characterizes his most troublesome students as *rebellious,* a state he would distinguish from *disturbed;* many of them had in fact been regarded as beyond hope by the public schools from which they came. To the extent that First Street was successful with these students, it was successful with just those children with whom the public schools are most conspiciously failing. Whether or not it would have succeeded with the nonrebellious may be argued, but I am inclined to believe that it would: few of the school's activities seem especially therapeutic, and for what the evidence is worth, my own eminently nonrebellious son attends a considerably posher private school whose spirit is remarkably Dennisonian (a judgment which might surprise his teachers), and in it he and his fellows thrive in ways and to degrees I would not have thought possible.

Dennison, then, is an educational reformer who comes to the world with ideas tested in realistic conditions and found not wanting. We ought, as Holt has said, to listen to him very carefully. Inasmuch as Dennison and Holt are generally invoked these days as part of a trinity usually completed by A. S. Neill, the reader may wonder how a critic with whom Holt had found so little favor can find Dennison so promising. The answer is fairly simple: although Dennison may bear a surface resemblance to the other romantics, he is at heart profoundly unlike them, whether he or they know it, and it is crucial to us all to be able to tell the difference.

If one were called upon to characterize Dennison in a phrase, the one which comes to mind first is "tough-minded romantic." As his experience has been limited to primary education, he is remarkably unlike Holt, who seems to see no difference in kind between the first grade in elementary school and sophomore year in college. Whether Dennison, after teaching in college, would agree with Holt is beside the point. In his conduct of the school, he frequently did things that are anathema to the movement in general: the best way to calm a hysterical child, he tells us, is often to shake him into exhaustion. If discipline of the no-chewing-gum sort was mercifully absent at First Street, behavior which endangered others was likely to lead to suspension. Although the school admitted one student who proved to be, in Dennison's judgment, disturbed, it was also to come to the conclusion that the admission had been a mistake, and that the school was incompetent to help him.

Dennison's theorizing, to be sure, can be as dubious as that of the others I have discussed:

> . . . with two exceptions, the parents of the children at First Street were not libertarians. They *thought* that they believed in compulsion, and rewards and punishments, and formal discipline, and report cards, and homework and elaborate school facilities. [Emphasis added.]

Now, the parents may well have been wrong in holding such beliefs, they may well have renounced them after experience with First Street, but I am at a loss to understand the concept of *thinking a belief*, if it means anything other than *believing*. Here Dennison condescends to his parents; he can also be surprisingly naive:

> It goes without saying that teachers must be competent (which does not *necessarily* mean passing courses in a teacher's college). Given this *sine qua non*, there is nothing mysterious. The present quagmire of public education is *entirely* the result of unworkable centralization and the lust for control that permeates every bureaucratic institution. [Emphasis added.]

SAMUEL McCRACKEN    33

To this one could answer that the relation of courses passed in a teacher's college to professional competence is somewhere near absolute zero, and that while it would be a happy thought that centralization and bureaucracy are the sole causes of all that is wrong with public education, there must be other causes, else the most centralized schools would be the worst, which is not necessarily so.

But in general, Dennison's theory, the product of carefully observed experience, and of a critical understanding of Tolstoy, Dewey, and A. S. Neill, is typified by the sort of caution and realism that entitle it to the label, "tough-minded." An example is his account of an imitation Summerhill. Such institutions have been mushrooming lately: one can follow their progress in a curious publication called the *New Schools Exchange Newsletter*, in which they publish self-descriptions. The *Newsletter* would be better named *The Journal of Educational Cant:* most of the accounts appear to have been plagiarized from last month's issue, and it is the rare school where education is not free, unstructured, and joyous, all at the same time. Most of the proprietors seem to view their students as a commodity ("We've got eight kids this term, and hope to get some more kids next"), and they are all just like Summerhill, except for two little differences. They do not appear to provide anything remotely like a classical education for those who want it, and none of them is run by that extraordinary genius A. S. Neill, or anything approaching a surrogate. Here is Dennison on one such school:

> I visited a school ostensibly modeled on Summerhill, but in fact (so I believe) not much like it. I noticed two teenagers who were pathologically depressed. I learned that they were suffering severe conflicts with their parents. I was informed, too, that their parents were small-minded, narrow, repressive, status-seeking petit-bourgeois; which is to say that the suffering of the two students had been invested with a programmatic, radical meaning: their detestation of their parents appeared as a form of loyalty to the school. The two students, in short, were being tugged in opposite directions by interested adults. To make matters worse, the tugging at school was largely *sub rosa*, implicit rather than overt, and the foreground was filled by "freedom," that is, by lack of contact, lack of guidance, lack of structure, lack of everything that children experiencing such disorders require. Let me hasten to say that such lacks cannot be filled by rules and regulations. They must be filled by persons, and not just any persons, but those capable of true encounter and decently motivated for work with the young. The problem at this school was that the director regarded staff and students less as people than as events in his own protracted

struggle against middle-class America. The faculty, too, consisted of True Believers, and I had never before seen such a listless, resentful bunch, or heard the words "creativity" and "spontaneity" bandied about quite so often.

It is not common for a member of a vanguard to be so clearsighted about his presumed allies. Where Dennison clearly differs from most of his fellow practitioners is in his fine understanding that the removal of external ordering devices requires replacement by internal ones, and that occasionally the external is justified in the absence of the internal. Thus, deciding that (a) Jose ought to learn to read, and (b) Jose would never decide on his own to start reading, Dennison simply began Jose's lessons in reading. Jose learned to read.

One of Dennison's particular strengths is his ability to see how quickly an innovator in theory can become treated as a guru and then misunderstood by a horde of Beatle-like followers. It is this critical ability, I believe, which proves Dennison no Postman or Weingartner, and which is pretty good evidence that he will not follow in Holt's footsteps. It seems very unlikely that Dennison will become no more than a self-exploiter, and he may well remain, as has Paul Goodman, a romantic to whom nonromantics must listen with absolute respect.

Holt, Postman and Weingartner, Leonard, and Dennison are likely to be the most influential of the authors the Grosses anthologize, for each of them has a program, and a program of a fairly fashionable sort. I therefore feel justified to a degree in neglecting to deal with other writers represented in the work (they include Jonathan Kozol, James Herndon, Herbert Kohl, and older, well-known writers like Paul Goodman, A. S. Neill, Edgar Z. Friedenberg, and Sylvia Ashton-Warner). All in all, *Radical School Reform* is a fair sampler of a movement, and its representativeness is hardly diminished by any doubts one may have about the validity of the movement itself. I do end by worrying about the book's possible influence on education; its publicists are already pushing it as a *vade mecum* for would-be reformers, and if there is anything than an already oversimplistic movement does not need, it is to be watered down for popular consumption in a general anthology. As a matter of fact, it is too bad for the movement to be defined, and its prophets identified, at all, for it is painful to see people like Paul Goodman and George Dennison entered on the same class lists with the Holts and the Postmans and Weingartners; for the genius of the former for simple solutions is balanced by a concomitant understanding of the complexities. If they begin to be read in capsule form, the distinction may begin to blur, and that would be most unfortunate.

AMITAI ETZIONI
# A REVIEW OF
# "CRISIS IN THE CLASSROOM"

Over the recent decades our ambition to fashion society in the shape of our values has swollen. We no longer accept society as a given, as a pre-existing state of nature. We view it as an arrangement, one which *we* can disassemble and then rearrange. We seek not merely to reform but to transform the relations among the races, the classes, the nations; we seek to deeply affect people's smoking, drug use, drinking, and eating habits, as well as to fundamentally change their education. Our economic, political, and intellectual capacity to affect these changes has increased, but much more slowly than our ambitions. We are now learning, as recent discussions of the "peace dividend" indicated, the full measure of this disparity between ambition and resources. Even if the war is finally terminated and the SALT talks do succeed, there apparently will be available only $15 to $20 new billions per annum for domestic reforms, which require at least $60 to $100 billions. As a nation, it seems, we are much more inclined to talk reform than to display the political will required to bring it about. In those domestic sectors where the nation does find the will and the resources, it frequently lacks the necessary know-how. The knowledge and skills needed to provide a *viable* plan for social engineering are still rudimentary. Frequently we are still guided by well meaning but inadequately conceptualized and poorly worked out blueprints, by semi-utopian programs of which Silberman's book is a recent example.

The problem is not Silberman's, but is a common one shared by most of our efforts at guided societal[1] change. Like several other such books, it is the result of a commission's study, involved extensive interviews, travel, and considerable staff work, and a $300,000 investment by the Carnegie Corporation. The study provides an opportunity to examine the problems encountered by those who seek to provide an intelligent input into the decisions of policy makers and into public debates as to what is to be done. Similar

From Amitai Etzioni, "Review of *Crisis in the Classroom*," *Harvard Educational Review*, 41, February 1971, 87-98. Copyright © 1971 by the President and Fellows of Harvard College.

questions raised by this book can be asked about the designs of the war against poverty, Title I, compensatory education, the Kerner Commission's report, and—more generally—the thinking which preceded and accompanied most of the four hundred odd domestic reform programs initiated in the U.S.A. since the early Sixties. (The limitations encountered by social thinkers of other societies, which include some of ours and some of their own, do not concern us here.)

Blueprints for a societal change may be usefully assessed in terms of: the definition of the problem (why is change needed); the goals subscribed to (where we ought to be); the specificity of the recommendations; the extent to which those are based on empirical evidence and on sound theory; the degree to which the recommendations take into account the linkages between the problem studied and others which inflict the same society, as well as the relationship between the policies recommended for the problem under study and those sought for other sectors of the same society; and the extent to which the analysis is anchored in an encompassing concept of the society and its dynamics.

## DEFINITION OF THE PROBLEM

I cannot summarize Silberman's definition of the problem more effectively than Christopher Lehmann-Haupt who wrote:

> Mr. Silberman has sailed up the shallow creek of American education, surveyed the landscape and pronounced it joyless, mindless, barren. The natives, he says, are pinched and crabbed, and stand before their children mumbling empty incantations; the children stare back silently, hollow-eyed, and pick their scabs. (*New York Times*, October 8, 1970).

Stylistically, Silberman, like most reform writers, utilizes straight English prose rather than sociologese. He is not reluctant to use terms which have normative and emotive connotations or to cue the reader to his general ideological posture which—unlike that of former Senators Tydings and Goodell—is radical-liberal. Typically, Silberman does not seek a revolution and is careful to disassociate himself from the more radical writers such as John Holt, Paul Goodman, and Edgar Z. Friedenberg. At the same time, he asks for *more* than piecemeal, limited reform. He believes that the total educational system of America must be transformed through the accumulation of sweeping, peaceful, and encompassing changes. In the course of these, the nation will be redone, since the ills of education are diagnosed as reflecting and reinforcing those of a society in deep crisis.

As in other such documents, for instance the Report of the Kerner Commission, the definition of the problem is by far the best part of the work. We recognize the symptoms pointed out; the challenge reads well; it arouses the desire to get out there and do something about all these horrors. They all deserve "A" for exhortation.

But these documents do not limit themselves to preaching or to outlining societal symptomatology; they do seek root-causes and they make what look like specific recommendations. Hence, they open themselves to the critique of their value as a guide to deliberate societal change. Silberman suggests that the crisis—education's loss of meaning and authority, and hence its reliance on discipline which *causes* disciplinary problems—results from the *rapid* changing of our world. As a consequence, the nation can no longer draw on an educational system whose purpose is to transfer the accumulated wisdom of earlier generations. A new system is needed which is highly "horizontal," participatory, and which stresses helping the pupil to evolve procedures for knowing rather than transmitting details. This new system should also focus on the evolution of the whole man rather than preparing manpower for a fragmented life in the obsolescent industrial-bureaucratic society. As I said, the definition of the problem is quite convincing. But what about the plan?

## THE PURPOSES OF THE NEW EDUCATION

Once the ills of the present are recited, setting the goals for the future becomes almost an inevitable step for the radical-liberal writer. But, as several commissions have discovered, setting goals is a very unrewarding enterprise.[2]

The twin traps which await the goal-setters are vagueness and dissension. To say, as Silberman does repeatedly, that the purpose of education should be to render our society "humane and just" is no more of a guidepost for school boards or community groups than the seven virtues and less so than the ten commandments. On the other hand, to specify what a just or a humane society entails is an inordinately difficult task, and one which would quickly elicit very considerable disagreements among those who are to accept the policy writer's advice.

Once it is recognized that consensus cannot be assumed, the policy writer must ask to what historical, societal, or political force or forces he addresses himself. Silberman and others write as if as long as their counsel is wise and worthy, it will be heeded. Actually, at the moment, there is very little reason to believe that America is headed toward either a humane or a just society or could be so transformed by any educational reforms the present system would tolerate. Why then design an educational system to serve such a transformed society?

While the answer is not to bless wherever the society is going anyhow, the writer whose interests go beyond preaching or fiction must constrain his prescriptions to the confines of where the society might be made to go. He must couple his work to goal-setting processes which grow out of the tensions and dynamics of the society he is addressing. The moralist can advocate anything *he* believes in. However, for societal designers to write policy to their own goals (or leave undocumented the assumption that their design is relevant to a viable societal, historical force) is to place themselves where God, history, the polity, or "the movement" belong, and to truncate analytic responsibilities.


## FROM THE CRISIS TO SILBERMAN'S FUTURE: HOW TO GET THERE?

The test for blueprints of reforms or societal transformations is not the acidity of their critical prolegomena or the placidity of their futuristic poetry but the sharpness of the cutting edge of their recommendations. Sharpness is to be found in making recommendations specific, spelling out the reasons one expects the proposed changes to have the projected impact, and in marshalling the necessary evidence to support such claims. Most blueprint makers escape such detailed specifications for any one of their recommendations, by briefly listing many recommendations. A typical example of this fallacy is the Kerner Commission Report which lists more than a hundred suggestions, none of which are spelled out. Silberman achieves a better balance. His core idea, the informalization of American schools, receives considerable treatment in his book. Many of the numerous recommendations he makes, concerning, for instance, changes in teacher education, follow from or supplement his core idea. How valid is the core conception?

The main features of informal schools, a subject to which we cannot do justice here, are the replacement of the teacher as directing a passively seated class of children, by several "interest areas" in which children *do*, at their own pace, a variety of things *they* are interested in, for varying time intervals, with the help of teachers and teacher-aides. Self-directed, self-disciplined, the children enjoy rather than work at their tasks. The teachers' main duty is to provide a stimulating, encouraging environment. This informalization of the schools entails more than reorganization. Teachers must be re-educated to be able to fulfill their roles in the new classroom. The substance of the curriculum must be adapted to be more meaningful, open to the child's interests, and "balanced" to include the affective next to the cognitive, and esthetics and ethics next to acquiring information and skills.

Informal schools were recommended by the Plowden Report of Great Britain and are being introduced there. "Open classroom" is a similar, albeit more radical, concept endorsed by a variety of American writers on education and practiced in a few places in this country. The progressive movement harbored a similar idea. Silberman stresses the differences between the idea he endorses, the informalizing schools, and the open or progressive mode of education. In the informal school, he says, the teacher does have a guiding role. Spontaneity, it is recognized, is not all that is needed; encouragement to growth is also to be provided.

Now we turn to the tough test: how valid are the prescriptions? If you come to a society and recommend that its schools (or welfare system, or prisons, or some other major institution) be remade, and your advice is faulty, energies and resources made available to reform will be wasted; frustrations will multiply; and the end result may be as bad or worse than where you started. (Silberman's report on the fate of all pre-Silberman educational reform movements in the U.S.A. provides convincing reading on this subject.) Hence, the responsible designer must be precise enough in his recommendations so that his ideas can be critically examined and tested. After all, a mere change in the direction of the traffic, as Sweden found out recently, costs millions of dollars and requires considerable other adaptations. Informalizing the American schools, if it can be done, is not much less of an undertaking then the war on proverty and may be an even match to desegregation.

The demand to provide an idea which would make a viable program, let me be the first to admit, is a harsh one. In each area of social endeavor, there are thousands of ideas, hundreds of programs, and, at best, a handful of effective reforms. That is, most ideas do not survive the trip from concept to reality and all are significantly modified on the way. The steps needed to select those ideas which could make viable programs of reconstruction are best depicted in terms of the "R and D" (for "research and development") sequence followed in engineering. In this field, a concept is first concretized into a rough sketch, which is followed by the production of detailed blueprints. These, in turn, are converted into small scale models, which are tested in laboratories. Models which survive these tests provide the basis for one or more full-scale prototypes which are built and tried. In social "engineering," the tendency is still to omit most or all of these stages and to jump from an idea to its implementation in a mass system. In this way, a theoretical postulate was written into the law, which required "maximum feasible participation of the poor," which view turned out to be quite unfeasible. A form of compensatory education for the disadvantaged was awarded $1.2 billion a year over four years under Title I before the Coleman Report, the key relevant research on the possible effects of such a drive, was available.

Silberman's informalize-the-schools offers an idea in the rough-sketch stage. He does point to live systems (in U.K. and U.S.) to support the viability of his plan. However, for reasons which will become evident below, these do *not* provide the test or specificity needed to evaluate the idea of informal schooling. Let me digress long enough to say that there is only so much one man can do, even with $300,000 and a team. Nor am I sorry to see an idea written up. Silberman's book does, though serve well to illustrate what is needed to advance a process he and many others start, but few care to advance, let alone to complete. How far does Silberman carry the scheme he favors? How specified and documented is his advice?

## SPECIFICITY

Critical to the whole idea of the informal classroom is the role of the teacher. If he overly exerts his influence by making children learn his ways, his lines, the informal school will be little more than the old system in a new disguise. However, if he is too passive allowing anarchy and indulgence to prevail, the new school may be rather like some of the least structured progressive schools. Silberman speaks about the "right balance" between allowing the child's interests to guide the educational process and allowing the teacher to guide the child toward the knowledge, skill, and development of self-discipline. However, he gives the reader no set of indicators by which he can discern if such a balance exists in a classroom under observation. Even in these general terms, he leaves the range quite open, stating at one point about the system he approves, ". . . the teachers and administrators with whom I talked and whose informal classrooms I observed were more than simply 'here'; they were very much in charge" (p. 210). Discussing Piaget's contribution to what educational practice ought to be, Silberman says that "the child is the principal agent in his own education and mental development" (p. 215).

Silberman recognizes the pivotal nature of teacher education for the translation of the informal school idea into practice. But several of the measures he suggests are so vague that they amount to a statement of faith or expression of sentiment. For instance, he urges that teachers should think about education, that the teacher should be infused with purpose. Hence, like many others, Silberman is frequently in the re-endorsing the banners stage rather than in the stage of program development (which in itself is only the second step on the long road to societal change).

Particularly naive are Silberman's implicit assumptions about the societal anchoring of the present structure and the conditions under which it may be unlocked and reshaped. The *I.D.E.A. Reporter* ("News from the World of Education") summarizes Silberman's message on this point: ". . . by and large, teachers, principals, and superintendents are decent, intelligent, and caring people who try to do their best by their lights. If they make a botch of it, and an uncomfortably large number do, it is because it simply never occurs to more than a handful to ask *why* they are doing what they are doing—to think seriously or deeply about the purposes or consequences of education."[3] Silberman's theory is not quite that simple, but almost so.

Silberman endorses the idea that all students should do some teaching as a major way to humanize them and that all university departments should make teacher education one of their prime goals. But, one must ask, is it accidental that these ideas, which are not completely novel, have not been implemented so far? Are there other values which will have to be sacrificed to maximize this educational one? Are there deep-seated interests which are being challenged? These are problems of substantive rationality (multiplicity of purposes) and politics (how sufficient support may be marshalled for the desired change). Without some answer to these kinds of questions, no idea can be realistically specified.

While Silberman generally stays on a level of generality, which in a sense protects the ideas he promotes, at one key juncture his vagueness casts doubt on the validity of the whole conception. This concerns his evidence.

## ON THE ROLE OF DATA

Ideas fly cheaply, evidence is hard to muster. Hence, ideas which are substantiated by evidence, supported by data that they "work," are to be particularly treasured. Before turning to the essence of the data on the merits of informal schools, let me say that, throughout the book, the research Silberman and his staff undertook is not of high quality. In their attempts to substantiate a point, they frequently draw on sources even vaguer and more immune to evidence than Silberman himself. For instance, so what if Paul Goodman "argues" that "technology *is* a branch of moral philosophy" or if Harold Taylor has said that "preparing to become a teacher is like preparing to become a poet?" Does this co-endorsement of banners make them wiser, more useful, and indeed more authoritative? Whole books, some of which are edited collections of papers, are cited as sources of evidence for specific points. And statistical data is used in a rather relaxed manner.

Silberman relies heavily on journalistic observations of the "I-have-seen-it-myself" type. I am among those sociologists who maintain that such data is often as good a source as quantitative data and that is almost invariably a valuable complement to quantitative data. However, one must separate credible from tendentious reporting. When I read that in a primary school in Oxfordshire "there is no ambivalence about authority and no confusion about roles" and that in an infant school in London we find ". . . the combination of great joy and spontaneity and activity with equally great self-control and order" and that "in every formal classroom that I went to visit in England, children were restless" and so on, I take it for granted that such statements are, at least, exaggerated, since very few social phenomena are that monolithic. As Silberman's reporting is loaded with such adjectives, I cannot but start wondering about the reliability of all his first-hand observations.

Second, the well-trained and qualified journalist, anthropologist, and historian has a special sense which allows him to tell the trivial from the consequential. It is a poor journalist who attempts to use the trivial to claim that it stands for the consequential, which he did not observe and hence cannot report from first hand. Too often Silberman reports relatively trivial items, as follows:

A child who has been seated at a table, writing, hurriedly leaves as she hears the call for physical education. "Come back, please, Michelle; your chair isn't put back," the teacher softly calls to her. "We don't have very many rules," the teacher tells the visitor, "but children must learn to look after the property and put things back where they belong." (p.227)

A school in Leicestershire. In a corner where two main corridors meet, is a large table with a sign in large letters reading, "Smell everything on this table." On the table are a number of jars, of rose petals, of mixed flowers, of vanilla, coffee, cloves, and various other herbs and spices. (p. 224)

Thus, it is not Silberman's journalistic approach to data which weakens his case, but his weak journalism softens the data.

This weakness chiefly concerns secondary points; the main empirical softness is found in the lack of clarity concerning schools which have been successfully informalized. Silberman recommends informal schools on the basis of "it has been done, successfully, in Britain" (and in a few cases in the U.S.A.). That is, there *are* viable prototypes. The evidence of success of these schools is, by necessity, limited and incomplete since the approach is fairly new and full evaluation is very difficult. But the very fact that schools can be organized in this way, and that they graduate students who are at least not very poorly educated, is itself of great significance. One must then ask—*which* schools have been informalized in Britain? Are these infant schools (age 5 to 7) *or* schools in general, including secondary ones? It is a very different proposition to state that the first grade should be quite similar to the Kindergarten and to limit the informalization largely to the first two school years, than to state that "schools" should be full of learn-through-play, do-your-own-thing and so on. At one point Silberman makes quite clear that the British experience is much more extensive in infant schools than in higher grades of primary schools. Infant schools provide much of the "it works" data and they are frequently cited as the source of his first-hand observations. However, in contrast to the factual materials presented, his discussion tends to imply that at least all grades of the primary school should be informalized and, to a somewhat lesser extent, also those of the secondary schools. To put it more sharply—where the evidence is relatively solid, for the "infant age,—the recommendations offer little that is new either for educational thought *or* practice; where the recommendation requires far-reaching changes, it has little grounding in empirical reality.[4]

Furthermore, the data gives an unclear picture as to the value of these schools for pupils from a working class or lower middle class background. It is also unclear whether there are special factors in Britain which are not transferable to American schools; for example, the role of the principal seems to be quite different in the two school systems. Finally, as long as attendance is required, children are evaluated (graded), and many parents demand "achievements," it is unclear if informalized schools will really be fundamentally different from the existing ones—an assumption which runs throughout Silberman's book.


## HUMAN NATURE, INSTITUTIONALIZATION, AND PIAGET

Any educational theory is predicated on certain implicit or explicit assumptions about human nature. To what extent is man open to instruction or is he biologically predetermined? And, is man straining toward the light of reason or must he be coaxed to look at it? The prevailing view of man's nature in the social sciences and in the educational establishment downgrades biological factors (often viewed as racist) and tends to assume that man is very educable. Silberman subscribes to this highly optimistic position.

Among the optimists, there are those who see man taking to education as naturally as a duck to water; this propensity approximates the unfolding of an instinct, which can be helped or hindered by the educational institutions, but which cannot be fundamentally shaped by them. Piaget's theory, which Silberman embraces, is interpreted as a major support of this view.

This great confidence in human nature is coupled with a great suspicion of institutions. Schools, at least as they are presently constituted, are viewed as hindering or distorting this natural development. The more extreme proponents favor doing away with schools as institutions. The more moderate counsellors, like Silberman, favor, in effect, curbing their scope, reducing their institutionalization, and restructuring the remaining elements in such a way that the child is helped in his growth rather than being directed. The informalizers stress the second element (of help), while the liberators concentrate on the first (reducing the scope). Silberman's program is rich in both, although he talks as if it is chiefly a matter of moving from control to assistance.

My view of human nature is less optimistic. Recent evidence suggests that physiological factors (such as nourishment) and social background factors (such as those recorded by the Coleman report and studies by compensatory educators) are quite powerful. As a result, we see that preschool and extraschool forces can damage many children to the point where their preprogrammed" sequence of capacities, as Piaget followers see them, are so severely disturbed that they will not unfold and can be tapped by the *educator only through very great efforts and costs.* For me, the normative conclusion derived from this evidence is *not* to reduce our educational efforts for the disadvantaged, but to start earlier, to move more broadly, to be more persistent, and to invest many more resources in such efforts. But, it also means that school organization and curriculum often cannot be based on an optimistic assumption about the unfolding natural powers of the child. Educators must recognize that the natural sequence is often derailed and that only large guided efforts *on their side* can put the child back on this high actualization track.

Also, it must be noted that Piaget's work refers to stages of learning in which the *inner capacities* blossom; but, there is no evidence to show that these capacities will be actualized unless actualization is *systematically* encouraged. One cannot derive from man's capacity to walk on two legs the assumption that he will unless he is actively taught to do so. Nor can one assume that a child, possessing a certain natural capacity, also possesses a natural motivation to exercise it.

The critical question becomes then—how much, how detailed, how encompassing a guiding hand is needed? Silberman does not hold the radical position, which in effect eliminates such guidance; he does see a role for a teacher. But, he philosophically leans towards a teacher who is child-centered, not in the sense of responding to the child's underlying capacities, but to his *expressed* needs. Informalization aims to give prime emphasis to the child's *interests*, which may or may not correspond with his natural capacities, and to construct the educational process around his wishes.

In my opinion, the majority of the children in *our* society need more of a guiding hand, a more institutionalized school than the highly informal school that the theorists advocate. A school system is needed which exercises less control than the present but provides more guidance than the one Silberman advocates. The exact mix cannot be spelled out within the limits of a review essay. Nor should it be based on idle speculation; different mixes should be tried and evaluated. It may well be established that children who come from privileged homes, often inconsistent or ultra permissive, may have to learn to function within a *somewhat* more structured environment. No society could function if all its members acted as selfishly as those who seek to maximize their freedoms, disregarding the costs such maximization imposes on others. Children from lower middle-class homes may have to be guided in learning to cope with more freedom than they are accustomed to, so that they will not backlash in frustration when they are given more of it. (Possibly here the first grades would be more formal than the later ones, within the primary school, to reduce the discontinuity in the transition from the authoritarian home to the informal school.) A still different approach may have to be designed for those whose natural potential capacities have been suppressed by the conditions which prevail in disadvantaged communities. The concept of the same school structure for all never had any broad reality in a society where children come from such divergent starting points. Children may now go to what looks like the same school but actually there are great differences among schools in the way the same rules and organizational principles are applied, and these differences are correlated with class background. Nor has the notion of one school for all, on the face of it a great equality, any normative validity. "Informality for all" is no more realistic than assuming you can teach all fifth graders the same math just because the Piaget scheme suggests that they all ought to be "ready" for it.

Most important of all, the school is unavoidably a funnel which leads from infancy at home to the adult occupational structure in the greater society. Hence, just as earlier grades are and ought to be much more like home, the later grades ought to be more like the society in which the students will live. This ought to be a better society than the present one; hence the higher grades may be geared not only to the present, but also to a brighter future, although not to a utopia. Otherwise, one burdens the educational system with more pressures than it can possibly sustain; this in turn could backfire both against the schools and their graduates. Therefore, an adequate theory of education requires a conception of the society from which the child comes and which he will enter as an adult—and an understanding of the amount of leverage the school can be reasonably expected to have on either of these aspects of society. To reiterate, I see the backgrounds of the majority of children as highly suppressive to their natural capacities and, hence, the school organization, first of all, must serve a corrective function for these. It is not only the disadvantaged who are in need of decompressive education, but also those from the silent majority and from ultra permissive or inconsistent homes.[5] It is precisely in this area that the school's greatest potential leverage lies, especially if it works in connection with other social institutions, ranging in scope from labor exchanges to housing authorities.

Considerations of the society into which the students will graduate are equally important; it is unfair and unrealistic to prepare them for the educator's favorite dream world because education does not have the force to transform society. Hence, educating students for life in a society which does not exist, say in Silberman's "humane and just society" or for one in which work is as much fun as play—will *not* yield such a society, but might well serve to prepare a frustrated and disillusioned generation of graduates. Moreover, the students mostly are much too smart for such schemes to suceed *in* school, especially in high school and college; they seek education which has a reality and when this is not given—the educator's utopianism becomes a major alienating factor.

Silberman correctly stresses that our schools are organized as if everyone will graduate either to work on an assembly line or in a civil service. They are best suited to preparing indifferent cogs for an industrial-bureaucratic machinery; that is, at best, to be part of yesterday's world. Schools must, hence, be reorganized, not just in the substance of their teaching but in the very educational environment and experience they provide, to prepare their students for the different societies of 1980 and even for the year 2000 and beyond. But, despite the hip talk about rapid societal change, as far as I can foresee, our society will continue to have major instrumental and technical needs. True, we will be able to work less, and less efficiently, and still be affluent. And we can realistically help prepare students for a world with more "work" and less "labor" (to use Hannah Arendt's terms) and a world in which more energy and time are devoted to personal and interpersonal growth, and less to productivity—all educational purposes for which informal schooling is suited. However, we must also recognize that the transition from one societal pattern to another will not be abrupt, even if there will be a radical revolution, and a revolution does not seem imminent. Hence, schools must help prepare the child for a better society; but, unfortunately, it is premature to prepare him for the good society. To cease to educate children for discipline or to put a ceiling on their spontaneity, to build up their intolerance for periods of labor, and their acceptance of rules and authority—is to prevent the educational system from helping to bring about that change for which the society is *ripe*. Our efforts to prepare students for a society that may exist at a later time or for a society which cannot exist *reduces* the impact of the educational system, as an agent of societal change. Its graduates will be too utopia-minded to join with other groups working for societal change, and this in turn will lead the graduates to withdraw into apathy, romantic revolutionary infantile acts, or to reject their education in favor of the world around them, as it is. The well-known principle of physical education applies here: one helps the pupil to evolve goals which require that he stretch his muscles, but not to run one mile in three minutes. One helps the pupil to raise his sights, as his actualized capacities (as distinct from his potential ones) grow. Such a posture would spell, for the organization of schools, moving from a relatively informal organization in the early years (subject to great variations according to varying decompressive needs) to a *relatively* less informal, more uniform, more specialized schooling as we move closer to graduation.

It may seem ungrateful to a book which raises many provocative issues to conclude by saying that the best we can hope to do is to outgrow it rapidly—both as a policy guide for educational reforms and as a form of policy research. But this recommendation seems appropriate not only for this work but for many which recently provided a stimulating but also "soft" basis for new policy making in education and societal guidance in general.

FRED M. HECHINGER

# VERSUS SUMMERHILL

Summerhill is not a school but a religion. That is why one can be intrigued by it—can even admire it—without being converted to it. To derive benefits from it for one's children requires religious faith in the efficacy of its myths. As with every religion, faith distilled into fanaticism can be dangerous. But there is so much essential goodness of intent and spirit in Summerhill that its doctrine may—in modified form—be most beneficial to ordinary parents who send their children to a variety of ordinary schools.

The underlying dogma of the Summerhill faith is that children, if not subjected to any adult pressures or influences, are perfect seeds that will turn into beings of predestined goodness. A. S. Neill actually goes beyond this when he says: "My view is that a child is innately wise and realistic. If left to himself without adult suggestion of any kind, he will develop as far as he is capable of developing."

This is not unlike the idea of Rousseau's Noble Savage, only presumably without the savagery. It is a difficult theory for parents to subscribe to when they have in fact experienced mean and contrary traits in their children; but Neill would (probably with much justification) dismiss such objections by pointing to the mean and contrary streaks in the parents and other adults and to the mean and contrary treatment to which the children have been subjected.

The holy writ of Summerhill says that if the mean and repressive influences could only be removed, the child would flower into a good adult according to his capacity. Whatever his accomplishments might turn out to be, he would be happy, and happiness is Summerhill's holy grail. It is not off in some distant promised land; it is attainable.

True to this belief, the original Summerhill therefore has been made into a place in which the mean and repressive influences have been removed, to the best human ability. It is not something that can be totally accomplished, any more than church or temple can be purged of human corruption and made into the original Eden; but it is fair to say that Summerhill has been startlingly successful in approaching its own ideal. Neill, by admitting that not all teachers nor even all children work out, and some have to be let go, defines the limitations of the experiment with characteristic honesty. But on the whole, Summerhill has created an oasis in which the children are left to develop without pressure and repression.

But even if it were not a religion and Neill its prophet and patron saint Summerhill would not be a school. It is really a family—an ideal family, to be sure, without overly possessive attachments—with an option to learn, but no compulsion to do so.

Size and arrangements alone make it a family rather than a school. It is very doubtful whether Summerhill, even given the funds and the facilities, could remain intact if it had many more than the 45 youngsters, subdivided into many smaller living and playing units.

It is more than doubtful—it is inconceivable—that Summerhill could exist without Neill. Whether one agrees or disagrees with him (and only the most computerized misanthrope could totally disagree with him) the fact is that he is a man of saintly strength and force. His intertwined belief in the child and the idea becomes, in the sweep of his eloquence, virtually irresistible. And this is so simply because all reservations are easily rejected by his conviction: it is the corruption of the world around, not any seed in body or soul, that corrupts the child. It is a conviction, unshakably held by Neill (without any shred of truculence), that can never be disproven. Unfortunately, in the face of continuing corruption, it cannot be proven either.

The rub is that—however some of the disciples and imitators are sure to dispute this—Summerhill cannot be reproduced. It is doubtful that even the original Summerhill will be able long to survive its founder. Indeed, the occasional playful exercise described by Neill in which he pretends that he has died and is succeeded by some dictatorial school master almost seems like a subconscious premonition. Neill's successor, of course, will not be a martinet or scoundrel, although he may seem so to the children, but he will at best be a disciple. Disciples rarely save any enterprise or idea.

But with or without Neill, Summerhill, not being a school, cannot be turned into the prototype of anything but an occasional small reproduction—private, selective, special.

This is inherently so because—as Neill makes unmistakably clear—the great majority of the world's parents do not believe in his basic concepts. They do not believe that children can be brought up without the customary restraints; that children can be groomed for a competitive world without competition in school; that children can be left to go about their growing up without being made to attend class or study certain subjects and learn certain skills.

As long as this is so, there is no way of setting up Summerhills for great numbers—or for any more than the occasional odd parents who march to Neill's drummer. Neill himself makes it quite clear that he cannot fight the realities outside. There is pathos in Neill's realization that, while he may write about what he feels is wrong with society and teach the children of the few who agree with him, if he tried to reform society by action, society would fight back. He even believes, perhaps a little too flamboyantly or pessimistically, that it would kill him "as a public danger."

"Hating compromise as I do, I have to compromise here, realizing that my primary job is not the reformation of society, but the bringing of happiness to some few children," he writes with disarming modesty.

And so, Summerhill remains, in his own words, "an island." (He would not even think of asking the local newspaper to publish success stories about his old pupils, and could you be more of an island in this age of the press agent, and expect to go into mass-production.)

Yet, despite its limitations as a model for mass-education, Summerhill is one of the world's most powerful ideas that is not likely ever to die. It has lived before Neill, although it has rarely been represented with such dynamic, charismatic power. It will outlast him—nuclear fission permitting—as long as men live and learn.

Parents who love their children should know about Summerhill. Even if they refuse to share Neill's total faith they should try to imagine how much happier their children might be if their natural childish drives, curiosities and creativity could be given their way.

Just as Freud opened the eyes of men and physicians to the terrible damage done by sterile repressions, those who bring up children need to question, day after day, whether many of the old restrictions and taboos are not in fact mental and physical chains which, though designed to shape them, actually weigh their children down and misshape their bodies and minds.

In an age when mothers worry about College Board test scores before their tots enter nursery school, the Summerhill contempt for the educational rat race—for the school that trains rather than liberates—is an antidote against a terrible pollution.

At a time of frantic affluence, the Summerhill contempt for educational upward mobility to material success is a reminder that parental ambition to shine through the accomplishments of one's children can be mental cruelty of tribal savagery.

FRED M. HECHINGER    51

To all but the most incorrigible reactionaries, it is clear that there is so much wrong with social and political values today that an affirmative appeal from the heart is a humanitarian service to all. Neill says:

> Most political newspapers are bristling with hate, hate all the time. Too many are socialistic because they hate the rich instead of loving the poor. . . . All the Greek and math and history in the world will not help to make the home more loving, the child free from inhibitions, the parent free from neurosis. . . . New generations must be given the chance to grow in freedom. The bestowal of freedom is the bestowal of love. And only love can save the world.

To Neill, the issue is simple, perhaps oversimplified in the view of some nonbelievers. He sees a civilization that is sick and unhappy, producing children who, being made unhappy, will grow into sick and oppressive adults. He is repelled by the ritual of stressing the negative—saying "don't" to children rather than "do;" relying on fear rather than love.

Unlike other reformers, Neill is not a man of bromides. Except when he lives at Summerhill, he is near despair, knowing that "the fight is an unequal one, for the haters control education, religion, the law, the armies, and the vile prisons."

To Neill, "it is a race between the believers in deadness and the believers in life." It is a race in which "no man dare remain neutral . . . the death side gives us the problem child; the life side will give us the healthy child."

Every parent and every teacher—whether he cares about the arrangements and the dogma of Summerhill—ought to carry this warning with him to the nursery and to the classroom.

I recommend Summerhill to parents and teachers—but not without misgivings. It is a religion based on love for, and understanding of, children; but it carries with it a religious mysticism that should not be accepted without critical analysis.

There is, in Neill himself, a strange streak of anti-intellectualism, almost a frantic rejection of all academic value judgments. Whatever the child likes, whatever makes him happy, is equal to any other enterprise. Bach equals Elvis Presley.

Neill can get upset about a ruined chisel but refuses to fuss about a book carelessly left in the rain "for books have little value for me."

This, I think, is a flaw that affects the Summerhill religion and the Neill philosophy. It claims to be noncoercive; but the model and the life style of those who teach do, in fact, coerce, however gently. The priorities of Summerhill are so nonintellectual as to place the book, the literary masterpiece, the evolution of thought at a disadvantage.

Neill is undoubtedly right in objecting—almost as much as to John Dewey's "learning by doing" reliance on the pragmatic consumer lesson—to the sugar-coated abomination of learning by playing or French without tears; but I am not convinced that the way to correct the subversion of honest play is to give it unlimited parity with work. Neither the history of man nor that of pedagogy has offered convincing proof that the child, if left without adult suggestion will (as Neill insists), "develop as far as he is capable of developing" by his own initiative.

Neill claims, and his disciples make an important point of it, that children who have the innate ability and wish to be scholars will be scholars, just as those who are only fit to sweep the streets will sweep the streets—and are likely, if left to their devices, to be happy street sweepers.

This, it seems to me, is an over-extension of the Freudian principle. It does not follow that men, merely by being free of sexual repressions, will lead happy lives—even only sexually—unless they are also positively guided into the proper use of their potential. While innate scholarly ability is essential to the development of scholars, it is not realistic to expect the wish to be a scholar to be present in every academically gifted child. Surely, the sampling of the delights and possibilities of scholarship—the function of good teaching, in contrast to the sterile or rote approach to learning—is part of the process. If repression and coercion are wrong, is not the absence of exposure, or sampling under expert guidance, equally deficient?

"Whether a school has or has not a special method for teaching long division is of no significance, for long division is of no importance except to those who *want* to learn it," says Neill. I find no logic in this. Only the rare—even odd—child is likely to want to learn long division, ever, unless he is given to understand what intellectual purpose it may ultimately serve. This is true of so much initial intellectual endeavor that it is very unlikely that intellectual progress—or the life of the mind—would get a fair shake under Summerhill auspices. Neill appears willing to sacrifice brain to heart.

Neill's criticism of the conventional teachers is that they lack "the power to subordinate thinking to feeling." He is distressed by any schooling that "goes on separating the head from the heart."

This is an immensely attractive concept. It is attractive, in part,

FRED M. HECHINGER    53

for very sound reasons—because there is, in truth, so much heart-less use of brain power. Much of the suffering in the world and in any community is caused by the highly intelligent who act without feeling and conscience. Much of what pretends to be government planning—particularly in the area of national defense—is based on computerized data, without concern for the consequences to humanity or human priorities.

But concern about the downgrading of the intellect and the excessive reliance on feelings and emotions is that, in the end, the results tend to be just about equally damaging to the only constituency that counts—people. The history of reforms is strewn with wreckage caused by kindly emotions defeated by lack of intellectual rigor.

This, too, is what worries me about the similarity between the Summerhill ideology and the present student unrest. Nowhere does the Summerhill dogma have as much appeal as among young rebels who seek happiness in activism. It is in the revolutionary occupation of buildings and the fellowship of the sit-in that youth finds emotional satisfaction based on the subordination of brain to emotion. Unfortunately, it also often seems to be an extension of just the kind of playing to which Summerhill accords such a key role. Yet, it is the playful, happiness-seeking campus revolution that is likely, not only to fragment and undermine the academic community, but frustrate and, in the end, disappoint and alienate those who seek concrete redress of just grievances. To uplift the poor and the deprived requires more than heart and sympathy; it calls for effective strategies of social and economic reforms. Perhaps the greatest risk of heart without intellect is that it is so easily fooled, and those in search of power inevitably know, and ruthlessly exploit, this.

There is natural appeal, too, in Neill's report that, no matter how long some youngsters might have decided to skip academic preparation, they quickly make up for lost time when they suddenly decide to aim for the university admissions examinations. This may offer some useful commentary on the nature of those tests—and the excessive and long-range worry expended on them traditionally by many parents and their children. On that score—if Summerhill manages to question and perhaps demolish some sterile myths—much is to be gained. But it does not answer my concern that much latent talent remains undeveloped in the process and that indeed the occasional decision to opt for the climb up the academic ladder is even more likely to be made on the basis of irrational, extraneous influences than under the system of more conventional pressures.

Her Majesty's Inspectors, who incidentally approached Summerhill with a model of understanding that might well be studied by those who have power over school accreditation and standards in the United States, in the end could not suppress some honest professional doubts.

"To have created a situation in which academic education of the most intelligent kind could flourish is an achievement; but in fact, it is not flourishing and a great opportunity is being lost," the inspectors said.

To Neill, this criticism meant that even the most sympathetic education officials could not completely "rise above their academic preoccupations" and that they overlooked the fact that the system does flourish when a child wants an academic education. The question on which, not unlike the inspectors, I part ways with Summerhill is whether tastes and wants need not be nourished, trained, acquired. I often feel that, had I been permitted to benefit a little more from the Neill philosophy in my schooling, I might have gained some of his facility with, and enjoyment of, the chisel and the rake. But I would not want to trade such tastes and wants for my greater concern with books. While I agree with his contempt for dessicated bookishness in the worst of traditional education, I cannot accept attitudes which, as a matter of experience and observation, give the nonintellectual drives a fast and clear track.

Summerhill is rightly opposed to fear as a pedagogical tool. But Neill admits that the search for approval is a strong human drive, and in the concern for lack of approval (even by Neill and the best, most saintly of his teachers) there is, of course, an element of fear.

The goal—and I think the Summerhill disciples might be persuaded to accept this revision of the absence-of-fear concept—ought to be to teach children to consider the consequences of their actions and inactions, and in the light of such considerations to curb their desires for instant gratification. What this calls for, however, is the abandonment of the search for immediate happiness in the hope of attaining greater happiness later—with lesser risks of creating unhappiness in others. Whether this can be expected of children, without more direct guidance and restraints than Summerhill admits (or without so much covert manipulation that it would make dishonest men and women of the faculty), seems to me highly questionable. Even if Neill, and an occasional genius like him, can bring it off, this seems to me the kind of success story that proves the exception rather than the rule.

There is a direct line from America's Progressive Education Movement of the 1920s to Summerhill. But in reality, there is nevertheless a fundamental difference. The old progressives believed fervently in what they thought of as life-adjustment education, and only the more radical among them also thought of the school as an instrument of social change or even revolution.

Neill clearly does not want to adjust children to the corruptions and sterile competition of a life that he sees around him. This is to his credit. Simply to train people to play the game, whatever it may be, and to aim for the jackpot under existing rules is surely a perversion of the educational process. It is not adjustment to life but to death-in-life, and I applaud Neill's refusal to have any part in such an enterprise.

But not to bring up children to understand, and cope with, the realities and the challenges of the competition "outside" is to offer them little more than an escape into their islands of happiness, impotent either to adjust to existing realities or to change them into better ones.

In the end, the impact of Summerhill is—as it ought to be—in the needs of the beholder. Much depends on the society in which the schools exist which Summerhill wants to reform. If it is true in Britain, for instance, as Neill indicated, that many babies are still subjected to the tyranny of a rigid feeding schedule, then the need to remove these irrational restraints from child care is great. Her Majesty's Inspectors may have been surprised (and, I hope, pleased) not to find youngsters at Summerhill jumping to attention as they entered the classroom; but most sensible American schools have long since abandoned this disruptive Teutonic ersatz respect.

At a time when permissiveness in the American home and school has often become a mindless exercise in the abolition of all value judgments and standards of conduct, the Summerhill lesson should be read with caution and discrimination; it should be read particularly with the clear understanding that Neill would never expect any part of his religion to work without an abiding faith in the joint enterprise—adults and children together—of the search for what is good and right and peaceful. He seeks, as a result of the removal of restraints, not orgiastic license but self-discipline.

Unless Summerhill is considered in such a light, it can be very potent poison, encouraging parents and teachers in a hands-off policy, without the compelling dedication and love and, even more important, the essential adult example of righteousness and—I hesitate to use the word because of its chronic abuse—goodness. Without these ingredients, the free-style approach is dynamite. It may well turn children (even if they are indeed Noble Savages, which I doubt) into Ignoble Savages when they grow up.

But taken with these cautions an infusion of Summerhill into the minds of those who rear or educate children and into educational institutions is an important antidote against the suspicions and rigidities that creep into the brains of adults and into the policies of schools.

I recoil when Neill says: "The child should not do anything until he comes to the opinion—his own opinion—that it should be done."

But then I realize that Neill and•his handpicked staff intend to be molders of opinion, though they would deny this, by way of demonstrated love and understanding—and with the added caveat that nobody's freedom must interfere with anybody else's.

This is why I agree with Neill that the future of Summerhill itself is of little import, while the future of the Summerhill idea is "of the greatest importance to humanity." My reservations about it are comparable to those I hold about many religious faiths and rituals in whose moral and ethical foundations I urgently concur.

SIDNEY HOOK

# JOHN DEWEY
# AND HIS BETRAYERS

During the last few years there has been an open season on the American school system from the most elementary to advanced levels. It has been indicted not only for its failure to teach the rudiments of the traditional disciplines, but for its repressive attitude towards the spontaneous activities and the outreaching natural curiosity of the child and student as learning animals. The schools have been compared to penal institutions not only because of the physical conditions that exist in some ghetto areas but even more so because of the manner, spirit, and methods of instruction.

Such criticism comes from those who regard themselves as libertarians and humanists and who either profess themselves inspired to some degree by the thought of John Dewey or are commonly regarded as continuing his influence—writers like Paul Goodman, Ivan Illich, John Holt, Jonathan Kozol, George Dennison,

From Sidney Hook, "John Dewey and His Betrayers," *Change* (November 1971), pp. 22-26.

Edgar Friedenberg, George Leonard. Their criticisms are exercising a surprising influence on educators and teachers: they are partly responsible for a phenomenon observable in liberal arts colleges from one end of the country to another, viz., the abandonment of required courses and even area distribution studies as unendurable forms of faculty paternalism and violations of the "student's autonomy, his moral freedom and responsibility." Since the student, in this conception, is the best judge of his own educational needs, it is a tyrannical imposition from without to require him to take any course that he thinks he does not need.

I am concerned here with the ways in which such views misinterpret the thought of John Dewey. It is an open question whether Dewey's educational philosophy has been more flagrantly distorted in the accounts given of it by some of his latter-day disciples than by the criticisms of his vociferous detractors. Both, it seems to me, have been intellectually irresponsible in disregarding his plain and easily available texts. But the moral failings of the professed followers of Dewey are graver than those of his critics: first, by the very virtue of their allegiance, which should impose a greater conscientiousness upon them, and second, because the fundamentalist critics of Dewey have as a rule seized upon *their* formulations, as professed followers of Dewey, as evidence of the validity of their fundamentalist reading of him.

The first misconception of John Dewey's philosophy stems from the notion that because he stressed the importance of freedom, he was therefore opposed to authority. Nothing could be farther removed from his true teaching. "The need for authority," he wrote, "is a constant need of man" (*Problems of Men*, p. 169). It is a constant need because conflicts, differences, incompatible desires, perspectives, and possibilities are ever present features of existence and experience. Some authority is therefore necessary, and for Dewey the supreme authority is intelligence. It is "the method of intelligence, exemplified in [but not identical with] science, [that should be] supreme in education" (*Experience and Education*, p. 100). Intelligence recognizes that not all forms of conduct are possible or desirable, that restriction and negation are as central to any discipline as affirmation, and that the growth which prepares the way for further desirable growth can be achieved only through a limitation of possibilities. Freedom outside the context of the authority of intelligence is the license of anarchy. The democratic idea of freedom, Dewey tells us again and again, is *not* the right of each individual to do as he pleases; instead the "basic freedom is that of freedom of *mind* and of whatever degree of freedom of action and experience is necessary to produce freedom of intelligence"

(*Problems of Men*, p. 61). Far from being an anti-intellectualist, he is more vulnerable—but only on a first glance—to the charge of intellectualism.

The second misconception of Dewey's philosophy—one more fateful because of its educational corollaries—is the equation drawn between education and experience. From this equation it is inferred that the experience itself is educative, and that any series of experiences—the more direct and dynamic the better—can be substituted for formal schooling, which is often disparaged as an artificial experience. Experiences of travel and living away from school are often considered as appropriate substitutes for study. In short, *having* an experience is identified with knowing or understanding it.

Dewey, however, makes a central distinction between experiences that are "educative" and experiences that are "noneducative" or "miseducative." The first are those that result in increased power and growth, in informed conviction, and sympathetic attitudes of understanding, in learning how to face and meet new experiences with some sense of mastery, without fear or panic or relying on the treadmill of blind routine. The second may give excitement but not genuine insight, may result in a mechanical training or conditioning that incapacitates individuals when the situations encountered in life change and must be met by intelligent improvisation.

But is it not true, some critics counter, that Dewey believes that we learn by doing? And does not that mean that anything a child or student desires or decides to do inside or out of school is *ipso facto* educational? No, emphatically, no! Doing is a part of learning only when it is directed by ideas which the doing tests. Doing in Dewey's sense is the experimenting that is guided by an hypothesis, not the blind action that never reaches the level of an experiment. It is true that we learn by doing: it is not true that all doing is a form of learning.

The fallacy that converts Dewey's statement that "all genuine education comes about through experience" into the belief that "all experiences are genuinely educational" is reflected today in two kinds of curricular abuse in our liberal arts colleges. The first is the tendency to assume that any subject matter is as good as any other subject matter for educational purposes and that all intellectual standards or hierarchies or grades of achievement and excellence merely reflect traditional prejudices that must be swept aside from the standpoint of the egalitarian ethic of a democratic education. This is a point of view held unfortunately not only by students eager to reform or reconstitute the curriculum but by some members of the faculty. One recent college reader titled *Starting Over*, apparently making a fresh start to get away from the prejudices of the past, declares in its preface to these selected readings: "We don't rule out the possibility that Lenny Bruce may have more to teach us than Alfred North Whitehead." They do not indicate *what* we can learn from Lenny Bruce that is of such moment that it dwarfs the many things that one can learn from Whitehead. Dewey, on the other hand, insists that "the central problem of an education based on experience is to select the kind of present experiences that live fruitfully and creatively in subsequent experiences" (*Experience and Education*, p. 17).

Dewey has two basic principles which still provide the direction for continued criticism not only of existing practices but of any proposed reforms: first, an equal concern that *all* children in the community develop themselves by appropriate schooling to the full reach of their powers and growth as persons; and second, a reliance upon the best available scientific methods in the psychology of learning to discover the means, methods, and materials by which the growth can best be achieved in the case of each individual child.

It should be obvious how absurd it is to attribute to Dewey a belief that *only* the child is important in the teaching process and not the subject matters that he is taught, and that therefore it is relatively unimportant what he is taught or what his present experiences are so long as they are enjoyed. What Dewey is saying simply is that unless we take into account the "powers and purposes of those taught," their needs, capacities, attention spans, and related phenomena, we cannot rely on the alleged inherent educational value of any subject to become meaningfully acquired in the child's present experience. Enjoyment, of course, is an aid, not a drawback, to learning, but it should come from interest and growing absorption in the tasks and problems to be mastered. He does not believe we can substitute for a sound psychology of learning a set of hunches, intuitions and impressionistic anecdotal accounts of what has occurred in teaching highly selected children in special circumstances without any objective controls. But the latter constitute the stock in trade of much of the recent writing of our school critics, who totally disregard the danger of extrapolating techniques and methods from episodic learning situations to a public school system that must provide structured and sequential courses of study. Their familiar assertion, that because children learn to speak and walk without formal schooling they can learn almost anything else they need to know in the same way, is evidence of how dogma can put out the eyes of common sense. It is not even true in most cases for learning how to read and write, divide and multiply. There are some skills which if not acquired when young by formal schooling are rarely completely mastered in later years.

The greatest damage of the new dogmas that equate experience and education is apparent not only in what students are offered in the ways of courses, and materials within courses, but what they are often permitted to do in fulfillment of their academic responsibilities. Much of this is covered by the euphemisms of "field work" or "independent study." These must be sharply distinguished from the clinical experience that is essential to the acquisition of knowledge and skills in many scholarly and professional areas. Genuine clinical experience is related to a definite body of knowledge or set of techniques that the student tests or applies in concrete situations continuous with those he will subsequently face; it is carefully supervised, the student's progress checked and evaluated so that he knows in what direction to continue. "Field work" today often means no field except what the student professes an interest in, and work means whatever he chooses to do.

*The New York Times* (April 26, 1971) revealed the kind of "field work" done at the New York State University College at Old Westbury under the presidency of Harris Wofford. According to this uncontested report, the independent study which students were allowed to pursue embraced:

> Almost any project that was neither illegal nor hazardous. Among selected topics were "Migrant Camps and Workers," "Liberation of the Ghetto Through Economics," "Film Study," "Guitar Country Blues," "The Craft of Sewing." . . . One student's project was called "Creative Candle-Making—learning how to (appreciate) and making candles." The professor's role in this five credit project was "to look at my candles when I make them and receive several as gifts." . . . The project of one woman student, for five credits, was called "Poetry of Life." Her project description reads as follows: "Now I hear beautiful music. Then I paint a mind picture. Later I walk in the wood. Reverently I study my wood, know it. Converse with a poet meaningful to me. Make Love."

These oddities undoubtedly are not representative of all institutions that offer "field work," although the chief architect of this curriculum was rewarded by being offered a post at a more prestigious educational institution. But Old Westbury marks a growing tendency to substitute a period of mere lived experience for a period of academic study. Unless undertaken in connection with a structured course of study and intelligently supervised by faculty it would be far better to terminate academic study at the point where the student is ready "to do his own thing," and hopefully earn his own living.

The issues I am discussing are raised in a fundamental way when any general requirements are proposed for educational institutions. The new critics of education are against all requirements on the ground that needs are personal and that students are the best judges of their educational needs. I find a threefold confusion in this point of view: the tendency to assume that, first, desire and impulse are synonymous with need; second, when not synonymous, desire is an unfailing index of need; and third, because needs are personal, they are unique and necessarily subjective.

Impulse and desire may sometimes be an expression of need, and desire is often a consequence of frustrated impulse. But our common experience shows that we sometimes desire things we don't need and that we sometimes, especially in an educational context, discover what we really need only when we have ascertained what our purposes are. One may need to acquire certain skills and knowledge in order to achieve a purpose. Therefore, as Dewey puts it, "the crucial educational problem is that of procuring the postponement of immediate action upon desire until observation and judgment have intervened" (*Education & Experience*, p. 81). Like Hume, Dewey believes that desires are the ultimate moving springs of action, but unlike Hume, he holds that we need not be enslaved by our desires, that they can be governed, modified, sublimated.

If this is true, desire is not always an unfailing index of genuine need. It depends on how and when the desire is expressed and whether our intelligence has disclosed the price to be paid in present and future for acting on it.

Finally, even if it is true that human needs are personal and individual, it doesn't follow that the student is the best judge of them or is even always aware of the needs required by his purposes. One can draw an analogy here with the medical needs a person has who wishes to live a healthy life. It does not follow that because they are *his* needs they may not also be common to others. Nor does it follow that he necessarily is the best judge of them. They are objective needs even if they are personal needs, and the physician is usually the better judge of them than the patient.

Let us apply this to the educational scene, particularly since the new progressive critics of education encourage the present student generation to assert itself against its "exploiters." Students demand the right to select their own courses on every level, and with a kind of democratic belligerence inquire: "Who are *you* to tell me, a grown person of 16 or 18 years of age, what my educational needs are? How can you prate about democracy in education? After all, I am neither an infant nor an idiot!" To which I believe we can reasonably answer:

We are qualified, professional educators who have been studying the educational needs of our students and our culture for many years. We gladly indicate what we believe your educational needs are and are prepared to set forth the grounds on which we select them, inviting your critical response. For example, we believe that you and your fellow students have a need to communicate clearly and effectively, to acquire a command of your own language, oral and written, no matter what your subsequent educational experience or career will be. You have that need whether you are presently aware of it or not. We believe you have a need to understand the essentials concerning the nature of your own bodies and mind, for what you don't know about these matters—as the current drug culture indicates —may hurt you, even kill you. Again, we believe that you have a need to understand something of the history of your own society, the political and economic forces shaping its future—all the more so because you have already indicated that you are aflame with reformist and revolutionary zeal to alter society.

Surely, you must understand the conditioning social, political, and technological factors of any social change that hopes to improve on the past. Your unwillingness to learn about these crucial matters would cast doubts on the sincerity of your professions. It was Karl Marx who pointed out to William Weitling that ignorance is not a revolutionary virtue. We believe that you have other intellectual needs that are requisite to the proper performance of your function as a citizen, especially now that you are or will soon be of voting age. These needs you have in common with all other students, and the courses we require are those designed to meet them. We welcome your suggestions. Of course, you have other educational needs that are not common but personal and reflect your own special aptitudes, interests and aspirations. Here we are prepared to guide you, and help you fashion your own educational purposes and curriculum. Gradually you must take complete responsibility for your own education. When you do, your decisions are more likely to be sensible if they are informed.

Most of the criticisms the new progressive critics make of the educational establishment have been launched from what they declare to be democratic and humanist premises. I want to say a few things about the roles proposed for students and teachers in the democratic reconstitution of institutions of higher learning. Does a commitment to democracy require or justify the recent demands that students have almost as great an influence as the faculty in deciding the curriculum and operating the university?

We must make some crucial distinctions. In the first instance democracy is a political concept. In a political democracy, however, it does not follow that all the major social institutions can or should be run on politically democratic lines according to which each individual counts for one and no more than one, and where a numerical majority makes a decision that binds the entire community. In a political democracy the army, the church, the museum, the orchestra, the family, and the school cannot be organized in a *politically* democratic manner if these institutions are to perform their proper specific functions. There is, to be sure, a sense in which we can speak of a democratic family, of a democratic army, orchestra, or university. This is the moral sense. This requires in the family, for example, not that children have an equal vote on all questions affecting them but that they be treated with respect, listened to, given rational answers to their questions, and not humiliated by arbitrary decisions. In a school or university the spirit of democracy can prevail, without students functioning as citizens do in the larger political community, by devising modes of participation that will make their educational experience more meaningful and without establishing a preposterous equation of intellectual authority between the learned and the unlearned, the mature and the immature. Such an equation is never drawn between masters and apprentices in any field, and in the field of education the overwhelming majority of students, except on advanced graduate levels, cannot be realistically regarded as apprentices.

Without vesting students with educational power equal to that of the faculty, they are always to be treated as persons, always consulted, always listened to, and given responsibilities commensurate with their growth and maturity in those areas where they have competence until they can take over their own education.

This brings me finally to the role of the teacher in education. Only those unfamiliar with Dewey's work can believe that he rejects the active role of the teacher in planning the classroom experience by properly organized subject matters. The teacher must have, he writes, "a positive and leading share in the direction of the activities of the [classroom] community" (*Experience & Education*, p. 66). Because he eschews the role of a drill master and refrains from imposing adult demands upon the growing child, the teacher's task is more difficult, requiring more intelligence and consequently more subtle and complex planning than was required in the days when pedagogues ruled with loud voice and big stick.

Some of the recent critics of education give the impression that all that is required for good teaching is a loving heart, that most courses in preparation for teaching are a waste, and that not only in teaching, but in all other vocations and professions, individuals learn best by the apprentice method or on the job. That anybody can teach something is probably true, but that anybody can become a *good* teacher merely by teaching on the job is demonstrably false. We may not be preparing teachers properly, but the remedy is not the abandonment of preparation and greater reliance upon volunteers and paraprofessionals but in the improvement of that preparation.

In assessing and selecting teachers, whatever other qualities and skills are sought, one should look for a sense of concern on the part of teachers, especially on the lower levels of instruction, and a sense of mission on all levels. By a sense of concern I mean something stronger than interest and less than affection. A teacher cannot love all children, and most children, except those that *are* genuinely preferred and loved, can see through the pretense of the profession, for they know that genuine love is discriminatory. Paul Goodman asserts that one must either love students or resent them, but this is typical of his false disjunctions. The good teacher respects all of his students, is concerned about them and recognizes his equal responsibility for the educational growth of all of them.

The teacher's sense of mission is troublesome, because it can easily be transformed into an indoctrinating zeal that uses the classroom for purposes foreign to the process of learning. Dewey was unalterably opposed to indoctrination, political or otherwise. He was aware of the great social reforms and reconstructions that were necessary in order for the schools to realize the moral ideals of the democratic society, and as a citizen he was always in the forefront of the battle for reform. But all the schools could legitimately do was "to form attitudes which will express themselves in intelligent social action." This, he says, "is something very different from indoctrination" (*Problems of Men,* p. 56) because intelligence, alone of all virtues, is self-critical. Only those indoctrinate who are unable or unwilling to establish their conclusions by intelligent inquiry. Dewey was confident that if his views about man and society had merit they would be recognized as valid by those whom the schools —in the proper exercise of their educational function—had taught to study and deal with the social world and its problems responsibly, i.e., intelligently, scientifically, conscientiously. He would have regarded any attempt to indoctrinate students with his own doctrines and proposals as an arrant betrayal of his educational philosophy.

The effort today to politicize schools and universities from within is foolish for many reasons, the most obvious being its counter-productive character. For nothing is more likely to bring about the politicizing of the university from without, and from a perspective extremely uncongenial to that of the new progressive critics of education. In combatting this internal politicizing, one of the most formidable problems is coping with the teacher who regards his class as a staging ground for revolutionizing society or for disrupting the local community if its norms of social morality fall short of his notions of the good society. In pursuit of a political commitment, he is often led to abandon elementary principles of professional ethics, and sometimes to deny in an apology for his political mission that any distinction can be drawn between objective teaching and indoctrination.

The following passage appears in a publication of Teachers College (*Perspectives in Education*, Fall, 1969), where John Dewey formulated the principles of education for a free society:

> It is the task of the teacher to educate—to educate for change —to educate through change. To educate for orderly planned revolution. If necessary to educate through more disruptive revolutionary action.

John Dewey would have been the first to repudiate this travesty of the role of a teacher in a free society. The task of the teacher is to educate students to their maximum growth as perceptive, informed, and reflective persons so that they can decide intelligently for themselves *what* is to be changed, *where* and *how*. It is not the teachers' function to indoctrinate his students in behalf of any cause, no matter how holy, to brainwash them into becoming partisans of revolution or counter-revolution. To declare as this teacher does—and unfortunately he is not alone—that students are to be educated for and through "disruptive revolutionary action" is to declare oneself morally and pedagogically unfit to inhabit the academy of reasoning.

John Dewey's philosophy is not understood in many of the places where he is honored as well as in many of the places he is denounced. He is not the father of permissiveness, nor the prophet of life adjustment. We can still learn from him without assuming that he said the last word about our problems in school or out. For him democracy was not merely a set of political mechanisms but a way of life in which we use all the arts of intelligence and imagination in behalf of human freedom.

SIDNEY HOOK

# ILLICH'S DE-SCHOOLED
# UTOPIA

We are beginning to understand that the rhetoric of revolutionary extremism is not simply a put-on or a form of exhibitionism or an outburst of politicized aesthetic fury that titillates the penthouse *rentiers* of the New Left. Not only have ideas consequences, words have consequences, too, even if the ideas they express are vague and somewhat incoherent. The inflammatory language of the Black Panthers and the blood-chilling manifestos of the Weathermen may be empty of serious content. There can be little doubt, however, that they have had a profound effect on the behaviour of some of their initiates. The terrorism of the word—even revolutionary bull—prepares the way for the terrorism of the deed.

Something analogous is observable in the field of education. Paralleling the extremist position and inflated rhetoric of the revolutionist decrying the possibility of democratic social reform is the development of extremist positions in education decrying the possibility of intelligent school reform. Here, too, what was listened to with indulgence as an exaggerated expression of a universally shared dissatisfaction with the present state of schooling is beginning to have practical consequences. The existence of the school itself and the system of compulsory public education has come under fire in the United States. The professional teachers and their organizations are becoming the scapegoats of our discontent.

Permanent tenure is under fierce attack in many quarters as primarily a shelter for incompetence at public expense. At the same time we are told that everyone has a natural birthright not only to learn but to teach. Every citizen is not only equally concerned with education, he is equally an authority about what should be learned and how. Those educational authorities, especially the professional teachers and administrators, who are dubious about this are really authoritarians masking themselves as adepts in the pseudo-science of pedagogy. In the interest of freedom we must abolish schools

From Sidney Hook, "Illich's De-Schooled Utopia," *Encounter*, 38:1 (January 1972), pp. 53–57.

whose inhibiting and demoralizing effects on the personalities of their charges are worse than those of our military and penal systems.

The most recent expression of this view is found in a slight volume, *De-schooling Society*, by Ivan Illich.[1] It is a book whose absurd extremism warrants little attention from anyone endowed with a normal portion of common sense. The only reason for taking it seriously is that some of its positions are influencing the new radical critics of American education who, without subscribing to Illich's panacea, are accepting some of his assumptions about schools and schooling to fortify their attacks on current educational theory and practice and on professional teachers as "buttresses of the Establishment." Also disquieting is the fact that Illich's views seem to have won the endorsement of some officials of educational institutes who purvey advice for liberal fees to the school systems of the nation.

Illich's thesis is a simple one—so simple that the reader hesitates for a moment in concluding that he really means what he writes. But he does. Our schools are unmitigatedly bad. All of them? Well, almost all. Then why not try to improve schooling by taking as a model the best schools? This is hopeless, a trap, says Illich. The "hidden curriculum" of schooling, of any formal schooling, inspires the "myth" that certified teachers—bureaucrats all —can use scientific knowledge to impart "humane and efficient" education. The only remedy is to abolish all formal schools and with it all compulsory education.

What do we put in its stead? Reliance upon "self-motivated" learning upon the processes of self-education in freedom through natural association with those who already possess skills and knowledge or who are willing to cooperate in a quest for them. This will be facilitated by four interrelated networks or "learning webs." The first will make accessible to children and students the necessary things and processes (in libraries, museums, theatres, factories, and farms); the second will facilitate the exchange of skills among learners; the third is called "peer-matching": persons will advertise their educational needs or interests "in the hope of finding a partner" for mutual advantage; and, finally, diligent use will be made of a Yellow Book of self-selected and self-advertised Educators-at-Large who will list their skills and addresses and the price of their services.

The only thing clear about the operation of these networks is that the government will pay the costs. Left completely vague is the answer to the question: Who will supervise and direct this educational experience and provide for the sequential organization of subject matters that can be mastered? Something like the invisible hand that guarantees the harmonious adjustment of the needs of buyers and sellers in the free market is presupposed. But even less than the free market in commodities, the free market in education may not meet genuine and desirable needs while gratifying some that are not so desirable. Some of the proposals for peer-matching are suggestive of the techniques used by genteel and literate prostitutes in arranging assignments through the columns of literary periodicals. Although Illich admits that his networks of learning may be abused, he is convinced that the perils of schooling are far worse because of their restrictions on the freedom of natural, self-motivated learners. How the child who is not self-motivated is to learn is left unexplained.

It is not only the school which in Illich's view prevents "personal, creative, and autonomous interaction" among learners and teachers but all the major institutions of society: the state, the church, the army, the medical services, the political party, the media, the family as we know it.

> Not only education but society as a whole needs "de-schooling."

One would imagine, therefore, that before any significant change in education can be effected we would need a total social and cultural revolution. Nonetheless Illich holds that the de-schooling of education can succeed in relative independence of the other equally necessary "de-schoolings."

Despite the extremism of his position Illich writes with an astonishing confidence and dogmatism, piling one questionable statement upon another in reckless disregard of evidence, logic, and common sense.

> Middle class parents commit their children to a teacher's care to keep them from learning what the poor learn on the streets.

But parents—poor ones no less than those of the middle class —usually commit their children to schools and teachers in the hopes that they will learn what they can't learn at home or in the street. (Illich seems unaware that a child who is well taught at home is not compelled to attend school.)

> Teachers more often than not obstruct such learning of subject matters as goes on in a school.

In order to know this Illich would have to know how much reading, writing, arithmetic, geography, history, etc., most children learn *without* benefit of any schooling. Since he does not and cannot know this today, his remark simply slanders school teachers whose dedication to their students is no less than his own. Teachers are painted as monsters sadistically exploiting and oppressing children whose "chronological age disqualifies [them] from safeguards which are routine for adults in a modern asylum—madhouse, monastery, or jail." They need the constitutional protection of the First and Fifth Amendments!

Why should all schools, not merely authoritarian ones but those that are avowedly liberal and progressive, be charged with totalitarian oppressiveness? Because they all operate with the idea that "one person's judgment should determine what and when another person must learn." Yet, surely, when the other person is a growing child and not an adult, an informed and sympathetic determination of what and when he should learn is no more improper than determining what and when he should eat. What is wrong is the imposition of the same learning (or feeding) schedules on children independently of their special needs and interests. But there is a world of difference between individualizing the curriculum and, as Illich proposes, abolishing it.

Actually it is both foolish and cruel to rely for education on the casual, chance encounters of the young. Illich's assurance that the young always learn something from their experiences or become aware of their needs through raw, unstructured experience is not less absurd than his implied view that with respect to health they should be liberated from the ministrations of compulsory medical care. The young are no more always aware of what they need to know in order to grow to their full powers than they are always aware of what to do and what to avoid to achieve health. In either case what they don't know may sometimes cripple them for life. If they waited until they experienced an acute need before learning certain things, they would discover what so many foolish adults have discovered who waited to see a doctor until they had an acute need for one, viz., that it was too late or costly to remedy what ailed them.

The basic question in education, explicitly denied by Illich and other New Left critics, is: "what should individuals learn" in modern society in order more readily to achieve their maximum growth as persons? The basic problem in teaching on every level (except the graduate school) is how to motivate the individual to learn joyfully, yet thoroughly what he should learn—as well as what he wants to learn—until he is mature enough to take over the direction of his own education. This, of course, is a gradual process that recognizes that each learner has individual needs as well as common needs.

For Illich and those he has influenced, on the other hand, the planning of new educational institutions must start with the question: "What kind of things and people might learners want to be in contact with in order to learn?" A parent who actually lived up to Illich's dictum might well find himself in difficulties with the Society for the Prevention of Cruelty to Children (if that worthy group hasn't also been abolished). Children might want to be in contact with anything from live wires and drugs to the glazed ridges of tenement roofs; they may never recover from the effects of learning about them and kindred things. Conversely, they might *not* want to be in contact with children of different races, religions, or nationalities. And yet such experiences of mixing and contact might be necessary to cure them of their prejudices and helpful in avoiding the stereotyped judgments of their elders. On Illich's view, whether anyone learns anything worthwhile is purely a matter of chance. On a more sensible view, our world is too dangerous to take such chances.

The flaws in this smart, silly book can be traced to a number of assumptions explicitly made by Illich but also widely held by other romantic critics of the school system who draw back from his extremist remedies. He assumes that because children learn to speak their own language casually without going to school and without explicit instruction, they learn most other things in the same way. To be sure, children have learned to speak and walk without schooling or explicit instruction since the emergence of man from more primitive species, but all human history testifies that they do not learn to read and write as effortlessly. Before compulsory schooling was introduced the vast majority of mankind remained illiterate. Illich holds no brief for illiteracy but he assumes that literacy can be more readily acquired by abolishing schools and relying upon the casual operation of his networks to effect mastery of elementary skills. To claim that we will all learn from and teach one another as need and interest manifest themselves is to invoke pious hope that flies in the face of overwhelming evidence. Not everyone who knows something, even when he knows it well, can teach it, not to mention teach it effectively. Not everyone who is able to teach is willing or in a position to do so. Even speech depends upon the models imitated and can be immensely improved by proper schooling.

Further, some skills are best learned in youth, like writing and arithmetical computation, as well as certain habits of work, and of thoughtfulness for others. Anyone who has seen a grown man, who has been raised in some foreign culture where no ball games were played, writhe as he vainly tries to throw a ball, understands the point. Accidents have been known to happen to persons who, never having learned when children to differentiate automatically between left and right, paused too long at the shouted advice to turn out of the path of an oncoming car.

Illich "hopes" that education will improve after society is deschooled. But his conception of "hope" indicates that he has not liberated himself from metaphysical superstition. He sharply contrasts "expectation" with "hope," and downgrades the former because it means "reliance upon results which are planned and controlled by man." Schooling is a form of expectation, since it uses plans and controls, and is therefore bad. Hope "means trusting faith in the goodness of nature." It is interference with nature and human nature that produces evil. Disease presumably is the product of medicine, not the consequence of natural causes. If Illich had the courage of his hope, he would opt for the free market as well as for education free of schools in order to avoid any kind of planning and controlling of the economy.

Illich has a flair for drawing absurd conclusions from truisms. "We have all learned most of what we know outside the school." From which he infers that schools are therefore unnecessary. But unless the kind of learning is specified it is just as true to say that most of what we learn outside of school we learn *because* of the skills, knowledge, and training we learned in school. Obviously, since formal schooling is comparatively recent, human beings have learned most things, for better or worse, in the course of living. In a sense they always will. But having an experience is not *ipso facto* educational. Schooling can make a difference to what we bring to an experience to make it educationally significant. Illich pretends that "schools are designed on the assumption that there is a secret to everything in life" and that only teachers hold the key to it. The truth is that the assumptions of modern schooling are much more modest. They are: that much knowledge and many skills are interesting and useful in helping people cope with their experience and in enhancing the quality of their lives; that they can be learned by systematic schooling more easily than by casual encounters with things and persons or by reliance on "the goodness of nature"; that the acquisition of knowledge and mastery of skills requires a grasp of sequential order in subject matter; that teachers can be helpful in the process of learning until students are in a position intelligently to choose their own patterns of growth.

Illich disputes all this. He claims that schools and teachers prevent children from learning by chaining them to alternating routines of trivial play and drill. According to him we tend to romanticize what we have learned in schools. No one, he claims, really learned how to read in school. We learned outside of school from parents or older siblings or from the boy across the way. He leaves unexplained how, in the U.S.A., entire generations of children of immigrant parents, who could neither speak, read, nor write English, learned English more or less adequately. He has read about all the weaknesses of the American public school; but he is ignorant of its achievements.

The animus against school teachers extends to a point where he resents and deplores reliance upon official certification by the state of the capacity to teach or to practice any profession. For all his talk about autonomy and independence and creative rediscovery in education he bemoans the passing of "personal discipleship." The Yellow Book of Educators-at-Large will probably have a special supplement on Gurus. Not unaware of the dangers, he nonetheless would abandon all official restraints or controls on those who hold themselves out to be healers of the sick in mind and body. Their expertise would be determined by popularity polls of students, patients, and clients. "The right to teach any skill"—including surgery and engineering?—"should come under the protection of free speech." For him academic freedom is not the right of *qualified* teachers to be free of ecclesiastical, political, and administrative interference. Academic freedom is a human right; it does not have to be earned. His open society, therefore, would be an open society for medical and educational quacks without any safeguards for their victims that intellectual scepticism, the by-product of effective teaching, can produce. Never mind the casualties! Of course, schools of medicine, engineering, and education today have their casualties, too. But the remedy for poor schools is better schools, not their abolition.

What makes Illich's proposal to abolish schools gratuitously foolish is that some of his suggested webs of learning, with appropriate revisions and safeguards, are in use today as supplementary aids to basic schooling. Compulsory education is an institution, not a process of learning. Students can no more be compelled to learn than to love. Compulsory education expresses the responsibility of society to all its children, especially where parental responsibility is absent. It does not go on forever. By the time students have reached the school-leaving age, they should be in a position to choose freely and intelligently the kind of continuing education, in school or out, they wish to pursue.

The meeting of extremes in politics is an old story. The voice of Bernadette Dohrn and the Weathermen is hardly distinguishable from that of Charles Manson and his Family. In education the mindless Right which opposes public education sounds very much like some factions among the mindless Left. For both the state is always the enemy whose interference with the natural order must be resisted even if it is the order of anarchy. The case in general for compulsory education, not necessarily through one kind of school or any formal school, is even better than the case for compulsory vaccination which in Illich's eyes must also appear as an abridgement of human freedom and a betrayal of hope "in the goodness of nature." In a democratic community the right to learn is a human right. The community owes a responsibility to all children to provide them with the opportunities to develop their powers to make informed and reflective choices not only for the sake of their survival but its own. Under certain circumstances this responsibility may override the rights of parents who are either indifferent or hostile to their children's development.

It is significant that in democratic societies the centres of dissent have usually been the schools and the schooled. Nor is it fortuitous that sophisticated apologists of oppressive regimes in the past have been hostile to universal compulsory education out of fear that "the lower classes," having caught glimpses of the great legacies of human culture, would seek to enlarge their share of it. Nothing would please those who are opposed to desegregation in American education today more than the abolition of compulsory schooling. Like so many other contemporary reactionaries on the new Left, Illich talks a great deal about freedom but neglects the principles of intellectual authority and organization necessary to negotiate the conflicts of freedoms. The result is that his free society is one in which everyone is free "to do one's thing," no matter if the consequences result, as in all anarchist utopias that rely on the goodness of nature, in the universal loss of hard-won freedoms.

MANFRED STANLEY

# ILLICH DEFROCKED

Essentially there are three criticisms that Ivan Illich is directing at the Western model of established education. First, education is doing nothing about the fundamental inaccessibility of the modern

Published by permission of Transaction Inc. from *Society* Vol. 9 (March 1972). © 1972 by Transaction Inc.

world—inaccessibility in the sense of both incomprehensibility on the level of knowledge and impermeability to participative action on the level of practice. Second, education in the West has been deeply corrupted by a technocratic orientation reflecting the psychology of a consumer society. Thus knowledge is defined in terms of accredited, prepackaged curricula, and educative action is circumscribed by tightly regulated, professionalized role structures. For Illich, a major effect of this sort of corruption is a supposedly educated public's inability to distinguish between true and false utilities. Finally, Western education is an elitist institution because it has been structured so as to undermine learner sovereignty, that is, the "free determination by each learner of his own reason for living and learning—the part that his knowledge is to play in his life."

I have little quarrel with Illich's first class of criticisms. His articulations of these, and some of the suggested remedies, are worth the price of admission for me. Illich's analysis of the technocratic dimensions of education also makes important points, although on the whole he seems strongly prone to ignore many manifest and latent functions of schooling that are benign from the standpoint of his own values. The brunt of the subsequent remarks, however, are addressed to Illich's major remedial strategy, that of deschooling in the name of learner sovereignty. This is not for the sake of having something critical to say. Illich has gone out of his way to encourage revolution through disestablishment—the deschooling of society and culture. In this program's name, he encourages total rejection of the Western model of education as schooling. Because Illich's arguments for disestablishment and learner sovereignty are currently so popular and because this reviewer regards them as obscuring the central issues of educational discourse, this review will closely examine learner sovereignty and its implications.

A commentary on the notion of learner sovereignty implied in Illich's discussion of educational disestablishment requires attention to at least four issues. These are (1) the status of coercion in education, (2) confusion between education and the process of learning as such, (3) connections between education and the moral ambiguities of a professionalized division of labor, and (4) possible consequences of disestablishment for the larger organization of society.

THE PROBLEM OF COERCION

Illich is quite direct about his denial of legitimacy to any kind of coercion in education:

Healthy students often redouble their resistance to teaching as they find themselves more comprehensively manipulated. This resistance is due not to the authoritarian style of a public school or the seductive style of some free schools, but to the fundamental approach common to all schools—the idea that one person's judgment should determine what and when another person must learn.

Again and again Illich denies that he is arguing for reforms of specific ills. Rather he is insisting upon "positive recognition of each person's independence in the face of school and of any other device designed to compel specific behavioral change or to measure man in the abstract rather than to measure man for a concrete job."

Illich seems to me a bit simplistic in this emphasis on removing coercion from educational life. He never states whether he actually believes that society can get along with no coercion at all, even the coercive effects of custom such as represented by socialization practices themselves. But let us examine the issue just from the logic of Illich's own proposals. He urges upon us a society that is noncoercive educationally in the sense that every individual should be free to decide throughout his life what sorts of skills and knowledge he wishes to acquire and when. Yet in some ways this notion of life-long opportunity for learning is an illusion. Certain things if not learned early cannot then serve as what we might call enabling functions later in life. That is, many forms of knowledge require sequential states of learning, the early stages of which—if not acquired during youth—must simply be acquired later. Sometimes they cannot be effectively acquired later at all. I have in mind habits related to the learning process and subtle patterns of interplay between skill, confidence, and knowledge. The performing arts provide good examples, but there are others.

Children and young people are often not aware of these demands of professionalism. From the standpoint of the mind, a wasted youth could be catastrophic for later life, certainly in the case of those individuals who subsequently discover that they desire a professional level of attainment in the arts or sciences. The cumulative effects upon a society's intellectual life could be as serious. Much of the learning process is simply not intrinsically interesting when one is young or at any other time. Schooling is—precisely— a form of coercion that can introduce and reinforce habits that the adult, a different person from the child in his insights and ambitions, is later very often simply grateful for, whatever he may have felt as a child. The fact that this may not be true in every case or indeed in a majority of cases might well be overbalanced by the contributions made to the intellectual, artistic, and professional life of a society by that minority for whom the schools did function in this manner. This argument is not necessarily vitiated by the well-known observation that some of the greatest achievers in the arts and sciences were indifferent students. It is not clear from this fact alone that they could have accomplished what they did without benefit of the many direct and indirect effects of schooling that do not show up in grades or even in motivation to stay in school. This point is even more relevant to some developing societies. One wonders, for example, where Japan would be today if her modernizing elites had not had recourse to schools as an instrument of mobilization and resocialization.

## REDUCTION OF EDUCATION TO LEARNING

According to Illich, "The learner must be guaranteed his freedom without guaranteeing to society what learning he will acquire and hold as his own. Each man must be guaranteed privacy in learning with the hope that he will assume the obligation of helping others to grow into uniqueness." Such arguments are tantamount to denying anyone the right to represent society in its dimension as a moral community. Community presupposes a certain continuity of tradition, moral insight, and cognitive literacy standards that set limits upon the range of uniqueness permitted each person. Education has never meant simply learning for the sake of learning. Yet Illich's discussion fudges such distinction radically. Samuel Mc-Cracken's comments about "Quackery in the Classroom" (*Commentary*, June 1970) express exactly my own sense of the matter.

## EDUCATION AND THE DIVISION OF LABOR

Illich's thought is part of the long debate on the moral effects of the division of labor upon civilization. For Illich, school is the paradigm of intervention into practical life by bureaucratized service agencies whose job it is to present people with packaged values to consume. The problem is not with one or another inefficiency of operation; it is inherent in the very notion of schooling itself. "Most learning is not the result of instruction. It is rather the result of unhampered participation in a meaningful setting." But, says Illich, school implies "transfer of responsibility from self to institution."

Allegedly it is school that first socializes the child into assuming that value of anything (in this case knowledge itself) lies in its identity as a specialized, technologically produced commodity.

Once trapped in a context of commodity consciousness, a man ceases to be self-consciously engaged in value-oriented social practices. Instead he becomes a consumer, one who encounters values as predefined products. As a consumer, his wants are encouraged to become endless, and eventually "the value of institutionalized man depends on his capacity as incinerator." Pollution, exhaustion of resources, and social polarizations follow. This chain of events must be broken at its source: the institution whose specialized task it is to induce children into a merchandised consciousness (curriculum) must be eliminated.

I will not explore the question here of whether Illich's uncompromisingly dim view of the functions of school would be sustained by empirical research designed to test it. Serious doubts could be raised about this. What is for me more striking than Illich's pessimism about schools is the optimistic expectations he apparently has about what would follow upon this radical liberation from school. It would seem that Illich has to believe that if from earliest childhood men are forced into the world (that is, deprived of institutionalized definitions of commodities to consume), they will discover beneath the chaos of relativism and immediate impulses an aesthetically intelligible hierarchy of values implicit in experience itself and accessible only through practical existence. If Illich does assume this, it would be a case of yet one more man aligning himself with John Stuart Mill who, against Jeremy Bentham's comment that "quantity of pleasure being equal, pushpin is as good as poetry," replied:

> It is better to be a human being dissatisfied than a pig satisfied; better to be Socrates dissatisfied than a fool satisfied. And if the fool or the pig is of a different opinion, it is because they only know their side of the question. The other party to the comparison knows both sides.

In attacking the elitism of schooling, Illich seems almost disingenuous in not pointing out the possible elitism of his own orientations. Schooling has, after all, liberated people from a variety of rather confined forms of ascribed elitism. What happens to those people who—in their wanderings through Illich's "learnings webs"—fail to discover that pushpin is not as good as poetry? School will not be there to make them feel guilty about this. But it is a little hard for me to imagine that Illich really believes that those who fail to make such a discovery will (or should) have terribly much to say about how society is governed. Before neo-Marxists and participatory ideologists clasp Illich to their ranks, they should perhaps ask if his ideas are not more congenial to a Platonic society of hierarchical orders fixed according to people's natural (rather than schooled) capacity for discovering the relationships between pushpin and poetry.

## CONSEQUENCES FOR THE LARGER STRUCTURE OF SOCIETY

Illich never considers, from a skeptic's point of view, what the structural effects of his proposals for deschooling culture are likely to be upon society at large. His view of society as a vast learning web seems as romantically optimistic as his picture of schooled society is pessimistic. Let us imagine for the moment that Illich's proposals are accepted and implemented as they stand within the next twenty-four hours. Here is a scenario of some possible problematic effects not accounted for in Illich's analysis.

Parental authority is drastically undermined as children struggle within what remains of the family to countermand their parents' wishes for their education on the ground that they want complete control over their own edu-credit voucher resources. With the elimination of extended childhood (one of Illich's themes) young people leave home earlier and parental opportunities for socializing their children are drastically curtailed. The effects upon families in the upper social strata are particularly pronounced since parents are decreasingly able to prevent the proletarianization of their young under the influence of romanticized street cultures and commercialized pop-fads.

The legal prohibition on any criteria for employability except skill performance places an undiluted premium on technical specialization that is greater than at any time in modern history. General liberal arts education is completely undermined and dies out as a major social force since there is no further indirect market support for it. Efforts at innovation and reform in general education give way to renewed concern with narrow vocational training programs.

All sorts of private certification programs are organized by agencies interested in creating their own general education (read indoctrination) programs. Examples are the Defense Department and other giant government bureaus, private think tanks like Rand Corporation, and large industrial organizations. Meanwhile, sectarian education flourishes, and militant organizations begin to set up their own educational programs on a large scale in order to mobilize the revolutionary consciousness of their members' children. This latter development is fueled by the increasing fragmentation of the larger society as social enclaves become ever more involuted due to people no longer being exposed to any countervailing, integrative influences of the sort once provided, however ineptly, by the schools. Instead, people are ever more trapped in their social classes and strata. They have been deprived of compulsory schooling which, by exposing people to new motivations and possibilities, often functioned as a potent conduit to social mobility. Likewise, politico-ideological attitudes harden and become more conservative throughout the more affluent population as the widely documented, liberalizing infiuence of exposure to higher levels of schooling becomes a thing of the past.

   This reviewer is grateful to Illich for refining the terms of social criticism in relation to modern society, including the moral ambiguities of schooling. I think Illich is right when he says, "School appropriates the money, men, and good will available for education and in addition discourages other institutions from assuming educational tasks." But one can substitute for school and its functions here the name of almost any other institution and its functions. This is the dilemma that school shares with all institutions; it is the problem of institutionalization itself. But surely the answer to radical misuse by human beings of their own inventions (be they machines or institutions) is not the abandonment of these, but the evolution of human awareness to a higher stage of effective control over the unintended consequences of social action itself. This is the task of education. Not all freely chosen learning contributes to this task.

JONATHAN KOZOL

# FREE SCHOOLS: A TIME FOR CANDOR

For the past six years free schools have almost been pets of the media. Too little of this coverage, however, has focused on the deep and often overwhelming problems that confront some of these schools: the terrible anguish about power and the paralyzing inhibition about the functions of the teacher.

The difficulties begin with a number of foolish, inaccurate, and dangerous clichés borrowed without much criticism or restraint from fashionable books by fashionable authors who do not know very much about either life within the cities or responsibilities that confront a free school for poor children in a time of torment and in a situation of great urgency and fear. It is almost axiomatic that the free schools that survive are those that start under the stimulus of a neighborhood in pain and that remain within the power of that neighborhood. Those that fail are, time and again, those that are begun on somebody's intellectual high or someone's infatuation with a couple of phrases from the latest book and then collapse after six months or a year of misery among the cuisenaire rods.

It is time for us to come right out and make some straightforward statements on the misleading and deceptive character of certain slogans that are now unthinkingly received as gospel. It is just not true that the best teacher is the one who most successfully pretends that he knows nothing. Nor is it true that the best answer to the blustering windbag of the oldtime public school is the free-school teacher who attempts to turn himself into a human inductive fan.

Free schools that exist under the siege conditions of New York, Boston, or one of the other Northern cities should not be ashamed to offer classroom experience in which the teacher does not hesitate to take a clear position as a knowledgeable adult. Neither should these free schools be intimidated in the face of those who come in from their college courses with old and tattered copies of *How Children Fail* and *Summerhill*. Many of these people, fans of John Holt or A. S. Neill though they may be, are surprisingly dogmatic in their imposition of modish slogans on the real world they enter. Many, moreover, have only the most vague and shadowy notion of what the free school represents.

Free schools at the present moment cover the full range of beliefs from the Third World Institute of all black kids and all black teachers, operated by a group of revolutionary leaders wearing military jackets, boots, and black berets, to a segregated Summerhill out in the woods of western Massachusetts, offering "freedom" of a rather different kind and charging something like $2,000 or $3,000 yearly for it. The free schools that I care most about stand somewhere in between, though surely closer to the first than to the second. The trouble, however, is that the intellectual imprecision of the school-reform movement as a whole, and the very special imprecision of the free schools in particular, allow *both* kinds of free schools to advertise themselves with the same slogans and to describe themselves with the same phrases.

The challenge, then, is to define ourselves with absolutely implacable precision—and to do so even in the face of economic danger, even in the certain knowledge of the loss of possible allies. "This is what we are like, and this is the kind of place that we are going to create. This is the kind of thing we mean by freedom, and this is the sort of thing we have in mind by words like 'teach' and 'learn.' This is the sort of thing we mean by competence, effectiveness, survival. If you like it, join us. If you don't go someplace else and start a good school of your own."

Such precision and directness are often the rarest commodities within free schools. Too many of us are frightened of the accusation of being headstrong, tough, authoritarian, and, resultingly, we have tried too hard to be all things to all potential friends. It is especially difficult to resist the offered assistance when we are most acutely conscious of the loneliness and isolation of an oppressive social structure.

The issue comes into focus in the choice of teachers and in the substance of curriculum. In an effort to avoid the standard brand of classroom tyranny that is identified so often with the domineering figure of the professional in the public system, innovative free-school teachers often make the grave mistake of reducing themselves to ethical and pedagogical neuters. The teacher too often takes the role of one who has *no* power.

The myth of this familiar pretense is that the teacher, by concealing his own views, can avoid making his influence felt in the classroom. This is not the case. No teacher, no matter what he does or does not say, can ever manage *not* to advertise his biases to the children.

A teacher "teaches" not only or even primarily by what he *says*. At least in part, he teaches by what he *is*, by what he *does*, by what he seems to *wish to be*. André Gide said, "Style is character." In the free school, life-style is at the heart of education. The teacher who talks of "redistribution of the wealth" yet dresses in expensive clothes among the poor and spends the Christmas holidays in San Juan gets across a certain message, with or without words, about his stake in some of the nice things privilege can offer. A black woman with a conspicuous Afro and a certain definite quality of suppressed intensity in her manner and voice gets across a whole world of feelings and biases concerning race and rage and revolution. A white woman who dresses in old sandals, blue work shirt, Mexican skirt, whose long hair is frequently uncombed, who wears love beads or a molded-steel medallion on her breast, who calls things "neat," "right on," "downers," and "together" presents a living advertisement for a whole body of implied ideas, political tendencies, and ideological directions.

In certain respects, the things a teacher does not even *wish* to say may well provide a deeper and more abiding lesson than the content of the textbooks or the conscious message of the posters on the wall. When war is raging and when millions of people in our land are going through a private and communal hell, no teacher—no matter what he does or does not do—can fail to influence his pupils. The secret curriculum is in the teacher's own lived values and convictions, in the lineaments of his face, and in the biography of passion (or self-exile) that is written in his eyes. The young teacher who appears to children to be vague or indirect in the face of human pain, infant death, or malnutrition may not teach children anything at all about pain, death, or hunger, but he will be teaching a great deal about the capability of an acceptable adult to abdicate the consequences of his own perception and, as it were, to vacate his own soul. By denying his convictions during class discussion, he does not teach objectivity. He gives, at the very least, a precedent for nonconviction.

It is particularly disabling when a strong and serious free school begun by parents of poor children in an urban situation finds itself bombarded by young teachers who adhere without restraint or self-examination to these values. Not only does such behavior advertise gutlessness and weakness to the children, it also represents a good deal of deception and direct bamboozlement. The willingness of the highly skilled white teacher to blur and disguise his own effectiveness and to behave as if he were less competent and effective than he really is provides the basis for a false democracy between himself and the young poor children he works with. The children, in all honesty, *can't do nothing*. The young man from Princeton only *acts* as if he can't. The consequence of this is a spurious level of egalitarian experience from which one party is always able to escape, but from which the other has no realistic exit.

I believe, for these reasons, in the kind of free school in which adults do not try to seem less vigorous or effective than they are. I believe in a school in which real power, leverage, and at least a certain degree of undisguised adult direction are not viewed with automatic condescension or disdain. I believe in a school in which the teacher does not strive to simulate the status or condition of either an accidental "resource-person," wandering mystic, or movable reading lab, but comes right out, in full view of the children, with all of the richness, humor, desperation, rage, self-contradiction, strength, and pathos that the would reveal to other grownups. Nevertheless, some of the free schools that describe and advertise their high-priced, all-white, innovative education in the pages of *New*

*Schools Exchange* seem literally to build the core of their life-style around the simulation of essential impotence, with competence admitted only in those areas of basic handiwork and back-to-nature skills where no serious competition from the outside world exists. "Wow!" I hear some of these free-school people say. "We made an Iroquois canoe out of a log!" Nobody, however, *needs* an Iroquois canoe. Even the Iroquois do not. The Iroquois can buy aluminum canoes if they should really need them. They don't, however. What they need are doctors, lawyers, teachers, organizers, labor leaders. The obvious simulation-character of the construction of an Iroquois canoe by a group of well-set North American children and adults in 1972 is only one vivid example of the total exercise of false removal from the scene of struggle that now typifies the counterculture. There may be some pedagogic value or therapeutic function in this form of simulation for the heartsick or disoriented son or grandson of a rich man. It does not, however, correspond to my idea of struggle and survival in the streets and cities I know.

In the face of many intelligent and respected statements on the subject of "spontaneous" and "ecstatic" education, the simple truth is that you do not learn calculus, biochemistry, physics, Latin grammar, mathematical logic, Constitutional law, brain surgery, or hydraulic engineering in the same organic fashion that you learn to walk and talk and breathe and make love. Months and years of long, involved, and—let us be quite honest—sometimes nonutopian labor in the acquisition of a single unit of complex and intricate knowledge go into the expertise that makes for power in this nation. The poor and black cannot survive the technological nightmare of the next ten years if they do not have this expertise.

There is no more terrifying evidence of the gulf of race and class that now separates oppressor and oppressed within this nation than that so many of those people who are rich and strong should toil with all their heart to simulate the hesitation, stammer, and awkward indirection of impotence, while blacks in Roxbury, in Harlem, and in East St. Louis must labor with all their soul to win one-tenth of the *real effectiveness* that those white people conspire to deny. If there is a need for some men and women to continue in that manner of existence and that frame of mind, and if it is a need that cannot be transcended, then let there be two very different kinds of free schools and two very different kinds of human transformation and human struggle. But, at least within the urban free schools that we build and labor to sustain, let us be willing to say who we are and what we think and where we stand, and let us also say what things *we do not want.*

Those who fear power in themselves fear it still more in those whom they select to lead them. Several free schools that I know firsthand have gone through nightmarish periods in which they all but pick apart the man or woman they have chosen to be their headmaster or headmistress. The process is dangerous and debilitating not only because it does so much direct damage in terms of simple pain and hurt to many decent and courageous men and women but also because it wastes our time in minor skirmishes and diverts us from the serious struggle for the well-being and real survival of our children.

More importantly, however, fear of power places a premium on mediocrity, nonvital leadership, insipid character, and unremarkable life-style. An organization, of whatever kind, that identifies real excellence, effectiveness, or compelling life-style with the terrifying risk of despotism and authoritarian manipulation will, little by little, drive away all interesting, brilliant, and exhilarating people and will establish in their stead norms of communal mediocrity. The label reserved for those who do not learn to respect these norms is "ego-tripper." Without question, there is a need for realistic caution, but not every straightforward, unequivocal statement of position can be construed as an instance of ego-tripping. The perfect way to avoid an ego trip, of course, is to create a community of utterly alienated, dull, and boring people. There is no risk of ego-tripping if there is no ego. But there isn't any life or strength or truth or passion, either.

Free schools, if they wish to stay alive and vital, must learn to separate the fear of domination from the fear of excellence. If a free school were ever able to discover or train a leader with the power and vision of a Jesse Jackson or, in a different sense, a George Dennison or a Truman Nelson, I hope it would have brains enough not to attempt to dull his edge or obscure his brilliant provocations with communal indecision. "Participation" and "the will of the full group," inherently eloquent and important aspects of a democratic and exciting free school, can easily turn into the code words for a stylized paralysis of operation and for a new tyranny of will and function.

It may well be that certain free schools, within a rural, safe, and insulated situation, will find it possible to function and survive without formal structure, leadership, or power apparatus. It is their choice if they should wish to do in that way; but those who look for leaders, place them in power, and invest them with the trust and confidence of numbers ought then to stand beside them and help to make them stronger and less frightened in the face of the dangers they confront. Angry parents who never before had power in their hands and young white people who have forever hated anyone who wielded it, can together paralyze the operations of a free school and can gradually destroy the finest qualities in anyone that they select to lead them.

Statements of this kind run counter to a large part of the jargon that the media tend to associate with the free schools. Jargon, however, does not often correspond to the realities of struggle and survival. In every free school that has lasted longer than two years there is—*there always is*—some deep down and abiding power center. Free schools do not hang photographs of unremarkable individuals. They put up photographs of Malcolm X, of Cesar Chavez, of Martin Luther King, of Tolstoy, of José Marti. What is true in history and on the poster-photographs is also true in our own numbers: Some women and some men *are* more powerful and more interesting than others. Behind every free school that survives are the special dedication, passion, and vocation of one woman, one man, or one small and trusted group of men and women. It is by now almost a rule of thumb that the less the free-school bylaws speak of "power" the more one person or one group turns out to hold it. It may be only by a look, a shrug, or a sense of peace within the quiet center of the pedagogic storm. Is A. S. Neill the "ego-tripper" or the "power center" or the "ethical fire" in the heart of his own school? Ask anyone who has ever been to Summerhill.

Still another dangerous tendency included in the syndrome of pretended impotence and threatening the survival of urban free schools is what Bernice Miller speaks of as an inclination toward "The Insufficient"—or what I think of sometimes as The Cult of Incompletion. It is the kind of hang-loose state of mind that views with scorn the need for strong, consistent, and uninterrupted processes of work and aspiration and, instead, makes a virtue of the interrupted venture, the unsuccessful campaign. I have in mind an almost classic picture of a group of rural free-school people I know, sitting on the lawn of someone's country farm or "radical estate" in an almost too comfortable mood of "resting on our elbows at a place of satisfying retrospect on our own failure" or at a kind of "interesting plateau of our half-success."

I think that it is time for us to face head on this problem of our own inherent fear of strength and effectiveness. We must be prepared to strive with all our hearts to be strong teachers, efficacious adults, unintimidated leaders, and straightforward and strong-minded provocators in the lives of children. We must work with all our hearts to overcome the verbal style of debilitation and subjunctive supposition—the interposition, for example, of the preposition or conjunction of arm's-length invalidation ("like") before all statements of intense commitment or denunciation. I know some free-school leaders and writers who now begin to justify and defend the will-to-failure by making a virtue of the capability to start and stop things in response to sudden impulse. It is a curious revolution that builds its ideology and its morale upon the cheerful prospect of surrender. Men who walk the city streets with minds uncluttered by their own internal need for self-defeat, aware of the pain around them, could not make barbarous recommendations of this kind.

The free-school press and writers speak more often of Bill Ayer's free school in Ann Arbor, Michigan, which did not work out, than they do of Edward Carpenter's remarkable and long-sustained success at Harlem Prep. I have a good deal of respect and admiration for Bill Ayers. Still, it cannot be ignored that, insofar as the free schools are concerned, Bill Ayers's experience is perhaps the prototype of the eloquent exercise in self-defeat. I believe we ought to honor people like Bill Ayers in the same way many of us revere the name of Che Guevara. There is also Fidel, however, who was not afraid to sit in the victor's chair, and there are also strong and stable people like Ed Carpenter. It would not hurt to have upon the walls or in the stairways of our little schools photographs not only of those who do not fear to die for their beliefs but also of those who do not fear to win. I think that the children of the black and poor ought to be able to know and believe, right from the first, that the struggle for liberation does not need to end with sickness in the mountains or with steel helmets in Chicago or with a T-group in Manhattan. It can also end with personal strength, political passion, psychological leverage, and the deepest kind of moral and pragmatic power.

I do not intend to mock young people, or myself, or my own friends, who really try and honestly do fail; but I am thinking also of the anguish in success and in "too much effectiveness" of those who look upon effectiveness itself as bearing the copyright of evil men. There is no need for us to choose between a contaminated sense of competence and a benign sense of ineptitude. The opposite of the cold and avaricious doctor earning his $350,000 yearly in the kingdom of lighted pools and begonia hedges in Lexington, Massachusetts, does not need to be the spaced-out flautist in the shepherd's jacket on a mountaintop in Colorado or the mystical builder of the Pakistani mud hut in New Hampshire; it can also be the radical, bold, and inexhaustible young doctor working his heart out in the store-front clinics of Chicago. The opposite of the sleek corporation lawyer spooning up the cool lime sherbet from a silver dish in the air-conditioned confines of the Harvard Club in Boston does not need to be the barefoot kid in blue jeans in New Hampshire; it can also be the strong and passionate young woman who nails down her law degree while working nights to tutor kids within the nightmare of the Pruitt-Igoe projects in St. Louis—and then comes back to be their representative before the law. The preference for the unsuccessful, for the interrupted enterprise, for hesitation and low-key aspiration is not surprising or inexplicable in a hard and driving nation such as our own.

One final point: Free schools often prove to be almost irresistibly attractive to some of the most unhappy and essentially aggressive people on the face of the wide earth. In many instances, the very same people who have been "evicted" from someone else's free school precisely for the pain and hurt they cause will shop around until they come to us. There is, as many people in the free schools find, a rather familiar kind of man or woman who does not, in fact, care a great deal about children but who enjoys a power struggle. There is a kind of "energy of devastation" in such people that can be helpful when it is directed at external obstacles but that can be incredibly destructive when it turns in on our own small numbers.

I have seen one of the kindest black people I know pause, and look gently, almost with sadness, into the eyes of someone of this sort and say quietly:

> "Well, you don't seem to be somebody that I want to work with. There has been too much unhappiness among us since you came. You do not seem to think we are sufficiently enlightened. You do not seem to think that we have read the right books. You may be right. We have not read many books in the past year. We have been too busy trying to build up our school and trying to keep off people who bring sadness and unhappiness into our ranks. We think that you are just that kind of person. We would rather have the courage of our errors than the kind of devastation forced upon us by your intellectual wisdom."

I do not like to end with a passage of this kind. It shows too much of the bitterness and the deep pain that have been part of the free schools I know. I am trying, however, to be as realistic and as candid as I can. There is a time when we must sit down and compose rhapsodic stories to raise money for the free schools; there is another time when we have to be as honest as we can. In 1972 the free schools have come into their own hour. It is the time for candor.

PART 2

# THE LEARNER
# AND THE
# CURRICULUM

The essays in this part will not resolve all the theoretical disputes about the goals of education and the nature of the curriculum. However, they will extend our critical discussion of the radical school-reform movement and offer several alternatives to the radical concepts of the teacher's role, the value of subject-matter disciplines, and the worth of a methodology called discovery learning.

In Part 1 the reader will have noticed the rather antiradical position taken by Jonathan Kozol, who defended the value of teacher competence (knowledge and methodology), the importance of the academic disciplines, basic skills, and structured learning activities. The authors in Part 2 would agree with this conception of teaching and learning, oversimplified as it is. They defend benign teacher authority, structured learning, the liberal arts disciplines, and related traditional values.

In the first article the British philosopher, G. H. Bantock, criticizes the very foundation of the radical humanist educational philosophy—the romantic views of Jean Jacques Rousseau. He reviews the major ideas and sentiments in *Emile*, including Rousseau's views on freedom, nature, the child, and learning. The weaknesses in each of Rousseau's views are sorted out and placed in perspective.

Bantock's rigorous assessment of Rousseau, the educational theorist, should provide the reader with an illustration of modern critical analysis. One of his telling arguments is the contention that Rousseau seemed to believe that cognitive growth is as natural (developmental) as ordinary biological growth. Consequently, leaving children alone should not hurt their intellectual development at all. A large body of psychological evidence, however, suggests a completely different conclusion: that cognitive growth requires structured learning situations and careful adult assistance of many kinds. The facilitation of child attention, language acquisition, concept development, perceptual abilities, and various cognitive abilities is carried on by various agents, the most effective of which is the classroom teacher.[1]

In the second article Paul Hirst defends the importance of the traditional liberal arts and sciences. Radical writers like Paul Goodman prefer that children learn whatever they are interested in; and it is true that in the free schools I visited the basic disciplines of knowledge, that is, physics, chemistry, history, literature, social studies, and art, are treated *only* as they arise out of the interests of the learners. In most free schools or informal classrooms, this "content" has no real structure and organization—and it is generally devalued compared to humanistic values such as self-expression. Hirst attempts to counter this antiintellectual thrust by pointing out features of the various disciplines and their meaning for curriculum development, teaching, and learning.

In the third essay, David Ausubel provides a balanced overview of discovery learning. Many radical reformers call forth discovery as their basic system of learning. Its strengths and weaknesses are therefore important to our entire discussion. Ausubel clearly retains enough doubt to cause any reformer to reflect upon the value of relatively unstructured learning ventures.

Although proposed solutions for school discipline problems vary considerably, no one today doubts that disorder and even chaos are widespread. Lawrence Vredevoe, who has studied such matters for many years, has documented this deplorable state of affairs. This condition seems to support some radical humanist claims about the inadequacy of our schools. Along with Vredevoe, this editor finds it ridiculous to assert that our schools are largely to blame for child misconduct and disrespect. Many changes in our society, including laissez-faire childrearing practices, may have far more to do with the disruptive classroom behavior than practices within the school itself. Although a permissive or open classroom may correspond closely to many modern home environments, this fact does not establish permissiveness as an effective means for reaching the ends defended in this book.

The final two essays, by Ausubel and J. Glenn Gray, discuss the teacher's role as authority. Ausubel concentrates upon discipline, and his views generally oppose the laissez-faire thinking of most radical reformers. Gray provides a gentle treatment of the authority relations between teacher and pupils, emphasizing the personality traits most likely to foster healthy relations, based upon mutual respect between teachers and students.

PAUL H. HIRST

# LIBERAL EDUCATION AND THE NATURE OF KNOWLEDGE

The phrase "liberal education" has today become something of a slogan which takes on different meanings according to its immediate context. It usually labels a form of education of which the author approves, but beyond that its meaning is often entirely negatively derived. Whatever else a liberal education is, it is *not* a vocational education, *not* an exclusively scientific education, or *not* a specialist education in any sense. The frequency with which the term is employed in this way certainly highlights the inadequacies of these other concepts and the need for a wider and, in the long run, more worthwhile form of education. But as long as the concept is merely negative in what it intimates, it has little more than debating value. Only when it is given explicit positive content can it be of use in the serious business of educational planning. It is my contention in this paper that whatever vagaries there have been in the use of the term, it is the appropriate label for a positive concept, that of an education based fairly and squarely on the nature of knowledge itself, a concept central to the discussion of education at any level.

From Paul H. Hirst, "Liberal Education and the Nature of Knowledge," in R. D. Archambault, ed., *Philosophical Analysis and Education* (New York: Humanities Press, Inc., 1965), pp. 113-138.

# THE GREEK NOTION OF LIBERAL EDUCATION

The fully developed Greek notion of liberal education was rooted in a number of related philosophical doctrines; first about the significance of knowledge for the mind, and secondly about the relationship between knowledge and reality. In the first category there was the doctrine that it is the peculiar and distinctive activity of the mind, because of its very nature, to pursue knowledge. The achievement of knowledge satisfied and fulfills the mind which thereby attains its own appropriate end. The pursuit of knowledge is thus the pursuit of the good of the mind and, therefore, an essential element in the good life. In addition, it was held that the achievement of knowledge is not only the attainment of the good of the mind itself, but also the chief means whereby the good life as a whole is to be found. Man is more than pure mind, yet mind is his essential distinguishing characteristic, and it is in terms of knowledge that his whole life is rightly directed.

That knowledge is equal to its task was guaranteed by the second group of doctrines. These asserted that the mind, in the right use of reason, comes to know the essential nature of things and can apprehend what is ultimately real and immutable. Consequently, man no longer needs to live in terms of deceptive appearances and doubtful opinions and beliefs. All his experiences, life and thought can be given shape and perspective by what is finally true, by knowledge that corresponds to what is ultimately real. Further, the particular way in which reason is here represented as attaining knowledge, results in a view of the whole of man's understanding as hierarchically structured in various levels. From the knowledge of mere particulars to that of pure being, all knowledge has its place in a comprehensive and harmonious scheme, the pattern of which is formed as knowledge is developed in apprehending reality in its many different manifestations.

From these doctrines there emerged the idea of liberal education as a process concerned simply and directly with the pursuit of knowledge. But the doctrines give to this general idea particular meaning and significance; for they lead to a clear definition of its scope and content, and to a clear justification for education in these terms. The definition is clear, because education is determined objectively in range, in structure and in content by the forms of knowledge itself and their harmonious, hierarchical interrelations. There is here no thought of defining education in terms of knowledge and skills that may be useful, or in terms of moral virtues and qualities of mind that may be considered desirable. The definition is stated strictly in terms of man's knowledge of what is the case.

The development of the mind to which it leads, be it in skills, virtues or other characteristics, is thought to be necessarily its greatest good.

The justification that the doctrines lend to this concept of education is threefold. First, such an education is based on what is true and not on uncertain opinions and beliefs or temporary values. It therefore has a finality which no other form of education has. Secondly, knowledge itself being a distinctive human virtue, liberal education has a value for the person as the fulfillment of the mind, a value which has nothing to do with utilitarian or vocational considerations. Thirdly, because of the significance of knowledge in the determination of the good life as a whole, liberal education is essential to man's understanding of how he ought to live, both individually and socially.

Here, then, the Greeks attained the concept of an education that was "liberal" not simply because it was the education of free men rather than slaves, but also because they saw it as freeing the mind to function according to its true nature, freeing reason from error and illusion and freeing man's conduct from wrong. And ever since Greek times this idea of education has had its place. Sometimes it has been modified or extended in detail to accommodate within its scheme new forms of knowledge: for instance Christian doctrines and the various branches of modern science. Sometimes the concept has been misinterpreted: as in Renaissance humanism when classical learning was equated with liberal education. Sometimes it has been strongly opposed on philosophical grounds: as by Dewey and the pragmatists. Yet at crucial points in the history of education the concept has constantly reappeared. It is not hard to understand why this should be so.

Education, being a deliberate, purposeful activity directed to the development of individuals, necessarily involves considerations of value. Where are these values to be found? What is to be their content? How are they to be justified? They can be, and often are, values that reflect the interests of a minority group in the society. They may be religious, political, or utilitarian in character. They are always open to debate and detailed criticism, and are always in need of particular justification. Is there not perhaps a more ultimate basis for the values that should determine education, some more objective ground? That final ground has, ever since the Greeks, been repeatedly located in man's conception of the diverse forms of knowledge he has achieved. And there has thus arisen the demand for an education whose definition and justification are based on the nature and significance of knowledge itself, and not on the predilections of pupils, the demands of society, or the whims of politicians.

Precisely this demand was behind the development by the Greeks of an education in the seven liberal arts, an introduction to and a pursuit of the forms of knowledge as they were then conceived. It was precisely this demand that prompted Newman and Arnold in the nineteenth century to call for an education that aimed at the cultivation and development of the mind in the full range of man's understanding. It is the same demand that today motivates such classical realists as Maritain and R. M. Hutchins.

## A TYPICAL MODERN STATEMENT: THE HARVARD REPORT

It may well be asked, however, whether those who do not hold the doctrines of metaphysical and epistemological realism can legitimately subscribe to a concept of education of this kind. Historically it seems to have had positive force only when presented in this particular philosophical framework. But historical association must be distinguished from logical connection and it is not by any means obvious that all the characteristic features of the concept are dependent on such philosophical realism. If the doctrines about mind, knowledge and reality mentioned at the beginning of this paper are regarded as at best too speculative a basis for educational planning, as well they may be, the possibility of an education defined and justified entirely in terms of the scope and character of knowledge needs re-examination. The significance of the concept originally came directly from the place the basic doctrines give to knowledge in a unified picture of the mind and its relation to reality. Knowledge is achieved when the mind attains its own satisfaction or good by corresponding to objective reality. A liberal education in the pursuit of knowledge is, therefore, seeking the development of the mind according to what is quite external to it, the structure and pattern of reality. But if once there is any serious questioning of this relationship between mind, knowledge and reality, the whole harmonious structure is liable to disintegrate. First there arise inevitably problems of definition. A liberal education defined in terms of knowledge alone is acceptable as long as knowledge is thought to be necessarily developing the mind in desirable ways, and hence promoting the good life. But if doubt is cast on these functions of knowledge, must not liberal education be redefined stating explicitly the qualities of mind and the moral virtues to which it is directed? And if knowledge is no longer seen as the understanding of reality but merely as the understanding of experience, what is to replace the harmonious, hierarchical scheme of knowledge that gave pattern and order to the education? Secondly there are equally serious problems of justification. For if knowledge is no longer thought to be rooted in some reality, or if its significance for the mind and the good life is questioned, what can be the justification for an education defined in terms of knowledge alone?

Difficulties of both kinds, but particularly those of definition, can be seen in the well-known Harvard Committee Report: *General Education in a Free Society.*[1] (In the Committee's terminology the aims of a "liberal" and a "general" education are identical.) Though certain of the doctrines that originally supported the concept of a liberal education are implicit in this work, the classical view of the significance of knowledge for the mind is considerably weakened, and the belief that in metaphysics man has knowledge of ultimate reality is ignored, if not rejected. The result is an ambiguous and unsatisfactory treatment of the problem of definition and a limited and debatable treatment of the question of justification. Some examination of the Report on both these scores, particularly the former, will serve to show that adequate definition and justification are not only not dependent on the classical doctrines, but can in fact be based directly on an explication of the concepts of "mind" and "knowledge" and their relationship

The Report attempts the definition of a liberal education in two distinct ways: in terms of the qualities of mind it ought to produce and the forms of knowledge with which it ought to be concerned. What the precise relationship is between these two is not clear. It is asserted that they are "images of each other," yet that there is no escape from "describing general education at one time looking to the good man in society and at another time as dictated by the nature of knowledge itself."[2] Which of the forms of description is to be given pride of place soon emerges, however. First, three areas of knowledge are distinguished, primarily by their distinctive methods: the natural sciences, the humanities, and social studies. But it made plain that "the cultivation of certain aptitudes of mind" is being aimed at, the elements of knowledge being the means for developing these. Liberal education is therefore best understood in terms of the characteristics of mind to which it leads. "By characteristics we mean aims so important as to prescribe how general education should be carried out and which abilities ought to be sought above all others in every part of it. These abilities in our opinion are: to think effectively, to communicate thought, to make relevant judgments, to discriminate among values."[3] The meaning of each of these four is elaborated at some length. Amongst the many things detailed of "effective thinking" it is first said to be logical thinking of a kind that is applicable to such practical matters as deciding who to vote for and what wife to choose: it is the ability to extract universal truths from particular cases and to infer particulars from general laws: it is the ability to analyse a problem and to recombine the elements by the use of imagination. This thinking goes further than mere logic, however. It includes the relational thinking of everday life, the ability to to think at a level appropriate to a problem whatever its character. It includes too the imaginative thinking of the poet, the inventor, and the revolutionary. "Communication," through "obviously inseparable from effective thinking," is said to involve another group of skills, those of speaking and listening, writing and reading. It includes certain moral qualities such as candour, it covers certain vital aspects of social and political life and even the high art of conversation. "The making of relevant value judgments" involves "the ability of the student to bring to bear the whole range of ideas upon the area of experience." It is the art of effectively relating theory to practice, of abstractions to facts, of thought to action. Finally there is "discrimination among values." This includes the distinction of various kinds of value and their relative importance, an awareness of the values of character like fair play and self-control, intellectual values like the love of truth, and aesthetic values like good taste, and, in addition, a commitment to such values in the conduct of life. [1]

As to how exactly these come to be those developed by the three types of knowledge, little is said. It is noted that "the three phases of effective thinking, logical, relational, and imaginative, correspond roughly to the three divisions of learning, the natural sciences, the social studies, and the humanities, respectively. [5] The difficult connection between education in the making of value judgments and the formation of moral character is noted. Otherwise the remarks are of a general nature, emphasizing that these abilities must be consciously developed in all studies and generalized far as possible.

This double, if one-sided, characterization of liberal education seems to me unsatisfactory and seriously misleading if what is said of the four abilities is examined more closely. In the first place, the notion that a liberal education can be directly characterized in terms of mental abilities and independently of fully specifying the forms of knowledge involved, is I think false. It is the result of a misunderstanding of the way in which mental abilities are in fact distinguishable. From what is said of "effective thinking," it is perfectly plain that the phrase is being used as a label for mental activity which results in an achievement of some sort, an achievement that is, at least in principle, both publicly describable and publicly testable—the solving of a mathematical problem, responsibly deciding whom to vote for, satisfactorily analysing a work of art. Indeed there can be effective thinking only when the outcome of mental activity can be recognised and judged by those who have the appropriate skills and knowledge, for otherwise the phrase has no significant application, Thus although the phrase labels a form of mental activity, and such mental processes may well be directly accessible only to the person whose processes they are, its description and evaluation must be in public terms occurring in public language. Terms which, like "effective thinking," describe activities involving achievements of some sort must have public criteria to mark them. But in that case, none of the four abilities can in fact be delineated except by means of their detailed public features. Such characterization is in fact forced on the Committee when they come to amplify what they mean. But their approach is simply illustrative, as if the abilities are directly intelligible in themselves, and the items and features of knowledge they give merely examples of areas where the abilities can be seen. If the public terms and criteria are logically necessary to specifying what the abilities are, however, then no adequate account of liberal education in terms of these can be given without a full account in terms of the public features of the forms of knowledge with which it is concerned. Indeed the latter is logically prior and the former secondary and derivative.

In the second place, the use of broad, general terms for these abilities serves in fact to unify misleadingly quite disparate achievements. For the public criteria whereby the exercise of any one of these abilities is to be judged are not all of a piece. Those that under the banner of "effective thinking" are appropriate in, say, aesthetic appreciation are, apart from certain very general considerations, inappropriate in, say, mathematical thinking. In each case the criteria are peculiar to the particular area of knowledge concerned. Similarly, for instance, "communication" in the sciences has only certain very basic features in common with communication in poetic terms. It is only when the abilities are fully divided out, as it were, into the various domains and we see what they refer to in public terms that it is at all clear what is involved in developing them. To talk of developing "effective thinking" is like talking of developing "successful games playing." Plainly that unifying label is thoroughly misleading when what constitutes playing cricket has practically nothing in common with what constitutes playing tiddlywinks. The implications of the term are not at all appreciated until what is wanted is given detailed specification. It is vitally important to realize the very real objective differences that there are in forms of knowledge, and therefore in our understanding of mental processes that are related to these. Maybe this unfortunate desire to use unifying concepts is a relic of the time when all forms of knowledge were thought to be similar, if not identical in logical structure, and that the "laws of logic" reflected the precise psychological operations involved in valid thinking. Be that as it may, the general terms used in the Report are liable both to blur essential distinctions and to direct the attention of educational planners into unprofitable descriptions of what they are after.

Thirdly, in spite of any protestations to the contrary, the impression is created by this terminology that it is possible to develop general unitary abilities of the stated kind. The extent to which this is true is a matter for empirical investigation into the transfer of training. Nevertheless such abilities must necessarily be characterized in terms of the public features of knowledge, and whatever general abilities there may be, the particular criteria for their application in diverse fields are vital to their significance for liberal education. But to think in these terms is to be in danger of looking for transfer of skills where none is discernible. We must not assume that skill at tiddlywinks will get us very far at cricket, or that if the skills have much in common, as in say squash and tennis, then the rules for one activity will do as the rules for the other.

Failure to appreciate these points leads all too readily to programmes of education for which quite unwarranted claims are made. It is sometimes said, for instance, that the study of one major science can in itself provide the elements of a liberal education—that it can lead to the development of such abilities as effective thinking, communication, the making of relevant judgments, and even to some extent, discrimination among values. But this facile view is seen to be quite untenable if it is once understood how these abilities are defined, and how any one form of knowledge is related to them. Much more plausible and much more common is the attempt to relate directly the study of particular subjects to the development of particular unitary abilities. The Harvard Committee do this with subdivisions of effective thinking when they suggest that, roughly speaking, logical thinking is developed by the sciences, relational thinking by social studies, and imaginative thinking by the humanities. This, of course, could be said to be true by definition if logical thinking were taken to be just that kind of thinking that is developed by the study of the sciences. But such a straight and limited connection is not at all what is indicated in the Report. The forms of thinking there are much more generalized. It follows then that logical, relational and imaginative thinking must be independently defined. Because of the vagueness of the terms it might appear that this would be simple enough. But in fact this very vagueness makes the task almost impossible, for any one of the three terms might, with considerable justice, be applied to almost any example of thinking. (And the appropriateness of using such a term as "imaginative" to describe a distinct type of thinking rather than its manner or style is very debatable.) Even if this most serious difficulty were overcome somehow, there would remain the problem of establishing empirical evidence for asserting both the existence of such an ability and that a particular study leads to its development. Generally speaking, there is little such evidence. What there is on transfer of training suggests that it occurs only where there is marked logical similarity in the elements studied.

Finally, the characterization of a liberal education in these terms is misleading owing to the tendency for the concept to be broadened so that it is concerned not only with the development of the mind that results from the pursuit of knowledge, but also with other aspects of personal development, particularly emotional and moral, that may or may not be judged desirable. This tendency can be clearly seen in the Report's comments on the abilities of communication, making relevant judgments and discriminating among values. Stretching the edges of the concept in these ways leads to a much wider, more generalised notion of education. It then ceases to be one defined directly in terms of the pursuit of knowledge as liberal education originally was, and thus cannot be justified by justifying that pursuit. But this is surely to give up the concept in favour of another one that needs independent justification. The analysis of such a concept is beyond our present concern.

## A REASSERTION AND A REINTERPRETATION

On logical grounds, then, it would seem that a consistent concept of liberal education must be worked out fully in terms of the forms of knowledge. By these is meant, of course, not collections of information, but the complex ways of understanding experience which man has achieved, which are publicly specifiable and which are gained through learning. An education in these terms does indeed develop its related abilities and qualities of mind, for the mind will be characterized to a greater or lesser degree by the features of the understanding it seeks. Each form of knowledge, if it is to be acquired beyond a general and superficial level, involves the development of creative imagination, judgment, thinking, communicative skills, etc., in ways that are peculiar to itself as a way of understanding experience. To list these elements, picking them out, as it were, across the forms of knowledge of which they are part and in each of which they have a different stamp, draws attention to many features that a liberal education must of course include. But it draws attention to them at the expense of the differences among them as they occur in the different areas. And of itself such listing contributes nothing to the basic determination of what a liberal education is. To be told that it is the development of effective thinking is of no value until this is explicated in terms of the forms of knowledge which give it meaning: for example, in terms of the solving of problems in Euclidean geometry or coming to understand the poems of John Donne. To be told instead that it is concerned with certain specified forms of knowledge, the essential characteristics of which are then detailed explicitly as far as possible, is to be given a clear understanding of the concept and one which is unambiguous as to the forms of thinking, judgment, imagination, and communication it involves.

In his Gulbenkian Foundation Report: *Arts and Science Sides in the Sixth Form*, Mr. A. D. C. Peterson comes considerably nearer than the Harvard Committee to the definition of a liberal education (once more termed here a "general education") by proceeding in just this fashion. Being concerned that this should not be worked out in terms of information, he shies away from any direct use of the term "knowledge" and defines the concept modestly as one that "develops the intellect in as many as possible of the main modes of thinking."[6] These are then listed as the logical, the empirical, the moral, and the aesthetic. The phrase "modes of thinking," it is true, refers directly to forms of mental activity, and Mr. Peterson's alternatives for it, "modes of human experience," "categories of mental experience," and (elsewhere) "types of judgment," all look in the same direction. Yet the "modes" are not different aspects of mind that cut across the forms that human knowledge takes, as the Harvard Report's "abilities" are. They are, rather, four parallel forms of mental development. To complete this treatment so that there is no ambiguity, however, it must be made clear in a way that Mr. Peterson does not make it clear, that the four forms can only be distinguished, in the last analysis, in terms of the public features that demarcate the areas of knowledge on which they stand. Logical, empirical, moral, and aesthetic forms of understanding are distinguishable from each other only by their distinctive concepts and expressions and their criteria for distinguishing the true from the false, the good from the bad. If Mr. Peterson's "modes" are strictly explicated on the basis of these features of knowledge, then his concept of education becomes one concerned with the development of the mind as that is determined by certain forms of knowledge. This is to be in sight of a modern equivalent of the traditional conception of liberal education.

But the reassertion of this concept implies that there is once more the acceptance of some kind of "harmony" between knowledge and the mind. This is, however, not now being maintained on metaphysical grounds. What is being suggested, rather, is that the "harmony" is a matter of the logical relationship between the concept of "mind" and the concept of "knowledge," from which it follows the achievement of knowledge is necessarily the development of mind—that is, the self-conscious, rational mind of man—in its most fundamental aspect.

Whatever else is implied in the phrase, to have "a rational mind" certainly implies experience structured under some form of conceptual scheme. The various manifestations of consciousness, in, for instance, different sense perceptions, different emotions, or different elements of intellectual understanding, are intelligible only by virtue of the conceptual apparatus by which they are articulated. Further, whatever private forms of awareness there may be, it is by means of symbols, particularly in language, that conceptual articulation becomes objectified, for the symbols give public embodiment to the concepts. The result of this is that men are able to come to understand both the external world and their own private states of mind in common ways, sharing the same conceptual schema by learning to use symbols in the same manner. The objectification of understanding is possible because commonly accepted criteria for using the terms are recognized even if these are never explicitly expressed. But further as the symbols derived from experience can be used to examine subsequent experience, assertions are possible which are testable as true or false, valid or invalid. There are thus also public criteria whereby certain forms of expression are assessable against experience. Whether the "objects" concerned are themselves private to the individual like mental processes, or publicly accessible like temperature readings, there are here tests for the assertions which are themselves publicly agreed and accepted.

It is by the use of such tests that we have come to have the whole domain of knowledge. The formulating and testing of symbolic expressions has enabled man to probe his experience for ever more complex relations and for finer and finer distinctions, these being fixed and held for public sharing in the symbolic systems that have been evolved. But it is important to realize that this progressive attainment of a cognitive framework with public criteria has significance not merely for knowledge itself, for it is by its terms that the life of man in every particular is patterned and ordered. Without its structure all other forms of consciousness, including, for example, emotional experiences, or mental attitudes and beliefs, would seem to be unintelligible. For the analysis of them reveals that they lack independent intelligible structure of themselves. Essentially private though they may be in many or all of their aspects, their characteristic forms are explicable only by means of the publicly rooted conceptual organizations we have achieved. They can be understood only by means of the objective features with which they are associated, round which they come to be organized and built. The forms of knowledge are thus the basic articulations whereby the whole of experience has become intelligible to man, they are the fundamental achievement of mind.

Knowledge, however, must never be thought of merely as vast bodies of tested symbolic expressions. These are only the public aspects of the ways in which human experience has come to have shape. They are significant because they are themselves the objective elements round which the development of mind has taken place. To acquire knowledge is to become aware of experience as structured, organized, and made meaningful in some quite specific way, and the varieties of human knowledge constitute the highly developed forms in which man has found this possible. To acquire knowledge is to learn to see, to experience the world in a way otherwise unknown, and thereby come to have a mind in a fuller sense. It is not that the mind is some kind of organ or muscle with its own inbuilt forms of operation, which if somehow developed, naturally lead to different kinds of knowledge. It is not that the mind has predetermined patterns of functioning. Nor is it that the mind is an entity which suitably directed by knowledge comes to take on the pattern of, is conformed to, some external reality. It is rather that to have a mind basically involves coming to have experience articulated by means of various conceptual schema. It is only because man has over millennia objectified and progressively developed these that he has achieved the forms of human knowledge, and the possibility of the development of mind as we know it is open to us today.

A liberal education is, then, one that, determined in scope and content by knowledge itself, is thereby concerned with the development of mind. The concept is thus once more clearly and objectively defined in precisely the same way as the original concept. It is however no longer supported by epistemological and metaphysical doctrines that result in a hierarchical organization of the various forms of knowledge. The detailed working out of the education will therefore be markedly different in certain respects. The distinctions between the various forms of knowledge which will principally govern the scheme of education will now be based entirely on analyses of their particular conceptual, logical, and methodological features. The comprehensive character of the education will of course remain, since this is essentially part of the definition of the concept, but any question of the harmonious organization of its various elements will depend on the relationships between them that are revealed by these analyses.

But if the concept is reasserted in these terms, what now of the question of its justification? The justification of a liberal education as supported by the doctrines of classical realism was based on the ultimacy of knowledge as ordered and determined by reality, and the significance of knowledge for the mind and for the good life. Having weakened these doctrines, the Harvard Committee's justification of their concept ignores the question of the relationship between knowledge and reality, and there is a specific rejection of the view that knowledge is in itself the good of the mind. They assert, however, the supreme significance of knowledge in the determination of all human activity, and supplement this, as is certainly necessary because of the extended nature of their concept, by general considerations of the desirability of their suggestions. When once more the concept is strictly confined so as to be determined by the forms of knowledge, the return to a justification of it without reference to what is generally thought desirable on social or similar grounds becomes possible. And such justification for the concept is essential if the education it delineates is to have the ultimate significance that, as was earlier suggested, is part of its raison d'être. This justification must now, however, stem from what has already been said of the nature of knowledge as no metaphysical doctrine of the connection between knowledge and reality is any longer being invoked.

If the achievement of knowledge is necessarily the development of mind in its most basic sense, then it can be readily seen that to ask for a justification for the pursuit of knowledge is not at all the same thing as to ask for the justification for, say, teaching all children a foreign language or making them orderly and punctual in their behaviour. It is in fact a peculiar question asking for justification for any development of the rational mind at all. To ask for the justification of any form of activity is significant only if one is in fact committed already to seeking rational knowledge. To ask for a justification of the pursuit of rational knowledge itself therefore presupposes some form of commitment to what one is seeking to justify. Justification is possible only if what is being justified is both intelligible under publicly rooted concepts and is assessable according to accepted criteria. It assumes a commitment to these two principles. But these very principles are in fact fundamental to the pursuit of knowledge in all its forms, be it, for instance, empirical knowledge or understanding in the arts. The forms of knowledge are in a sense simply the working out of these general principles in particular ways. To give justification to any kind of knowledge therefore involves using the principles in one specific form to assess their use in another. Any particular activity can be examined for its rational character, for its adherence to these principles, and thus justified on the assumption of them. Indeed in so far as activities are rational this will be possible. It is commitment to them that characterizes any rational activity as such. But the principles themselves have no such assessable status, for justification outside the use of the principles is not logically possible. This does not mean that rational pursuits in the end lack justification, for they could equally well be said to have their justification written into them. Nor is any form of viciously circular justification involved by assuming in the procedure what is being looked for. The situation is that we have here reached the ultimate point where the question of justification ceases to be significantly applicable. The apparent circularity is the result of the interrelation between the concepts of rational justification and the pursuit of knowledge.

Perhaps the finality of these principles can be brought out further by noting a negative form of the same argument. From this point of view, to question the pursuit of any kind of rational knowledge is in the end self-defeating, for the questioning itself depends on accepting the very principles whose use is finally being called in question.

It is because it is based on these ultimate principles that characterize knowledge itself and not merely on lower level forms of justification that a liberal education is in a very real sense the ultimate form of education. In spite of the absence of any metaphysical doctrine about reality this idea of liberal education has a significance parallel to that of the original Greek concept. It is an education concerned directly with the development of the mind in rational knowledge, whatever form that freely takes. This parallels the original concept in that according to the doctrine of function liberal education was the freeing of the mind to achieve its own good in knowledge. In each case it is a form of education knowing no limits other than those necessarily imposed by the nature of rational knowledge and thereby itself developing in man the final court of appeal in all human affairs.

As here reformulated the concept has, again like the original, objectivity, though this is no longer backed by metaphysical realism. For it is a necessary feature of knowledge as such that there be public criteria whereby the true is distinguishable from the false, the good from the bad, the right from the wrong. It is the existence of these criteria which gives objectivity to knowledge; and this in its turn gives objectivity to the concept of liberal education. A parallel to another form of justification thus remains, and the concept continues to warrant its label as that of an education that frees the mind from error and illusion. Further, as the determination of the good life is now considered to be itself the pursuit of a particular form of rational knowledge, that in which what ought to be done is justified by the giving of reasons, this is seen as a necessary part of a liberal education. And as all other forms of knowledge contribute in their way to moral understanding, the concept as a whole is once more given a kind of justification in its importance for the moral life. But this justification, like that of objectivity, no longer has the distinct significance which it once had, for it is again simply a necessary consequence of what the pursuit of knowledge entails. Nevertheless, liberal education remains basic to the freeing of human conduct from wrong.


## CERTAIN BASIC PHILOSOPHICAL CONSIDERATIONS

Having attempted a reinstatement of the concept without its original philosophical backing, what of the implications of this for the practical conduct of education? In working these out it is necessary first to try to distinguish the various forms of knowledge and then to relate them in some way to the organization of the school or college curriculum. The first of these is a strictly philosophical task. The second is a matter of practical planning that involves many considerations other than the purely philosophical, and to this I will return when certain broad distinctions between forms of knowledge have been outlined.

As stated earlier, by a form of knowledge is meant a distinct way in which our experience becomes structured round the use of accepted public symbols. The symbols thus having public meaning, their use is in some way testable against experience, and there is the progressive development of series of tested symbolic expressions. In this way experience has been probed further and further by extending and elaborating the use of the symbols, and by means of these it has become possible for the personal experience of individuals to become more fully structured, more fully understood. The various forms of knowledge can be seen in low level developments within the common area of our knowledge of the everyday world. From this there branch out the developed forms which, taking certain elements in our common knowledge as a basis, have grown in distinctive ways. In the developed forms of knowledge the following related, distinguishing features can be seen.

1. They each involve certain central concepts that are peculiar in character to the form. For example, those of gravity, acceleration,

hydrogen, and photosynthesis characteristic of the sciences; number, integral, and matrix in mathematics; God, sin, and predestination in religion; ought, good, and wrong in moral knowledge.

2. In a given form of knowledge these and other concepts that denote, if perhaps in a very complex way, certain aspects of experience form a network of possible relationships in which experience can be understood. As a result the form has a distinctive logical structure. For example, the terms and statements of mechanics can be meaningfully related in certain strictly limited ways only, and the same is true of historical explanation.

3. The form, by virtue of its particular terms and logic, has expressions or statements (possibly answering a distinctive type of question) that in some way or other, however indirect it may be, are testable against experience. This is the case in scientific knowledge, moral knowledge, and in the arts, though in the arts no questions are explicit and the criteria for the tests are only partially expressible in words. Each form, then, has distinctive expressions that are testable against experience in accordance with particular criteria that are peculiar to the form.

4. The forms have developed particular techniques and skills for exploring experience and testing their distinctive expressions, for instance the techniques of the sciences and those of the various literary arts. The result has been the amassing of all the symbolically expressed knowledge that we now have in the arts and the sciences.

Though the various forms of knowledge are distinguishable in these ways it must not be assumed that all there is to them can be made clear and explicit by these means. All knowledge involves the use of symbols and the making of judgments in ways that cannot be expressed in words and can only be learnt in a tradition. The art of scientific investigation and the development of appropriate experimental tests, the forming of an historical explanation and the assessment of its truth, the appreciation of a poem: all of these activities are high arts that are not in themselves communicable simply by words. Acquiring knowledge of any form is therefore to a greater or lesser extent something that cannot be done simply by solitary study of the symbolic expressions of knowledge, it must be learnt from a master on the job. No doubt it is because the forms require particular training of this kind in distinct worlds of discourse, because they necessitate the development of high critical standards according to complex criteria, because they involve our coming to look at experience in particular ways, that we refer to them as disciplines. They are indeed disciplines that form the mind.

Yet the dividing lines that can be drawn between different disciplines by means of the four suggested distinguishing marks are neither clear enough nor sufficient for demarcating the whole world of modern knowledge as we know it. The central feature to which they point is that the major forms of knowledge, or disciplines, can each be distinguished by their dependence on some particular kind of test against experience for their distinctive expressions. On this ground alone however certain broad divisions are apparent. The sciences depend crucially on empirical experimental and observational tests, mathematics depends on deductive demonstrations from certain sets of axioms. Similarly moral knowledge and the arts involve distinct forms of critical tests though in these cases both what the tests are and the ways in which they are applied are only partially statable. (Some would in fact dispute the status of the arts as forms of knowledge for this very reason.) Because of their particular logical features it seems to me necessary to distinguish also as separate disciplines both historical and religious knowledge, and there is perhaps an equally good case, because of the nature of their empirical concepts, for regarding the human sciences separately from the physical sciences. But within these areas further distinctions must be made. These are usually the result of the groupings of knowledge round a number of related concepts, or round particular skills or techniques. The various sciences and the various arts can be demarcated within the larger units of which they are in varying degrees representative in their structure, by these means.

But three other important classifications of knowledge must in addition be recognized. First there are those organizations which are not themselves disciplines or subdivisions of any discipline. They are formed by building together round specific objects, or phenomena, or practical pursuits, knowledge that is characteristically rooted elsewhere in more than one discipline. It is not just that these organizations make use of several forms of knowledge, for after all the sciences use mathematics, the arts use historical knowledge and so on. Many of the disciplines borrow from each other. But these organizations are not concerned, as the disciplines are, to validate any one logically distinct form of expression. They are not concerned with developing a particular structuring of experience. They are held together simply by their subject matter, drawing on all forms of knowledge that can contribute to them. Geography, as the study of man in relation to his environment, is an example of a theoretical study of this kind, engineering an example of a practical nature. I see no reason why such organizations of knowledge, which I shall refer to as "fields," should not be endlessly constructed according to particular theoretical or practical interests. Secondly, whilst moral knowledge is a distinct form, concerned with answering questions as to what ought to be done in practical affairs, no specialized subdivisions of this have been developed. In practical affairs, moral questions, because of their character, naturally arise alongside questions of fact and technique, so that there have been formed "fields" of practical knowledge that include distinct moral elements within them, rather than the subdivisions of a particular discipline. Political, legal and educational theory are perhaps the clearest examples of fields where moral knowledge of a developed kind is to be found. Thirdly, there are certain second order forms of knowledge which are dependent for their existence on the other primary areas. On the one hand there are the essentially scientific studies of language and symbolism as in grammar and philology. On the other hand there are the logical and philosophical studies of meaning and justification. These would seem to constitute a distinct discipline by virtue of their particular concepts and criteria of judgment.

In summary, then, it is suggested that the forms of knowledge as we have them can be classified as follows:

1. Distinct disciplines or forms of knowledge (subdivisible): mathematics, physical sciences, human sciences, history, religion, literature and the fine arts, philosophy.
2. Fields of knowledge: theoretical, practical (these may or may not include elements of moral knowledge).

It is the distinct disciplines that basically constitute the range of unique ways we have of understanding experience if to these is added the category of moral knowledge.


## THE PLANNING AND PRACTICAL CONDUCT
## OF LIBERAL EDUCATION

Turning now to the bearing of this discussion on the planning and conduct of a liberal education, certain very general comments about its characteristic features can be made though detailed treatment would involve psychological and other considerations that are quite beyond the scope of this paper.

In the first place, as liberal education is concerned with the comprehensive development of the mind in acquiring knowledge, it is aimed at achieving an understanding of experience in many different ways. This means the acquisition by critical training and discipline not only of facts but also of complex conceptual schemes and of the arts and techniques of different types of reasoning and judgment. Syllabuses and curricula cannot therefore be constructed simply in terms of information and isolated skills. They must be constructed so as to introduce pupils as far as possible into the interrelated aspects of each of the basic forms of knowledge, each of the several disciplines. And they must be constructed to cover at least in some measure the range of knowledge as a whole.

In a programme of liberal education that is based directly on the study of the specific disciplines, examples of each of the different areas must of course be chosen. Selection of this kind is not, however, simply an inevitable practical consequence of the vast growth of knowledge. It is equally in keeping with what a liberal education is aiming at. Though its aim is comprehensive it is not after the acquisition of encyclopaedic information. Nor is it after the specialist knowledge of the person fully trained in all the particular details of a branch of knowledge. Such a specialist can not only accurately employ the concepts, logic, and criteria of a domain but also knows the skills and techniques involved in the pursuit of knowledge quite beyond the immediate areas of common human experience. Nor is liberal education concerned with the technician's knowledge of the detailed application of the disciplines in practical and theoretical fields. What is being sought is, first, sufficient immersion in the concepts, logic, and criteria of the discipline for a person to come to know the distinctive way in which it "works" by pursuing these in particular cases; and then sufficient generalization of these over the whole range of the discipline so that his experience begins to be widely structured in this distinctive manner. It is this coming to look at things in a certain way that is being aimed at, not the ability to work out in minute particulars all the details that can in fact be discerned. It is the ability to recognize empirical assertions or aesthetic judgments for what they are, and to know the kind of considerations on which their validity will depend, that matters. Beyond this an outline of the major achievements in each area provides some grasp of the range and scope of experience that has thus become intelligible. Perhaps this kind of understanding is in fact most readily distinguishable in the literary arts as critical appreciation in contrast to the achievement of the creative writer or the literary hack. But the distinction is surely applicable to other forms of knowledge as well.

This is not to assert that "critical appreciation" in any form of knowledge can be adequately achieved without some development of the understanding of the specialist or technician. Nor is it to imply that this understanding in the sciences, the arts, or moral issues can be had without participation in many relevant creative and practical pursuits. The extent to which this is true will vary from discipline to discipline and is in fact in need of much investigation, particularly because of its importance for moral and aesthetic education. But it is to say that the aim of the study of a discipline in liberal education is not that of its study in a specialist or technical course. The first is concerned with developing a person's ways of understanding experience, the others are concerned with mastering the details of knowledge, how it is established, and the use of it in other enterprises, particularly those of a practical nature. It is of course perfectly possible for a course in physics, for example, to be devoted to a double purpose if it is deliberately so designed. It may provide both a specialist knowledge of the subject and at the same time a genuine introduction to the form of scientific knowledge. But the two purposes are quite distinct and there is no reason to suppose that by aiming at one the other can automatically be achieved as well. Yet it would seem to be true that some specialist study within a discipline, if it is at all typical of the discipline, is necessary to understanding the form of knowledge in any developed sense. The study of a discipline as part of liberal education, however, contributes practically nothing directly to any specialist study of it, though it does serve to put the specialism into a much wider context.

A liberal education approached directly in terms of the disciplines will thus be composed of the study of at least paradigm examples of all the various forms of knowledge. This study will be sufficiently detailed and sustained to give genuine insight so that pupils come to think in these terms, using the concepts, logic, and criteria accurately in the different domains. It will then include generalization of the particular examples used so as to show the range of understanding in the various forms. It will also include some indication of the relations between the forms where these overlap and their significance in the major fields of knowledge, particularly the practical fields, that have been developed. This is particularly important for moral education, as moral questions can frequently be solved only by calling on the widest possible range of human understanding. As there is in fact no developed discipline of moral knowledge, education in moral understanding must necessarily be approached in a rather different way. For if it is to cover more than everyday personal matters this has to be by the study of issues that occur in certain particular fields of knowledge. The major difficulty this presents will be referred to briefly later. The important point here is that though moral understanding has to be pursued in contexts where it is not the only dominant interest, the aim of its pursuit is precisely the same as for all other elements in a liberal education, the understanding of experience in a unique way. What is wanted (just as in the study of the disciplines *per se*) is, basically, the use of the appropriate concepts, logic, and criteria, and the appreciation of the range of understanding in this form.

It is perhaps important to stress the fact that this education will be one in the forms of knowledge themselves and not merely a self-conscious philosophical treatment of their characteristics. Scientific and historical knowledge are wanted, not knowledge of the philosophy of science and the philosophy of history as substitutes. A liberal education can only be planned if distinctions in the forms of knowledge are clearly understood, and that is a philosophical matter. But the education itself is only partly in philosophy, and that is only possible when pupils have some grasp of the other disciplines themselves.

Precisely what sections of the various disciplines are best suited to the aims of liberal education cannot be gone into here. It is apparent that on philosophical grounds alone some branches of the sciences, for instance, would seem to be much more satisfactory as paradigms of scientific thinking than others. Many sections of physics are probably more comprehensive and clear in logical character, more typical of the well-developed physical sciences than, say, botany. If so, they would, all other things being equal, serve better as an introduction to scientific knowledge. Perhaps in literature and the fine arts the paradigm principle is less easy to apply though probably many would favour a course in literature to any one other. But whatever the discipline, in practice all other things are not in fact equal and decisions about the content of courses cannot be taken without careful regard to the abilities and interests of the students for whom they are designed.

Yet hovering round such decisions and questions of syllabus planning there is frequently found the belief that the inherent logical structure of a discipline, or a branch of a discipline necessarily determines exactly what and exactly how the subject is to be taught and learnt. The small amount of truth and the large amount of error in this belief can only be distinguished by clarifying what the logic of a subject is. It is not a series of intellectual steps that must be climbed in strict order. It is not a specific psychological channel along which the mind must travel if there is to be understanding. This is to confuse logical characteristics with psychological processes. The logic of a form of knowledge shows the meaningful and valid ways in which its terms and criteria are used. It constitutes the publicly accepted framework of knowledge. The psychological activities of the individual when concerned with this knowledge are not in general prescribed in any temporal order and the mind, as it were, plays freely within and around the framework. It is simply that the framework lays down the general formal relations of the concepts if there is to be knowledge. The logic as publicly expressed consists of the general formal principles to which the terms must conform in knowledge. Coming to understand a form of knowledge involves coming to think in relations that satisfy the public criteria. How the mind plays round and within these is not itself being laid down at all, there is no dragooning of psychological processes, only a marking out of the territory in which the mind can wander more or less at will. Indeed, understanding a form of knowledge is far more like coming to know a country than climbing a ladder. Some places in a territory may only be get-at-able by a single specified route and cannot be understood without first understanding certain others. But that countries are explorable only in one way is in general false, and even in mathematics, the most strictly sequential form of knowledge we have, many ways of coming to know the territory are possible. The logic of a subject is relevant to what is being taught, for its patterns must be accepted as essential to the form of knowledge. But how those patterns are best discerned is a matter for empirical investigation.

School subjects in the disciplines as we at present have them are in no way sacrosanct on either logical or psychological grounds. They are necessarily selections from the forms of knowledge that we have and may or may not be good as introductions for the purposes of liberal education. In most cases they have developed under a number of diverse influences. The historical growth of the subjects has sometimes dominated the programmes. The usefulness of certain elements, the demands of higher specialist education, certain general "psychological" principles such as progressing from the simple to the complex, from the particular to the general, the concrete to the abstract, all these factors and many others have left their marks. This being so, many well established courses need to be critically reexamined both philosophically and psychologically before they can be accepted as suitable for liberal education. Superficially at least most of them would seem to be quite inappropriate for this purpose.

Though a liberal education is most usually approached directly in the study of various branches of the disciplines, I see no reason to think that this must necessarily be so. It is surely possible to construct programmes that are in the first place organized round certain fields of knowledge either theoretical or practical. The study of aspects of power, natural as well as social and political, might for instance be one element in such a scheme; or a regional study that introduces historical, geographical, industrial, and social considerations; or a practical project of design and building involving the sciences, mathematics and visual arts. In this case, however, it must be recognized that the fields are chosen because together they can be used to develop understanding of all the various forms of knowledge, and explicit steps must be taken to see that this end is achieved. There will necessarily be the strongest tendency for liberal education to be lost sight of and for the fields to be pursued in their own right developing the techniques and skills which they need. These may be valuable and useful in many ways, and perhaps essential in many a person's whole education. (Certainly liberal education as is here being understood is only one part of the education a person ought to have, for it omits quite deliberately, for instance, specialist education, physical education, and character training.) But a course in various fields of knowledge will not in fact be a liberal education unless that aim is kept absolutely clear and every opportunity is taken to lead to a fuller grasp of the disciplines. Again some fields of study will be better for this purpose than others but all will demand the highest skill from the teacher, who must be under no misapprehension as to what the object of the exercise really is. Yet it is difficult to see how this kind of approach can be fully adequate if it does not in the end lead to a certain amount of study of the distinct disciplines themselves. For whatever ground may have been covered indirectly, a satisfactory understanding of the characteristically distinct approaches of the different forms is hardly possible without some direct gathering together of the elements of the disciplines that have been implicit in all that has been done.

Whatever the pattern of a liberal education in its later stages, it must not be forgotten that there is being presupposed a broad basic education in the common area of everyday knowledge where the various disciplines can be seen in embryo and from which they branch out as distinct units. In such a basic primary education, the ever growing range of a child's experience and the increasing use of linguistic and symbolic forms lays the foundation for the various modes of understanding, scientific, historical, religious, moral, and so on. Out of this general pool of knowledge the disciplines have slowly become ever more differentiated and it is this that the student must come to understand, not confusing the forms of knowledge but appreciating them for what they are in themselves, and recognizing their necessary limitations.

But is, then, the outcome of a liberal education to be simply the achievement of a series of discreet ways of understanding experience? In a very real sense yes, but in another sense not entirely. For one thing, we have as yet not begun to understand the complex interrelations of the different forms of knowledge themselves, for they do not only have unique features but common features too, and in addition one discipline often makes extensive use of the achievements of another. But we must also not forget that the various forms are firmly rooted in that common world of persons and things which we all share, and into this they take back in subtle as well as simple ways the understanding they have achieved. The outcome of a liberal education must therefore not be thought of as producing ever greater disintegration of the mind but rather the growth of ever clearer and finer distinctions in our experience. If the result is not some quasi-aesthetic unity of the mind neither is it in any sense chaos. Perhaps the most suggestive picture of the outcome is that used by Professor Michael Oakeshott, though for him it has more literal truth than is here intended. In this the various forms of knowledge are seen as voices in a conversation, a conversation to which they each contribute in a distinctive way. If taken figuratively, his words express more succinctly than mine can precisely what it seems to me a liberal education is and what its outcome will be.

> As civilized human beings, we are the inheritors, neither of an inquiry about ourselves and the world, nor of an accumulating body of information, but of a conversation, begun in the primeval forests and extended and made more articulate in the course of centuries. It is a conversation which goes on both in public and within each of ourselves. Of course there is argument and inquiry and information, but wherever these are profitable they are to be recognized as passages in this conversation, and perhaps they are not the most captivating of the passages. . . . Conversation is not an enterprise designed to yield an extrinsic profit, a contest where a winner gets a prize, nor is it an activity of exegesis; it is an unrehearsed intellectual adventure. . . . Education, properly speaking, is an initiation into the skill and partnership of this conversation in which we learn to recognize the voices, to distinguish the proper occasions of utterance, and in which we acquire the intellectual and moral habits appropriate to conversation. And it is this conversation which, in the end, gives place and character to every human activity and utterance.[7]

DAVID P. AUSUBEL
# LEARNING BY DISCOVERY

Even the most cursory examination of new curriculum proposals indicates that there is presently a strong movement toward introducing a larger component of "discovery" experiences into the elementary and secondary schools. In many school systems where such ideas are being tried out, the discovery approach is like a breath of fresh air in what has been frequently a depressing and restrictive school environment. However, while one's educational convictions should be argued with passion, it seems a sensible requirement that they should also be informed with reason. And it was a sensed lack of realism and reasoned argument among the more extreme discovery enthusiasts which prompted a critique of the "mystique" which seems to have grown up around this approach.[1]

During the preparation of this book, our first inclination was to omit a detailed discussion of the merits and pitfalls of discovery learning, on the assumption that the wave of enthusiasm evidenced in the early 1960s had passed and that more sober viewpoints now prevailed. However, a survey of current professional literature, after-dinner talks to teachers' conventions, the pronouncements of many educational psychologists themselves, and the opinions of elementary-school teachers who have come into our courses has convinced us that our initial opinion is entirely unfounded. For example, in the province in which one of the authors is located, a prestigious government commission has recently issued a report containing an unequivocal (and virtually unqualified) endorsement of discovery learning, without serious reference to reasoned counter-arguments of potential weakness.[2] It is our firm conviction, therefore, that the issues of half a decade ago are still very much alive; for that reason we present here an abridged version of the 1963 statement, together with further analyses and recommendations.

# AN OVERVIEW OF DISCOVERY LEARNING

## Historical Background

To what may the present enthusiasm for discovery methods be attributed? To begin with, the progressive education movement undoubtedly furnished a major impetus to its utilization and appeal. One aspect of this movement was a growing dissatisfaction with the empty formalism of much educational content in the latter part of the nineteenth and the early part of the twentieth century; with stultifying drill and catechism-like methods of teaching; with the curriculum's lack of relatedness to the everyday experience of the child, his physical world and social environment; and with pupils' rote verbalization and memorization of ideas for which they had no adequate referents in experience. The progressive educator's overreaction to these faults took the form of an exaggerated emphasis on direct, immediate, and concrete experience as a prerequisite for genuine understanding, on problem solving and inquiry, and on incidental learning and learning in natural, uncontrived situations. From this type of emphasis grew activity programs and project methods and the belief in "learning for and by problem solving."

A second aspect of the evolution of the discovery method was the child-centered approach to instruction that originated in the educational philosophies of Rousseau and Froebel. The adherents of this approach emphasized the importance of structuring the curriculum in terms of the nature of the child and of his participation in the educational process, that is, in terms of his current interests, his endogenously derived needs, and his state of intellectual and emotional readiness. According to this point of view, the educational environment facilitates development best by providing a maximally permissive field that does not interfere with the predetermined process of spontaneous maturation. The child himself, it was asserted, is in the most strategic position to know and select those educational ingredients that correspond most closely to his current developmental needs, and hence are most conducive to his optimal growth. Propositions such as these clearly make a fetish of autonomy and self-discovery, and take an extremely dim view of any form of guidance or direction in learning, particularly the communication of insights or generalizations by teacher to students. Herein lies, in part, the origin of the notion that expository teaching is, on developmental needs, and hence are most conducive to his optimal discovered insights are uniquely and transcendentally endowed with meaning and understanding that can be achieved through no other means.

These two strands—emphasis on the child's direct experience and spontaneous interests, and insistence upon autonomously achieved insight free of all directive manipulation of the learning environment—set the stage for the subsequent adulation of problem solving, laboratory work, and questionable emulation of the scientific method. Many mathematics and science teachers were made self-conscious about systematically presenting and explaining to their students the basic concepts and principles of their fields because it was held that this procedure would promote glib verbalization and rote memorization. Although enthusiasts are reluctant to admit it, the new emphasis on problem solving often meant little more than that the students ceased to memorize *specific* formulas but memorized instead *type* problems, learning how to work exemplars of all the kinds of problems they were responsible for, and memorizing not only the form of each type but the solution as well. This was paralleled in science courses by laboratory experiences in which the student proceeded mechanically through a set of instructions without any real appreciation of the concepts or hypotheses at issue, arriving finally at the predetermined conclusion set out in the manual. The result of these experiences was far from the hoped-for aim of self-discovered generalizations. In the final analysis it produced an approach to problem solving which was frequently just as formalistic, mechanical, passive, and rote as the worst form of verbal exposition.

The previously mentioned factors contributing to the advocacy of the discovery method have been in operation over long periods of time, and do not in themselves explain the intensity of current interest. These attitudes and beliefs, existing both in latent and active forms in many educational circles for several generations, were galvanized into widespread overt expression by at least three recent occurrences. The first was the curriculum "revolution," commencing in the early postwar period and accelerating thereafter, which brought with it a great emphasis on the "heuristics of discovery"; this emphasis was itself premised on the argument that, given the inevitability of change, the student is best prepared for life by "learning how to learn." A concurrent influence was the rediscovery of the writings of Piaget by North American educational psychologists and the questionable assertion that his theoretical speculations and research results argue conclusively for the necessity of a discovery approach to the learning of concepts.[3] Finally, it seems that many contemporary high-school and college officials are looking toward greater student activity and initiative with respect to their own learning (for example, through a heavier emphasis on inquiry and discovery methods) as one means of combatting apparent student disenchantment with both the substance and method of instruction at these levels. However, it is not our purpose in this chapter to discuss the reasonableness of the latter arguments, but rather to analyze the discovery method in more detail so that its potential advantages and weakness can be better understood.

Nature of Discovery Learning in School Settings

The essential criterion for discovery learning is that the material to be learned is *not* presented to the learner in final form, but that he must reorganize or transform it in some fashion prior to its incorporation into cognitive structure. As we saw earlier, discovery learning ranges in complexity from concept formation and the formation of generalizations to problem solving and creativity. In these particular kinds of learning *there is no alternative* to discovery learning, so that a discovery-reception controversy makes no sense there.

The real controversy then is not whether discovery learning is desirable or undesirable (since under certain circumstances it is unavoidable), but rather the *relative emphasis* upon these respective modes of learning which is most appropriate at various stages of the learner's development. While the opportunity for discovery learning exists across the whole behavioral hierarchy, the controversy concerning this approach has been centered at the level of generalization learning. The reason for this is that the generalization or principle expresses the utlimate result of most investigations or experiments which the student might undertake.

While we tend, for convenience, to speak of reception and discovery as though we were dealing with a true dichotomy, analysis of teaching methods employed in the classroom indicates that there are a variety of approaches which can be ordered along a dimension of *increasing direction* on the part of the teacher. Consider, for example, the various ways in which we might attempt to have a child come to understand the proposition that "the sum of the angles in a triangle equals 180 degrees." In a "pure discovery" approach (only very occasionally found in the school), we would provide the child with numerous triangles and such measuring instruments as rulers, compasses, and protractors and simply allow him to "play" with the materials, giving no specific directions whatsoever. While the child might well make some useful discoveries, the probability that he would arrive at the desired generalization entirely on his own seems rather remote.

At a second level of directedness the teacher would attempt at least to steer the child's thinking in the direction of the intended generalization, as for example by asking him to "see if you can find any interesting facts about the angles of triangles." Again the probability of the emergence of the correct generalization seems rather remote but is distinctly higher than in the first case.

At a third level of directedness, the child might be given the instructions: "Measure the angles of a triangle and add the results together. Repeat this for a number of triangles and see if you can state any conclusion which applies to all the triangles." The directions now have become quite specific and would in most cases be sufficient to allow the child to formulate the generalization.

At a fourth level—where we encounter a procedure commonly used in classrooms—the teacher would draw a number of triangles on the board and ask various students to come forward to measure the angles and perform the requisite addition, and would then invite the class to formulate a generalization. Here the teacher exerts even greater control over the learning process (insuring, for example, that the angles are added properly) and most of the children are deprived of the opportunity to measure the angles themselves; but an opportunity still exists for each child to formulate the generalization independently. Consequently, this approach could still qualify as discovery learning.

At the fifth level of directedness, the teacher would probably first enunciate the generalization and then have various children confirm it with examples drawn on the board, or have each child verify it in his workbook. We have now passed into reception learning, since it is no longer the child but the *teacher* who formulates the generalization.

Finally, at the sixth level—which might be appropriate to adolescents and adults—the teacher would merely enunciate the generalization and, without offering corroborative evidence, utilize it as the basis for further learning (for example, the fact that the sum of the angles in a rectangle—comprising two triangles—must equal 360 degrees).

It is clear then that generalizations concerning the relative merits of discovery (as compared with reception) approaches must take into account the degree of direction or guidance involved in the particular discovery method in question. For example, while the most extreme form of reception learning would take considerably less time than most of the discovery approaches, the difference in learning time between the fourth level (discovery) and the fifth level (reception) would seem to be minimal.

In the same vein, we should recognize that the current change in emphasis in schools is not from pure reception to pure discovery learning. Probably it would be far more accurate to say that while most teachers have traditionally chosen methods at the fourth or fifth level, schools are currently introducing a larger proportion of activities at the second and third levels. It is also interesting to note that in teaching which can be classified at the fourth level—where the teacher typically calls upon one child to formulate the generalization—it is difficult to say whether any other particular child is engaged in guided discovery learning (that is, is formulating the generalization himself) or reception learning (that is, relating to his cognitive structure a generalization formulated by *another student*).

## Psychological and Educational Rationale of the Discovery Method

What are some of the legitimate claims, the defensible uses, and the palpable advantages of the discovery method? Several can be cited under the headings indicated in the paragraphs below.

*Transmission of Subject Matter*   In the first place, under certain circumstances some variants of the discovery method may have advantages over reception learning in the transmission of subject matter itself. In particular, occasional use of inductive discovery techniques for teaching subject-matter content is didactically defensible when pupils are in the *concrete operational* stage of cognitive development. It is true, of course, that only the availability of some concrete empirical experience is necessary to generate the semi-abstract level of meaningfulness characteristic of this stage of cognitive development. Hence, either simple verbal exposition, using concrete empirical props, or a semi-autonomous type of discovery accelerated by the judicious use of prompts and hints, is adequate for teaching simple and relatively familiar new ideas. But when the learning task is more difficult and unfamiliar, a more autonomous measure of discovery learning probably enhances intuitive meaningfulness by intensifying and personalizing both the concreteness of the experience and the operation of abstracting and generalizing from empirical data. In these circumstances, also, the time/cost disadvantage of discovery learning is not very serious, since the time-consuming, concrete empirical aspect of learning must take place anyway.

To a lesser degree this same rationale also applies to adolescents and adults who are relatively unsophisticated in the basic concepts and terminology of a given discipline. The older individual, however, has the benefit of greater cognitive sophistication and linguistic facility, as well as of past successful experience in meaningfully relating abstractions to each other without the aid of concrete empirical props. He will therefore move through the intuitive, subverbal phase of insightful understanding much more rapidly than the unsophisticated child and, unlike the latter, will soon dispense with this phase entirely.

*Testing Meaningfulness of Learning*   One obviously *necessary* use of the discovery method is in evaluating the meaningfulness and depth of the learning of a particular concept or generalization. For example, if the child has been taught (via reception learning) the generalization that objects expand when heated, the learner's understanding might be tested by asking him to supply specific examples of this generalization from the environment. Again, if the learner has been taught a formula (that is, a principle) for determining the area of a triangle, an appropriate test of his comprehension would be to have him apply this generalization to a number of exemplars which he had not seen before. In both cases there is a modicum of discovery required. In the first instance the child is not presented with the exemplars, but must select them from a variety of environmental stimuli, and in the second case the child must select various lines as representing the base, height, and so on of the triangle. In both cases, then, there may be said to be some transformation of perceptual data to fit the conditions of the generalization prior to the incorporation of the exemplars into cognitive structure as derivatives of the generalization.

*Problem Solving*   Discovery learning is, of course, crucially implicated in problem solving. One can teach strategies (verbal rules) by a reception approach, but one can never tell whether they are comprehended and utilizable until the learner attempts to apply them to novel cases. Moreover, even though the strategy offers guidance to the learner there is still a considerable need for "discovery" within the resulting procedural framework. In the pendulum problem, for example, the learner operating under the general strategy provided must identify the independent variables and, after manipulating data, formulate a generalization relating the variables to the period of the pendulum. Similarly, in our geometry problem, the strategy does not determine an invariant order for combining or manipulating relevant propositions, but merely defines choice points at each of which the learner must discover which of a number of relevant propositions might be applied, and what further conditions must hold before this application can be made.

*Transfer*   One might expect greater transfer, particularly of the lateral type, if the student actually formulates his own generalizations. This would be true because such a learner would tend to have experiences with a greater variety of exemplars and should therefore be able to recognize these more easily when they occur in different contexts. Such facilitation or transfer would compensate, to some extent, for the longer time usually required in discovery approaches.

*Motivation*　The last advantage of discovery learning which we will cite, and this perhaps its most salient one, has to do with the enhancement of motivation. One would think, for example, that the student whose motivation is based primarily on ego-enhancement drive would obtain a greater feeling of self-esteem from independent discovery than from being told a result or principle. Certainly in our contemporary value system discovery learning is accorded a higher status and would therefore seem to have more potential for ego-enhancement than reception learning. Similar arguments would apply to the efficacy of discovery learning in satisfying affiliative drive, for parents and teachers are more likely to recognize, and therefore show explicit approval of, the child who makes a discovery on his own (frequently a more conspicuous activity than the deceptively passive-appearing reception learning). Where the advantage might lie in respect to cognitive drive is a rather difficult question, for if there exists a "desire to know' to understand, and to acquire knowledge for its own sake" then this drive could equally well be satisfied by both discovery and reception modes of learning. However if, in accordance with our definition, cognitive drive also includes the desire to solve problems, then in this particular respect the discovery approach would provide opportunities for enhancement not available in reception learning.

## PSYCHOLOGICAL AND EDUCATIONAL
## LIMITATIONS OF LEARNING BY DISCOVERY

If proponents of discovery learning confined their assertions to the legitimate claims outlined above there would be no cause for concern. Unfortunately, many present claims go so far beyond that to which one can reasonably subscribe that it seems necessary to analyze and refute some of the arguments advanced in its support. Such arguments can be conveniently considered under the following ten headings.[1]

### 1.　All Real Knowledge Is Self-Discovered

The most general and metaphysical of the ten propositions is the familiar assertion that to *really* possess knowledge or acquire an idea the learner must discover it by himself or through his own insight. It is true that one cannot simply soak up one's culture like a piece of blotting paper and expect it to be meaningful. The very processes of perception and cognition necessarily require that the cultural stimulus world must first be filtered through each individual's personal sensory apparatus and cognitive structure before it can have any meaning. Meaning can never be anything more than a *personal* phenomenal product that emerges when potentially meaningful ideas are integrated within an individually unique cognitive structure. All of this, however, is recognized and accounted for in any program of meaningful expository learning.

In the final analysis the proposition that everyone must discover for himself every bit of knowledge that he *really* wishes to possess is a repudiation of the very concept of culture. For perhaps the most unique attribute of human culture, which distinguishes it from every other kind of social organization in the animal kingdom, is precisely the fact that the accumulated discoveries of millenia can be transmitted to each succeeding generation in the course of childhood and youth, and need not be discovered anew by each generation. This miracle of culture is made possible only because it is so much less time consuming to communicate and explain an idea meaningfully to others than to have them discover it by themselves.

## 2. Meaning as an Exclusive Product of Nonverbal Discovery

A related proposition holds that abstract concepts and propositions are forms of empty verbalism unless the learner discovers them directly out of his own concrete, empirical, nonverbal experience. This assertion concerning "empty verbalism" seems to rest on the following three logical errors: (a) a misinterpretation of verbal learning as a passive rote phenomenon; (b) confusion between the reception/discovery and rote/meaningful dimensions of learning; and (c) an unwarranted generalization to adolescents and adults of the child's dependence upon concrete empirical props in comprehending and manipulating abstract ideas. Meaningful knowledge, however, is not an exclusive product of creative nonverbal discovery; for potentially meaningful *presented* material to become meaningful knowledge, the learner need only adopt a set to relate and incorporate its substantive import nonarbitrarily within his cognitive structure.

## 3. Subverbal Awareness as the Key to Transfer

Hendrix, in attempting to construct a more systematic and sophisticated pedagogic rationale for the discovery method than had been attempted previously, denied that verbal

> generalizing is the primary generator of transfer power. . . . As far as transfer power [is] concerned the whole thing [is] there as soon as the nonverbal awareness [dawns]. . . . The separation of discovery phenomena from the process of composing sentences which express these discoveries is the big new breakthrough in pedagogical theory (pp. 290, 292).[5]

Support for this position was adduced from an experiment involving three matched groups of elementary-school children working in arithmetic.[6] Two groups acquired meaningful, nonverbal awareness of a principle; the first group immediately attempted to verbalize the principle, the second did not, and both groups subsequently attempted to transfer this understanding to a new problem. The third group had the principle explained to them verbally. Although differences were not large enough to be statistically significant, the group which did *not* attempt to verbalize their subverbal awareness made better transfer scores than the group which did, and both groups out-performed the group which had been taught the principle by verbal exposition.

The generalization formulated from these results is that the state of awareness constituting the discovery is generated in an initial nonverbal stage and that it is only when this stage is complete that there exists something which can be transferred. It is asserted, moreover, that verbalization is not only unnecessary for the generation and transfer of ideas and understanding, but is also positively harmful when used for these purposes. Language only enters the picture because of the need to attach a symbol or label to the emerging subverbal insight, so that it can be recorded, verified, classified, and communicated to others; but the entire substance of the idea inheres in the subverbal insight itself. The resulting problem then, according to Hendrix (1961), becomes one of how to plan and execute teaching so that language can be used for these necessary secondary functions *"without* damage to the dynamic quality of the learning itself." Clearly this view is not congenial to the notion of reception learning advocated in this book.

The unqualified generalization that verbalization of an insight prior to its use inhibits transfer lacks both logical cogency and empirical support. Nonverbal understanding of principles undoubtedly exists, especially in children and unsophisticated adults, as a precursor to some verbal understanding.[7] This, of course, does not mean that *nonverbal* concept meanings and propositions are actually used in the *generation* of new insights. Such a feat would be very difficult because ideas that are not represented by words lack sufficient manipulability to be used in any complex type of thought process. It merely suggests that a preliminary intuitive (subverbal) stage exists in the *product* of thought when the emerging new insight is not clearly and precisely defined. However, when this product is eventually refined through verbalizing, it acquires thereby a much greater transfer power.[8] The verbalization of the insight that takes place at this point is actually a later phase of the thought process itself and is not to be confused with the still later representational process of *naming* verbalized meanings, as a result of which the latter meanings become more manipulable for purposes of thought.

In light of the foregoing remarks, what explanation can be offered for Hendrix's (1947) finding that immediate verbalization of newly acquired subverbal insight apparently renders that insight less transferable than when verbalization is not attempted? First, it seems likely that *premature* verbalization of nonverbal insight—before such insight is adequately clear, stable, complete, and consolidated further by extensive use—may well interfere with its more adequate emergence and consolidation at this level, as well as encourage rote memorization of the marginal and ineptly stated verbal proposition. Even more important, however, is the likelihood that a verbally expressed insight—when ambiguous, unstable, unconsolidated, ineptly expressed, and only marginally competent—possesses less functional utility and transferability than the ordinarily more primitive and less transferable subverbal insight that is more adequate in these latter respects. This is particularly true in the case of children, because of their limited linguistic facility and their relative incompetence in formal propositional logic.

Drawing these various strands of argument together, what can we legitimately conclude at this point? First, verbalization does more than just encode subverbal insight into words. The use of manipulable words to represent ideas makes possible, to begin with, the very process of transforming these ideas into new insights. Moreover, the verbalization of emerging subverbal insights into sentences is an integral part of the thought process that greatly enhances the precision and explicitness of its products. It therefore makes possible a qualitatively higher level of understanding with greatly enhanced transfer power. Second, direct acquisition of ideas from verbally presented abstract propositions presupposes both that the learner has attained the stage of formal logical operations and that he possesses minimal sophistication in the particular subject matter in question. The typical elementary-school child, therefore, tends to be limited to an intuitive, semi-abstract awareness of difficult abstractions. The older, cognitively mature individual, however, who is also unsophisticated in a particular subject-matter area, is able to dispense with the semi-abstract phase of awareness rather quickly, that is, as soon as he attains the necessary degree of sophistication. Once he attains it, he probably short-circuits the semi-abstract phase completely. Lastly, premature verbalization of a nonverbal insight, when this latter insight is still incomplete, unclear, and inadequately consolidated, probably decreases its transferability.

### 4. The Discovery Method in Transmitting Subject-Matter Content

Educators who are convinced that abstractions are mere glib verbalisms unless independently discovered by the learner have no logical alternative to advocating the use of discovery techniques—in high school and university as well as in the elementary school—as a principal method of transmitting the substantive content of subject matter. Easley,[9] for example, argues strenuously for reorganizing, in whole or in part, the curricula of science, mathematics, and other secondary-school and college-level subjects along lines of inductive discovery. He also insists that nonverbal understanding and application of principles should be required of and demonstrated by students before they are permitted to use them in verbal form.

The first argument which must be brought against this claim resides in the time/cost factor. As we saw earlier, a case can be made for some use of the discovery method in the concrete operational period, particularly when the material to be learned is complex or abstract and where one would normally resort to empirical props in any case. However, the fact that most discovery approaches are incomparably more time consuming (and, therefore, more costly) than reception approaches presents a strong argument against more than their limited use (confined mainly to highly directed kinds) for transmitting subject matter at the high-school level and beyond.

Another difficulty in using discovery as a *major* source of acquiring subject matter is that children (even when quite young) usually start with some preconceptions or spontaneous models derived from their own experience or from prevailing folklore. Hence when they are supposedly discovering principles inductively, they may be really attempting to use empirical experience to confirm their existing preconceptions. It is "unpromising to base a teaching program on the expectation that children can invent . . . modern scientific concepts, because their spontaneously invented concepts . . . present too much of a block." A more realistic approach "is for the teacher to *introduce* . . . modern scientific concepts . . . [and] follow the introduction with opportunities for the children to discover that new observations can also be interpreted by the use of the concept."[10]

A further disadvantage in using a discovery approach for the presentation of subject-matter content inheres in the difficulties caused by children's subjectivism and by their exaggerated tendency to jump to conclusions, to overgeneralize on the basis of limited experience, and to consider only one aspect of a problem at a time.[11] It is true that one objective of the elementary-school science curriculum (to enhance appreciation of scientific method) implies an effort to educate them out of these tendencies. But it is one thing to do so as part of a limited and directed laboratory program, and quite another to struggle full-time with this handicap as children are required to self-discover everything they have to learn.

## 5. Problem-Solving Ability as a Primary Goal of Education

A fifth proposition underlying the learning-by-discovery thesis is a belief that the development of problem-solving ability is the primary goal of education. The development of problem-solving ability is, of course, a legitimate and significant educational objective in its own right. Hence it is highly defensible to utilize a certain proportion of classroom time in developing appreciation of, and facility in the use of, scientific methods of inquiry and of other empirical, inductive, and deductive problem-solving procedures. But this is a far cry from advocating that the enhancement of problem-solving ability is *the* major function of the school. As the reader will appreciate from earlier sections, it is the consistent thesis of this book that the acquisition of subject-matter knowledge is itself a major goal of the school, and one which should not be subjugated to problem solving—as important as the latter may be. Although these two sets of objectives can be mutually supportive, they are far from being identical. Hence it cannot be argued that methods promoting one objective necessarily promote the other. In particular it cannot be assumed that the learner will acquire all the subject-matter content he needs in the course of learning how to solve problems autonomously.

On a related matter, many current writers[12] in the field of science education express the view that the principal objective of science instruction is the acquisition of general inquiry skills, of appropriate attitudes about science, and of training in the "heuristics of discovery." Implicit or explicit in this view is the belief that the particular choice of subject matter chosen to implement these goals is a matter of indifference so long as it is suitable for the operations of inquiry. Thus, Hibbs (1961) states:

> It does not matter whether the student learns any particular set of facts, but it does matter whether he learns how much fun it is to learn—to observe and experiment, to question and analyze the world without any ready-made set of answers and without any premium on the accuracy of his factual results, at least in the field of science.

The significant difficulty with this approach is that its proponents are, in effect, asserting that the goals of the scientist are identical to the goals of the science student and that students can learn science most effectively by playing the role of junior scientist. Yet the scientist is engaged in a full-time search for new general or applied principles in his field, while the student should be primarily engaged in an effort to learn the same basic subject matter in this field which the scientist learned in his student days, and also to learn something of the method and spirit of scientific inquiry. Thus while it makes perfectly good sense for the scientist to work full-time formulating and testing new principles, it is quite indefensible (in our opinion) for the student to be doing the same thing—either in real discovery, or in the sense of rediscovery. It is the student's business to learn these principles as meaningfully and critically as possible, and then *after* his background is adequate, to try to improve on them if he can. If he is ever to discover, he must first learn. He cannot learn adequately by pretending that he is a junior scientist.

In our opinion, then, any realistic science curriculum must be concerned with the systematic presentation of an organized body of knowledge as an explicit end in itself. Even if it is relatively superficial and organized on an intuitive basis, as it must be in the elementary school, the science curriculum should make a start in this direction and give the student a feeling for science as a selectively and sequentially organized structure. This is no less important than imparting the view that science is a method of inquiry.

6. "Every Child a Creative Thinker"

Discovery methods are often rationalized in terms of the currently fashionable notion that the school's chief responsibility is to make every child (or nearly every child) a creative thinker. This extreme notion is based on the highly questionable assumption that all discovery activity, irrespective of degree of originality, is qualitatively of one piece; on a watered-down, "democratic" definition of creativity broad enough to include any type of independent discovery; on the belief that the very multiplicity of human abilities gives every individual a good chance, genically speaking, of being creative in at least one area; and on naive *tabula rasa* conceptions of human plasticity which maintain that even if a given child has no creative potentialities, good teachers can take the place of missing genes.

The general plausibility of these arguments will be examined in a later chapter. At this point we need only say that they are highly unrealistic, and that while efforts must be made to develop creative potential in those children who possess it, schools should give priority to the as yet unattained task of having each child master the basic intellectual skills as well as a reasonable proportion of the more important subject-matter content of the major disciplines.


7. Expository Teaching as Authoritarianism

Advocates of the discovery method also take advantage of the disfavor attached to authoritarianism in education to discredit didactic exposition. When a teacher stands in front of a classroom and presents facts, concepts, and principles, he is—according to some discovery enthusiasts—behaving in an authoritarian fashion. In his role of expositor the teacher is allegedly coercing pupils, by the prestige of his position and by his power to dispense reward and punishment, into unquestioningly accepting on faith his own version of "the truth," instead of giving them an opportunity to discover it for themselves.

This distressing picture of expository teaching seems a bit overdrawn. We do not deny that schools and colleges abound in such teachers. But this characterization is certainly not true of all didactic exposition, nor is it inherent in the method itself. There is nothing inherently authoritarian in presenting or explaining ideas to others so long as the hearers are not obliged—either explicitly or implicitly—to accept them on faith. The deference to authority implied in accepting already discovered knowledge has been condemned out of all reason, for if students were required to validate independently every proposition presented by their instructors before accepting it, they would never progress beyond the rudiments of any discipline. We can only ask that established knowledge be presented to them as rationally and nonarbitrarily as possible and that they accept it tentatively and critically, as only the best available approximation of the "truth."

## 8. Discovery Organizes Learning Effectively for Later Use

We turn now to three recently propounded propositions which, taken together, may be said to constitute a proposed psychological—rather than philosophical—rationale for the discovery method.[13] First, it is suggested that emphasis upon discovery in learning has the effect upon the learner of leading him to be a constructionist, to organize what he is encountering in a way not only designed to uncover regularity and relatedness, but also to avoid the kind of information drift that fails to keep account of the kind of uses to which information might have to be put.

However, learning by discovery—in our opinion—does not *necessarily* lead to more orderly, integrated, and viable organization, transformation, and use of knowledge. It does so only insofar as the learning situation is highly structured, simplified, and skillfully programmed to include a large number of diversified exemplars of the same principle, carefully graded in order of difficulty. But under the circumstances one must, in all fairness, attribute these latter outcomes to the teacher's or the textbook writer's organization of the data from which the discovery is made, rather than to the act of discovery itself.

Concern with the "structure" of a discipline is certainly not indigenous to the discovery method, since it is also the basis of all modern approaches to expository teaching or reception learning. In fact, concern with presenting the unifying principles of a discipline is the main substantive rationale of expository teaching. The more unstructured discovery methods, on the other hand, tend to ignore the particular substantive content of a discipline as long as this content can be used to further problem-solving or inquiry processes. In Suchman's "Inquiry Training," for example, there is no attempt to present systematically the content of a scientific discipline. Content is largely a matter of indifference, or incidental to the process of discovery. Any kind of content is as good as any other so long as it lends itself to discovery and inquiry. Hence unsystematic and haphazard sampling of scientific concepts is characteristic of his inquiry Training Program.

## 9. Discovery as a Unique Generator of Motivation and Self-Confidence

Discovery enthusiasts perceive learning by discovery as a unique and unexcelled generator of self-confidence, of intellectual excitement and of motivation for sustained problem solving and creative thinking.[14] While certain motivational advantages have already been mentioned, including the fact that the successful discovery experience enhances the individual's feeling of confidence, it seems a mistake to believe that positive motivational effects accrue exclusively to this method. For, as any student who has been exposed to competent teaching knows, the skillful exposition of ideas can also generate considerable intellectual excitement and motivation for genuine inquiry. Moreover, self-confidence can certainly be bolstered by the act of simply understanding arguments on a reception basis. Most of us, for example, could recieve a considerable boost in our self-estimate—as well as a great deal of sheer intellectual pleasure—if we could meaningfully comprehend the lofty speculations of the general theory of relativity.

## 10. Discovery as a Prime Source for Intrinsic Motivation

A related motivational proposition states that "to the degree that one is able to approach learning as a task of discovering something rather than 'learning about it,' to that degree there will be a tendency for the child to carry out his learning activities with the autonomy of self-reward or, more properly, by reward that is discovery itself." Bruner feels that learning by discovery frees the child from the immediate control of such extrinsic motives as high marks, desire for parental and teacher approval, and the need to conform to the expectations of authority figures.

In our opinion, however, there appears to be no *necessary* association between a discovery approach to learning and intrinsic motivation, on the one hand, and the reception approach and extrinsic motivation, on the other. At the same time, one must acknowledge that independent discovery, in our culture, has come to acquire considerable prestige—whose acquisition is, of course, satisfying to the ego-enhancement drive. Consequently it could be argued that rather than being uniquely powered by intrinsic motivation, learning by discovery may appeal relatively more to the extrinsic ego-enhancement drive. Moreover, since high achievement at a prestigious task is essential for children who lack intrinsic self-esteem, we might speculate that it will be the latter child in particular who will aspire to successful discovery performance.[15] To be sure, there are individuals who are driven to discover principally because of a compelling need to express their individuality or creative urges, to find the answers to haunting problems, or to discharge their feelings of moral obligation to the social community.

But in our particular culture with its emphasis on status, prestige, ego-aggrandizement, and material rewards—especially among individuals who lack intrinsic self-esteem—such motives for discovery tend to be the exception rather than the rule.


## RESEARCH EVIDENCE

In this section we will examine a representative sample of the more significant published research bearing on the discovery method. The professional literature on "learning by discovery" regrettably exemplifies, as clearly as any research in education, the all too frequent hollowness of the phrase "research shows." Careful examination of what research supposedly "shows" in this instance yields these three disheartening conclusions: (1) that most of the articles most commonly cited in the literature as reporting results supporting discovery techniques actually report no research findings whatsoever, and consist mainly of theoretical discussion, assertion, and conjecture, of descriptions of existing programs utilizing discovery methods, and of enthusiastic but wholly subjective testimonials regarding the efficacy of discovery approaches; (2) that most of the reasonably well-controlled studies report neutral findings at best; and (3) that most studies reporting positive findings either fail to control other significant variables or employ questionable techniques of statistical analysis. Thus, actual examination of the research literature allegedly supporting learning by discovery reveals that valid evidence of this nature is virtually nonexistent. Moreover it appears that enthusiasts of discovery methods have been supporting each other by citing one another's opinions and assertions as evidence and by generalizing extravagantly from questionable findings.


### Long-Term Studies

Despite their frequent espousal of discovery principles, the various curriculum reform projects have failed thus far to yield any research evidence in support of the discovery method. This is not to say that the evidence is negative, but rather that there just is not any evidence one way or the other. One reason for the lack of evidence is that the sponsors of some of these projects have not been particularly concerned about proving the superior efficacy of their programs, since they have been thoroughly convinced of this from the outset. Hence in many instances they have not even attempted to obtain comparable achievement test data from matched control groups. And only rarely has any effort been expended to prevent the operation of the crucial "Hawthorne Effect," that is, to make sure that evidence of superior achievement outcomes is attributable to the influence of the new pedagogical techniques or materials in question rather than to the fact that the experimental group is the recipient of some form of conspicuous special attention, that something new and interesting is being tried, or that the teachers involved are especially competent, dedicated, and enthusiastic—and receive special training, attend expense-free conventions and summer institutes, and are assigned lighter teaching loads.

A number of long-term curriculum studies in the older literature are frequently cited as providing empirical support for the discovery method. Using basically identical research designs. T. R. McConnell,[16] C. L. Thiele,[17] and E. J. Swenson[18] compared the so-called "drill" and "generalization" methods of teaching number facts to second-grade pupils. The drill approach emphasized rote rules, whereas the generalization method stressed meaningful perception of relationships and derivation of generalizations. Students taught by the generalization method also had the added benefit of concrete props in the McConnell study, and of organized grouping of materials in the Swenson study. A well-known study by G. L. Anderson[19] was also conducted along very similar lines, but used fourth-grade pupils.

Needless to say, the generalization method was found to be superior in all four studies, except in criterion situations calling for immediate and automatic recall of knowledge relatively unchanged in form from that learned in the training situation. Much more salient than the *discovery* variable in each of these studies, however, is the *rote-meaningful* factor. In two of the studies, the differential availability to the "generalization" group of visual aids or of organized grouping of learning materials, further complicated interpretation of the findings. It should be remembered also that it is precisely in relation to this age group of young learners first entering the stage of concrete logical operations, and still completely unsophisticated in a new, difficult, and abstract subject matter, that the efficacy and feasibility of the discovery method are least disputed.


Short-Term Studies in the Gestalt Tradition

The well-known Gestalt writings on insightful problem solving by Köhler,[20] Wertheimer,[21] Duncker,[22] and Katona[23] are traditionally cited in the "discovery" literature as supporting the discovery method of teaching. Wertheimer, for example, found that students who have been taught (via relatively rote reception learning) a procedure for finding the area of a parallelogram (dropping lines from the two top corners perpendicular to the base—thus forming a rectangle) and who could do routine examples, became confused when the orientation of the parallelogram was changed (for example, stood on its narrow base). On the other hand, some children who had obtained insight into the structure of the parallelogram—in effect seeing it as a distortion of a rectangle—were able to handle much more difficult cases. Without disputing these results, it should be observed that this and other studies following the Gestalt emphasis on insight (like the early "generalization" studies) deal far more with the rote/meaningful dimension of problem solving than with the relative efficacy of the expository (reception) and discovery approaches. And as pointed out earlier, both reception and discovery learning may each be either rote or meaningful, depending on the conditions under which learning occurs.

Köhler's, Wertheimer's, and Dunckers' monographs also do not really report research findings in the usual sense of that term. They are, rather, sophisticated analyses of the nature and conditions of insightful problem solving from the Gestalt point of view, which use observations, informal experiments, anecdotes, and demonstrations to illustrate the principles under discussion. Katona's studies, on the other hand, are more genuinely experimental but, at the very most, demonstrate that the understanding of a principle, as opposed to rote memorization, leads to superior retention and transfer. One experiment in particular shows that a rotely memorized verbal principle is less transferable to new problems than is mere empirical experience with problems exemplifying the principle in question. But this indicates only that understanding of a principle, even when it is unverbalized, is more transferable than *rote* memorization, not that newly emerging nonverbal awareness is *always* more transferable than verbal understanding.[24]

Studies Involving Varying Amounts of Directedness

We finally come to a series of experimental studies in which varying amounts of guidance were furnished to different groups of subjects in problem-solving situations. Stacey[25] studied the effects of directed *versus* independent discovery on solving a group of simple meaningful "problems," each of which required subjects to identify the one item in a set of five that did not "belong." He found that active participation and self-discovery were more efficacious for learning than was "passive participation involving only recognition or identification of information" presented to the learner. This finding, of course, was wholly predictable since the fostering of such complete passivity in problem-solving experience as providing the correct answer for each problem, as well as the reason for the answer, seems inadvisable and is seldom if ever practiced today. But even so—and this is rather surprising—significant differences were not found between these extreme treatment groups on a transfer test.

Using similar kinds of material, but with college students rather than sixth-grade pupils, Craig[26] obtained results even less favorable for the discovery method. His "directed" group, which received a brief verbal explanation of principles during the training period, learned and retained significantly more principles than did his "independent group," which had no help whatsoever in the training situation. As in the Stacey study, however, the two groups were not significantly different with respect to mean score on a transfer test. Kittell's[27] findings in a similar type of experiment with sixth-grade pupils were, if anything, even more damaging to the discovery cause than were Craig's. The group in his experiment which received an "intermediate" amount of guidance, but nevertheless an amount which was somewhat *greater* than that received by Craig's "directed" group (that is, explanation of principles *plus* organization of materials) was superior in learning, retention, *and* transfer to groups receiving either less or more direction. Pooling the findings of these three studies, therefore, the evidence supports the conclusion that in this type of "problem-solving" exercise, guidance in the form of providing information about underlying principles facilitates learning, retention, and possibly transfer, more than either the provision of less guidance or the furnishing of specific rules for each of the problems.

Haselrud and Meyers[28] conducted a coding study with college students, which was explicitly designed to rebut the Craig and Kittell findings. However, their subjects exhibited significantly better learning on problems where the coding rules were given than where they had to be independently derived. Furthermore, on a delayed transfer test there was *no* difference whatsoever in the number of correct code identifications made for the problems learned originally with the rule given and the problems learned originally by independent derivation of the code.

Other studies in this area by Kersh[29] yielded results practically identical to those of Craig, Kittell, and Haselrud and Meyers on the test of original learning, but results opposite to those of Kittell on the delayed retest. By using an ingenious research design, however, Kersh was able to explain this latter finding on the basis of the greater interest and motivation, on the part of the "independent discovery" group, to continue practicing the task during the test-retest interval. Kersh concluded that discovery experience per se does not enhance understanding or meaningfulness.

Larson[30] found that at least part of the superior retention of Kersh's discovery group was attributable to the Zeigarnik effect, that is, a tendency to remember more incompleted than completed tasks. Craig's[31] findings suggest that providing continuing tasks and not stating the rule at the conclusion of initial learning, rather than discovery per se, enhance motivation to learn in this context.

In another group of studies on the effects of varying amounts of guidance on problem solving, either no differences were found between treatment groups, or a limited amount of guidance ("guided discovery") was found to be superior both to no guidance whatsoever or to complete guidance. J. Moss,[32] Maltzman and others,[33] Tomlinson,[34] and Forgus and Schwartz[35] reported no significant differences in delayed retention and transfer between "direct-detailed"[36] and "guided discovery" types of learning groups. W. E. Ray[37] and Rowlett,[38] on the other hand, found that guided discovery was superior to direct-detailed instruction in remembering and transferring principles of micrometer use and orthographic projection. In a study of programmed learning, Gagné and Brown[39] reported that a small-step, guided discovery method of programming was superior both to the "ruleg" method (in which generalizations are provided first and then a supporting example) and to a large-step, prompted discovery procedure. Corman's findings[40] were differentiated with respect to the ability level of his subjects; highly explicit instructions were most effective with his more able subjects, whereas his less able subjects benefited equally from more and less explicit instructions. Grote[41] found that the direct-detailed method was superior for high-ability students and that the guided discovery procedure was superior for average-ability students in learning a lever principle.

## Concluding Statement

The reader will recognize that there is no simple way of "adding up" the results of the various experiments. The principal difficulty is that these studies vary in many significant details, the most important of which are probably the amount of actual guidance or direction in the "guided discovery" treatment, and the taxonomic level of the task involved (for example, comprehension, application, problem solving). In addition, it is not always clear—even in the published research reports, unfortunately—whether all treatment groups received an equal allotment of learning time or, if they did, how the most "directed" group could have been profitably employed on the task to be learned while the most "undirected" group went through the time-consuming task of formulating the principles themselves.

The foregoing reservations notwithstanding, the research literature does provide us with a range of serious attempts to measure the effect of various degrees of directedness in instruction over a variety of tasks similar to those which are now (or might be) taught in school. Our assessment of the evidence is that, if any conclusion can be drawn, it must be that the traditional emphasis of capable teachers has *not* been shown to be demonstrably in error. That is, there is nothing in the research evidence to suggest that it is inappropriate to use a fairly high level of directedness (perhaps the fourth or even the fifth level in our earlier example) with, of course, a concomitant use of props appropriate to the stage of cognitive development in question—when the intention is adequate comprehension of a principle or concept. When application or genuine problem solving are hoped for, however, there is some warrant for a less directed teaching of the principles to be employed in the criterion task; but even here, a degree of structuring at the third (or fourth) level of our initial example seems clearly preferable to more autonomous discovery. Finally, little evidence of advantage exists for minimally structured or completely unstructured instructional methods. It would seem that they should be used sparingly and on the acknowledged gamble that even their theoretical advantage— that is, a possible enhancement of long-term cognitive drive—has simply not been assessed in the (essentially short-term) studies which comprise the research literature.

## SOME CONSIDERATIONS IN ORGANIZING CLASSROOM DISCOVERY EXPERIENCES

In view of the foregoing remarks, considerable caution is necessary in planning discovery learning experiences for school children. The vigorous statements of support for discovery learning in many new curriculum projects, coupled with the equally strong convictions of teachers who are using these new approaches, lead us to believe that most of the extreme views discussed earlier are very much in evidence today. The authors have found, for example, that it is extremely difficult to get a teacher who is "sold" on the discovery method even to entertain the proposition that a child might learn as much or more in a learning situation within which reception learning plays a larger part.

Having set out the pros and cons—as is the educational psychologist's customary stance—we must now declare more directly our personal beliefs as to how the educator should proceed. There seems little doubt that a certain amount of planned discovery (of generalizations or principles) is desirable for the child, although experience at the undirected end of the discovery/reception scale should not take up a very large proportion of total instructional time. In our opinion, the benefits of discovery approach to the acquisition of knowledge can be realized in the elementary school if, among the half-dozen or more subject areas in which the student works at any one time, the program in *one* area currently involves a preponderance of minimally directed student discovery experiences (that is, a combination of activities from the first, second, and third levels indicated earlier). Planned discovery-oriented units of several weeks' duration—embedded in a larger program of reception-oriented instruction and rotated among the subject areas—would seem well suited to provide students with scope for independent activity in each area, without jeopardizing the acquisition of a coherent body of content.[42]

At the same time, of course, the elementary-school teacher will use strongly guided approaches as a regular teaching strategy in most subjects. Such methods, while allowing the child to formulate generalizations himself, both provide necessary consolidation of the ideas learned (Carlow, 1967) and move the student along at a steady pace. Moreover, genuine problem-solving experiences, which involve the utilization of learned principles in the "discovery" of solutions, should also constitute a regular part of the child's education from the earliest school years.

## Precautions

It seems very important that teachers develop realistic attitudes concerning the advantages and disadvantages of the discovery method, for those who now harbor fantastic or one-sided views are inviting disillusionment at a later stage. Perhaps the only way for "sold" teachers to acquire such attitudes is to obtain first-hand evidence as to how more directed (even reception) approaches would work in the same circumstances. In respect to making realistic comparisons, teachers are at a disadvantage because the discovery approaches characteristic of the new curricula not only change a *teaching method* (that is, from reception to discovery) but involve as well changes in *content*, degree of *teacher freedom* to set independent goals, incidence of *team approaches* to learning (that is, a group of students cooperating to make discoveries), and in some instances utilization of the teaching staff itself (for example, team teaching). The change in content may in itself be highly significant, since many new programs utilize more careful sequencing and a greater preponderance of organizing themes and concepts than do traditional texts.

Over and above this is the fact that many of the new approaches involve more expensive materials, equipment, and classroom facilities than reception learning methods. Consequently, the teacher is in no position to determine—by casual inspection alone —to which of these many variables any observed improvement in student performance can be attributed, and singling out the discovery method as the causal variable may frequently be erroneous. Under the circumstances the temptation is strong to fall back upon student enthusiasm as the criterion of success. This is extremely hazardous because heightened student enthusiasm tends to appear in most new programs and need not reflect superior achievement.

An illustration of these dangers can be seen in a study on the Cuisenaire method conducted in one Canadian city.[43] In this particular school system a group of competent and highly interested elementary-school teachers produced achievement in arithmetic with the Cuisenaire rod approach which clearly exceeded that which children had been making in traditional classes. Initially it was widely concluded that this effect could be attributed to the new method itself. However, as a check on this hypothesis, an experiment was conducted in which an equally competent and well-motivated group of teachers was given the same freedom as the Cuisenaire teachers to set higher standards, to meet together to discuss their common instructional problems, and to enjoy the "Hawthorne Effects" which are usually found in experimental ventures. The interesting finding was that this second group, although using essentially *traditional* methods, also produced achievement which was vastly in excess of that typically obtained. In fact, the second group actually out-performed the Cuisenaire group, although not by a statistically significant amount. The conclusion which one must draw is that it was not the method itself that had been effective, as had been postulated, but rather such other factors as increased expectations and greater opportunities to plan and to exchange ideas with colleagues.

Because of the lack of specific research-documented prescriptions on the proper use of discovery learning, it is our conviction that schools which are moving into more widespread use of this technique—particularly of the free inquiry variety—should attempt to set up some internal comparisons which will allow teachers to attain the realistic attitudes which are so badly needed. For example, in a large school with a number of classes at the primary level, it would seem feasible for the teachers involved to agree on a common set of goals (that is, concepts, skills, and generalizations to be learned) and for a number of clearly formulated teaching approaches—which vary in the degree of discovery—to be tried out for a period of time. At the end of this period the approaches should be compared on a broad range of criteria including the mastery of concepts and skills produced, resulting ability to solve problems, attitude effects, time required to attain this mastery, and transfer or side effects accruing outside the particular subject area in question. Very careful attention will have to be given—and appropriate tests devised—to determine whether children who have discovered generalizations themselves have any firmer or deeper appreciation of these generalizations than children who have learned them through more reception-oriented approaches. Such informal "experimental" arrangements, although lacking the rigor of laboratory studies, provide a much better basis for reaching informed conclusions about teaching procedures than mere speculation unaided by any objective comparisons.

G. H. BANTOCK

# "EMILE" RECONSIDERED

What is interesting about Emile is the combination of observation and "idealization"—idealization both in the sense of pursuing that which is looked upon as most desirable, and in D. H. Lawrence's sense of working in terms of an abstract conception of the thing.

From G. H. Bantock, *Education and Values: Essays in the Theory of Education.* Reprinted by permission of Faber and Faber Ltd.

The inhibiting effects of Jean Jacques's self-regard and lack of self-knowledge display themselves; he cannot fully appreciate child nature because he cannot really see it as bearing much resemblance to his own—"no conclusions could be drawn from it in regard to others": he must trust to external observation and thus simplify: "The child must come first, and you must devote yourself entirely to him. Watch him, study him constantly, without his knowing it." It cannot ultimately be as satisfactory as observation implemented by self-awareness because there is no standard of reference for interpretation. It is a curious paradox that many who have depended so much on the inner life (Froebel is another example who springs to mind) have shown so little awareness of it in others, and of its possible corruptions.

Rousseau called his "idealization" the "natural man"; to arrive at some more precise understanding of what he implied by "natural" and by "nature" will help to indicate more concretely the sort of individual he attempted to form and that individual's relations with his environment.

The word "nature" is one of protean ambiguity, and Rousseau himself uses it in a number of different senses. The term has exercised a great influence in many fields of thought, including that of educational theory.[1] One sense in which Rousseau uses "nature" is to designate the phenomenal world apart from man, especially the world of plants and animals. Thus, in speaking of the custom of adding wine to the warm water in which the infant is first bathed, he asserts that "I think the wine might be dispensed with. As nature does not produce fermented liquors, it is not likely that they are of much value to her creatures" (*Emile*, pp. 26-7). Such a meaning is implied by his analogies drawn from animal life: the example, for instance, of the way in which puppies practice their budding teeth. Such a conception of "nature" not only has the power, often, of positive example; it also provides the permanent background of instruction and observation:

"Men are not made to be crowded together in ant-hills, but scattered over the earth to till it. . . .

"Men are devoured by our towns. In a few generations the race dies out or becomes degenerate; it needs renewal, and it is always renewed from the country" (*Emile*, p. 26).

It also forms the subject-matter of learning, through observation of the behaviour of "natural" objects: "Teach your scholar to

---

*Emile* is the title of Jean Jacques Rousseau's classic work on education. Published in 1762, it contains a doctrine of extreme individualism embodied in a set of recommendations for the education of Emile from infancy to adulthood.—Ed.

observe the phenomena of nature; you will soon rouse his curiosity.
. . . Let him not be taught science, let him discover it" (*Emile*, p.
131). It is important to realize, once more, that Rousseau drew no
deep resources of wisdom, as did Wordsworth, from an appreciation of man's organic relationship with this "nature." There is no
sense of fusion, no wisdom derived from the "imaginative" appre-
hension of the "Wisdom and Spirit" of the Universe; no "plastic
power," permitting

> observations of affinities
> In objects where no brother-hood exists
> To passive minds,

moved Rousseau's soul in subservience "strictly to external things."
"Nature," in this sense, for Rousseau, seems to have provided
either a background for fantasy life, a retreat and a "solitude"
in which he did not have to face up to the responsibilities of social
living: "I sometimes exclaimed with emotion, 'O Nature! O my
mother! behold me under thy protection alone! Here there is no
cunning or knavish mortal to thrust himself between me and thee' "
(*Confessions*, ii, p. 282), or to have provided the material for a series
of observations of a biological or botanical kind which could be
applied more or less mechanically (at least with too little concern for
the implications of some of the analogies) to the education of the
"natural" man; or to have afforded a subject-matter for control and
investigation in the manner indicated by such sources of prudential
management as *Robinson Crusoe*, a book Rousseau is concerned to
recommend as supplying "the best treatise on natural education";
and, as we shall see, a great deal of Rousseau's education is intended to make the child at home in the midst of this "natural" environment.[2]

Several other equally significant meanings of "nature" and
"natural," need to be indicated. Thus, "natural" comes to signify
"that which is in accord with the behaviour of primitive, precivil-
ized, savage man" (though this meaning is not as frequent as some
commentators on Rousseau have made out). Hence, in expatiating
on the desire for self-preservation, he remarks: "In a natural state
man is only eager to preserve his life while he has the means for its
preservation; when self-preservation is no longer possible, he re-
signs himself to his fate and dies without vain torments. Nature
teaches the first law of resignation. Savages, like wild beasts, make
very little struggle against death, and meet it almost without a
murmur. When this natural law is overthrown reason establishes
another, but few discern it, and man's resignation is never so com-

plete as nature's" (*Emile*, p. 46). (The division between the law of nature and that of reason is worth noting.) Hence nature sometimes comes to mean "that which is opposed to nurture, to all training given by other men": "Drawn this way by nature and that way by man, compelled to yield to both forces, we make a compromise and reach neither goal" (*Emile*, p. 9). Also, it takes on the significance of "that which is opposed to historical situation." Thus, in speaking of matters of religion, immediately after the testimony of the Savoyard Vicar, Rousseau states: "So long as we yield nothing to human authority, nor to the prejudices of our native land, the light of reason alone, in a state of nature, can lead us no further than to natural religion" (*Emile*, p. 278). And Rousseau's "natural religion" involves a further important meaning: "that which can be deduced from the abstract psychological tendencies common to all men." There is the Vicar's testimony: "all that man knows by nature I am capable of knowing" (*Emile*, p. 261).

There is now emerging a conscious view of human nature, one in which "conscience" and "reason" play a predominant part and which therefore leads "naturally" to a certain type of deistic belief. Here, Rousseau draws on the uniformitarian beliefs of the eighteenth century; the "natural man" comes to be equivalent to the "real" man discoverable under all forms and pretences; he is equated with those common gifts, those rules discovered "at the very centre of my being, indelibly inscribed by nature," behind all the "masks" which ordinary social life provides to hide a man's "true" nature: "Hitherto I have made no distinction of condition, rank, station, or fortune; nor shall I distinguish between them in the future, since man is the same in every station; the rich man's stomach is no bigger than the poor man's, nor is his digestion any better; . . . a great man is no taller than one of the people, and indeed the natural needs are the same to all, and the means of satisfying them should be equally within the reach of all. Fit a man's education to his real self, not to what is no part of him" (*Emile*, pp. 156-7).

Thus, we arrive at the significance: "that which is in line with a certain order of human development through which Rousseau believes that man realizes his true inner potentialities." This is probably the heart of the conception of "natural man." No human regression to a primitive state is intended, but the achievement of a harmony between man and his environment through which man will attain his true happiness and "being." *L'amour de soi-même* was to be encouraged and *amour-propre* avoided, which latter, as Rousseau pointed out in the *Discourse on Inequality*, was a "factitious feeling, arising only in society, which leads each man to think more highly of himself than of any other." This last significance of "nature" is implicit in such comments as: "l'homme naturel est pour lui," and: "Before his parents chose a calling for him nature called him to be a man. Life is the trade I would teach him. When he leaves me, I grant you, he will be neither a magistrate, a soldier, nor a priest; he will be a man. All that becomes a man he will learn as quickly as another. In vain will fate change his station, he will always be in his right place" (*Emile*, p. 9). And, of course, in practice, this meaning often equates itself with that "order of human existence which Rousseau, for a variety of reasons, considers desirable." This meaning harmonizes all the rest; if we bear in mind the characteristic stresses of Rousseau's work rather than individual phrases torn from context (the products frequently of an ill-adjusted vehemence), it enables us to summarize his ultimate conception of human life, to which Emile's education is directed. Thus, whereas it is true that the savage state is not in Rousseau's eyes the most desirable, and he believes that man must learn to live among other men, the general emphasis of his work in *Emile* is to depreciate the social, the sophisticated, the urban, the "civilized" in the sense which is prepared to accept conventional forms of society and conventional disciplines of learning through books and the traditions built up by others, and to stress man's need to learn from a carefully selected series of observations drawn from animal and especially rustic life, and thus to follow some quintessential conception of manhood beneath all the forms of conventional existence and the particular trainings implied in such social occupations, to accept the discipline of "things," to maintain an independence of others and to find in practical utility the true criterion of learning, to prefer the less sophisticated forms of human activity to the more: "Now, of all the pursuits by which a man may earn his living, the nearest to a state of nature is manual labour" (*Emile*, p. 158).[3]

As Arthur Lovejoy has said, for Rousseau "man's good lay in departing from his 'natural' (in the sense of primitive, savage) state—but not too much; 'perfectibility' up to a certain point was desirable, though beyond that point an evil. Not its infancy but its *jeunesse* was the best age of the human race."[4] Rousseau wants, in fact, the imagined freedom of a simpler life ("Emile, having been brought up in full freedom like young peasants and savages[5]) with such advantages of civilization as are necessary to preserve a certain competence. He sees none of the disadvantages of the simple life, the essential strains of living, in whatever context. Nor does he appreciate the profound difficulties of tacking on this type of existence to the historically evolved society of his time, a society which, by its very existence, makes certain demands, involves certain inherited modes and memories of living which cannot simply be ignored or forgotten. Such modes form the essential background against which any idea of "reform" must measure itself or at least accept as primary data. This aspect of Rousseau's "romanticism" has affected modern educational thinking which, in certain of its manifestations, looks to the lifting of restraint as the essential element in the truly educative process.

*Emile*, of course, is directed towards indicating how this ideal, "natural" and, in effect, highly abstract, human being could be produced. This explains the cryptic letter to Cramer:

> You say, quite rightly, that it is impossible to produce an Emile; but do you really believe that that was my aim and that the book which carries such a title is a treatise on education? It's a work basically philosophical on the principle put forward by the author in other writings that man is naturally good.
>
> To bring this notion into line with another, no less certain, truth, that men are evil, it was necessary to show how all the vices developed in the human heart. This is what I have done in this book. . . . [6] (13th October 1764.)

For, in indicating how the "natural" man should be formed, Rousseau was largely concerned with what should be avoided so that man's evil propensities should not be permitted to develop.

The basic inadequacy of *Emile* lies in its treatment of human egotism. One can see, in fact, that the need to assert the natural goodness of man, and the consequent distortions of emphasis which such an assertion has entailed, have thrown the whole treatment of education out of gear. For it has forced Rousseau to adopt what is, in effect, a highly artificial system, and to assert a rigid dichotomy between man and society which has no basis in experience and which immediately perverts the "practical" possibilities of the treatise. It begins with the highly disputable dogmatic assertion that childish egotism comes from ill-teaching, not from "nature: "This is how they become tiresome, masterful, imperious, naughty, and unmanageable; a development which does not spring from a natural love of power, but one which has been taught them, for it does not need much experience to realize how pleasant it is to set others to work and to move the world by a word" (*Emile*, p. 34). How that which is not there can be evoked even by bad training is a possible sophistication that Rousseau does not appreciate.[7] Even Rousseau, however, has to admit that egotism (*amour-propre*, or *fantaisie*) is unavoidable in society; he is thus forced to impose a peculiar isolation on both tutor and child, and to demand a perceptiveness on the part of the tutor, whose function it is to ". . . study carefully their speech and gestures, so that at an age when they are incapable of deceit you may discriminate between those desires which come from nature and those which spring from perversity" (*Emile*, p. 35), which could only be adequately fulfilled by someone having superhuman powers of intuition. And, indeed, Rousseau, by stressing the necessity of meeting the true "needs" of children: "He is only subject to others because of his needs, and because they see better than he what he really needs, what may help or hinder his existence" (*Emile*, p. 48), avoids, as does so much current educational theorizing, the precise assessment of what constitutes a human "need." Thus it was an important step on Rousseau's part to stress the need for child activity, as, for instance, against the pervasive tyranny of the *maillot*; what is insufficiently valid is the ultimate end which this activity is intended to subserve; moreover he neglects the equally valid need for receptivity. Thus, what I am concerned to criticize is not the importance of Rousseau's stress on the necessity to consider the "needs" of children, but the fact that in Rousseau these "needs" are stressed in relationship to a too inadequate conception of the nature of life and of the ends of human existence—an inadequacy briefly indicated above. One needs to temper praise for Rousseau's perceptiveness in recognizing children's "needs" with a regret that such "needs" were not stressed by one whose realization of need at any stage of existence was supplemented by a fuller appreciation of such need in relation to end; the second term in Rousseau's diagnosis: "because they see better than he what he really needs" is the weaker link in his argument.[8]

It is important to appreciate the effect of Rousseau's emphasis on the education of "things"; even the tutor is to become a "thing" in order to avoid arousing the egotism of the child: "Keep the child dependent on things only. By this course of education you will have followed the order of nature" (*Emile*, p. 49). One obvious advantage Rousseau derives from making the tutor like a "thing" lies in avoiding the possibility of those emotional disturbances between pupil and tutor which his own experience as a teacher had revealed to him: ". . . when things went wrong, I was a devil. When my pupils did not understand me, I raved like a madman; when they showed signs of insubordination, I could have killed them, which was not the way to make them either learned or well-disposed." (*Confessions*, i, pp. 245—6.)[9]

In his concrete recommendations, Rousseau falls into that verbal ambiguity which dogs the progress of modern education. He intends to free the child, on the grounds we have noted that "the first impulses of nature are always right; there is no original sin in the human heart" (*Emile*, p. 56). Thus, he urges such precepts as: "The only habit the child should be allowed to contract is that of having no habits" (p. 30), which obviously form an important element in the idea of "negative education": "Give nature time to work before you take over her business, lest you interfere with her dealings" (*Emile*, p. 71). Yet, at the same time, there is implicit in many of his recommendations an active human authoritative interference. The sort of environment in which the child is to be placed is to be chosen most carefully: "As soon as the child begins to take notice, what is shown to him must be carefully chosen" (*Emile*, p. 30). Even more explicit is the recommendation: "While the child is still unconscious there is time to prepare his surroundings, so that nothing shall strike his eye but what is fit for his sight" (*Emile*, p. 59). A great deal of this is consistent with modern practice, and provides one of the sources from which modern education has learnt its technique of infant management. From such precepts springs that confusion of freedom and authority characteristic of many modern expositions. Rousseau himself is led to his ambiguous position because of his assumption that man only learns evil from others.

To learn from "things" has none of those disadvantages to which learning from men lay itself open; for "it is in man's nature to bear patiently with the nature of things, but not with the ill-will of another" (*Emile*, p. 55). At the same time, he realizes that some order of presentation is necessary to the growing mind and explicitly admits that the child is so feeble that "il craint tout ce qu'il ne connaît pas" (*Emile*, p. 37). He must thus smuggle in a human intervention which is confined to the careful presentation of data, but which is, none the less, real for all the apparent restriction of its incidence. The most perfect example of this ambivalence of Rousseau's attitude occurs when he asserts that Emile "should always do what he wants to do, but he should only want to do what you want him to do." One is reminded that Rousseau was the originator of Totalitarian as well as of Liberal Democracy.[10] And, indeed, *Emile* is much more subtly authoritarian than might at first appear.

Thus the idea of learning from the environment, of subservience to the authority of "things" rather than of people was considerably advanced by this eighteenth-century writer's indignation against a society with which he was unable to come to terms. He was aided by the pervasive tendency of the time to find in sense experience, the source of scientific understanding, the chief source of "real" knowledge. (Both Comenius—following Bacon—and Locke had urged the vital importance of learning through the senses; such learning formed the basis of Locke's psychology.) Knowledge, according to Rousseau, was either sensational or intuitive; it came either from the environment, or from the intuitive perceptions of the "Inner Light"; other people, the authority imposed by conventional, social and intellectual arrangements constituted the danger to the integral and pure heart of man. Modern education, largely unaware of the origin of its techniques, emerges from a shift in assumptions about man's nature which stresses at once his conceit of himself in terms of innate goodness, and his uniform capability to learn; and one strain in modern egalitarianism springs as much from the conception that everything which comes from others spells corruption (is, in fact, a protective device) as it does from a positive belief in man's equality of endowment. It finds its roots in a desire to shift responsibility for evil on to others; and that desire to shift responsibility on to something other than self is peculiarly characteristic of Rousseau's own psychology. In this, he is a true representative figure of the modern world.[11]

Rousseau's exposition of the learning process disingenuously fails to discriminate between two sorts of learning. There is the learning involved in biological development, the need for activity so that muscles, etc., can expand: "Let them run, jump and shout to their heart's content" (Emile, p. 50). Such learning is, of course, largely spontaneous; it needs to be distinguished from that mental learning which results from perception and realization of the environment, where spontaneity and nurture intermingle in a way which requires more careful elucidation than Rousseau seems to realize:

> Without the study of books, such a memory as the child may possess is not left idle; everything he sees and hears makes an impression on him, he keeps a record of men's sayings and doings, and his whole environment is the book from which he unconsciously enriches his memory, till his judgment is able to profit by it.
>
> To select these objects, to take care to present him constantly with those he may know, to conceal from him those he ought not to know, this is the real way of training his early memory (Emile, p. 76).

Organic development, maturation, will go on to a certain extent irrespective of usage (though, even here, development will be better if there *is* usage, and Rousseau seems to be aware of this, for he emphasizes the need for physical exercise and movement).[12] Mental growth only proceeds from usage and conscious employment, once the necessary organic development has taken place; there is something ambiguous in the injunction: "The mind should be left undisturbed till its faculties have developed" (*Emile*, p. 57). And from the ensuing remarks, it is obvious that Rousseau is confusing the two sorts of growth:

> If only you could let well alone, and get others to follow your example; if you could bring your scholar to the age of twelve strong and healthy, but unable to tell his right hand from his left, the eyes of his understanding would be open to reason as soon as you began to teach him. Free from prejudices and free from habits, there would be nothing in him to counteract the effects of your labours. In your hands he would soon become the wisest of men; by doing nothing to begin with, you would end with a prodigy of education. (*Emile*, pp. 57—8)

Without exercise of mental "faculties" there is no intellectual growth at all: Rousseau's following of nature involves too rigid an application of analogy from organic development. It is not true that mental growth follows the same patterns, and that the policy of noninterference in the one will have equally good results in the other; only skilled intervention can bring to mental maturity, can, even within the limited purview of Rousseau's conception of experience, bring about the appreciation of stress and importance.

Moreover, it is important to note the implications of the sort of "reason" involved in this type of learning. Emile's earlier education is very much one of learning "how things work," of gaining a measure of control over his environment; and the sort of "reason" which Rousseau allows to pre-adolescent children is that which enables them to see relations of sense experience. The need for *present* interest is stressed. The possible contingencies of a later period are to be ignored, for the child may die at any time, and preparation for such a hypothetical future would be so much time wasted. The type of education designated is one which will help the child to be at home in the world in the here and now.

> On the other hand, he exercises discrimination and forethought, he reasons about everything that concerns himself. He does not chatter, he acts. Not a word does he know of what is going on in the world at large, but he knows very thoroughly what affects himself. As he is always stirring he is compelled to notice many things, to recognize many effects; he soon acquires a good deal of experience. Nature, not man, is his schoolmaster,

and he learns all the quicker because he is not aware that he has any lesson to learn. So mind and body work together. He is always carrying out his own ideas, not those of other people, and thus he unites thought and action; as he grows in health and strength he grows in wisdom and discernment. (*Emile*, p. 84)

In this way, the only sort of reason of which Rousseau considers children are capable is developed, for: "our first teachers in natural philosophy are our feet, hands, and eyes. To substitute books for them does not teach us to reason, it teaches us to use the reason of others rather than our own" (*Emile*, p. 90).

There are several points worth noting about this type of education. It involves a principle of considerable importance, one in which there is a certain degree of psychological truth and one which modern education has not been slow to take advantage of. Nevertheless, learning by this kind of discovery develops only certain approaches to the nature of experience; it helps the "practically"-minded child. But the world of practical experience does not involve the whole of the human potentiality, even where pre-adolescent children are concerned; and even within its limited purview, Rousseau depends overmuch on the assumed "spontaneous" curiosity of the child—and the child's ability to appreciate points of significance in what is presented. The *Robinson Crusoe* approach is artificial in normal community life because it assumes a motivation lacking outside the pressure to survival on desert islands. There is too little obligation on the child to "reason" even in the way which is allowed him, and, indeed, too much reliance seems to be placed on incidental encounters which happen to throw into the way temporary inducements for learning. Present interest and a certain natural curiosity, the twin bastions of Rousseau's system, do not always have the efficacy that is alleged on their behalf. Thus it is not true, necessarily, that "every concrete example suggests another and always points to the next in the series. This succession, which stimulates the curiosity and so arouses the attention required by every object in turn, is the order followed by most men, and it is the right order for all children" (*Emile*, p. 135). Such a generalization depends too much on culturally induced conceptions of cause and effect. The appreciation of a chain of relationships is no more "natural" than any other mode of systematizing phenomena or of inducing some method of order into the presented chaos of sense impression. Furthermore, the importance of language is overlooked.

Again, too much emphasis is placed on novelty of discovery. For instance, Rousseau, in his example of the magnet and the duck, an experiment which is supposed to lead to the study of physics, assumes a power of generalizing in the child only possible to those who are already habituated to the mode of drawing general inferences from the observation of a number of individual phenomena, or of otherwise relating phenomena which, unaided, he would not necessarily connect: "Let the child learn all these facts, let him learn those that are within his reach by experiment, and discover the rest by induction; but I would far rather he knew nothing at all about them, than that you should tell him" (*Emile*, p. 113). Thus, to make the leap from the observation of the behaviour of the duck to the discovery of the compass ("the study of physics has begun") implies a mental leap which can only result from a certain type of conscious training inhibited by Rousseau's injunctions.

Again, the general principle enunciated in the following is certainly untrue:

> Undoubtedly the notions of things thus acquired for oneself are clearer and much more convincing than those acquired from the teaching of others; and not only is our reason not accustomed to a slavish submission to authority, but we develop greater ingenuity in discovering relations, connecting ideas and inventing apparatus, than when we merely accept what is given us and allow our minds to be enfeebled by indifference. (*Emile*, p. 139)

Not only are there certain types of learning which can only be attained on the word of others, and which such a principle would remove from the "syllabus" (an omission which Rousseau, to do him justice, is prepared to face); it is certainly not true that "it is only objects which can be perceived by the senses which can have any interest for children."[13] In objecting to verbal explanation, Rousseau was revolting with good reason against an over-verbal type of education; but he reacted too far. He completely banishes imaginative literature for young children, for instance. His comment on the fable of La Fontaine involves a notorious literalness of interpretation which it is safe to assume children are not bothered about; (the empirical argument about the distance at which a cheese can be smelt is sufficient to illustrate the criteria brought to bear by Rousseau). The apposite comment, the product of a mind working on a very different level of imaginative insight, is that of Coleridge:

> For from my early reading of fairy tales and genii, etc., etc., my mind had been habituated *to the Vast*, and I never regarded *my senses* in any way as the criteria of my belief. I regulated all my creeds by my conceptions, not by my sight, even at that age.

Should children be permitted to read romances, and relations of giants and magicians and genii? I know all that has been said against it; but I have formed my faith in the affirmative. I know no other way of giving the mind a love of the Great and the Whole. Those who have been led to the same truths step by step, through the constant testimony of their senses, seem to me to want a sense which I possess. They contemplate nothing but *parts*, and all *parts* are necessarily little. And the universe to them is but a mass of *little things*. It is true, that the mind *may* become credulous and prone to superstition by the former method; but are not the experimentalists credulous even to madness in believing any absurdity, rather than believe the grandest truths, if they have not the testimony of their own senses in their favour? I have known some who have been rationally educated, as it is styled. They were marked by a microscopic acuteness, but when they looked at great things, all became a blank and they saw nothing, and denied (very illogically) that anything could be seen, and uniformly put the negation of a power for the possession of a power, and called the want of imagination judgment and the never being moved to rapture philosophy! (Letter to Poole, 16 October 1797.)

It is significant that Rousseau, himself so influenced as a child by romantic literature, should be opposed to any imaginative reading by the child, not on the grounds that children should be kept from certain types of literature (a prohibition which Jean-Jacques might well support from personal experience) but because he is concerned to omit altogether the need for the sort of training that literature can supply.

Thus Rousseau constantly inveighs against book learning: "Reading is the scourge of childhood," and "Books! What sorry clutter for a child of that age." He claims that he is allowing the child to gather the skills of learning: "You teach science; well and good; I am busy fashioning the necessary tools for its acquisition" (*Emile*, p. 90). Yet one of the chief skills, that of reading, is deprecated. It is quite unjustifiable to urge that "The child who reads does not think. He only knows how to read" (*Emile*, p. 179), as should be obvious enough. Reading can set up an "activity" in the mind, no less inferior to that provided by environmental stimuli. Like many "progressive" educationalists Rousseau is too taken up with physical activity to appreciate the full value of mental exercise. Rousseau's emphasis on the "natural" man leads, in fact, to a misconception of man's nature;[14] what was "natural" to man, as an older view made clear, was precisely his capacity for complex development, his ability to respond to training and nurture, his building up on an assimilation of previous knowledge and wisdom; this most obviously marks him off from the animals.

The implications of Rousseau's own peculiar psychology, then, are becoming clearer; his theory of "negative" education involves basically an unwillingess to measure up to the full complexities involved in growing up in society. The education of "things" avoids all those complications of egotism and emotion which are specifically characteristic of man and through which a child must develop. Rousseau's pedagogy, in *Emile*, like some modern theorizing, is one of self-development and evolution rather than of conflict involving self-transcendence; and such straightforward evolution can only exist within a system which ignores many of the incongruities inherent in the development of human beings. He is concerned to eliminate conflict from his scheme—the education of things "being non-moral does no injury to liberty and begets no vices."[15] The same desire is manifested in the bringing up of adolescents, who, no longer free, even in Rousseau's view, from the possibilities of emotional disturbances, are yet to be sheltered from emotional experience: "we must take the opposite way from that hitherto followed, and instruct the youth rather through the experience of others than through his own" (*Emile*, p. 198). Yet, as Keats pointed out, only out of such experience can maturity come: "axioms in philosophy are not axioms until they are proved upon our pulses." The choice of Sophie through the tutor has often been commented upon as one of the less happy recommendations of Rousseau; yet its significance has been little realized. It represents yet another aspect of Rousseau's fear of emotional complication. It demonstrates how little he learnt from such emotional situations as they affected his own life. His whole picture of the Emile-Sophie relationship is marred by an inhibiting sentimentality which seems to indicate how little Rousseau understood about such relationships; even "reverie," to deserve attention, requires a somewhat closer contact with life as we know it than Rousseau displays.

The implication, in *Emile*, then, all too frequently is that ignorance implies innocence and virtue; an assumption which too easily panders to the complacency of modern man, who like Rousseau himself, is willing to be relieved of the effort needed to undertake that slow and painful attempt at the clarification of what is involved in human existence which is what education at its best implies. An apposite comparison is with a man like Newman, whose dogmatism, in the modern view, appears to contrast unfavourably with the advocate of the Inner Light. Yet Newman is content to exist within a system which assumes man's essential imperfection, and he therefore stresses the painful effort necessary to bring him to even a reasonable degree of enlightenment; for, as Newman appreciated, there is "... no true culture without acquirements, and philosophy presupposes knowledge. It requires a great deal of reading or a wide range of information, to warrant us putting forth our opinions on any serious subject" (*The Idea of a University*). Newman remains the true advocate of civilization; Rousseau's educational ideas involve a regression to simpler modes of living. Behind the apparent humility of "negative" education there is a certain complacency of ignorance, a lack of patience before the careful unravelling of what human knowledge has so carefully built up.[16]

What Rousseau has done for education has rightfully had its meed of praise; he is capable of much acute observation and the revolution of approach he instigated has conferred considerable benefits on education. At the same time, in criticizing him, one must not blame him for failing to observe what only half a century of patient child study has revealed. Nevertheless, near contemporaries, like Wordsworth and Coleridge, achieved a deeper insight; and Rousseau must take some of the blame for errors of observation because such errors are inherent in the mental immaturities of the man and are not essentially in the inadequacies of the time. As John Stuart Mill pointed out, no one's synthesis can comprise more than the elements of his analysis; and Rousseau's understanding of life would appear to contain some considerable gaps.

DAVID P. AUSUBEL

# A NEW LOOK AT CLASSROOM DISCIPLINE

A few years ago, in one of our better New England high schools two members of the school's counseling staff happened to be walking in the building when their attention was drawn to sounds of a disturbance in an adjoining corridor. Investigating further, they

From David P. Ausubel, "A New Look at Classroom Discipline," *Phi Delta Kappan* (October 1961).

found that two boys, surrounded by a knot of curious onlookers, were engaged in an all-out switchblade fight. One counselor quickly whispered to the other, "We'd better break this up in a hurry before there's bloodshed." The latter replied heatedly, "For heaven's sake leave them alone or you'll ruin everything! Do you want the kids to think we are *disciplinarians?*" Fortunately, however, the native common sense of the first counselor prevailed over the doctrinaire permissiveness of his colleague, and a near-tragedy was averted.

This true story is admittedly a bit extreme and unrepresentative of disciplinary attitudes in American public schools. Nevertheless, somewhat less extreme versions occur frequently enough to suggest that American teachers are more confused and disturbed about matters of discipline today than at any previous time in the history of our public school system.

It is true that superficial observation does not support this conclusion. On the surface, practically everything *appears* the same as it was ten years ago when, except in the so-called "Blackboard Jungles," these same teachers seemed supremely confident that the ideal of democratic discipline had been achieved in the American classroom. Substantially the same disciplinary philosophy is still preached in our teachers colleges; and teachers, by and large, still practice the same kind of discipline they practiced a decade ago.

To be sure, there is still an appreciable gap between the theory or discipline as taught in colleges of education and discipline as it is actually conceived and practiced in the schools. For example, in a recent survey conducted by the National Education Association, 72 per cent of the responding classroom teachers favored the judicious use of corporal punishment in the elementary school. But the gap is no greater now than it has ever been. In everyday disciplinary practice, American teachers have never gone along completely with the more extreme ideas of educational theorists. Elementary and high-school teachers, after all, have to be realistic in handling problems of discipline because they encounter them daily in doing their jobs. Unlike professors of education, who rarely if ever have to cope with disciplinary problems in the classroom, they can ill afford to be starry-eyed about these matters.

Why then should teachers be suddenly confused and disturbed about issues of discipline? Closer scrutiny reveals that everything is not *really* the same as it used to be. One important factor in the situation has undergone significant change: Although educational theory in the field of classroom discipline has remained virtually unchanged over the past two decades, the pendulum of public opinion in recent years has been swinging further and further away from the formerly fashionable cult of permissiveness. As a result, a growing estrangement has arisen between the general public, on the one hand, and educational and psychological theorists on the other—with the classroom teacher and the rank-and-file school administrator caught squarely in the middle. Teachers, of course, were also in the middle throughout the entire period of approximately 1935—1955, when American classroom discipline underwent a process of extensive democratization. But this middle position was decidedly more comfortable then than it is now, because all three groups—educational theorists, teachers, and the public at large—were moving toward the same culturally desirable goal of a less authoritarian classroom climate.

It is true that these three groups were moving toward this goal at quite different rates. Permissiveness, nondirective guidance, and the cults of extroversion, conformity, and social adjustment were much more extreme among child-centered educators, client-centered counselors, and psychoanalytically trained child-study experts than among American parents and teachers generally. By 1955, however, the entirely laudable objective of more democratic pupil-teacher relationships had been reached, and perhaps overreached. Public opinion began moving away from permissiveness, but educational and psychological theorists and professors of education, with few exceptions, stood their ground tenaciously. The same relatively extreme permissive doctrines of discipline are still dominant in teachers colleges, even though educational philosophy in the post-Sputnik era has generally become less permissive in most other areas, such as curriculum.

Now, it was one thing for teachers to swim in the middle of two streams moving in the same historically necessary direction, and to enjoy the approbation of both the general public and of their own professional leaders. It is quite another for them to be caught between two opposing streams, and to be faced with the problem of having to choose between the spirit of the times, on the one hand, and the historically obsolete ideological extremism of their former professors on the other.

## HISTORICAL AND CULTURAL PERSPECTIVE

Before examining how particular concepts and practices of discipline have gone astray, it might be profitable first to view the problem in historical perspective within a broader cultural context. The revolution in classroom discipline that swept American schools between 1935 and 1955 was as necessary as it was inevitable. Teacher-pupil relationships had to be brought into closer alignment with the general spirit of adult egalitarianism in American society; and a more desirable balance had to be achieved between the actual dependence of children on adult direction and their realistic capacities for exercising self-direction and self-discipline. It was inevitable, of course, that we would go too far in redressing the balance—in overdoing the permissiveness and in cutting back adult control and guidance too drastically. Much more serious, however, were the deplorable consequences of deemphasizing certain other traditional American values in the enthusiasm of democratizing adult-child relationships.

Thus, in stressing the inherent right of children to receive the consideration to which they are entitled, we have neglected the equally valid claims of age and maturity. In debunking superficial and unilateral forms of etiquette, we have lost sight of the importance of genuine courtesy in human relationships. And in attacking despotic and abusive adult rule, we have failed to cultivate appropriate respect for just and rightful authority.

By respect for age I do not mean uncritical veneration or ancestor worship, but simply the consideration that is due all human beings at any stage in the life cycle. Yet our cultural attitude toward middle-aged and elderly persons tends to be patronizing and slightly contemptuous. Because they quite understandably lack the exuberance and venturesomeness of youth, they are often cavalierly dismissed as "has-beens" or as bumbling, ineffectual fuddy-duddies.

Courtesy is another of our most valuable cultural assets that was over looked in the frenzy of extending democracy to home and school. It is fashionable in many quarters—not only among the younger set—to regard good manners and the more subtle amenities of interpersonal relationships as hollow formalities. But even the highly stylized bowing ceremony of the Japanese is far from being an empty gesture. It symbolizes deep and culturally ingrained respect for the dignity of the individual and genuine concern for his pride and feelings. Although bowing is obviously incongruous with our modern way of life, concern for the pride, feelings, and dignity of every human being is one of our most cherished American values. Hence, since courtesy is basically an institutionalized set of rules designed to safeguard and implement this legitimate cultural concern, those who sneer at courtesy, whether they realize it or not, sneer at nothing less than human dignity.

Finally, our culture has tended to put authority figures in an anomalous and untenable position, particularly in the school environment. We have assigned them the necessary and often distasteful task of authority figures the world over, that is, to enforce certain basic standards of conduct; but in too many instances we have failed to give them the respect, the authority, and the protection commensurate with this responsibility. When they conscientiously attempt to apply without fear or favor the community approved sanctions for violating these standards, we accuse them of being punitive, vindictive, and authoritarian. School administrators, of course, are not above criticism and reproach when they use poor judgment or exceed their authority; but society has an obligation to protect them from disrespect and abuse for simply doing their duty and exercising their just and necessary disciplinary prerogatives. In our present cultural climate, therefore, it is small wonder that many principals and superintendents of schools are more concerned with courting general popularity than with enforcing desirable norms of pupil behavior.

## THE BRIGHTER SIDE OF THE COIN

In pointing out some of the failings of our recent approach to discipline, I do not mean to detract in any way from our genuine accomplishments. The latter are extremely impressive when compared with disciplinary practices in many other countries. I recently had an opportunity to study secondary schools in New Zealand, an English-speaking welfare state of British origin with a pioneering tradition not unlike our own. School discipline in New Zealand high schools connotes explicit subjection to authority and implicit habits of obedience that are enforced by a very heavy-handed set of controls and punishments. It implies a very identifiable atmosphere of classroom control which the teacher maintains with much deliberate effort—in much the same sense that he strives to have his pupils understand and assimilate the subject matter he teaches. For example, it is not uncommon for a New Zealand high-school teacher to begin the school year by exhibiting a cane to his class and announcing that he fully intends to use it on the first pupil who steps out of line.

By contrast, the American approach to discipline seems laudably incidental. Our teachers tend to feel that the cause of discipline is adequately served if pupils exercise sufficient self-control and observe a minimum set of rules with sufficient decorum to enable classroom work to proceed in an orderly, efficient manner. They do not, in other words, strive deliberately for discipline as an explicit goal in its own right. They assume instead that good discipline is *ordinarily* a natural by-product of interesting lessons and of a wholesome teacher-pupil relationship; that the vast majority of pupils respond positively to fair and kindly treatment; that respect for the teacher is a usual accompaniment of the latter's superior knowledge, experience, and status as a leader, and does not have to be reinforced by such artificial props and status symbols as differences in clothing, mode of address, and fear ot the strap. Hence they treat adolescents as maturing young adults rather than as unruly children, and implicitly expect them to respond in kind—which they usually do. And it was a very gratifying experience to discover that despite the absence of strict authoritarian controls, American high-school students, on the whole, behave more decorously than their New Zealand counterparts—particularly when not under direct supervision.

## SCIENCE OR OPINION?

Discipline today is much less a science than a matter of opinion. It not only shifts in response to various social, economic, and ideological factors, but also manifests all of the cyclical properties of fads and fashions. Objective scientific evidence about the relative merits of different types of discipline is extremely sparse. Indeed it is highly questionable to what extent valid objective data are obtainable and even relevant in matters of discipline. Whether or not particular disciplinary practices are appropriate depends, in the first place, on the particular values, institutions, and kinds of personal relationships prevailing in a given culture; and, second, any definitive empirical test of appropriateness would have to be conducted over such an extended period of time that its conclusions would tend to be rendered obsolete by intervening changes in significant social conditions. For all practical purposes, therefore, the choice of disciplinary policy involves taking a rationally defensible and self-consistent position based on value preferences, on relevant considerations of child development, and on individual experience and judgment.

The fact that discipline cannot be placed on a largely scientific basis, however, does not mean that one position is as good as another or that no public policy whatsoever is warranted. Society is continually obligated to resolve issues of much greater moment with even less objective evidence on which to base a decision. Under the circumstances, all we can reasonably expect is greater humility and less dogmatism on the part of those engaged in formulating disciplinary policy. Thus, the most disturbing aspect of the entire problem is not the fact that there is precious little scientific evidence to support the disciplinary doctrines expounded in our colleges of education and educational journals and textbooks, but rather the ubiquitous tendency to represent purely personal opinions and biases as if they were the incontrovertibly established findings of scientific research.

## THE DEFINITION AND FUNCTIONS OF DISCIPLINE

By discipline I mean the imposition of *external* standards and controls on individual conduct. Permissiveness, on the other hand, refers to the absence of such standards and controls. To be permissive is to "let alone," to adopt a laissez-faire policy. Authoritarianism is an excessive, arbitrary, and autocratic type of control which is diametrically opposite to permissiveness. Between the extremes of laissez-faire permissiveness and authoritarianism are many varieties and degrees of control. One of these, to be described discipline.

Discipline is a universal cultural phenomenon which generally serves four important functions in the training of the young. First, it is necessary for socialization—for learning the standards of conduct that are approved and tolerated in any culture. Second, it is necessary for normal personality maturation—for acquiring such adult personality traits as dependability, self-reliance, self-control, persistence, and ability to tolerate frustration. These aspects of maturation do not occur spontaneously, but only in response to sustained social demands and expectations. Third, it is necessary for the internalization of moral standards and obligations or, in other words, for the development of conscience. Standards obviously cannot be internalized unless they also exist in external form; and even after they are effectively internalized universal cultural experience suggests that external sanctions are still required to insure the stability of the social order. Lastly, discipline is necessary for children's emotional security. Without the guidance provided by unambiguous external controls, the young tend to feel bewildered and apprehensive. Too great a burden is placed on their own limited capacity for self-control.

## DEMOCRATIC DISCIPLINE

The proponents of democratic classroom discipline believe in imposing the minimal degree of external control necessary for socialization, personality maturation, conscience development, and the emotional security of the child. Discipline and obedience are not regarded as ends in themselves but only as means to these latter ends. They are not striven for deliberately, but are expected to follow naturally in the wake of friendly and realistic teacher-pupil relationships. Explicit limits are not set routinely or as ways of showing "who is boss," but only as the need arises, i.e., when they are not implicitly understood or accepted by pupils.

Democratic discipline is as rational, nonarbitrary, and bilateral as possible. It provides explanations, permits discussion, and invites the participation of children in the setting of standards whenever they are qualified to do so. Above all, it implies respect for the dignity of the individual and avoids exaggerated emphasis on status differences and barriers between free communication. Hence it repudiates harsh, abusive, and vindictive forms of punishment, and the use of sarcasm, ridicule, and intimidation.

The aforementioned attributes to democratic classroom discipline are obviously appropriate in cultures such as ours where social relationships tend to be egalitarian. This type of discipline also becomes increasingly more feasible as children become older, more responsible, and more capable of understanding and formulating rules of conduct based on concepts of equity and reciprocal obligation. But contrary to what the extreme permissivists would have us believe, democratic school discipline does not imply freedom from all external constraints, standards, and direction, or freedom and discipline as an end in itself. And under no circumstances does it presuppose the eradication of all distinctions between pupil and teacher roles, or require that teachers abdicate responsibility for making the final decisions in the classroom.

## DISTORTIONS OF DEMOCRATIC DISCIPLINE

Many educational theorists have misinterpreted and distorted the ideal of democratic discipline by equating it with an extreme form of permissiveness. These distortions have been dogmatically expressed in various psychologically unsound and unrealistic propositions that are considered sacrosanct in many teachers colleges. Fortunately, however, most classroom teachers have only accepted them for examination purposes—while still in training—and have discarded them in actual practice as thoroughly unworkable.

According to one widely held doctrine, only "positive" forms of discipline are constructive and democratic. It is asserted that children must only be guided by reward and approval; that reproof and punishment are authoritarian, repressive, and reactionary expressions of adult hostility which leave permanent emotional scars on children's personalities. What these theorists conveniently choose to ignore, however, is the fact that it is impossible for children to learn what is *not* approved and tolerated simply by generalizing in inverse from the approval they receive for behavior that *is* acceptable. Merely by rewarding honesty and good manners one cannot, for example, teach children that dishonesty and rudeness are socially unacceptable traits. Even adults are manifestly incapable of learning and respecting the limits of acceptable conduct unless the distinction between what is proscribed and what is approved is reinforced by punishment as well as by reward. Futhermore, there is good reason to believe that acknowledgement of wrongdoing and acceptance of punishment are part and parcel of learning moral accountability and developing a sound conscience. Few if any children are quite so fragile that they cannot take deserved reproof and punishment in stride.

A second widespread distortion of democratic discipline is reflected in the popular notion that there are no culpably misbehaving children in the classroom, but only culpably aggressive, unsympathetic, and punitive teachers. If children misbehave, according to this point of view, one can implicitly assume that they must have been provoked beyond endurance by repressive and authoritarian classroom discipline. Similarly, if they are disrespectful, then the teacher, by definition, must not have been deserving of respect. It is true, of course, that some pupil misconduct *is* instigated by harsh and abusive school discipline; but there are also innumerable reasons for out-of-bounds behavior that are completely independent of the teacher's attitudes and disciplinary practices. Pupils are also influenced by factors originating in the home, the neighborhood, the peer group, and the mass media. Some children are emotionally disturbed, others are brain-damaged, and still others are aggressive by temperament; and there are times when even the best-behaved children from the nicest homes develop an irresistible impulse—without any provocation whatsoever—to test the limits of a teacher's forebearance.

Both of the aforementioned distortions of classroom democracy are used to justify the commonly held belief among educators that pupils should not be reproved or punished for disorderly or discourteous conduct. I have, for example, observed classrooms where everybody talks at once; where pupils turn their backs on the teacher and engage in private conversation while the latter is endeavoring to instruct them; and where pupils verbally abuse teachers for exercising their rightful disciplinary prerogatives. Some educators contend that all of this is compatible with wholesome, democratic teacher-pupil relationships. Other educators deplore this type of pupil behavior but insist, nevertheless, that punishment is unwarranted under these circumstances. In the first place, they assert, reproof or punishment constitutes a "negative" and hence axiomatically undesirable approach to classroom management; and, secondly, the misbehavior would assuredly have never occurred to begin with, if the teacher's attitudes had been less autocratic or antagonistic. I have already answered the second group of educators, and to the first group I can only say that I am still sufficiently old-fashioned to believe that rudeness and unruliness are not normally desirable classroom behavior in any culture.

When such misconduct occurs, I believe pupils have to be unambiguously informed that it will not be tolerated and that any repetition of the same behavior will be punished. This action does not preclude in any way either an earnest attempt to discover why the misbehavior occurred or suitable preventive measures aimed at correcting the underlying causes. But, by the same token, the mere fact that a pupil has a valid psychological reason for misbehaving does not mean that he is thereby absolved from moral accountability or rendered no longer subject to punishment.

Still another related distortion of democratic discipline is reflected in the proposition that it is repressive and authoritarian to request pupils to apologize for discourteous behavior or offensive language. However, if we take seriously the idea that the dignity of the human being is important, we must be willing to protect it from affront; and apology is the most civilized and effective means mankind has yet evolved for accomplishing this goal. In a democratic society nobody is so important that he is above apologizing to those persons whom he wrongfully offends. Everybody's dignity is important—the teacher's as well as the pupil's. It is no less wrong for a pupil to abuse a teacher than for a teacher to abuse a pupil.

If apologies are to have any real significance in moral training, however, it is obvious that, even though they are explicitly requested, they must be made voluntarily, and they must be reflective of genuine appreciation of wrong-doing and of sincere regret and remorse. Purely formal and mechanical statements of apology made under coercion are less than worthless. Apologies are also without real ethical import unless their basis is reciprocal, i.e., unless it is fully understood that under comparable circumstances the teacher would be willing to apologize to his pupils.

A final distortion of democratic classroom discipline associated with the extreme child-centered approach to education is the notion that children are equipped in some mysterious fashion for knowing precisely what is best for them. "Scientific proof" of this proposition is adduced from the fact that nutrition is adequately maintained and existing deficiency conditions are spontaneously corrected when infants are permitted to select their own diet. If the child can successfully choose his diet, runs the argument, he must certainly know what is best for him in *all* areas, including curriculum and classroom management.

This doctrine, however, has even less face validity than the three other distorted concepts of school discipline. Because the human being is sensitive in early childhood to internal cues of physiological needs, we cannot conclude that he is similarly sensitive to complex intellectual and moral needs, or that he has sufficient experience, perspective, and judgment to make intelligent decisions in these latter areas. Even in the field of nutrition, self-selection is a reliable criterion of need only during early infancy. The current interests and opinions of immature pupils can hardly be considered reliable guideposts and adequate substitutes for seasoned judgment in designing a curriculum or in formulating rules of classroom behavior. Hence, while it is reasonable to consider the views of pupils in these matters, teachers and school administrators cannot abdicate their responsibility for making the final decisions.


WHAT NEEDS TO BE DONE

In seeking to correct these undesirable permissive distortions of classroom democracy, it would be foolhardy to return to the equally undesirable opposite extreme of authoritarianism that flourished in this country up to a quarter of a century ago, and still prevails in many Western nations. Democratic school discipline is still an appropriate and realistic goal for American education; hence there is no need to throw away the baby with the bath water. It is only necessary to discard the aforementioned permissivist doctrines masquerading under the banners of democracy and behavioral science, and to restore certain other traditional American values that have been neglected in the enthusiasm of extending democracy to home and school.

More specifically, we first have to clear up the semantic confusion. We should stop equating permissiveness with democratic discipline, and realistic adult control and guidance with authoritarianism. Permissiveness, by definition, is the absence of discipline, democratic or otherwise. We should cease instructing teachers that it is repressive and reactionary to reprove or punish pupils for misconduct, or to request them to apologize for offensive and discourteous behavior.

Second, we should stop misinterpreting what little reputable evidence we have about discipline, and refrain from misrepresenting our personal biases on the subject as the indisputable established findings of scientific research. The available evidence merely suggests that, in our type of cultural setting, authoritarian discipline has certain undesirable effects—*not* that the consequences of laissez-faire permissiveness are desirable. As a matter of fact, research studies show that the effects of extreme permissiveness are just as unwholesome as are those of authoritarianism. In the school situation a laissez-faire policy leads to confusion, insecurity, and competition for power among pupils. Assertive pupils tend to become aggressive and ruthless, whereas retiring pupils tend to withdraw further from classroom participation. The child who is handled too permissively at home tends to regard himself as a specially privileged person. He fails to learn the normative standards and expectations of society, to set realistic goals for himself, or to make reasonable demands on others. In his dealings with adults and other children he is domineering, aggressive, petulant, and capricious.

Third, we should stop making teachers feel guilty and personally responsible for all instances of misconduct and disrespect in the classroom. We do this whenever we take for granted, without any actual supporting evidence, that these behavior problems would never have arisen in the first place if the teachers involved were truly deserving of respect and had been administering genuinely wholesome and democratic discipline.

Finally, teachers colleges should terminate the prevailing conspiracy of silence they maintain about the existence of disciplinary problems in the public schools. Although discipline is the one aspect of teaching that the beginning teacher is most worried about, he receives little or no practical instruction in handling this problem. Colleges of education, as pointed out above, rationalize their inadequacies in this regard by pretending that disciplinary problems are relatively rare occurrences involving the disturbed child, or more typically the disturbed teacher. Due respect for the facts of life, however, suggests that prospective teachers today not only need to be taught more realistic propositions about the nature and purposes of democratic discipline, but also require adequately supervised, down-to-earth experience in coping with classroom discipline.

J. GLENN GRAY

# AUTHORITY IN TEACHER AND TAUGHT

As a practical people, we Americans are tempted to believe that the real issues of life and education concern means and not ends. Goals are thought to be easier to determine and delineate than are the ways of attaining them. Hence, problems of method are usually at the forefront of our planning and action. At times we are nearly obsessed with the urge to reduce the complexities of individual and collective life to question of "how to do" this or that, rather than "why do it" or "what is it" I am trying to do. It would be an interesting, if idle, task for a computer to determine the number of books our presses turn out yearly that are devoted to problems of method with the interrogative How in their titles. They certainly run the gamut from *How To Be Happy Though Married, How I Made a Million on the Stock Exchange, How To Study, How To Be the Life of the Party,* to *How To Be Paul Tillich.* This faith of ours is at once naïve, even amusing, and full of pathos, attesting a boundless optimism underlying our view of the world. It expresses a kind of innocence native to youth, a confidence that the riddles of existence have a hidden handle by which they can be got hold of and resolved.

A profounder explanation for our faith in method doubtless lies in the gradual coming to dominance of modern science in Europe and America. Recognition of this powerful cultural influence can be attributed as much to philosophers as to scientists, though they were until recently hardly distinguished from each other. It was René Descartes, commonly called the father of modern philosophy, who was among the first to proclaim that most problems could be solved if only men applied the method of mathematics to every imaginable subject matter and every human concern. Since him we have become accustomed to learned discourse about methodology and to devoting inordinate amounts of energy and intelligence to the search for right methods in every field. The latest, though

From J. Glenn Gray, *The Promise of Wisdom* (Philadelphia: J. B. Lippincott, 1968), chap. 6.

doubtless not the last, school of philosophy to put major emphasis on method are the language analysts, who are devoted to the proposition that most philosophical problems will disappear if and when we learn to use our language correctly.

Formal education and educators have likewise been preoccupied with method. Not long ago, students preparing to teach were under the impression that the "how" question was the primary one. At its extreme, such pedagogy asserted, in substance, that anyone could teach anything provided he had the right method. Methods courses proliferated in teachers' colleges and elsewhere until they became a scandal on the educational scene. Now, as everyone knows, we are in full retreat from this extreme, and emphasizing knowledge of subject matter as primary. As usual in such sharp reactions we are in peril of going too far, to the point of forgetting the vital, if subordinate, role that methods play in both schooling and education as a whole. The more perceptive students of educational theory clearly understand that problems of method dare not be neglected—as little in colleges and graduate schools as in elementary and high schools.

Many questions of method, however, are not mainly philosophical; they do not involve principles so much as educational psychology, sociology, and the practice of administration. For our philosophical purposes in this study the major questions of method become the kinds of relationships between teacher and student which promote the aims of education already outlined. In this relationship—and our focus will clearly be now on schooling—the teacher is primarily a means or a method. In simplest terms, the problem of method is this: how can the teacher best promote self-discipline in his students; how can he encourage them to care sufficiently for the values of individuality, artistry in conduct, and happiness to be able to realize them without him?

If it is true that individuality implies responsible freedom, it can be equally asserted that authority must be shifted from outside to within the growing youth in order to achieve this goal. Freedom and authority mutually imply each other. That individual is free who can control his impulses, discipline his desires and emotions, command himself in the pursuit of the goods his reasonable nature requires. So long as he is pushed and pulled this way and that by momentary moods and vagrant passions, he is in bondage and must be controlled from without. Unless he achieves self-discipline and learns to direct his life toward certain steady ends, he has no chance of gaining freedom. Hence the development of authority in individual life is the other pole of freedom. Without authority there can be no freedom, and so long as it stems from outside ourselves we are limited in our moral choices. So long as we are in the power of another we cannot be fully responsible. Until we learn to obey ourselves, we must obey others. Authority, as Hannah Arendt has stated it, implies obedience in which men retain their freedom.

One of the oldest educational doctrines is that the best kind of discipline is self-discipline. At every level the teacher's task is to impose order and to establish obedience in such a fashion that they gradually be transferred from the exterior forum to the interior. In the early grades this discipline is closely associated with maintaining physical order. That teacher has "good discipline," we say, whose pupils are quiet, obedient, and reasonably responsive to his or her directives. At more advanced levels discipline is grasped in more sophisticated ways. If students are mentally attentive and progressively ordering the subject matter they are studying into the pattern of their previous knowledge, their teacher is thought to possess good discipline. At a more advanced level still we sometimes feel that good discipline means "learning how to learn."

However, we commonly consider too little how much discipline is a continuity in education from first grade through graduate school. Unthinkingly we are likely to limit it to the sphere of outward behavior. The college professor may be as poor a disciplinarian as any primary teacher. His students have learned the elements of courtesy, but they may be making no advance whatever in control of impulse and attention. Morally his failure to command is far more culpable than that of one who has to impose physical restraints on the very young. If we try to think of authority in its essentials we will see it as a single problem throughout education.

That inner power to command obedience without force or violence in such a way as to transfer itself gradually from the teacher to the taught deserves the most careful reflection. For it is close to the secret of good teaching not merely of subject matter but of necessary values by which a free people live. The person who can speak with authority is a natural teacher, even though he may be a mere child. In the New Testament it is recorded of the boy Jesus that he taught in the temple "as one having authority," to the astonishment of the elders. It sometimes happens in the classroom that a student may have more actual authority than his teacher. I have observed students taking notes when one of their classmates gave his opinions and failing to do so when their teacher lectured. Though authority issues from many sources, its impact on us is likely to be single. In its absence there can be no real growth in autonomy and all teaching is in vain. The will to obey requires to be learned as truly as the will to command. Unless we discover authority in others as a compelling power to inspire our subordination of impulse, we shall assuredly never find it in ourselves.

Nothing concerns the beginning teacher in grade school and secondary education so much as his ability to keep good discipline in the classroom. Perhaps more young people turn away from teaching from fear of this inability than for any other reason. Thousands desert the profession after a few years' trial for the same, often unconfessed, failure. And those who stick it out will tell you that they find the problem of "keeping order" the chief liability of their calling. It wears them out, frays their nerves, and subtly undermines the real joys they discover in instructing the young. Thousands of American teachers are enthusiastic about their subject matter and gain incomparable fulfillment in the discovery that they can convey this enthusiasm to children and observe their growth in knowledge and understanding. But all too often they perceive little similar growth in the power of the taught to discipline themselves.

In nearly every class there are two or three "troublemakers," children who demand far more than their share of the teacher's attention, reproofs, angry expostulation and frequently punishment. Not only do they hinder the progress of their classmates, but they often infect them with the spirit of disobedience as well. In order to deal with these youngsters, a teacher finds himself adopting a harsh tone, which is frightening to the more timid spirits and likely to inhibit all the spontaneity and naturalness which the best learning situation requires. He finds it necessary to change his tone and mood a dozen times in the course of a morning, to become distracted from his main tasks, and to draw on the last reserves of his nervous energy. Because of a few students he discovers that he is turning into an image of himself that he most dislikes. The two or three students who provide him with the greatest joy of teaching are commonly balanced by a like number who sour his existence. So it is in a million classrooms over the land on every school day. Such conditions may be said to be among the most enduring features of school life in every generation. They do not always prevail, but they are the rule.

There are two kinds of problem children who need to be distinguished and treated quite separately: the disturbed or incorrigible children and those who are merely difficult. The former for one reason or another, usually discoverable to anyone who investigates their home background, have become pathological in their rejection of anyone placed in authority. Punishment of whatever kind only increases their defiance and resentment and their teacher soon realizes that he is incapable of teaching them anything of value so long as they reject the social situation entirely. Belatedly we are recognizing that such children must be taken out of the average classroom and taught in special institutions under the guidance of counselors and other experts who can often rescue them from outright delinquency and restore them to society. A few of our larger school systems have taken the lead in attempting to educate these incorrigibles separately. It is one of the tragedies of our educational organization that such children are not earlier removed in every community and given special care for their own sake as well as from consideration of the teachers they harass. While all of us recognize that no clear line can be drawn between the pathological, the borderline case, and the high-spirited child who is quick to resent authority, every teacher with experience is adept at distinguishing differences in a general way. In the following discussion of the sources of authority, we shall not be concerned with the seriously disturbed.

There are many elements of authority in the early years of school, but one of the most obvious is the status of the teacher as an adult. It was Aristotle who pointed out with the simplicity of genius that education is a process of age instructing youth. There is a natural deference which children at the pre-teen years pay to maturity. When they come from permissive homes in twentieth century America, this fact may not be obvious at first, but it is relatively easily established by a teacher with a modicum of assurance. However familiar the home environment has come to be, the youngster in school is dependent on direction and control by the adult world. He wants to be under supervision of a superior in the physical sense, and authority that is measurably different from that of his parents. The source of authority the teacher exerts by virtue of his age is not the same as that of the parents, but is easily assimilated to theirs. That is, the child transfers his habits of obedience, provided he has acquired any, from mother and father to teacher. He expects to be told and his teacher is the only one available while he is at school. The teacher has not brought him up from the condition of infant helplessness, hence school authority is derived and transmitted from parents. The important thing to notice is that it need not be won in the first instance, as must authority of other sorts.

Nevertheless, this elementary authority is very limited in its effects and particularly in modern America. In a society where the status of teachers as figures of authority is more secure, this natural deference exerts a far more powerful influence. Writers who complain constantly about the breakdown of authority in our society might well emphasize more than they have the popular image of the teacher. Problems of poor discipline stem not simply from the inadequacies of teachers, but also from our social failure to provide teachers with sufficient independence to assume authority easily. We are currently engaged in a national effort to raise teachers' salaries and to redeem the profession from the neglect into which it has fallen. But the struggle to regain the respect and dignity inherent in the position as such will not be easily gained by more adequate compensation or higher social status. These are certainly necessary prerequisites in the sense that they will attract abler people into the profession. But community attitudes toward teachers will be the decisive factor. When parents learn to regard the instructors of their offspring as professionals and not simply employees of the local school board, some of the natural authority will be rewon. And when teachers come to regard themselves as persons of key importance in the society, they will retain much longer than at present something of the respect in which the young should naturally hold them.

Not long ago a middle-aged woman introduced herself to me as "only a grade-school teacher." It represents a frequent extension of the "merely a housewife" syndrome of which we have heard so much. When youngsters are introduced to authority by mothers and teachers who think so little of themselves as this, small wonder that the problem of instilling authority into the souls of the young gets a poor start. Such teachers are in constant dread of their Principals and Superintendents, who are, in too many American communities, fearful in turn of ths displeasure of two or three influential families of the school district. Though obedience is rendered by most of the young to adults in school as a natural consequence of age difference, it does not endure long when those adults reveal their servile fear of superior authority.

In the nineteenth century and lasting well into the twentieth, the problem of keeping order in the classroom was more easily solved by simple reliance on fear. Teachers were usually authority figures in a dreaded sense. Physical punishment was a commonplace and discipline was held to be a separate function, a precondition of any worthwhile instruction. A teacher's ability to "keep order" was the criterion of success and, as John Dewey somewhere remarks, too many of them did little more than this. Obedience was regarded as an absolute duty, needing to be attained in home and school by physical force. The teacher as stern taskmaster from whose slightest wish there was no recourse made school a hated experience from which the young escaped at the earliest opportunity. The notion of an inherent relation between freedom and authority even in youthful hearts was farthest from the mind in that earlier day. But the revolution against the excessive reliance on fear was not long in coming. A whole generation of writers and teachers appeared to denounce its relevance for a society seeking to become more democratic and equalitarian.

The complex movement we now loosely term progressivism—and few of us yet fully understand—was dominated by the conviction that self-discipline could never be instilled by fear. Keeping order in the classroom involved radically different methods. The teacher was enjoined to renounce his fear-inspiring authority and become a counselor, guide, and friend. School must be, above all, a happy experience where children were loved, their wishes respected, and their wills gently matured into responsibility. Teachers were failures only when they were unable to secure the enthusiastic cooperation of their charges in whatever project the class was engaged. The argument of the progressivists ran that once the interests of the children were engaged, the problem of keeping order would take care of itself. In any event, order was not the prime requisite for learning. A classroom in which the best learning was taking place would normally be one of creative confusion. The theory held that youth must achieve the precious boon of self-discipline through a liberation of their powers in school tasks which appealed to their stage of development.

Philosophically the chief difference between the old and the progressive concepts of discipline lay in the interpretation of child nature. The followers of John Dewey in education were thoroughgoing naturalists who thought of children in terms of the new biology and evolutionary theory of Darwin, Huxley, and others. The child's nature, they held, is not different in essence from that of any other organism; its chief activity is adaptation of itself to the environment. But the human species alone is able to adapt the environment, within limits, to its own needs by the use of intelligence and manipulation. Hence, schooling is the progressive induction of the child into the natural and social life of his time in such a fashion that his active nature may not simply adjust to the external but transform the world around him by a developing, creative intelligence. The problem of discipline is not to break the will of the child in order to subject it to adult culture, but rather to give it free rein to seek its own place and level in an organic order. Whatever is wrong with society—and the progressivists were highly critical—is not due to original human nature but to bad traditions, authoritarianism and false dualisms between man and the rest of nature, between reason and emotions, science and religion, and many others. The new pedagogy was nothing if not optimistic about child nature and looked forward confidently to a time when the scientific spirit would transform existing social institutions.

By contrast, the older view was pessimistic in doubting that the young were naturally directed toward the good. Permeated by the religious consciousness of a rebirth into a second nature as a condition of responsible maturity, the authoritarian tradition assumed an inevitable recalcitrance of youth. Goodness was an achievement in the mortal struggle with the merely animal and natural. Left to their own devices boys and girls would unfailingly seek the path of disorder and sin. How much the Christian distrust of the natural was responsible for the reliance on fear and punishment as primary aids to discipline depended on the pervasiveness of the Calvinistic persuasion. Progressivists were given to painting their opponents' view in somewhat lurid colors. Undoubtedly, the conviction that Adam's sin of disobedience would be repeated in his offspring if they were left free to pursue their natural impulses played a role in this older conception of discipline. Yet anyone who knows the history of education will discover this distrust of child nature in non-Christian cultures as well and will not too hastily conclude that Puritanism was a major ingredient. In any event, the belief that "to spare the rod spoil the child" and that "he who loves his child will not hesitate to reprove it" found solid Biblical support. There seems little question that before progressivism it was a widespread persuasion of the American public, whatever the origin. Such punishment and reliance on fear, it hardly needs to be added, were not inconsistent with love of children. Even the old schoolmaster of fearsome memory used sternness and the rod in the belief that these methods were best designed for the improvement of the young.

Today we are no longer so sure about the methods of discipline best designed to internalize authority. Though our society is in full retreat from the excesses of progressive education, there is little disposition to return to the nineteenth-century conception. Essentially we are looking for some kind of synthesis of the old and the new, whereby freedom and authority can be progressively related to each other as the child advances. The authoritarian teacher is regarded in more thoughtful circles to be as harmful to this enterprise as the one who has effectively lost control. We are aware that this problem is much more complex and subtle under the conditions of modern life than once it was thought to be.

Nevertheless, the dangers of extremism are very much present. Under the impact of the reform movement, there was a widespread revulsion against the harshness of the older discipline. Most American states established laws against physical punishment in the classroom. Now some are repealing these laws and there is active debate about the merits of punishment under carefully controlled conditions. A whole literature of extremism is growing up according to which progressive education is held to be responsible not only for our intellectual deficiencies in education but for moral failings as well. In the state of alarm into which we have fallen as a nation, there is danger of losing many of the great gains of the past half century. It is of the greatest importance to assess correctly the basic elements of discipline at the various stages of growth and to avoid dogmatism in a subject of the greatest difficulty where any generalization will be subject to numerous exceptions. As always, in dealing with education, it is helpful to keep in view the end toward which discipline in the teacher-student relationship is directed.

Surely we know enough about child nature by this time to reject some of the dogmas of the past. Children are born neither corrupt nor incorrupt. We cannot say with Rousseau that it is "an incontrovertible rule that the first impulses of nature are always right" and that therefore children are by nature directed toward the good, every vice being attributable to malign social influences. Nor would most of us hold that human nature is inherently corrupt in the literal sense of being predisposed to wickedness. It does not follow, of course, that children are born morally neutral, hence completely moldable to whatever experience writes on a blank tablet. We now believe that they bring to school dispositions that are still plastic, bundles of potentialities and powers that can be directed either toward constructive or destructive behavior. Some of these tendencies require suppression in the interests of giving others full play; many need nourishment and careful guidance in order to turn them in social rather than anti-social directions. In short, every youngster stands in need of authority, fitted to his own potentialities, that will enable him to achieve step by step free self-development.

What is the role of fear in establishing such creative authority? Is it at all consistent with the relationship of respect and confidence which should form the essence of authority in the early years? The answer is far from easy, given the variety in every classroom. With many children respect is easily won through confidence, friendliness, and the assurance that his teacher accepts him as an important member of the group. With others it must be established through a kind of friendly neutrality which insists on a line beyond which the child cannot go in refusing obedience to a teacher's command. With difficult children respect appears to be a subtle blending of love and fear or of trust and dread, and this blending forms the endless dilemma of the conscientious teacher. All of us have known teachers who were intent on "loving children into goodness" as well as those who did not scruple to rely on fear as a primary instrument. Both fail with many children at different stages of development. Fear does not necessarily breed hatred, as many allege. As an emotion it can be salutary not only for children but for adults as well.

Soft pedagogy always undervalues its effect. The difficulty arises when fear is not mixed with other sentiments and displays itself as an arbitrary force.

Should teachers be permitted to punish troublesome children in order to induce the necessary respect for authority? Certainly every teacher must be permitted some means of correction; the question concerns only physical punishment. So long as such punishment remains within clearly defined limits there is probably little harm in it. Pupils quickly learn the limits of the teacher's power to punish in those systems where physical correction is prohibited and some take advantage of it. All depends on the way such punishment is administered as well as on the degree of severity. The wise teacher will pay great attention to the pragmatic factor. With some children such physical correction engenders resentment and further defiance, a sure sign that the teacher has failed in an important function. With others mild punishment of a corporal kind appears to work wonders. On occasion nothing clears the air, when repeated threats fail, so much as a mild but well administered spanking or slap. But the teacher who finds himself relying on such punishment as a regular measure can be very sure that he is a failure. The fear of the the teacher may be the beginning of wisdom, but unless it gets transformed into deference for other qualities in his authority, it cannot produce the desired results.

The discipline acquired through fear and love should yield preeminence early in the school career to the discipline inherent in subject matter. Between the teacher and his students lies the material to be learned, the fundamental reason for their relationship in the first place. The teacher's ability to make relevant this objective factor in the situation determines in great part his success in imparting discipline to his charges. At first the authority of subject matter lies outside the teacher, but his skill and enthusiasm in appropriating this material and transmitting it can cause it to lose its impersonal character and become vital. Subject matter can remain, as it does for many students, something detached, external, and inert. As such it hinders the development of discipline and alienates teacher from student. But if the will of the student is made to confront this body of material, enter into it little by little and follow the structure of knowledge incorporated there, his energies are subtly if gradually transformed.

We speak glibly of the teacher's ability to make his subject interesting. There is, however, an interestingness which is external and relatively unimportant. Many a teacher gains a pseudo-authority by his capacity to dazzle students with isolated facts and facets of the material. Their attention is caught and held more by what the teacher does to the subject than what it does to him. There is a subjectivizing of material, a popularization that destroys the authority inherent in knowledge. Only as the teacher loses himself in his subject can he speak with authority about it or, more exactly, from within it. And only as the student learns that he is confronted with material that he must master, that has its own laws not dependent on his subjective will, does he begin to learn that primary lesson of self-discipline, namely, the overcoming of immediate impulse.

The teacher's authority as a knower, therefore, lies not so much in his ability to make material interesting as to make it appear relevant. For the majority of youth the vast store of human knowledge appears not only dead but irrelevant to their present concerns. They experience an initial resistance to mastering such patterns of the adult world. So much of it appears to belong to the past whereas the future is their primary interest. The teacher must impose his will by persuading them that, in the words of a recent novelist, "the past is not dead, it is not even past." He must constantly win their reluctant allegiance to lose the immediacy of the moment and so expand the narrow circle of their experience by adding to it material which yesterday lay outside their horizons.

Nothing tests a teacher's ability to utilize fully the discipline of subject matter so much as his success in absorbing students in material for which they felt a prior aversion. The required course in any curriculum frequently meets a resistance that exceeds the natural reluctance of youth to exert themselves on foreign material. Such a teacher may never succeed in interesting them greatly in such material. Yet he may nevertheless induce them to a mastery of the content of the course that exceeds all expectations. Most of us remember courses somewhere in our school career for which we felt a positive dislike, but in which we learned uncommonly much almost in spite of ourselves. Even though we quickly forgot most of the content and confess that we hated every minute of it, we can hardly deny its beneficial effects in promoting self-mastery.

Why is this so? And what is the secret of such teaching? The answer to the first question can certainly be found in the challenge of the difficult for the young. Of first importance is the exhilaration of exerting effort on unyielding material. Youth always doubt their powers. They are especially reluctant to undertake studies in which, in Aristotle's phrase, "there is no natural sweetness," the sweetness of pleasure. But if they discover that they can succeed, even to a moderate extent, in conquering that material which holds little intrinsic interest, their sense of triumph is all the greater. The pride in mastery for its own sake causes them to boast ever after of passing such a course and the effects linger on when more popular courses have been forgotten.

It is hard to exaggerate the disciplining power of material that is difficult when it is presided over by the truly authoritative teacher. Without a word being spoken about the meaning of freedom and authority in such a course, more may be learned about their substance than in others where these concepts are part of the subject matter. It is a serious mistake on the part of some devotees of the humanities to hold that students cannot acquire moral values from the study of the exact sciences. For self-discipline is acquired precisely where the material permits no concessions to subjectivity. Such material will not contribute greatly to the student's understanding of the world. If isolated from other aspects of knowledge and from his practical concerns it may quickly be forgotten. But in its sheer factuality and emptiness of the usual attractions, it can represent something of the necessary austerity involved in all self-discipline of the advanced sort. I agree with John Stuart Mill and others who hold that every student needs to be confronted at some point in his career with material that is without any external appeal. If he chances to have a teacher who is a master, it may well turn out to be a decisive experience in the course of his moral maturity.

One of the refreshing aspects of higher education is the fact that many students do at times seek such subject matter on the reputation of the teacher whose discipline they wish to submit to. As often as not they never learn to care much for the subject matter, but they do acquire that steel in the character which all of us so badly need for a life of democratic responsibility. There is, of course, a tremendous difference in effect when students are permitted to elect such courses rather than having them forced upon them. In this discussion we are not concerned with the problem of the required versus elective curriculum. There exists sufficient evidence against introducing requirements for the sake of self-discipline alone. And the goal of educating for individuality demands that we insist on students' rights to choose their subject matter at the earliest point consistent with responsible freedom. Doubtless there are subject matters which our educational system must require as a necessity for life in the modern world. Such prescription should not be undertaken as lightly as is commonly done. For without freedom, discipline cannot be learned, whereas external discipline can be imposed years on end without much growth of freedom. Also it is foolish to deny the importance of interest as a primary motivation, above all in the early stages of education.

It was, however, an error of progressive pedagogy to overemphasize the importance of building on already formed interests of youth. We are now coming to recognize, in Jerome Bruner's words, that new interests can be created. It is the teacher's primary concern, indeed, at nearly all levels of education to create these new interests. There is so much knowledge which all of us need to acquire for which we have no ready-made inclination. It is, in fact, startling to realize how much one needs to know in our complex civilization in order simply to escape the common dangers of life. The chasm between what many of us *want* to know and what we actually *need* to know even to lead a humdrum existence has surely never been so wide. Hence the central importance of constantly creating new interests is everywhere becoming apparent. Little can be credited to the teacher's authority when he succeeds in advancing knowledge and enthusiasm for material his students already like and for which they find immediate application. We who teach should not congratulate ourselves so much for success with students like these. They do not gain greatly in the kind of discipline freedom requires so long as they merely follow the paths of aptitude and interest in subject matter. The sensitive teacher rejoices more over the lost sheep he has rescued than in the ninety and nine already in the fold.

In creating these new interests, the level of difficulty of the material presented is a perennial issue for teachers concerned with helping students mature in self-discipline. Ideally, of course, all subject matter should be difficult enough to stretch students' abilities to their utmost without going beyond their present powers. The too easy will bore them, the too difficult discourage, and both are equally destructive of authority. Given the wide range of intelligence and diversity of previous preparation in any heterogenous class, such an ideal is rarely achieved. This fact in itself is one of the best arguments for the track system or homogenous grouping, as we have already noted in the preceding chapter. Even when everything possible is done to narrow diversity in students, there are within every academic discipline facts and concepts of widely varying degrees of sophistication. Consequently, every teacher must reconcile himself to failing to challenge his classes part of the time. No one has the right to expect that he can constantly advance the cause of authority in learning or in life. But unless we who teach are always alert to the problem of keeping students straining at the boundaries of their knowledge and abilities during a reasonable proportion of the learning period, we will miss precious opportunities. The tendency in earlier decades of this century to take it easy has given critics a ready weapon in their outcry for more rigor in learning.

The response of teachers to this criticism in the last few years has not, however, been uniformly favorable to the cause of self-discipline. Too many of late aspire to the reputation of being "tough" and fear unduly the reputation of teaching a course that is easy to pass. In many cases the young from grade school through college are being overloaded with work, with assignments that do not challenge their intellects so much as their endurance. The demand is for quality too often translated into increase in quantity. And the growing emphasis on grades is again a return to the external emphasis of an earlier discipline, which relied on fear alone. So long as the teaching profession is as insecure as at present, it will never achieve the golden mean.

There is as little to be said for the "tough" teacher as for the easy mark, for both commonly misconceive the discipline of their subject matter. The teacher who does not make allowance for inherent difficulties in what he teaches and does not recognize that students have only a limited time to devote to his course invariably undermines self-confidence. And the easy teacher who assigns too little material, and that of an elementary sort, and fails to hold students responsible for their work earns contempt. But the teacher who is reasonable in his demands on students time and comprehension will never be known as tough or easy and can congratulate himself that it rarely occurs to students to classify him in such ways.

At the more advanced levels of education the authority implicit in the materials of instruction becomes ever more important. As subject matter becomes more complex and intricate, its possibilities for discipline increase accordingly. A teacher of difficult material who aspires to influence his students in intellectual discipline must be made of no ordinary stuff. For he must, in the first instance, be in complete control of his material. The loss of authority arising from ignorance on the part of the teacher is an almost tangible thing. Most of us who teach have experienced the deep dismay which rises to choke us when students discover that we are unable to deal with a central concept on which knowledge must be presupposed. There are many ways of covering up such ignorance, but the perceptive student is not fooled by any of them. He may accept a frank confession of not knowing where details are concerned, but not on essentials. With startling suddenness student confidence is shattered and can only be rebuilt with the greatest difficulty. If the teacher does not "know his stuff," in student language, where the material is already of intrinsic interest, the damage may not be nearly so great. Many a student in such situations finds refuge in the text book or the library and allows them to share authority with his teacher. But where material is not immediately appealing there is no help. The teacher has failed and his discipline is imperiled in a fundamental way. More advanced students will continue to struggle with the material, but they will not take into their souls the value of such effort.

Yet competence is not enough; it is a necessary but not sufficient condition. Hundreds of teachers who are "authorities" in their fields do not succeed in being authorities for their students. The spectacle of a teacher who is a master of his specialty yet cannot "put it across," as students are wont to say, is an all too common one. The scholar is, alas, by no practical definition a teacher. He may or he may not be. What he requires where no ready interest is available is an imaginative understanding of the effect of this material on immature minds. He must possess the gift for logical and psychological presentation calculated to gather his students into the framework of his world. If he simply forgets himself in his material, he may speak like an inspired man yet not carry his students with him. Without the intuitive understanding of youth in all its perversity and its disturbing unpredictability such a teacher is unlikely to succeed. Until he learns the art of playing upon the expectations, hopes, fears, and capacities of the youth before him, of expecting neither too much nor too little, of being patient at the right time and impatient at others, he will not induce them into assaulting the obstacle which his material represents. He must possess, in the Biblical phrase, the wisdom of the serpent, but not the harmlessness of the dove. For even at more advanced levels a teacher can rarely do without a measure of fear in his authority, at least the fear of failure.

There are cherished occasions in the classroom when material may become such a dominant force that students forget themselves completely, speak out and speak up in their eagerness to understand or to contribute. All the wonderful qualities of young minds are suddenly released upon a common problem, absorbed in it, and able to communicate with each other without self-consciousness. Time can be forgotten and with it all one's private problems for the moment. From being a collection of heterogeneous individuals the class is fused into something like complex unity. Even then the teacher much guard against forgetting his role. Though he will fear to break the spell and be unable to control all the forces let loose, he will nonetheless notice when some students get behind or get "lost" and skillfully herd such stragglers into the play of thought.

There is another kind of discipline, connected with, but separated from, that of subject matter, which inheres in the teacher's manner of dealing with students. So much has been written on this subject that one hesitates to add more, yet its importance in the growth of moral authority will limit our focus. It is a commonplace that a teacher must respect his students if he is to gain their respect. Such generalizations are not very helpful unless we analyze what it means to treat youth with respect. Doubtless the central element is how much the teacher cares about students as individuals. On this point every young person is sensitive to the last degree. His liking or disliking a teacher is governed by this factor almost alone. It can be argued that liking or disliking a teacher can be fairly irrelevant to the acquisition of subject matter. And a few students can surely acquire worthwhile values from teachers they dislike. The great majority, however, cannot, above all if their disapproval is a strong one. It remains as true as when the Greek philosophers first pointed it out that youth learn much in terms of character from imitation and we rarely imitate those we dislike. Rightly or wrongly, young people give their inner allegiance only to those teachers in whom they sense a concern for them as individuals.

This concern expresses itself differently in personal interviews and in the classroom situation, a fact too infrequently noticed. The teacher is one and the students many and it is frequently difficult for any teacher to shift in manner from teaching to conversing face to face. After a wearing class hour or day, he is all too likely to indicate in subtle ways that the student who wishes to confer with him is intruding. His caring is revealed in how carefully he listens to what the student says, for teachers fall so quickly into the habit of talking too much and listening too little. It is revealed in his way of discovering the necessary facts of the student's history that are relevant to the matter being discussed. Most of all, caring is revealed by the tone of voice, the endeavor to avoid that impersonality of manner of one in authority over the group. One teacher can say harsh things in private to a student without wounding him, where another can be patronizing and offensive in the effort to be kind. Nothing offends so much as the teacher's making light of a student's endeavor to meet him at the personal level, to break through the official mask and to discover the human being. Unless the teacher relaxes his guard in such interviews, he will miss the chance to show he cares.

In the classroom situation caring is most easily demonstrated by the seriousness with which a teacher prepares himself for his work. It is hard to avoid fierce anger at the thought of how careless teachers can be with the precious time of their students. There is sufficient waste in the educational process that is unavoidable without teachers adding to it by lack of planning and preparation. Though the young may seem infinitely careless themselves in this respect, they are quick to resent the implication of their superiors that wasted time is of no importance to them. The teacher who improvises a lecture, repeats himself, and allows digressions for anecdotes of doubtful relevance can fritter away hard-won respect. In class discussions or recitations, sensitivity to student reaction and response to questions under discussion mark all too clearly how much a teacher cares. Those who are always kindly and endlessly patient with students' fumbling are nearly as destructive as those who are brusque and feelingless. The demoralization that besets a class with a teacher who suffers fools too gladly or who permits a strong-willed student to monopolize time is irreparable.

The dominance that holds a class under tension and yet never tyrannizes is possible only to that teacher who cares passionately and without sentimentality. Toughness or softness in a teacher is in this respect all-important. The student who succeeds in pretense to knowledge or to preparation he has not made will mark the teacher who is himself without discipline. Harshness with such pretense, an unrelenting demandingness, and a no-nonsense attitude is the mark of authority. Under the stress of being singled out, a timid student will sometimes speak thoughtlessly and incur the amused laughter of his classmates. Such situations are often decisive. The teacher can either save the student from his embarrassment by turning his meaning into a reasonable one or crush him by exposing him to further ridicule. Kindliness on these repeated occasions is wholly consistent with rigor and stringency of thought. By his consideration for the feeling of that student he can not only win his gratitude but impress the rest of the class. There is as little to be said for the authority of a teacher who is all tolerance as there is for one who demands perfection from his students.

The mistake a young teacher frequently commits is to believe that he can be a friend of his students. The term is used loosely, of course, but on any strict construction the teacher-student relation is not one of friendship. Friends do not normally serve as authority to each other, since friendship in its very nature implies equality. Students are often more perceptive in this matter than are teachers. They do not want their teacher to be a friend, though they appreciate friendliness on his part. The reason is not only a difference in age and attainments, but an intuitive perception that teaching requires psychological distance. Unless the teacher receives a deference which the mind willingly gives as compared with an external politeness, he is simply not one's teacher. We may learn from such a one as we normally do learn from all manner of people, but the meaning of authority in its relation to freedom is not acquired this way. The teacher must be to a youth in some sense a superior; not

only must he know more but must also stand for qualities of character the youth has not yet attained. Understood philosophically,
our teacher is only he who embodies a kind of freedom we lack. We
listen in an inner sense to those we admire, who embody in their
whole personality a good we want, however imperfectly and
vaguely we intuit it. Though a youngster has many teachers in the
formal sense, only a few of them can develop that discipline which
is the other side of freedom's coin.

Teachers, like students, are often insecure. Hence they cross the
line and seek a camaraderie with their students in the effort to win
their consent to be taught. At very advanced levels in graduate
school this behavior may be successful. Certainly there are informal
occasions when the teacher should relax with his students and reveal his common humanity, though he must do that, too, at every
level. But he should never reach the point of familiarity where it
will be difficult for him to resume his role of teacher. Human beings
are capable only up to a point of changing roles. And the teacher
who believes that he can be "one of the boys" on a festive evening
or afternoon and enter the classroom the following morning to step
into the old position is simply unwise. His students may consent to
play the game, but inwardly something significant has happened.
They will learn the facts of his field as before; they will hardly gain
in self-discipline. He has lost status as an authority.

Though the authority inherent in possession of knowledge and
in daily association with students is great, all of us are convinced
there is something more. If we reflect on our experience in school,
as too few of us are wont to do, we are nearly certain to discover
that the authority of our best teachers lay even deeper than in their
mastery of their fields and their personal relations with us. It matters little what we call this something more; there is inevitably
something mysterious about it. Perhaps the term "force of character" is as good as any. Some teachers hold an interest for students
year after year that has little to do with their knowledge or with
anything else that is very tangible. They may not be the best
teachers on a faculty or in some sense the most admirable of persons. They may not always be easy to get along with, and colleagues
and administrators may find them on occasion positively difficult.
Nor are they the teachers who have disciples or coteries, being
much too independent for that. They are their own men or women,
intent on an integrity that is inseparable from their very being.
Though they may well be moody from time to time, they are incapable of playing roles, of being different human beings in the mani-
fold relationships of life.

Such teachers have that indefinable quality called stature as persons. They escape that typing, a sort of "professional deformation," which the vocation of teaching fixes indelibly on so many of us. We may feel that they could just as easily have been business men or Congressmen or even military officers as successfully as what they are, though we would in all likelihood be mistaken, for they are born teachers. That is to say, they are natural leaders of men. If our society understood better than it does the importance of teaching, it would seek out such people and lure them into the classroom at almost any price. For they are, in any culture, the superlative formers of character in the young. They attract without willing it, yet hold themselves at a distance. The reserves of emotional power they possess are such that, always giving, they are rarely exhausted. Generosity understood in its deeper sense of a plenitude of spending power is what they have in common.

It is all too easy to build up an unreal image of an individual in the attempt to describe something called force of character. Perhaps it is not embodied in any single person so much as it is in the leadership quality in anyone who is a genuine teacher. One is ever tempted to repeat Whitehead's dictum when he spoke of greatness as the indispensable quality in all who teach character. But greatness is, of course, an abstraction and what we should attempt to do is to specify its qualities. Surely independence of mind and generosity are two of them. A certain intensity is likewise part of this complex of qualities. A teacher can be very quiet and yet assertive; he can dominate without perceptible effort. His moral reserve is such that students are unable to compass him, to find him out. Once a teacher is no longer interesting to students as a person, he can no longer be their moral instructor. If he himself ceases to advance in inner reserves, his students will catch up and surpass him. Such eventualities are inevitable, of course, the distribution of abilities being what it is. No teacher can be expected to be authoritative for students at every level. Enough if he beings them past a stage in the long growth toward self-mastery. And the best teacher does not aspire to more, since he recognizes himself as a means only and disdains to make the young a carbon image of his own values. The true authority in teaching is always intent on making itself dispensable, the master teachers those who point us beyond themselves. We leave them behind usually without much thanks, for such appears inappropriate. But in latter vicissitudes we bless them as men or women who have made it possible for us to hold out. The moral force they instilled in our characters by power of example may make all the difference as to whether we acquit ourselves like men in the lonely hours.

In conclusion, perhaps it needs to be emphasized that such

teaching and teachers are becoming ever more important on the American scene. To many critics it appears that authority in the wider society is rapidly eroding away. They speak of a crisis of authority in our time. The primary institution of the family as a source of authority has allegedly lessened its hold; that of the church is surely not so strong as once it was. And the political institutions that could trace their origins to the founding fathers and provide for our youth secure values, in this realm at least, are no longer compelling in the first global age. As a consequence, education has become for many a last desperate hope for a new foundation of authority that will save our society from dangerous drift. For most youth education begins with schooling and school continues to play a larger and longer role in the lives of the majority than ever before. On any calculation it is difficult to deny that schools have inherited, usually without willing it, a larger share in forming our future *ethos* than is perhaps desirable. In the absence of other authorities young people are forced to rely on teaching and teachers not merely for the knowledge they need but also for the values which will help to rescue them from confusion and inner anarchy. In short, teachers are increasingly important in a society adrift; their burden, assumed or neglected, is a heavy one. Sooner or later nearly all students of educational theory come to the conclusion that qualities in the teacher are the alpha and omega of educational method.

# PART 3

# THE TEACHING
# OF VALUES

In the realm of values the radical school-reform movement poses its most serious threat to responsible education and to freedom under intelligent and just law. Imbedded in its talk about spontaneity, joy, and freedom is a philosophy of anarchism. The values of the counter-culture are there, with the exception of advocating violence as a legitimate tactic for producing social and political change.

Violence, however, is not actively discouraged in free schools and open classrooms. Children frequently punch each other and indulge often in obscenity, verbal and physical harassment, and exploitation. Radical educators talk of lifting repressive forces, developing the ability to express openly all our emotions, including the aggressive ones, and encouraging values such as self-esteem, instant gratification, openness, flexibility, authority of the learner, and decision-making by group consensus.

Moral relativism, both cultural and subjective, permeate free-school and open-classroom activities. The individual achievements of great men are normally underplayed, and institutional authority suffers continual and inevitable devaluation. This moral relativism is not only insupportable philosophically, it has undesirable practical consequences; it deprives children of a rational basis from which to challenge evolving values that may well pertain to drugs, criminal behavior, sex, peer loyalty, loyalty to family, country, and government, and rights, obligations, and duties in a democratic society.

Radical humanism encompasses many values of the counter-culture. In education these tendencies would overwhelm such traditional values as objectivity, problem-solving, and critical thinking.

Deeply distrustful of our technological order and its alarming excess, including the alienation and interpersonal lack of love and feeling, the radical educators overcompensate through sensitivity training and many humanistic techniques, some of which are described in Part 4. The full development of man's capacities includes the cultivation of the intellect and aesthetic judgment, which are indeed related. Emotions, in fact, are a powerful aspect of human learning and problem-solving, so the attempt to de-emphasize our intellectual powers, because of some notorious abuses of those powers, smacks of logical inconsistency.

While competition, grades, and analytical thinking are being devalued, the autonomy of the learner comes to include notions that are incompatible with a healthy and critical sense of reality. Empirical claims are often judged on an individual basis; that is, the individual privately decides what is correct and incorrect, valid or invalid, just as he decides what is right or wrong *by simple preference.* Evidence is often regarded as irrelevant.

The debasement of standards of excellence, the glorification of private choice, aggression, arrogance, and disrespect for all authority mark the free-school and open-classroom movement as the educational branch of the counter-culture movement. Most Americans, despite their permissiveness in some areas, reject with justification the bulk of anarchist values that include self-interest, psychedelic consciousness, irrationality, sexual promiscuity.

To the extent to which genuine humanistic values like moral autonomy, love, cooperation, tolerance, and altruism are intelligently encouraged, the radical school-reform movement can make a positive contribution to American education. However, its emphasis on freedom and private choice is so extreme that this possibility is virtually precluded.

Affective education, including the expression of a range of emotions and concerns, can be useful to any educational program. My own visits to free schools and open classrooms militate against such optimism, however, for too much noise, obscenity, arrogance, and self-indulgence make such an approach presently unfeasible.

The cultivation of aggression and private choice moreover, flies in the face of traditional humanist values. Moreover it interferes with the development of an aesthetic sense. Awe, wonder, and fantasy have no place in a classroom devoted to instant gratification, high noise levels, and intolerance.

By indulging the individual learner, by exalting his choices, by dismissing the hard-won standards of civilization, the open-classroom devotee contributes to the dissolution of our civilization. Academic performance, artistic achievement, scientific findings, behavioral abnormalities, and moral decisions must be judged by the best available rational criteria. Without such judgments we cannot for long sustain the existence of a civilized community.

The authors in Part 3 offer guidance in the area of teaching values. The reader would do well to compare their judgments with the prescriptions of radicals like John Holt and Paul Goodman.

In the first essay, Sidney Hook provides guidelines for using the scientific method in the area of values. Hook's approach to teaching values is far more comprehensive than that of the radical reformers, who prescribe little more than facilitation of the expression of values as they appear in a free educational context. In Hook's scheme a responsible teacher would assist learners in judging the consequences of their value choices. Radical educators often underplay the importance of such judgments; they prefer to have children act upon their choices, then later reflect upon the consequences, if they are in the mood for it. Since there is often no responsible adult to guide even that kind of moral experimentation, few children will become morally committed to rules or principles relating to various classes of consequences.

In the second article Thomas Green offers an interesting treatment of making judgments of value. Green carefully distinguishes such judgments from guessing and expressing preferences and tastes. Through an analysis of language, Green tries to demonstrate that judgments of value in domains like aesthetics, character, and policy are at least partially empirical or truth-functional in nature. His stress upon the use of evaluative criteria is especially important.

Green's stress upon criteria or reasons ties in very well with the view Peters argues for moral objectivism both at the very general level, that is, goodness, equality, justice, and truth, and at the concrete, situational level, thus allowing for flexibility in specific situations, such as the abortion or euthanasia issues.

R. S. Peters applies his idea of moral levels to the prevailing concepts of child development. He concludes that some conditioning of "good behavior" seems essential to sound moral development. Habit and tradition should precede the rational morality of the adult. Such thinking is an anathema to the radical reformers, who value "natural moral development." That is, they believe that children will evoke their own morality as the need for it arises.

Just as the *manner* of conducting moral education is important to Peters, it is also emphasized by Nancy Gayer. Miss Gayer discusses teaching strategies related to the planned and unplanned modes of instruction.

The author distinguishes between the words "authoritarian"

and "authority" and recommends the latter as being extremely important in a program of moral education. Miss Gayer provides interesting practical guidelines, including the idea of children-made rules, but insists that the teacher's mandatory rules must circumscribe the children's area of freedom. Needless to say, such proposals directly conflict with the views of the radical humanists.

---

SIDNEY HOOK

# THE TEACHING OF VALUES

---

The great challenge to the centrality of scientific method in the process of education arises from the presence of values. How, on this view, are they to be approached? Can they be understood, can they be evaluated, without breaking free from the general pattern of inquiry? To this I now turn.

No matter what his *theory* of value is, every educator is committed to the proposition that one of the tasks of education is to teach values. Since not all values can be taught, and some selection must be made, every educator assumes that some values are better than others. What does it mean to reach values? What does it mean to teach that some values are better than others?

To teach values properly is to do a variety of related things. First, it is to make students *aware* of their attitudes of preference expressed in their choices and organized in their habits. By the time an individual reaches the stage when he can differentiate between himself and others he already has acquired a whole set of values. Every child imbibes values as he learns how to speak; and he learns how to speak before he learns how to think. By the time he is confronted by an experience that provokes moral doubt he is already in possession of many values. He does not start from scratch. He is committed to many values that may be more eloquently attested in his behavior than in his speech. These values are rarely organized and even their conflicts selfom lead to clear articulation unless certain intellectual habits have already been acquired. The existence of

From Sidney Hook, *Education for Modern Man: A New Perspective* (New York: Knopf, 1963), pp. 177—185. Reprinted by permission.

these values, rather than their source, is the important thing to note for our subsequent analysis.

To teach values is not only to make students aware of their commitments. It is also to make them aware of attitudes of evaluation to which not they but *others* are committed. This is not easily done. For it requires more than the realization that their own value commitment formally excludes its opposite. If they recognize themselves as ambitious, they must, of course, also be capable of formally recognizing what it means to be not ambitious. But this is not enough by far. For to be properly aware of what it means to be not ambitious is to understand it in relation to the psychological, historical, social, or other contexts which make *that* commitment as natural or plausible to the person who holds it as being ambitious is to oneself. Here a good teacher working with good books in the fields of literature and history can make the value commitments of others appear as vital options, actively competing with the students' own, instead of abstract negations. If we want to understand what "intolerance" means, we must make some historical or literary character who was self-righteously intolerant come alive. Assuming for the moment that our values are "goods"—I am trying to use language innocently—we must make the "bads" credible in the sense that imaginatively we can conceive ourselves holding them.

Finally, to teach values means to develop within students a willingness to commit themselves to new values, and to reaffirm or to reject the values to which they find themselves previously committed. When this is done after the value alternatives which are being excluded have been presented, then it can be said we are teaching that some values are better than others. When this willingness is developed by rhetoric and the hortatory arts, by promises of personal reward or fear of punishment, we have indoctrination. When this willingness results from a rational consideration of the evidence for one or the other commitment, then we have scientific determination of value judgments.

The retort comes at once: then in either case indoctrination is unavoidable, for there is no way of establishing scientifically that one judgment of value is better or truer than another without circularity. Only judgments of fact can be established scientifically.

The view that what is generically called scientific method, as distinct from the specific techniques of the special sciences, is irrelevant in establishing the validity of judgments of value, is what unites all philosophers—whether Thomist or narrow positivist, whether intuitionist or reductive materialist—against the experimentalist philosophy. To do justice to the claims and criticisms of these various schools of ethical thought would require a treatise.

But I propose in lieu of this to outline in a positive way an experimental approach to value judgments insofar as they enter into the content of education, and to see how far it will carry us before differences in philosophical theory obtrude.

A scientific or rational approach to judgments of value consists in (a) the investigation of the causes of such judgment, (b) their logical implications, and (c) their probable consequences. This investigation is always to be undertaken in relation to alternative values which limit freedom of choice.

(a) That judgments of value have histories, that they are related to interests, that they grow out of *problems* of valuation and appraisal are truths that no one denies. What is often denied is the relevance of these factors to the specific quality of value in any situation. Yet we are all aware of the simple fact that knowledge of the causes of value judgment often aids us in understanding what we are valuing. All who are not theoretically doctrinaire will grant that our knowledge that this man is starving makes some difference to our understanding of the good and bad quality of an action that flows from his acute need.

To discover why a man comes to value what he does, does not necessarily lead us to justify his value, but it enables us to be more intelligent about its character. What is true for individual values is true for group values. The whole of modern anthropology consists in removing the shock of difference, when one value system is confronted with another, by providing the cultural and historical perspectives within which both are surveyed—not rationalized—as responses to some need. One of the differences between moral insularity and parochialism on the one hand, and moral sophistication and wisdom on the other, is that the latter is aware of the conditions out of which values grow. We may not countenance these values when we have such knowledge; but we at least are not completely baffled by them. We know what they are an outgrowth of and response to.

(b) Value judgments are understood not only through knowledge of their origins and causes but through knowledge of their structural interrelations. What does it mean to say that an action is "courageous," "loyal," or "just"? Each value has a quality that we experience as specifically its own, but the meaning of the quality is enriched by the perception of the relations it bears to other values. Values come in clusters and constellations. They supplement and complement each other like colors. The *interpretation* of the nature of the relations between values may depend upon conflicting theories of their ontological, psychological, and social status. But the *ex-*

*istence* of these relations has been recognized by thinkers as far apart as Aristotle and Pascal, Scheler and Dewey. Because these relationships are general, they are never sufficient in enabling us to grasp the meaning of the value qualities in any specific situation. Nonetheless, they contribute to enlarging our understanding and sharpening our perceptions in particular cases. When we are familiar with the ways in which values call to values, we know what to look for, what to reinforce or guard against, what to affirm or reject.

We have called this immanent relationship between values logical. It might just as well be called dramatic. For it involves the conflict and clash or reinforcement and support of human attitudes as they develop in time. This development is funded in the meanings of the values. The analysis of value relations therefore discloses something significant about the history and nature of men.

(c) The third avenue to an understanding of values is perhaps the most important. It consists in grasping the consequences of judgments proposing that something should be done, anticipating their effects on the original difficulties which set the problem of moral choice, and noting their bearing upon other values to which we are implicitly committed. To ignore or discount the consequences of a proposed course of conduct is the mark of fanaticism. And even fanatics often pretend that they have taken the costs of their actions into consideration. But these other values to which we are committed—are they not finally valid independent of consequences? No—they can be challenged, too, if a problem arises about them. And if we take our problems, as we should, one at a time, and remember that a moral problem is created not merely by asking a question but by discovering an objective difficulty in a concrete situation, we avoid narrow circularity and a vicious infinite regress. Whether life is worth living is a serious and legitimate question under certain circumstances when honor or health are at stake, but it is frivolous to introduce it as if it were necessarily involved in every moral problem that arises. Those who believe that all value deliberation *must* at some point anchor itself to ultimate or intrinsic values which are beyond all possibility of scientific validation are as mistaken as those who hold that scientific judgments of fact *must* be based upon incontrovertible first truths for which no evidence can be given.[1]

The advantages of this approach to value judgments are independent of the specific analysis of the nature of value judgments. Whether we consider them as descriptions in the indicative mood, or commands in the imperative mood, or wishes in the optative mood, is not as important as that we should be able to answer the question "*Why?*" about them and uncover the nexus of relations, of causes and consequences, which makes one judgment, command, or wish more reasonable than another.

This does not in the least deny that there is a distinction between our knowledge of what it is right to do and our attitude toward the doing of it. Many who are aware of the injustice of racial discrimination are unable to liberate themselves from what they admit to be unfounded prejudice. The problem of inducing a change in attitude, of bridging the gap between recognition of moral truth and practical acceptance, is a perennial and basic educational task. Modern psychology has contributed powerful techniques of effecting voluntary persuasion that bear on this problem. But the point I wish to stress is that the transformation of attitude, no matter how subtly undertaken, is logically completely subordinate to the discovery of moral truth. Otherwise we have not risen above the level of non-rational indoctrination.

Nor am I denying that a legitimate distinction can be drawn between the judgments of fact and the judgments of value based upon them. But the stress should be placed upon their interrelation in any specific problem of evaluation, and above all on the method by which evaluations are justified. Whether this method is called "critical," "scientific," "experimental," or "rational" is a matter of indifference. The significant issue is whether in reaching conclusions regarded as true in considering questions of value we depart from the basic pattern observable in reaching conclusions regarded as true in considering questions of fact.

One fundamental cleavage on this point is between those who believe that moral statements are really not cognitive assertions at all and those who believe they are. The first denies that the term "truth" has any intelligible meaning when applied to moral statements. But they exempt all moral judgments which can be construed as instrumental or purposive and limit their taboo only to statements concerning "ultimate" or "intrinsic" values. For educational uses there is a sufficient margin of agreement between these two philosophical schools as to what can be investigated and what not, to justify a common procedure. For as we have seen it is one of the hypotheses of the experimentalists that all statements which invoke "ultimate" values will be found to be instrumental or purposive in concrete situations involving other values.

Another fundamental cleavage divides those who believe that value statements are cognitive. The first maintain that the pattern of confirmation is, in essentials, the same as that which obtains in scientific inquiry. The second asserts that the pattern is different; that a "scientific" inquiry into values is relevant only to the contexts of values, not to their essential qualities; and that these are authenticated by a direct intuitive grasp. The opposition between these two approaches is unbridgeable on a theoretical level. Nonetheless, here too a theoretical impasse need not hold up educational co-operation. Practice can be based on a minimum agreement. Supernaturalists, traditionalists and a priorists in insisting that *something more* is required than investigation into causes, structure, and consequences of values need not necessarily be opposed to such investigation. If it doesn't take us far enough there will be sufficient opportunity to try other methods. But a *beginning* can be made with such investigation without prejudging the theoretical issue. Those who believe that one common pattern of inquiry operates in all fields of investigation will be content to abide by the educative effects of the investigation they propose. All they ask is that the obstacles to such investigation be removed, and that it be wholeheartedly undertaken in fields in which it has hitherto been taboo.

It must be frankly recognized that this proposal is not innocent and that it will be fought tooth and nail by groups who hold to beliefs that are allegedly inaccessible to investigation by critical method but which in actuality may be affected once the authority of method replaces the authority of creed—religious, social, or political. Surely there is an inconsistency in maintaining that certain truths are beyond reach of, or comparison with, truths established by scientific method, and refusing to permit them to be investigated scientifically. For by definition they cannot be imperilled by this approach. Such opposition raises the suspicion that these beliefs may in fact be invalid and that those who are fearful of the *attempt* to approach them scientifically are fearful of their possible invalidity.

If we conceive of science, as John Dewey has suggested, in terms of methods of dealing with subject matter instead of uniform traits of subject matter, we can establish the living bond between the scientific and liberal spirit. This lies not in the methods of physics, or the methods of the humanities, but in the method of intelligence which uses the devices and techniques appropriate to specific subject matters. Method is central in a liberal philosophy as in science because it undercuts the absolutisms that would arrest the flow of new knowledge and new insights. Method should be central in educational activity because it not only evaluates the funded tradition of the past but enhances the capacity to enrich it. This is the meaning of liberalism in education. "Like science," writes Morris R. Cohen, "liberalism insists on a critical examination of the content of all our beliefs, principles, or initial hypotheses and on submitting them to a continuous process of verification so that they will be progressively better founded in experience and reason."[2]

---

THOMAS F. GREEN

# JUDGING

---

## THE ANALYSIS: ASSESSING, JUDGING, AND KNOWING

The term "judgment" is used in at least two ways. In the eighteenth century, and still sometimes in our own, logicians used the term "judgment" as synonymous with "assertion," "statement," or "proposition." The three topics of classical logic were "terms," "judgments," and "arguments." But "judgment" is used also to refer not simply to propositions or statements but to a certain capacity of human beings. We say, for example, "He has good judgment" or "He is a man of good judgment," and in this kind of assertion we are not commenting on a proposition or statement but on a human capability. Good judgment, in this sense, is a kind of wisdom. But this kind of wisdom, this ability to judge well, is usually displayed by a person in the assertions he makes. Thus, we use the term "judgment" both to designate a kind of human activity or capacity and also to refer to the assertions or statements through which this activity or capacity is expressed.

### Judgment as a Part of Teaching and as an Aim of Teaching

There can be no doubt that the exercise of judgment is among the activities included in teaching. Teachers must make judgments almost daily concerning the effects of their actions on other people, the relative merits of different performances among students, and the relative importance of different topics to be discussed. Nearly

---

From *The Activities of Teaching* by Thomas F. Green. Copyright © 1971 by McGraw-Hill, Inc. Used with permission of McGraw-Hill Book Company.

every decision a teacher makes reflects his capacity for good judgment. Moreover, there can be little doubt that one of the aims of education must be to develop in young people the capacity to judge well. There is hardly a skill taught in the school that does not involve the capacity to make discriminating judgments. Even learning the use of one's own language, for example, requires not only a capacity to make discriminating judgments about good and bad speech according to certain rules and principles; it also involves the capacity to decide what is better or worse and more or less appropriate. It involves, in short, the development of good taste. In one sense of "taste," the development of good taste is simply the development of the capacity to make such discriminating judgments. Thus, one of the activities inescapably involved in teaching is the exercise of the human capacity for judgment, and one of the pervasive goals of education must be the development of that capacity. How can we describe this activity? How can we get some clearer grasp of its nature and of what is involved in its cultivation?

Let us begin as before. Let us consider how it is that we sometimes use the concepts "judge" and "judgment" in ordinary and noneducational contexts. We might speak of a person as a good or bad judge, or as exercising good judgment, in respect to a variety of matters. A person, for example, may be

1. a good judge of wine
2. a poor judge of distance
3. a good judge of character
4. an equitable judge between disputants
5. a good judge of horses.

In some of these examples, judging involves ranking or grading; in some, estimating; and in others, predicting. The first and last examples are clearly cases of ranking or grading. The chief difference between judging wine, on the one hand, and judging horses, on the other, may lie in the exactness and precision with which the standards for ranking are formulated. In judging horses, there are some fairly explicit standards against which a knowledgeable judge will make his ranking. For example, in judging palomino horses, one standard is that the horse must be neither two shades lighter nor darker than a newly minted gold piece. Despite its vagueness, this is probably a more precisely drawn and objective standard than it is possible to formulate in judging wines. But the point, in any case, is that whatever the standards for judgment may be, our first and final examples are both instances of judging in the sense of ranking. And it is clear in both instances that acquiring a capacity to judge in this sense involves learning the standards against which judgments should be made.

The second example is a clear case of estimating; and the third, an example of predicting. To judge distances is to estimate, usually according to some rule of thumb or according to past successes and failures in estimating distances. To judge character is similarly to predict behavior, and such predictions are usually formulated according to some folk wisdom or other experience accumulated in trying to type men and foresee the kinds of behavior one might expect from them.

A banker, for example, must be a good judge of character when he considers making a loan. He must rely upon his past experience with other men, as well as upon past records of the particular borrower in question, and thus arrive at a judgment as to whether the man is reliable.

Our fourth example is somewhat more complex since it may require knowledge not only of human character but also of some commonly received rules or principles of equity. Judging equitably between disputants involves not only a wisdom about human character but also of some wisdom in applying the standards of justice and fairness. That is what makes our fourth example somewhat different from the others. It requires not simply ranking and estimating but being fair or just.

Nonetheless, for all of their differences, each of these cases illustrates the fact that the terms "judge," "judgment," and "judging" imply the application of some standards, grounds, reasons, or principles in predicting, estimating, ranking, or adjudicating. In many other respects, these activities are all quite different; but in this one respect—that they involve standards, grounds, or reasons—they are quite alike.


Judging Contrasted with Guessing

The second point is a negative one. It has to do with what judgment is not. A judgment is not a *mere* guess, hunch, or conjecture. One of the salient features of a mere guess, hunch, or conjecture is that it is groundless or very nearly groundless. This observation rests upon a perfectly normal and familiar distinction between a guess and a *mere* guess. We might give reasons for guessing that this whiskey is better than that one, but when we cannot give *any* reasons, then we say we have made a mere guess, however right it may be. It would be natural in such circumstances for a person to say, "I cannot really give a judgment; I can only guess." And this way of speaking suggests that we often contrast judging and guessing in relation to the grounds for judgment at our disposal.

For example, we would not say a person was making judgments of distances or character if his opinion was groundless and he could offer no evidence in the form of past experiences or any standards, however rough, on which to base his statement. We would not say that a man is a good judge of horses if he ranked them without recourse to any standards or principles and could offer no grounds for his decisions. When he nevertheless announces a decision, in that sense no doubt he renders a judgment. But that his pronouncement is the consequence of exercising judgment can certainly be questioned. We would say that his ranking is the expression not of judgment but of a guess. And a judge of horses who behaved in that fashion would be quickly disqualified. The concept of judgment, in short, is more closely related to the demand for grounds, reasons, standards, or evidence than is the notion of a mere guess or hunch. In that respect, judging is opposed to guessing. Judging and guessing are different things.

Judging in the Absence of Knowledge

But if the exercise of judgment is opposed to guessing by its stronger relation to grounds or reasons, then what shall we say when the grounds or reasons are decisive? When we are wholly without any grounds for ranking, estimating, or predicting, then we cannot be said to be in a position to render a judgment. But conversely, when our grounds or evidence are conclusive, then we do not need to render a judgment. In short, if the exercise of judgment is opposed to guessing in one respect, then it is opposed to a state of certitude or knowledge in another respect. We might think of these three concepts—guessing, judging, and knowing—as distributed on a continuum representing different degrees of certitude.

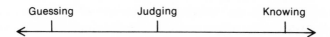

Think, for example, of the contest that until recently was so popular at county fairs, and consider the following directions:

1. Judge how many beans are in the jar.
2. Guess how many beans are in the jar.

Do these directions order you to do two different things? The answer to that question depends upon whether it makes any difference to one's procedure that he has some relevant knowledge of the volume of jars and the average size of beans. If I have some such knowledge, then I can arrive at an estimate, and if someone were to ask how I arrived at my judgment, I could give a method. On the other hand, if someone asked me how I arrived at my entry, I might answer, "I just guessed," and that reply would be taken to mean that I had not exercised judgment. But the interesting thing about this contest is that the prize goes to the person whose entry is most nearly correct, and this presupposes that there are circumstances in which one does not have to exercise judgment. One can pour the beans out on the table and count. Moreover, one can count without error. Thus, no entry can be allowed which is arrived at by actually counting all the beans. The person who does that cannot render a judgment, for he knows how many there are. Indeed, you could not have this contest at all were it not for the fact that there are circumstances in which judgment, being replaced by knowledge, is no longer required. The need to judge is replaced by counting. "Count all the beans in the jar, and then give me your judgment as to how many there are!" This kind of order makes sense only if counting is *not* regarded as offering certainty to the correct number.

It is easy to judge whether a rug is small enough to go in a certain room. But it is difficult to judge whether it is 12 feet and 1 inch long or 12 feet and 2 inches. Fortunately, we do not have to judge because we can know. We can measure. And so it is also with judgments of ranking or judgments of predicting. Just as we cannot exercise judgment in the total absence of reasons or grounds, so we do not *need* to exercise it when our grounds or reasons are conclusive. The concept of judgment as a human capacity, at least in relation to grounds or evidence, falls somewhere between a guess or hunch, on the one hand, and absolute certainty on the other. We might summarize these observations in the following general principle. *To exercise good judgment is to get optimum results under less than optimum conditions or on grounds which are less than decisive.* That is to say, good judgment is the capacity to maximize the accuracy of one's estimates, ranking, or predictions under conditions where knowledge is either unattainable or inaccessible. It follows from this that good judgment is never exercised when one's grounds for decision are conclusive, but neither is it exercised apart from some grounds or reasons.

Judgments, then, are truth claims made in the absence of conclusive grounds. This is one reason why we are often inclined to relate good judgment in practical affairs to a kind of wisdom. This point is especially important for the administrator or the policymaker, but it is also important in everyone's moral life. Policies, administrative decisions, and just plain moral choices are almost never made with sufficient knowledge to determine what the correct choice may be. The policy-maker never has all the information he needs. He must make choices and take action in the absence of enough information. In political affairs, policy formulation, and moral decisions as well, what is required is not certitude as to the right course of action but wise judgment in the absence of such knowledge. Aristotle understood this well. He recognized that the exercise of what he called phronesis, practical wisdom, was central to both politics and morality. Phronesis, according to Aristotle, was one of the intellectual virtues, and it was simultaneously a necessary ingredient in the exercise of any of the moral virtues and was incapable of being exercised independently of the moral virtues. He recognized, in short, that practical judgment is central to both politics and morality.

Good judgment, then, is a kind of practical wisdom, a sort of sixth sense. A banker who loans money might do so on the basis of his judgments about the character of people. If he is a good judge of character, then he manifests a kind of wisdom based upon insight and a considerable body of past experience. Making such predictions about character, about what you may reasonably expect this or that man to do in the future, can never be done with all the evidence in. But neither are such judgments made apart from all evidence. People who manifest good judgment in matters of character can almost always offer grounds for their judgments, though rarely enough evidence to make them indisputable.

Judgments, therefore, cannot be subjective. They are never subjective in the sense of having sole reference to the feelings, preferences, or subjective states of the speaker. They are never subjective in the sense that statements about one's feelings, preferences, and dispositions are subjective. They are always objective in the sense that they rest upon reasons, grounds, rules, or principles. But the grounds of judgment are never conclusive, and therefore it is perfectly possible for different men to give different judgments on the same matter and even in relation to the same grounds; and it may also be the case that such different judgments are equally reasonable. This point is immensely important in education. The fact that reasonable men may differ in matters of judgment is often construed by teachers as evidence that certain kinds of judgments are subjective or that, as opposed to judgments of fact, they are merely expressions of opinion. Nothing could be further from the truth. The fact that reasonable men may differ in their judgments does not imply that they are merely expressing some personal preference or a mere groundless opinion. It implies only that the subject matter of their views is appropriate for judgment rather than knowledge. Nor does it imply that in such matters any man's opinion is as good as another's. Clearly, there is a difference between discerning judgments and mere flippant or casual opinions; and that difference is roughly the same as the contrast between making a judgment and offering a mere guess or hunch. Good judgment, then, is always an expression of practical wisdom. Such judgments are always objective in the sense that they rest upon evidence, reasons, standards, or some other kinds of grounds. Like statements of probability, judgments have implicit reference to grounds or evidence.


Preferences and Value Judgments

These observations bear upon two perpetual and pervasive problems of education. The first has to do with the way we try to teach matters of appreciation, taste, or artistic sense. The second has to do with the much larger problem of how to teach values. Each of these is an enormously complex topic. In a brief and introductory exploration, we cannot hope to do more than suggest some questions and reveal some problems for further investigation. For this reason, it may be well to treat the two topics as one and to consider the matter of teaching taste as an example of what we might find in a more carefully wrought study of teaching values.

Consider the phrase "value judgment" as a special case of what we have been studying under the more general heading of "judgment." If we attend carefully to what is being said around us when people speak of value judgments, we will discover that the phrase is often used to refer to expressions of opinion that are purely subjective. From this popular perspective, a value judgment is an expression of a settled opinion which is beyond the reach of reasonable argument. It is an expression of purely individual likings, preferences, or subjective feelings. For example, when students are discussing the relative merits of a work of art, a particular social practice, or a proposed course of action, it often happens that an evaluative remark will be greeted with the comment, "Well, that's just a value judgment." The remark is an irrefutable argument-stopper. The implication is that value judgments are of an inferior sort and cannot be discussed among reasonable men. Sometimes, indeed, it seems that to advance a value judgment for serious consideration is to commit a kind of faux pas analogous to a violation of common courtesy. We are all supposed to know that values differ from man to man; and we learn early that it is a sign of an emancipated mind to recognize the fact and learn to live with such differences without expecting to find any rational procedure for discussing, to say nothing of surmounting, them.

When I inform you that I like asparagus and you counter with the statement that you do not, there is really no dispute between us. I cannot hope to demonstrate to you that you are wrong since there is no question here of being correct or incorrect. It is true that I like asparagus, but that is not a truth in any way contradicted by the truth that you do not. Do not ask me why I like asparagus, on what grounds or for what reasons. The request for reasons does not make sense. We are concerned here purely with a matter of personal preference. The difference between us on this important matter of asparagus is not a difference of belief or of knowledge and therefore cannot be discussed as though it were. Philosophers are disposed to express this fact by saying that the difference between us is noncognitive. I pity you, dear reader, for your aversion to asparagus, but I must be content in my pity, perhaps with the hope that you may someday acquire a more mature taste for the good things in life. There is an ancient saying, *de gustibus non disputandum est*—there is no disputing taste. This saying is true, at least in matters like our differences about asparagus.

The popular view about value judgments—what I shall call the view of the amateur philosopher—is that they are all noncognitive, all like my statement expressing a liking for asparagus. Our analysis of the activity of judging, however, would suggest that value judgments are not like that at all. Imagine a person who goes into an art gallery, looks at a painting, and says, "I don't know anything about art, but I know what I like, and I don't like that." According to our amateur view, that is a value judgment. But according to the analysis up to this point, such a remark does not constitute a judgment at all, much less a value judgment. Such a comment tells us a great deal about the speaker. It tells us, for example, that he has an intense distaste for a certain painting, but it tells us nothing whatever about the painting. Such a remark renders no judgment about the painting at all. It is as though, like Lucy, he simply threw up his arms and said A-A-A-A-A-G-H! As such, it is not a statement about the work of art, nor is it even about his feelings toward it. It is, instead, an *expression of* those feelings. A value judgment, however, is not the same thing as an expression of preference, liking, or subjective feeling.


Judgments of Value and Judgments of Taste

In one sense of "taste" it is true that there is no disputing taste; but in another sense of "taste" it is not true. When I say, "My taste tells me that the sauce is salty" or "The sauce tastes salty to me," I am using the word *taste* in a sense that does not admit of dispute. But when I say, "It is bad taste to wear that kind of coat with those trousers" or "It is bad taste to wear shorts to a drawing-room concert," I am using *taste* in a way that deals with judgments and which therefore makes implicit reference to standards. Such judgments are in the nature of rankings and are related to grounds, reasons, or standards. They express more than a mere preference or a mere report of my own feelings or sensations. Such judgments can be debated, and honest men may differ with respect to them. A judgment, we have said, is a truth claim made in the absence of decisive grounds in circumstances where decisive grounds are not attainable. There is a sense of "taste" in which good taste is simply the capacity to make discriminating judgments in this sense of "judgment." A man of good taste is simply a man who is able to make discriminating judgments about good food, good art, adornment, and so forth. Indeed, it makes no sense to suppose that a person makes discriminating judgments of art, dress, decoration, and so forth, and at the same time to suppose that he does not have good taste. Having good taste in this sense is not the same thing as simply liking or preferring good things; it involves also the capacity to make discriminating judgments. Indeed, a man's judgment might lead him to a high evaluation of a work of art, and yet it need not follow that he will like it. For example, one might appraise the Grunewald Isenheim altarpiece as a great work, yet one could hardly *like* it.

There may be, and in fact are, people of good taste who like bad movies, who find them entertaining and funny and yet would not commend them as good comedy. The point is that good artistic judgment—which after all is a kind of value judgment—is conceptually distinct from liking or mere preferring. Whether one's judgment is an expression of good taste will depend upon the grounds for his judgment. Indeed, whether it is a judgment at all will depend upon whether it rests upon some grounds. And if it makes sense at all to speak of the grounds for a value judgment in art, it follows that such judgments are not mere expressions of preference or of subjective feeling. It is incumbent upon a critic of art or an evaluator of art to address himself to the art he is appraising; he must point to the successes and failures he finds in it and not simply to his feelings about it. It is the work, after all, that is to be appraised, and not the attitudes or sentiments of the critic.

We should not expect artistic judges to agree in their estimates of artistic works any more than we would expect horse judges to agree in ranking animals or bankers to agree in their estimates of character. The fact that they do not agree does not mean that their judgments are subjective in the sense in which my affection for asparagus is subjective. Nor does it mean that the standards of judgment are hopelessly subjective. In painting, for example, there are certain principles of design, of color, of rest and unrest which are used, which can be studied and learned, and which constitute in large measure the communicative language of the artist. We can understand these conventions and learn to judge in relation to them. For example, we learn the language of the cinema with its "wipes" and "fades." The "dissolve," used in a motion picture to indicate a time lapse, is such a convention. To learn the language of the medium is part of what is involved in acquiring good taste. The use of these conventions enters into the formulation of standards of judgment. And formulating judgments that appeal to those conventions, under the tutelage of creative and more experienced judges, is one of the ways we learn the art of making such judgments. As Aristotle would put it, we learn to make such judgments by making them ourselves. Sometimes we witness differences among judges concerning the standards and conventions. But even in the case of popular or folk culture, such disputes usually occur among the experts and the artists themselves, and what we see emerging in the controversy is a refinement of old conventions, a new application of them, or even an addition to the grounds or standards of artistic judgment.

The point I wish to stress, in any case, is that *in this sense*, value judgments are never subjective if they are genuine judgments; and, therefore, good taste can be taught. Teaching good taste is much like teaching good judgment in any other field with its implicit reference to grounds, evidence, or reasons; and success in such teaching involves transmitting the special standards or communicative conventions appropriate to the sphere of activity within which the judgments are to be made. The fact that men's judgments in relation to values frequently differ does not mean that their judgments are beyond the reach of argument or dispute, nor does it mean that the capacity to make such judgments is something that cannot be taught. It does not mean that their differences are non-cognitive or that teachers who attempt to teach good taste are simply imposing their own opinions. Sometimes they are; but often they are not. Rather, the fact that men differ in such judgments means only that their appraisals are, in fact, judgments—having neither the subjectivity of mere preferences, nor the certainty of knowledge, nor the insubstantial quality of a mere guess.

Preferences and Judgments Related

Nonetheless, there is a close relation between aesthetic and moral judgments on the one hand and preferences, favorings, and likings on the other. Arthur Murphy, in a gentle dig at the "cinematic aesthetes," once remarked that the measure of one's aesthetic sophistication seemed to be to like as little as possible.[1] It is impossible to maintain a rigorous and thorough separation between value judgments and expressions of preference or mere personal likings. We would not know what to make of a person who showed discriminating judgment in matters of art and adornment and yet never liked what he judged good. Although liking and judging are not the same thing, they are nonetheless closely related. We would not know what a person was talking about who judged a series of works as excellent and yet displayed an obvious dislike for them. Such behavior would be like regarding an act as benevolent, good, and noble and then urging its punishment. No matter how discriminating his judgment, we would not say that a person had good taste if he manifested utter dislike for everything he judged good.

Why is there this close connection between liking or favoring on the one hand and rendering judgments of value on the other? We must consider this question more carefully, because it relates directly to what is involved in teaching discrimination in matters of value. Up to this point, I have been concerned to show that what we mean by a value judgment is conceptually distinct from what we mean by an expression of feeling, preference, or favoring. Now I seem to be claiming, nonetheless, that feelings, preferences, and favorings are conveyed in value judgments. Isn't that contradictory? Not really. The point is that, so far, I have chosen to focus upon the term "judgment" in the phrase "value judgment." I have been arguing—or rather, assuming up to now—that value judgments are a special class of judgments. They are judgments of value, but judgments nonetheless, and, therefore, they share the basic features of other judgments in the sense of estimates, rankings, or predictions. But now I want to focus attention upon the term "value" in the phrase "value judgment." Insofar as value judgments are judgments, they are implicitly grounded in reasons, standards, evidence, or grounds of some kind and are not essentially expressions of liking, preference, or favorings. But insofar as they are judgments of *value*, they are closely related to favorings, likings, and preferences.

Judgments of Appraisal and Judgments of Bestowal

Perhaps the point can be made more clearly if we attend to a further distinction between valuation or prizing, on the one hand, and evaluation or appraising, on the other. The difference is that an appraisal or evaluation is always a judgment in the sense of "judgment" we have been discussing. But a prizing or valuation is not. An act of appraisal is an estimate of a thing's value, but an act of prizing a bestowal of value on a thing. When you take a piece of fine jewelry to a craftsman for an appraisal, you are asking for his expert judgment of its worth. He must examine the craftsmanship, the materials, the quality of the stones and setting, compare it with other similar works, and then arrive at an estimate of its worth. Futhermore, he could provide grounds, reasons, or evidence for his judgment. You would not want a mere guess. Nor would you expect certitude. In short, he must render a judgment. But when you then turn away and say, "Nonetheless, it is worth the world to me" or "Despite its small value, it is precious," then you are expressing a prizing rather than an appraisal. You have indicated not what value it has as a matter of objective and public judgment but what value you bestow upon it as a possession. You are expressing a preference, feeling, attitude, or favoring. Appraisal, then, is a matter of judgment; but prizing, we might say, is a matter of love. Prizing, then, is not so much a skill one learns to perform as it is an attitude one learns to feel.

If we keep in mind the difference between these two things —prizing and appraising—then we can formulate some useful observations as to why, on the one hand, value judgments are unrelated to mere likings, preference, or favorings, and why, on the other hand, they are in a sense related. Value judgments are appraisals insofar as they are judgments. But it is also one of the functions of value judgments to express our prizings and to commend those prizings to others. Indeed, the most straightforward—and, regrettably, the most general—formulation of our aim in teaching values is to bring about a state in which one prizes those things which, according to competent appraisal, have worth. Indeed, one who has attained that objective is precisely what we normally mean by an expert in matters of taste. He is a man who can make discriminating and accurate judgments; that is, appraisals. But he is also a person who has learned to prize what, according to his appraisals, has worth. Hence, his value judgments will be simultaneously an expression of his judgment and an expression of his prizings. They will be both expressions of his judgments based upon grounds or reasons and also expressions of his preferences, likes, or favorings. Thus, the man who says, "I don't know anything about art, but I know what I like, and I don't like that!"—is not expressing a value *judgment* at all. He is expressing a personal valuation. But if he is to acquire what we commonly recognize as good taste, he must attain the capacity to make appraisals as well as prizings. He must be able to say, "That is a bad piece of art because . . . ."

In teaching values in general, and good taste in particular, appraisal and prizing are closely related. It might be argued that, though prizing can be learned, nonetheless it cannot be taught. But surely there can be no doubt that appraisal—the capacity to make discriminating judgments of value—can be taught or that such a capacity is fundamental to good taste, morality, and political judgment and is a good start toward shaping preferences and prizings. It seems to me, moreover, that those who retreat from dealings with value judgments in their teaching on the grounds that they are always expressions of mere opinion are wrong in their understanding of judgment and too timid in their view of the limits of teaching. Surely to omit from the precinct of teaching any concern with the formation of judgment on the grounds that it deals with opinion instead of knowledge is to perform the most disastrous surgery. It is to make teaching a dead thing and to remove from the corpus of education its very soul. For good judgment is crucial to the moral and social life of men, and good taste is essential to its excellence.

THE METHOD: THE USES OF LANGUAGE

In these chapters, the claim has been repeated—and exemplified —that language is a tool. It is a marvelously complex instrument that can be used in many ways. The underlying principle has been that the meaning of a term is its use. We identify its meaning by describing the way in which it is used. Similar remarks may be made about sentences or more extended units of linguistic expressions; they too must be understood in relation to their use. The attempt to develop a systematic account of precisely *how* words and sentences mean is the proper subject matter of the philosophy of language. A full and orderly treatment of those topics is impossible within the limits of these brief methodological discussions. But we cannot avoid them altogether, for the study of how words and sentences mean is so basic to our thinking that it must figure prominently in shaping not only how we think but what we think about. For example, the natures of metaphor, vagueness, and ambiguity must become topics of interest in their own right because they so strongly influence the ways we think about other concepts of more direct concern to the philosophy of education. And so attention to the uses of language becomes of interest not simply because it influences how we think about educational concepts. It becomes a central substantive topic of philosophy itself. Philosophy is peculiar in that it is one of the few areas of inquiry in which the methods of study become themselves part of the subject for study.

The analytic essay in this chapter illustrates the point rather well. It began with a study of a certain concept—the concept of "judgment." The initial point of study was the use of a certain term—"judgment." But the essay then moved on to the somewhat different question as to how certain kinds of judgments or quasi-judgments are really used to express feeling, emotions, or preferences rather than to render judgments. At other times, language is used not to render judgments, but to commend some attitude to another person. The direction of the argument, on the whole, was to show that the failure to recognize these different uses of language is itself the source of much confusion about value judgments and consequently about what can or cannot be taught. The capacity to recognize different uses of language is, therefore, an important tool for the analyst; and setting forth the features of those different uses becomes a significant topic for philosophical analysis.

The distinctions important for our purposes can be gathered together under two headings—the informative and directive uses of language, and the emotive or expressive uses of language. In gathering the uses of language under these headings, there is no need that the categories be either exhaustive or mutually exclusive. Once we get used to the idea that language is a tool, we may be able to think of ways to use that tool that are not included in these distinctions. Moreover, the fact that someone is using language in one of these ways need not exclude the possibility that he is using it also and at the same time in another way. It will often happen that in the same linguistic context the user of language will mix these categories. Language may be simultaneously informative, directive, and emotive. The purpose in distinguishing the uses of language is not to formulate rigorous principles of classification but to provide us with useful questions. In any context of analysis we want to be able to ask, "Is the language expressive, informative, directive, or what?" because the answer to that question will lead to somewhat different modes of analysis. To have added some such useful questions may be as much of a methodological gain as can be expected from any of these illustrative studies.

## Informative Language and Directive Language

The essential distinction is simple. Sometimes language is used primarily to inform and at other times primarily to direct people to do something. The important differences between these uses of language can be formulated in three basic points. First, language in the informative mode is always truth-functional; language in the directive mode is not. Secondly, language in the informative mode is typically expressible in the indicative mood; language in the directive mode is usually expressible in the imperative mood. Thirdly, language in the informative mode is always factual; language in the directive mode is nonfactual.

Let us consider each of these points. By saying that a certain use of language is always truth-functional we mean simply that, no matter what may be expressible in that mode of language, we can always ask whether it is true or false. That is a sensible question to ask about some utterances but not about others. Some utterances are truth-functional, and some are not. Consider the following:

1. My shirt is torn.
2. I ordered my steak rare.
3. The steak is well done.
4. Tomorrow will be a sunny day.
5. The cube root of 27 is 3.

In any usual context in which one of these statements might be used, we could ask whether the statement is true or whether it is false. Such assertions are truth-functional. They are uses of language in the informative mode. Consider, however, the following parallel examples:

6. Mend my shirt.
7. Bring me a rare steak.
8. Take the steak back.
9. Get out your bikini.
10. Find the cube root of 27.

We cannot ask whether any of these utterances is true or false. The question makes no sense. They are directive utterances.

I do not wish to suggest that a particular utterance is directive because it is not truth-functional. I mean to suggest the contrary. *If* a particular utterance is directive, *then* it will not be truth-functional. There are other non-truth-functional uses of language besides the directive mode. The point can be framed exactly if we make use of the technical formulas set forth in Chapter 5. The fact that a particular utterance is in the directive mode is a sufficient condition for concluding that it is not truth-functional. But the fact that a particular utterance is not truth-functional is not a sufficient condition for concluding that it is a directive use of language.

In these illustrations, I have drawn a somewhat more rigorous contrast than is typically the case. The clarity of the contrast arises primarily because I have taken examples in the indicative mood and for each have provided a parallel utterance in the imperative mood. For each declarative sentence, I have framed a parallel command. That is the clearest and most extreme form in which the difference between informative and directive uses of language can be shown. But consider the following example. We are in a restaurant. The meal is over, but the waitress is nowhere is sight. So I call the hostess and ask her, "Please get me another cup of coffee." That is an assertion in the directive mode. She then locates the waitress and tells her, "He wants another cup of coffee." That is an assertion in the informative mode. But even though the latter assertion is informative, the point of it is to direct the waitress to do something. That is, an assertion in the informative mode is being used as a directive tool.

One might argue that there is a kind of suppressed premise in the situation. The hostess is really telling the waitress, "He wants another cup of coffee. He is your customer. Get him one." Then the directive purpose of her comment is clear and explicit. It results in an utterance in the imperative mood. Similarly, I might tell my wife that my shirt is torn, and it may be that all I intend is to let her know that fact. But it could also be that such a remark, ostensibly in the informative mode of discourse, is in fact only a domesticated way of saying, "Mend it."

Whenever we set out to examine a certain type of language, we need to view the context and fathom the purpose. Language is a tool. How is the tool being used? We need to ask, "Is the language informative or directive in purpose?" This is a particularly important question when we wish to consider the kind of language involved in such things as value judgments. What kind of language do such judgments contain? How are they being used? What are they being used for? The reason we need to ask such questions is that if the language is strictly informative, then considerations of truth and falsity are relevant. If value judgments, for example, are that kind of tool (which they clearly are to some extent), then they can be debated (or debated to some extent). If their purpose is directive (as it clearly is to some extent), then such considerations are not relevant. If the use of language is informative, then we want to know what the facts are. Is the claim being made true, or is it false? But when the language is directive, we want to know whether the action recommended is a good one or a bad one. Should we do it or should we not? These are different kinds of questions, and they require different sorts of answer.

Finally, it is worth observing that the informative use of language is generally employed to communicate facts or information.

That is not the case with the directive use of language. There are, of course, mixed cases in which the communication of information is, in fact, directive in purpose. But I want to stress the point that by "information or facts" are meant not only contingent statements but also a priori claims as opposed to commands which are not, in the strict sense, assertions, propositions, or statements at all.

Emotive and Expressive Language

The assertion "It is wrong to kill" appears to be an instance of the informative use of language. Philosophers have sometimes argued, however, that the assertion is equivalent to the statement "Thou shalt not kill" or simply "Don't kill." Therefore, the statement "It is wrong to kill" is equivalent to a command and, consequently, can be neither true nor false. It follows that it can be neither true nor false that it is wrong to kill.

One way to attack this argument is as follows: We have seen that informative language can be used for a directive purpose. "My shirt is torn" means, in some sense, "Mend it." This insight might be reversed. Isn't it equally possible that an utterance framed as a command might be used to convey information? "Mend my shirt" tells my wife, "My shirt needs mending." "Get me a cup of coffee" will lead the hostess to report, "He wants a cup of coffee." We need to examine not simply the form of the sentence—whether it is indicative or imperative—but also its use. Thus, the fact that a sentence *expresses* a command does not imply that the sentence *is* a command.

This sort of argument was appealed to in the analytic essay on judgment. There it was argued that although value judgments may *express* our feelings, preferences, or desires, nonetheless they are not *expressions* of feelings, preferences, or desires. There is implicit in this kind of remark still another distinction in the uses of language. Consider the following locutions:

1. Oh, what a beautiful morning!
2. How can you possibly do a thing like that?
3. Eeeeeeeeeeek!
4. My God! My God! What has he done?

You will note immediately that none of these expressions is truth-functional. Nor is it ordinarily the case that expressions like these are directive. They are locutions of the sort that we use to give vent to our feelings of ecstasy, horror, fright, or despair. They are clear cases of language used to *express* our feelings or emotions. They are expressions of emotion or feeling in the same class with any number of physical and physilolgical expressions—the flushed face of anger or fear, the arms thrown up in despair, the beaming face and laughter of joy, the tears of love and of sorrow, and so forth. The only difference is that these particular expressions of emotion happen to take the form of linguistic utterances.

Here again I have taken prototypic cases of emotive or expressive language in order to make clear the logical type of linguistic entity we are trying to distinguish. It would be odd, however, if some expressions of emotion never appeared in other types of locutions. Language without feeling—what would that be like? It would not be what we know at all. Thus, when a person says during a meal, "This is a good steak—a really good steak," he is expressing his feelings or emotions. But it may be true that he is doing something else besides. He is commenting on the quality of the steak. That his remark is not simply an expression of feeling is evident in the fact that we can treat his remark as truth-functional. We could say that such a person is using expressive or emotive language; but it would be more accurate to say that, *among other things,* he is using language *in an emotive or expressive way.*

It is important to see the difference between using emotive or expressive language and using language in an emotive or expressive way. Consider the sentence "Today is Thursday." Ordinarily, without any special context painted in, we would be inclined to say that this sentence expresses a statement. It is language in the informative mode. It is either true or false. But suppose that someone utters that sentence as he rises on his wedding day, a day he has looked forward to all week long. In that case, "Today is Thursday" might be a way of saying, "Oh, what a beautiful morning!" The statement is truth-functional, but it can be used as an expression of emotion. Here is a case in which a person is not using emotive language, but he is using language in an emotive or expressive way. Or again, imagine a man who is judging meat. He might say, "This is a good steak—a really good steak!" and though we would understand how he felt about good meat and about this meat in particular, still we would be less inclined to say that he is simply expressing his feelings and more inclined to say that he is expressing an expert judgment on well-known technical criteria. Note, then, that the expressive or emotive use of language is identified not so much by a particular set of words or expressions as it is by a particular employment of a wide range of locutions. Still, the prototype of expressive or emotive language is found in those linguistic out-bursts and spontaneous locutions that we employ to give vent to our feelings and emotions.

We are now in a better position to see what was happening in the analytic essay at the beginning of this chapter. There is an expert view, related to what I called "the amateur view," according to which value judgments without exception are noncognitive. There are two forms of such a view. According to this view, statements of the form X is good" are to be analyzed as asserting: (i) "I approve of X" and (ii) "Do likewise." The two versions arise because the first of these statements can be understood in two different ways. On the one hand, the statement "I approve of X" can be interpreted as an assertion expressed in the informative mode of discourse. It is amenable to truth-functional treatment; but also, whether true or false, the statement will turn out to be a report of someone's feelings, attitudes, or dispositions. It is not a statement essentially about X itself. On the other hand, the statement "I approve of X" can be interpreted as a locution in the expressive or emotive mode of discourse in which case it is not truth-functional at all. It is, rather, an expression of a feeling, attitude, or disposition. Thus, in the one version, value judgments are analyzed as consisting of one part informative language about the subjective states or feelings of the speaker and one part directive language. In the other view, value judgments are analyzed as consisting of one part expressive language and one part directive language.

Allow me one more technical term before the point is made. In the essay on judgment the point was made that when the reports of two people on their respective preferences, likes, or feelings disagree, there is nonetheless no conflict between them. The fact that I like asparagus does not conflict with the fact that you do not. Each report, expressed in the informative mode of discourse, may be true, yet there is no question of truth at issue between the two claims. They do not conflict. This is part of what is meant when philosophers sometimes say that such reports, though truth-functional in the sense in which I defined that term, are nonetheless noncognitive. There is no point of knowledge or truth at stake between different reports of different people. Another part of what is meant is that expressive language or directive language, not being truth-functional, must also be noncognitive.

If we follow this line of reasoning, then we shall end with the view that value judgments, without exception, are noncognitive. There is no cognitive issue at stake between conflicting value claims. There are only differences of feeling, preference, or attitude. The issues are important; they belong largely to the philosophy of language. They have to do partly with trying to give appropriate weight to the different uses of language that enter into the formulation and use of value judgments. Instead of trying to meet the noncognitive view head on, I have tried to find a different way of viewing the problem. Value judgments of character, in aesthetics, in decorum, and to some extent in matters of policy are much more like judgments of other sorts than the noncognitive view would allow us to believe.

R. S. PETERS

# CONCRETE PRINCIPLES AND THE RATIONAL PASSIONS

## INTRODUCTION

In education content is crucial. There is some point in raising aloft the romantic banners of "development," "growth," and "discovery" when children are being bored or bullied. Romanticism is always valuable as a protest. But another sort of trouble starts when romantics themselves get into positions of authority and demand that children shall scamper around being "creative" and spontaneously "discovering" what it has taken civilized man centuries to understand. Some synthesis has to be worked out between established content and individual inventiveness. The basis for such a synthesis is to be found mainly in those public historically developed modes of experience whose immanent principles enable individuals to build up and revise an established content and to make something of themselves within it. In science, for instance, merely learning a lot of facts is a weariness of the spirit; but a Robinson Crusoe, untutored in a scientific tradition, could not ask a scientific question, let alone exhibit "creativity." Originality is possible only for those who have assimilated some content and mastered the mode of experience, with its immanent principles, by means of which this content has been established and repeatedly revised.

Reprinted by permission of the publishers from *Moral Education: Five Lectures.* Cambridge, Mass.: Harvard University Press, Copyright, 1970, by the President and Fellows of Harvard College.

The same sort of Hegelian progression is detectable in morality. "Morality" to many still conjures up a "code" prohibiting things relating to sex, stealing, and selfishness. The very word "code" suggests a body of rules, perhaps of an arbitrary sort, that all hang together but that have no rational basis. To others, however, morality suggests much more individualistic and romantic notions, such as criterionless choices, individual autonomy, and subjective preferences. Whether one experiences anguish in the attempt to be "authentic," produces one's commitment, like the white rabbit producing his watch from his waistcoat pocket, or proclaims, like Bertrand Russell, that one simply does not *like* the Nazis, the picture is roughly the same—that of the romantic protest. Synthesis must be sought by making explicit the mode of experience which has gradually enabled civilized people to distinguish what is a matter of morals from what is a matter of custom or law, and which has enabled them to revise and criticize the code in which they have been brought up, and gradually to stand on their own feet as autonomous moral beings. This they could never have done without a grasp of principles.

It is the details of this sort of snythesis that I propose to explore in this essay as a preliminary to discussing moral education; for it is no good talking about moral education until we have a more determinate conception of what is involved in being "moral." Because they are uncertain about this, many well-meaning parents and teachers are hamstrung in their attempts at moral education. If they incline toward the code conception, they tend to be authoritarian in their approach; if, on the other hand, they favor some variant of the romantic reaction, they may expect that children will go it alone and decide it all for themselves. A more adequate view of morality should reveal the proper place for both authority and self-directed learning in moral education. But I shall not have space to deal with details of such educational procedures in this essay—only to explore a middle road between these two extreme positions and to view the general contours of moral education from this vantagepoint.


THE FUNCTION OF PRINCIPLES

There are some, like Alasdair MacIntyre, who seem to hold that we have no middle way between allegiance to a surviving code and some kind of romantic protest. For, it is argued, moral terms such as "good" and "duty," once had determinate application within a close-knit society with clear-cut purposes and well-defined roles; but now, because of social change, they have broken adrift from these concrete moorings. A pale substitute is left in generalized notions such as "happiness" instead of concrete goals, and duty for duty's sake instead of duties connected with role performances that were manifestly related to the goals of the community. So we have a kind of moral schizophrenia in the form of irresolvable conflicts between "interest" and "duty" and no determinate criteria for applying these general notions, because their natural home has passed away. It is no wonder, on this view, that those who have not been brought up in one of the surviving tribalisms make such a fuss about commitment and criterionless choice; for there is nothing else except those ancient realities to get a grip on.

## The Emergence of a Rational Morality Based on Principles

But even if this is how concepts such as "good" and "duty" originated, why this nostalgic fixation on those stuffy, self-contained little communities, such as Sparta, where they could be unambiguously applied? Could not one be equally impressed by the Stoic concept of a citizen of the world, by the law of nations forged by the Roman jurisprudents, and by the labors of lawyers such as Grotius to hammer out laws of the sea against piracy? The point is that both science and a more rational, universalistic type of morality gradually emerged precisely because social change, economic expansion, and conquest led to a clash of codes and to conflict between competing views of the world. Men were led to reflect about which story about the world was true, which code was correct. In discussing and reflecting on these matters they came to accept higher order principles of a procedural sort for determining such questions.

MacIntyre, it is true, applauds those like Spinoza who drew attention to values connected with freedom and reason. He admits the supreme importance of truth-telling; he notes the massive consensus about basic rules for social living first emphasized by the natural law theorists, which H. L. Hart has recently revived as the cornerstone of a moral system. Why then is he so unimpressed by this consensus that he gives such a onesided presentation of the predicament of modern man? Mainly, so it seems, because an appeal to such principles and basic rules cannot give specific guidance to any individual who is perplexed about what he ought to do.

## Difficulties about Concrete Guidance

Two connected difficulties are incorporated in this type of objection to principles. The first, already mentioned, is that no concrete guidance can be provided by them for an individual who wants to know what he ought to do. This is usually illustrated by the case of the young man who came to Sartre wanting guidance about whether he should stay at home and look after his aged mother or go abroad and join the Free French. How could an appeal to principles help him? Well, surely he only had a problem because he already acknowledged duties connected with his status as a son and as a citizen. Would Sartre have said to him, "You have to decide this for yourself," if the alternative to joining the Free French had been presented as staying at home and accepting bribes from the Germans for information? And surely if what is claimed to be missing is a principle for deciding between these duties, there are principles which would rule out some reasons which he might give for pursuing one of the alternatives. Supposing, for instance, he said that he was inclined toward going abroad because he wanted to determine precisely the height of St. Paul's Cathedral. Would Sartre have applauded his exercise of criterionless choice?

The existentialist emphasis on "choice" is salutary, of course, in certain contexts. It is important, for instance, to stress man's general responsibility for the moral system which he accepts. This needs to be said against those who smugly assume that it is just there to be read off. It needs to be said, too, in the context of atrocities such as Belsen. It also emphasizes the extent to which character is destiny and the role which choices play in shaping the individual's character. In this kind of development, conflict situations are particularly important, and if fundamental principles conflict there is not much more that one can say than that the individual must make up his own mind or use his "judgment." But we do not decide on our fundamental principles such as avoiding pain or being fair; still less do we "choose" them. Indeed, I would feel very uneasy in dealing with a man who did. And why should a moral theory be judged by its capacity to enable the individual to answer the question "What ought I to do now?" as distinct from the question "What, in general, are there reasons for doing?" Do we expect casuistry from a moral philosopher or criteria for making up our own minds?

The more important difficulty is the one MacIntyre has in mind, that fundamental principles such as "fairness" or "considering people's interests" give us such abstract criteria that they are useless because they always have to be interpreted in terms of a concrete tradition. I am very sympathetic to this objection, but I think that it also applies in varying degrees to all rational activities. To take a parallel: all scientists accept some higher order principle such as that one ought to test competing hypotheses by comparing the deduced consequences with observations. But this does not give them concrete guidance for proceeding. It has to be interpreted. To start with what is to count as an observation? The amount of social tradition and previous theory built into most observation procedures, especially in the social sciences, is obvious enough. And how is the importance of one set of observations to be assessed in relation to others? This is not unlike saying in the moral case: Consider impartially the suffering of people affected by a social practice. But what is to count as suffering and how is one person's suffering to be weighed against another's? But do difficulties of this sort render the procedural principles of science useless? If not, why should fundamental moral principles be regarded as useless?

Fundamental principles of morality such as fairness and the consideration of interests only give us general criteria of relevance for determining moral issues. They prescribe what sort of considerations are to count as reasons. Within such a framework men have to work out arrangements for organizing their lives together. And just as in science there is a fair degree of consensus at a low level of laws, so in the moral case there are basic rules, e.g., concerning contracts, property, and the care of the young, which any rational man can see to be necessary to any continuing form of social life, man being what he is and the conditions of life on earth being what they are. For, given that the consideration of interests is a fundamental principle of morality and given that there is room for a vast amount of disagreement about what, ultimately, a man's interests are, there are nevertheless certain general conditions which it is in any man's interest to preserve however idiosyncratic his view of his interests. These include not only the avoidance of pain and injury but also the minimal rules for living together of the type already mentioned. Above this basic level there is room for any amount of disagreement and development. People are too apt to conclude that just because some moral matters are controversial and variable, for instance sexual matters, the whole moral fabric is unstable. It is as if they reason: In Africa men have several wives, in Europe only one, in the U.S.A. only one at a time; therefore all morals are a matter of taste! As evils, murder and theft are just as culture-bound as spitting in the street!

The point surely is that stability and consensus at a basic level are quite compatible with change and experiment at other levels. Indeed to expect any final "solution," any secure resting place in social or personal life, is to be a victim of the basic illusion which is shared by most opponents of democracy, that of belief in some kind of certainty or perfection. But in determining what are basic rules and in seeking above this level ways of living which may be improvements on those we may have inherited, we make use of principles. Such principles have to be interpreted in terms of concrete traditions; they cannot prescribe precisely what we ought to do, but at least they rule out certain courses of action and sensitize us to features of a situation which are morally relevant. They function more as signposts than as guidebooks.


## The Nature of Principles

A place for principles in the moral life must therefore be insisted on without making too far-flung claims for what they can prescribe without interpretation by means of a concrete tradition. Indeed I want to insist on the importance of such traditions for the learning of principles as well as for their interpretation. Before, however, this theme is developed in detail, more must be said about the nature of principles in order to remove widespread misunderstandings.

First of all, what are principles? A principle is that which makes a consideration relevant. Suppose that a man is wondering whether gambling is wrong and, in thinking about this, he takes account of the misery caused to the families of gamblers he has known. This shows that he accepts the principle of considering people's interests, for he is sensitized to the suffering caused by gambling rather than horror-struck at the amount of greenness in the world created by the demand for green tables. He does not, in other words, accept the principle of the minimization of greenness. He may or may not be able to formulate a principle explicitly. But this does not matter; for acceptance of a principle does not depend on the ability to formulate it and to defend it against criticism, as some, like Oakeshott who are allergic to principles, suggest. Rather it depends on whether a man is sensitized to some considerations and not to others.

Of course, formulation is necessary if one intends to embark on some moral philosophy in the attempt to justify principles. And it might well be said that the task of justifying them is a crucial one for anyone who is according them the importance I am according them. As, however, the central part of my *Ethics and Education* was concerned with this very problem it would be otiose for me to present more than a thumbnail sketch of the arguments here. What I argued was that there are a limited number of principles which are fundamental but nonarbitrary in the sense that they are presuppositions of the form of discourse in which the question "What are there reasons for doing?" is asked seriously. The principles which have this sort of status are those of impartiality, the consideration of interests, freedom, respect for persons, and probably truth-telling. Such principles are of a procedural sort in that they do not tell us precisely what rules there should be in a society but lay down general guidance about the ways in which we should go about deciding such matters and indicate general criteria of relevance. It was argued that these principles are presuppositions of what is called the democratic way of life, which is based on the conviction that there is a better and a worse way of arranging our social life and that this should be determined by discussion rather than by arbitrary fiat.

Even if it is granted that arguments along these lines might be sustained for a few fundamental principles, further difficulties might still be raised. It might be said, for instance, that stress on the importance of principles in morality implies rigidity in the moral life. A picture is conjured up of Hardy-like characters dourly doing their duty whilst the heavens fall about them. Certainly some kind of firmness is suggested by the phrase "a man of principle." But here again, there are misunderstandings. A man of principle is one who is *consistent* in acting in the light of his sensitivity to aspects of a situation that are made morally relevant by a principle. But this does not preclude adaptability due to differences in situations, especially if there is more than one principle which makes different factors in a situation morally important.

Another time-honored objection is that principles are products of reason and hence inert. We may mouth them or assent to them, but this may be a substitute for acting in a morally appropriate way. Part of the answer to this objection is to be found in the answer to the criticism that links having principles with the ability to formulate them and to defend them. But there is a further point that needs to be made. Notions such as "fairness" and "the consideration of interests" are not affectively neutral. "That is unfair" is an appraisal which has more affinities with an appraisal such as "that is dangerous" than it has with a colorless judgment such as "that is oblong." Pointing out that someone is in pain is not at all like pointing out that he is 5 feet 6 inches tall.

The strength of the emotive theory of ethics derives from the fact that moral principles pick out features of situations which are not affectively neutral. This, however, does not make them inconsistent with living a life guided by reason; for this sort of life presupposes a whole constellation of such appraisals, e.g., that one should be consistent, impartial, and truthful, that one should have regard to relevance, accuracy, and clarity, and that one should respect evidence and other people as the source of arguments. It is only an irrationalist who welcomes contradictions in an argument, who laughs with delight when accused of inconsistency, or who is nonchalant when convicted of irrelevance. Science and any other rational activity presuppose such normative standards which are intimately connected with the passion for truth which gives point to rational activities. Unless people cared about relevance and had feelings about inconsistency science would not flourish as a form of human life. The usual contrast between reason and feeling is misconceived; for there are attitudes and appraisals which are the passionate side of the life of reason.

So much, then, for the usual objections to the conception of the moral life in which prominence is accorded to principles. I hope I have said enough to establish their place in it. I now want to show how they can be seen to function in relation to concrete traditions to which MacIntyre ascribes so much importance and how they can save us from the existentialist predicament which he views as the logical alternative to being encased in a surviving code.


## THE COMPLEXITY AND CONCRETENESS
## OF THE MORAL LIFE

A man who accepts principles is too often represented as living in some kind of social vacuum and attempting to deduce from his principles a concrete way of living. This is an absurd suggestion. To start with, the disposition to appeal to principles is not something that men have by nature, any more than reason itself is some kind of inner gadget that men switch on when the occasion arises. If thinking is the soul's dialogue with itself, the dialogue within mirrors the dialogue without. To be critical is to have kept critical company, to have identified oneself with that segment of society which accepts certain principles in considering its practices. Rationality, of which science is a supreme example, is itself a tradition. Rational men are brought up in the tradition that traditions are not immune from criticism.

But criticism, thinking things out for oneself, and other such activities connected with a rational type of morality, cannot be exercised without some concrete content. For how can one be critical without being brought up in something to be critical of? How can one think things out for oneself unless one's routines break down or one's roles conflict? Adherence to principles must not be conceived of as self-contained; it must be conceived of as being bound up with and modifying some kind of content. Scientists cannot think scientifically without having any content to think about.

## Complexity

In an open society this content is considerably more complex than in those small, self-contained communities where, according to MacIntyre, concepts such as "good" and "duty" had their natural home. The notion, for instance, that people are persons with rights and duties distinct from those connected with their roles is an alien notion in such close-knit communities. But once this is admitted, as was widely the case with the coming of Stoicism and Christianity, the content of the moral life becomes immediately much more complicated. For the norms connected with treating people as persons begin to interpenetrate those connected with roles and with the accepted goals of life. In trying to get a clear idea, therefore, about the contours of our moral life it is necessary to consider its complexity before we can grasp the concrete ways in which principles enter into it. At least five facets of our moral life must be distinguished.

First of all, under concepts such as "good," "desirable," and "worthwhile," fall those activities which are thought to be so important that time must be spent on initiating children into them. These include things such as science, poetry, and engineering and possibly a variety of games and pastimes. Most of these are intimately connected not only with occupations and professions but also with possible vocations and ideals of life. In our type of society they provide a variety of options within which an individual can make something of himself if he is encouraged to pursue his own bent as the principle of freedom demands.

Second, under the concepts of "obligation" and "duty," fall ways of behaving connected with social roles. Much of a person's moral life is taken up with his station and its duties, with what is required of him as a husband, father, citizen, and member of a profession or occupation.

Third, there are those duties, more prominent in an open society, which are not specifically connected with any social role but which relate to the following of general rules governing conduct between members of a society. Rules such as those of unselfishness, fairness, and honesty are examples. These affect the manner in which an individual conducts himself within a role as well as in his noninstitutionalized relationships with others. They are personalized as character traits.

Fourth, there are equally wide-ranging goals of life which are personalized in the form of "motives." These are purposes not confined to particular activities or roles, which derive from non-neutral appraisals of a man's situation. Examples are ambition, envy, benevolence, and greed. An ambitious man, for instance, is one who is moved by the thought of getting ahead of others in a whole variety of contexts. Both traits of character and motives can be thought of as virtues and vices. The traits of fairness and honesty are virtues; those of meanness and selfishness are vices. The motives of benevolence and gratitude are virtues; those of greed and lust are vices. Both character traits and motives, when looked at in a justificatory context, incorporate considerations that can be regarded as fundamental principles. Examples would be fairness and benevolence, which can be appealed to in order to criticize or justify not only other traits and motives, but also conduct covered by activities and role performances.

There are, finally, very general traits of character which relate not so much to the rules a man follows or to the purposes he pursues as to the manner in which he follows or pursues them. Examples would be integrity, persistence, determination, conscientiousness, and consistency. These are all connected with what used to be called "the will."

The point in spelling out this complexity of our moral life is to rid us straightaway of any simpleminded view that moral education is just a matter of getting children to have "good personal relationships" or to observe interpersonal rules like those relating to sex, stealing, and selfishness. It emphatically is not. To get a boy committed to some worthwhile activity, such as chemistry or engineering, is no less part of his moral education than damping down his selfishness; so also is getting him really committed to the duties defining his role as a husband or teacher. These duties, of course, must be interpreted in a way which is sensitized by the principle of respect for persons; but no adequate morality could be constituted purely out of free-floating personal obligations.

Concreteness

So much for the complexity of the content of the moral life which is to form the basis for any rational morality that appeals to principles. Let me now turn to the matter of concreteness in the interpretation of fundamental principles and moral ideals. The burden of the attack on principles by people like MacIntyre and Winch is to be found in Edmund Burke; it is that they are too abstract. "The lines of morality are not like the ideal lines of mathematics." My contention is that principles can be conceived of and must be conceived of as entering into the moral life in a perfectly concrete way without making them completely culture-bound.

*Impartiality* The most fundamental principle of all practical reasoning is that of impartiality. This is really the demand that excludes arbitrariness, which maintains that distinctions shall be made only where there are relevant differences. This is essential to reasoning, in that what is meant by a reason for doing A rather than B is some aspect under which it is viewed which makes it relevantly different. But though this principle gives negative guidance in that it rules out arbitrariness, making an exception of oneself, and so on, it is immediately obvious that it is quite impossible to apply without some other principle which determines criteria of relevance. The most obvious principle to supply such criteria is that of the consideration of interests, which is personalized in virtues such as benevolence and kindness.

*The Consideration of Interests* In practice the rays of this principle are largely refracted through the prism of our social roles and general duties as members of a society. If we are teachers, for instance, considering people's interests amounts, to a large extent, to considering the interests of children entrusted to our care. I once taught with a man who had such a wide-ranging concern for people's interests that he used to tell his class to get on with some work and to sit there with them, writing letters to old scholars, in order to get them to subscribe to an "Aid to India" fund. His present scholars were, of course, bored to death! He certainly had a somewhat abstract approach to considering people's interests!

Most Utilitarians, following Mill and Sidgwick, have stressed the importance of Mill's "secondary principles" in morality. The Utilitarian, Mill argued, has not got to be constantly weighing the effects of his actions on people's interests any more than a Christian has to read through the Bible every time before he acts. The experience of a society with regard to the tendencies of actions in relation to people's interests lies behind its roles and general rules. The principle that one should consider people's interests acts also as an ever-present corrective to, and possible ground of criticism of, rules and social practices which can also be appealed to when rules conflict. This point is well made by Stephen Toulmin in his book on ethics. A man could stick too closely to his role and accept too uncritically what was expected of him generally as a member of society. He might be very much an organization man or a man of puritanical disposition, riddled with rules that might have lost their point, or without sensitivity to the suffering caused by unthinking insistence on the letter of the law. What would be lacking would be that sensitivity to suffering caused by actions and social practices which finds expression in virtues such as benevolence, kindness, and what Hume called "the sentiment of humanity."

*Freedom*   Giving interpersonal support to the consideration of interests is the principle of freedom which lays it down that, other things being equal, people should be allowed to do what they want, or that, in other words, reasons should be given for constraining people in their pursuit of what they take to be good. This combines two notions, that of "wants" and that of "constraints," and immediately the concrete questions crowd in "What is it that people might want to do?" and "What sorts of constraints should be absent?" What, too, is to count as a constraint? Is it the want to walk about nude or to speak one's mind in public that is at issue? And are the constraints those of the bully or those of public opinion? The situation becomes even more complicated once we realize that, men being what they are, we are only in fact free from obnoxious constraints like those of the bully if we are willing to accept the milder and more leveling constraints of law. And so concreteness asserts itself. The principle only provides a general presumption, albeit one of far-reaching importance. At what point we decide that there are good reasons for constraining people because, for instance, they are damaging the interests of others, is a matter of judgment.

Closely related to the principle of freedom are ideals like "the self-development of the individual" and personal autonomy. But here again, concreteness is imperative, for what can "development" mean unless we build into the concept those modes of experience that it has taken the human race so long to evolve? And what sort of "self" is going to develop? Granted that this must come to a certain extent from the individual, who does this partly by his "choices," must not this "self" be fairly closely related to the normal stock of motives and character traits which are called virtues? And is it not desirable that higher order character traits, such as persistence and integrity, be exhibited in the development of this "self"? And how can the pressure for independence and the making of choices arise unless the individual genuinely feels conflicting obligations deriving from his occupancy of social roles and his acceptance of the general rules of a society? And what point is there in choice unless the individual thinks that what he decides can be better or worse, wise or foolish? And if he thinks that any particular act is not a pointless performance he must already accept that there are general principles which pick out relevant features of the alternatives open to him.

All of this adds up to the general conclusion that the ideals connected with the principle of freedom are unintelligible except against a background of desirable activities, roles, and rules between which the individual has to choose and that any proper choice (as distinct from random plumping) presupposes principles other than freedom in the light of which alternatives can be assessed.

*Respect for Persons*   The same sort of point can be made about respect for persons, another fundamental principle which underlies and acts as a corrective to so many of our formalized dealings with other men. Indeed, much of the content of this principle has to be defined negatively in such concrete contexts. To show lack of respect for a person is, for instance, to treat him in a role situation as merely a functionary, to be impervious to the fact that he, like us, has aspirations that matter to him, is a center of evaluation and choice, takes pride in his achievements, and has his own unique point of view on the world. Or it is to treat him merely as a participant in an activity who is to be assessed purely in terms of his skill and competence in that activity. Worse at something becomes generalized to worse as a human being. In a similar way an excess of group loyalty or fellow-feeling can make a man seem not just different in some respects but generally inferior as a human being. Respect for persons, too, is at the bottom of our conviction that some motives are vices—lust, for instance, and envy and a certain kind of humility.

So much, then, by way of a brief sketch to illustrate the way in which I conceive of fundamental principles as entering into the moral life in a manner perfectly consistent with its complexity and concreteness. I now want to end by outlining my conception of moral education, which goes with this conception of the moral life.

## MORAL EDUCATION

One or two general remarks must first be made about the meaning of "education." There is a well-established generalized use of "education" which refers, roughly, to any processes of "rearing," "instruction," "training," etc., that go on at home and at school. But there is a more specific sense of education which emerged in the nineteenth century in which education is distinguished from training and which is used to pick out processes that lead to the development of an "educated man." In this more specific sense, education involves getting people to make something of themselves within activities that are thought to be worthwhile, in a way which involves an understanding that has some kind of depth and breadth to it. In this more specific sense of education, employed by most educators when they are thinking about their tasks, all education is, therefore, moral education, if we are to include the pursuit of good in morals and not just confine it to codes and more general dealings with other men. Again, we will have to leave on one side the vexatious question of justification in the sphere of "the good," of why, in other words, chemistry is more worthwhile than base-ball or sun-bathing. We can pursue the implications of this view of education without getting immersed in that issue, which is a veritable "Serbonian bog where armies whole have sunk."

The first implication is that educating people has very much to do with getting them "on the inside" of what is worthwhile, so that they come to pursue and appreciate it for what there is in it as dis-tinct from what they may conceive of is as leading on to. It is in re-lation to this criterion of education that I want to make sense of no-tions such as commitment and being authentic, which starkly confront the instrumental attitude of "What is the use of it?" and "Where is this going to get one?" I have sympathy for the philoso-pher who was pressed at an interview for a chair to commit himself to the view that philosophy must have some practical use—whatever that means. He exclaimed in exasperation, "Look, we may have to say that sort of thing in order to get money from governments and businessmen for universities, but for heaven's sake do not let us become victims of our own propaganda."

The second implication is that educating people must involve knowledge and understanding. To be educated is not just to have mastered a know-how or knack, even if it is in the sphere of some very worthwhile activity such as cookery or ballet dancing. The Spartans were highly trained and skilled, but they are almost para-digms of a people who were not educated. Though depth of under-standing is necessary to being educated, it is not sufficient, for a scientist can have a deep understanding of the "reasons why" of things and still be uneducated if all he understands is a specialized branch of science. "Education is of the whole man" is a conceptual truth in that being educated is inconsistent with being only par-tially developed in one's understanding—with seeing a car, for in-stance, as only a piece of machinery without aesthetic grace, without a history, and without potentialities for human good or ill. Let me now relate these two implications to the different facets of the moral life in order to show the indispensability of both content and principles and the proper place for the romantic ideal.


Commitment and Authenticity

One of the great enemies of education, in this specific sense, is second-handedness and instrumentality; hence Whitehead's polemic against inert ideas. What seems deplorable is not just that children should mug up some science because it is the done thing or in order to get good grades but that teachers should grind through their day with that dreadful fixed smile, or that people should be polite without sensing the point of it. Doing the done thing for conformity's sake seems a stifling corruption of the moral life, and, of course, it is an inherently unstable view; for a secondhand form of behavior is very susceptible to temptations and disintegrates when external pressures and incentives are withdrawn. This is tantamount to saying that moral education is centrally concerned with the development of certain types of motives, especially with what I have called the rational passions. When looked at in a justificatory context, some of these, e.g., benevolence, respect for persons, and the sense of justice, function as fundamental principles. But if such principles are to be operative in a person's conduct, they must become *his* principles. That means that they must come to function as motives, as considerations of a far-ranging sort that actually move him to act. Let us now consider the different facets of the moral life in the light of this commitment criterion of education.

*Activities and Role-Performances*    The trouble with the situation in which we are placed in education is not just that children do not always come to us glistening with a desire to learn what is worthwhile or with a predisposition toward mastering their duties; it is also that they are incapable of firsthand attitudes toward these activities and role performances until they are sufficiently on the inside of them to grasp them and be committed to what they involve. Although a child may have some degree of curiosity there is a great difference between this and the passion for truth which lies at the heart of an activity such as science, and until he feels strongly about this all-pervading principle that permeates science, it is difficult to see how his viewpoint can be anything but a bit external. He must, to a certain extent, be induced to go through the motions before he is in a position to grasp their point, and the point is given by the underlying principle, which personalizes one of the rational passions. To be rational is to care about truth; similarly, in the interpersonal sphere he must come to care about persons as centers of evaluation.

Of course there are all sorts of devices for bringing this about. In the old days, teachers, modeling the school on the army, used to employ a variety of coercive techniques. The progressives, in revolt, model the school more on the supermarket and try to gear their wares to children's wants and preferences. Then there are the less dramatic devices of stimulating by example and employing general guiding words such as "good" and "ought," which suggest that there are reasons but do not intimate clearly what the reasons are. The teacher's hope is that the proper reasons for doing things will become the pupil's actual reasons. This may come about by some process of identification. Admiration for a teacher may be turned outward toward involvement in the activities and forms of behavior to which he is committed, or an existing predisposition in the child, such as curiosity, may be gradually transformed by appropriate experience into the rational passion of respect for truth. This is likely to be greatly facilitated if the enthusiasm of the peer group is also enlisted, but this takes time and training. Let me illustrate this.

To be on the inside of an activity such as science or philosophy is not to have just a general curiosity or a merely abstract concern for truth. It is to be concretely concerned about whether particular points of view are true or false. These particularities are only intelligible within a continuing tradition of thought, which has been developed by people who adhere to a public stock of procedural principles. It is because of this concrete concern that they care desperately about things like the relevance of remarks, cogency in argument, and clarity of exposition; for how can one get to the bottom of anything without a concern about standards such as these which are indispensable to serious discussion? Sporadic curiosity is not enough; it has to be fanned into a steady flame and disciplined by adherence to the standards which regulate a common pursuit. The problem of education, as Whitehead saw only too well, is not just that of contriving the initial romance, it is that of bringing about acceptance of the precision and discipline required to wed a person to a pursuit. In this the support of the peer group is probably as important as the example and insistence of the teacher.

The judgment and skill which come with firsthand experience render activities more absorbing and worthwhile. The cultivation of personal relationships, for instance, and even sitting on committees, can become more and more absorbing as occupations for those who have a shrewd grasp of human behavior. Politics, as an activity, was quite different when practiced by Caesar rather than by Pompey, because of the skill and understanding Caesar brought to it. Although it is satisfying sometimes to relapse into routine activities requiring little effort (a point, I think, which Dewey appreciated too little), and although there is something to be said for occasional incursions into simple, and sometimes more brutish forms of enjoyment, it would be intolerable for a rational man to spend most of his life in such a circumscribed way. A minimum task of moral education is surely to equip people so that they will not be perpetually bored. Therefore, the case for skill and understanding, on grounds purely of individual satisfaction, is a strong one. There is also the point that, as soon as knowledge enters in as an important ingredient in an activity, an additional dimension of value, deriving from the concern for truth, is opened up.

In a pluralistic society like ours there must be a high degree of consensus at the level of those fundamental principles which underlie democratic procedures and, as I have already argued, it is obvious enough that there must be agreement about a level of basic rules which provide conditions necessary for anyone to pursue his interests. But above this level there is bound to be controversy. In this sphere of "the good" or of personal ideals, with which we are at the moment concerned, there are any number of options open to individuals. And the principle of freedom demands that there should be. It is in this sphere that talk of commitment and authenticity is particularly pertinent. One man may develop a lifelong passion for science. Another, more influenced by the Christian ideal, may find that his main sphere of commitment is in the sphere of personal relationships and the relief of suffering. Another may opt for an aesthetic type of activity.

On the other hand, another person may find almost complete fulfillment in devoting himself to the fulfillment of a role, that of a teacher for instance. There has been a lot of loose talk, deriving from Sartre's celebrated example of the waiter, about the incompatibility of authenticity with occupying a role. Playing a role, which involves either simulation or second-handedness, should not be confused with a genuine commitment to a role. And, of course, as has been emphasized repeatedly, there is no role which can *completely* contain one's concerns and duties as a human being.

*Interpersonal Rules*  In the interpersonal sphere there may have to be firm insistence from the start on rules like those of keeping contracts, not stealing, punctuality, and honesty. And why should children not *enjoy* mastering these rules as well as those of games? Unless, however, the reasons behind these rules eventually become the individual's reasons, the job is only half done. And this does not mean fostering a theoretical grasp of the conduciveness of such rules to the general good. That kind of notion never induced anyone to do anything except to preach theoretical revolution. Neither does it mean being swept by occasional gusts of sympathy when it dawns that somebody has suffered because he has been let down. It means, on the contrary, a steady but intense sensitivity to the consequences of actions, a constant and imaginative realization that in interpersonal relations one is dealing with persons who also have their unique point of view on the world and that this is something about them which matters supremely. In other words, it means the

R. S. PETERS    231

development of motives which personalize fundamental principles. It means also the development of judgment about particular moral matters that can only come to a person who has really got on the inside of this mode of experience. Making decisions and choices is too often represented as agonizing. For those who have attained some degree of wisdom it can be both a challenge and a delight.

It is not for a philosopher to pronounce on how children can be got on the inside of this more rational form of life, or on how the rational passions, which personalize fundamental principles, can best be awakened and developed. That is a matter for psychologists. The philosopher's role is only to indicate the sort of job that has to be done. But what he *can* say is that all talk of commitment and being authentic is vacuous unless this sort of job *is* done; for it is pointless to mouth these general injunctions unless concrete provision is made to implement them. What is to be lamented about young people today is not their lack of idealism but the difficulty of harnessing it to concrete tasks. Demonstrations, like mourning, are often symbolic expressions of feelngs that have no obvious channel of discharge in appropriate action.

*The Will* The importance of the rational passions can also be shown in the sphere of what used to be called "the will," where notions like those of integrity, determination, and resoluteness have their place. Of course this form of consistency is possible for people who adhere conscientiously to a simple code, perhaps because, like the colonel in *The Bridge over the River Kwai*, they accept unthinkingly some role-regulating principle such as "one ought always to obey orders" or "an officer must always care for his men." But such consistency is also possible for people with a more complicated morality if they genuinely care about the considerations which are incorporated in fundamental principles. Strength of character is so often represented in negative terms as saying no to temptation, as standing firm, as being impervious to social pressure. My guess is that rational people are able to do this only if they are passionately devoted to fairness, freedom, and the pursuit of truth and if they have a genuine respect for others and are intensely concerned if they suffer. As Spinoza put it: "Blessedness is not the reward of right living; it is the right living itself; nor should we rejoice in it because we restrain our desires, but, on the contrary, it is because we rejoice in it that we restrain them." So much, then, for the first aspect of education, which concerns commitment to what is worthwhile. I now pass briefly to the second: that concerned with depth and breadth of understanding.

# Depth and Breadth of Understanding

In any worthwhile activity or form of behavior there is a mode of acting or thinking, with its underlying principles, and some kind of established content which incorporates the experience of those who are skilled in this sphere. Depth is provided partly by the principles immanent in the mode of experience and partly by the degree to which it has been possible to discern the one in the many in the content.

The sin, of course, of the old formalism was to hand on content in a secondhand way without encouraging children to get on the inside of activities and to master the appropriate mode of experience for themselves. The converse sin of the progressive was to imagine that children could go it alone without any proper grasp of content or of the underlying mode of experience with its immanent principles. A more modern sin is to assume that a mode of experience, or a methodology, can be formalized and handed out and children saved the trouble of mastering any content. Don't bother, it is said, to teach children any historical facts, just teach them to think historically. This reminds me of the yearning, which one so often encounters, that one should hand out rules for Clear Thinking in twelve easy lessons or that one should set out philosophical method in advance of dealing with particular philosophical arguments. Enough, I hope, has been said about the intimate relationship between principles and concrete content to avoid that particular rationalistic delusion.

In the interpersonal sphere of morality there is, of course, a basic content, which every child must master, of rules to do with noninjury, property, contracts, and so on; but depth of understanding in this sphere is rather different. It is not like depth of understanding in the sciences, which consists in grasping more and more abstract theories; for in morality one comes very quickly to nonarbitrary stopping points in fundamental principles, such as the consideration of interests. Depth consists rather in the development of the imagination so that one can become more acutely aware of content to be given to these principles. What, for instance, is a man's interest? Above the level of physical and mental health what is to count? Surely not just what he thinks his interest to be? And so we start trying to understand various forms of worthwhile activity and personal ideals, not only in general but in relation to the capacity of particular individuals.

Respect for persons also opens up endless vistas for the imagination in making us vividly aware of the extent to which we drag our feet in failing to treat individuals and classes of people as persons in a full sense. It opens up, too, the whole realm of our understanding of persons. For understanding a person is more than being able to interpret his behavior in terms of wide-ranging psychological generalizations—even if there were any such generalizations that had been established—and it is not a mystic confrontation of "I" with "thou," about which there is little coherent that can be said. It is something about which a great deal can be said which is of cardinal importance for the moral life—about the way in which an individual's outlook is shaped by his roles, about his traits, and about his motives and aspirations. But most of this sort of knowledge we obtain by being with a person and sharing a common life with him, not by delving in psychological textbooks. This sort of knowledge is probably the most important sort for any moral agent to have; for our detailed appraisals of people are very closely intertwined with explanatory notions. Indeed, I made the point earlier that most motives and traits are also virtues or vices. And it may take a whole novel such as *Howards End* to explore concretely the range of an emotion like indignation.

Breadth of understanding, however, is of equal importance to depth in any concrete approach to the moral life. It has been argued that this life itself is a complex affair involving roles, activities, motives, and interpersonal rules. It also involves the disposition to be critical of this wideranging content in which any generation must necessarily be nurtured. The individual, too, may be confronted with conflicts arising from this heritage. How is he to be critical in an intelligent way about a social practice or about a particular feature of government policy unless he has some understanding of history and of the sorts of facts and unintended consequences of actions with which the social sciences are concerned? How is he to choose realistically between alternatives open to him unless he knows some facts?

It is absurd to encourage children to be critical and autonomous and not to insist on them learning facts which may inform their criticism and choices. In England, at the moment, we have all sorts of variants on the topic-centered curriculum, which is meant to induce moral commitment and to sensitize children to social issues. Discussion, of course, is the thing; it is regarded as almost sinful nowadays to instruct children in anything! But too often all that such discussions achieve is to confirm people's existing prejudices. They are not used as launching pads to dispatch children to the realm of some hard facts in the light of which they might make up their minds in an informed manner.

The same sort of point can be made about the necessity of breadth if children are to choose for themselves the sphere of activity within the wide range of what is desirable, to which they are to become personally committed and which may form the nucleus of a personal ideal. Not only must they have some breadth of content in order to be provided with concrete samples of the sorts of things between which they must choose; they must also make a concrete study of some of the forms of experience which have a special position in informing their choice. By this I mean studies such as literature, history, religion, and the social sciences, which, if imaginatively entered into, enlarge one's prespective of the predicament of man and so put one's own choice in a less abstract setting. The romantic ideal must at least have a classical background, if it is to function as more than a mere protest.


CONCLUSION

It might be said that my conception of moral education is indistinguishable from the ideal of a liberal education. I do not mind putting it this way provided that "liberal" implies no wishy-washiness and is used with awareness of the distinct emphases that it intimates.

A liberal education, to start with, is one that stresses the pursuit of what is worthwhile for what is intrinsic to it. It is hostile to a purely instrumental view of activities, to the bonds that link whatever is done to some palpable extrinsic end. The moral life, I have argued, rests upon rational passions which permeate a whole range of activities and which make them worthwhile for their own sake.

A liberal education is secondly one that is not narrowly confined to particular perspectives. I have argued both for a broad interpretaion of the moral life and for the necessity of breadth of understanding to give concrete backing to the ideal of freedom, which is the most obvious ideal of liberalism.

Thirdly, a liberal education is one that is incompatible with authoritarianism and dogmatism. This is because a liberal education is based ultimately on respect for truth which depends on reasons and not on the word or will of any man, body, or book. This means, of course, not that there is not an important place for authority in social life, but that it has to be rationally justified—as indeed it can be in the bringing up of children. The use of authority must not be confused with authoritarianism. Respect for truth is intimately connected with fairness, and respect for persons, which, together with freedom, are fundamental principles which underlie our moral life and which are personalized in the form of the rational passions. The central purpose, however, of my essay, has been to show that adherence to such principles is a passionate business and that they can and should enter in a very concrete way into a man's activities, roles, and more personal dealings with other men.

NANCY GAYER

# ON MAKING
# MORALITY OPERATIONAL

Moral education is inevitably with us. Since we cannot eliminate it, the school's responsibility is to find out more about it and improve it, so that it will result in a moral people.

If the phrase "a moral people" makes you wince, never mind. Morality doesn't necessarily imply adherence to a repressive, rigid, narrow code of behavior. The morality concept is large enough to include freedom and innovation, liberation and progress, rationality and discipline. Remember that its crucial criterion is goodness—whatever is good for man.

It is time that we stop identifying the moral man with the bore and the prig, or the prying censor, and understand that he can be anyone whose character exemplifies the values that we truly admire, that he can epitomize a way of life we think pleasant and rewarding for ourselves and desirable for those whose futures we are helping to shape. "Morality" need not be a nasty word.

## THE OVERT AND THE COVERT

Values, as everybody knows, are culturally transmitted. The nature of the interaction between human beings is such that moral attitudes are instilled by means of the very words used in communicating. Nonmoral values are no different from moral values in this

From Nancy Gayer, "On Making Morality Operational," *Phi Delta Kappan* (October 1964).

respect. Both are as much imbedded in the terms of everyday language as the experience of color is in our seeing.

Instead, then, of asking the fruitless question whether moral education *should* be given, we must inquire what values and moral outlooks actually *are* being given and investigate the *manner* in which they are being given. Then, when we become aware of the mechanism and content of the moral instruction which actually permeates all of our educational activities, we shall be in a better position to answer such questions as what values *ought* the schools to teach. A still further problem is the need to justify whatever values we decide are good. But before we discuss what ought to be done, we should find out what we are actually doing. For this preliminary purpose, I want to illustrate some of the ways in which teachers, in using the ordinary language of subject and skill instruction and classroom management, also succeed, somewhat unconsciously, in passing on to their pupils certain moral values as well.

## PLANNED MORAL TEACHING

There are, of course, many methods of deliberately teaching moral values. I shall summarize some in passing for the sake of clarifying the distinction between planned and unplanned moral education. My categories are rough and ready and are not meant to be definitive.

*Direct*, as when a teacher lectures or conducts a discussion on why one ought to be honest.

By *example*, as when a teacher influences his pupils to be trustworthy by conscientiously being a model of reliability himself.

By *intended by-product*, as when a teacher, in using problem-solving techniques to teach his subject, also instills an appreciation of critical thinking in his pupils.

By *training*, as when children become democratic through being in classrooms specifically designed to give guided experiences in self-government and in the common loyalties.

By *discovery*, as when a teacher uses role-playing procedures to help pupils examine and create their own values as well as to discover the values held by others.

## UNPLANNED MORAL TEACHING

I made a contrast between two modes of moral education, the conscious or planned, and the unplanned or linguistic. Words take on a characteristic import or force from the way they are used within a context. Although both modes are linguistic, I am confining "linguistic" to the latter, the unplanned mode, for the sake of emphasizing that the largely unintended and unnoticed transmission of values which characterizes it is derived from the logical function of language. Unplanned moral instruction comes about in the very act of speaking, whether one is actually talking about values or not.

When one describes a pupil as being alert, one is also expressing a *favorable attitude* towards alertness and *commending* the pupil for being alert. Certain values are imbedded in the words we use in ways that we mistakenly suppose are purely descriptive (evaluatively neutral) and are passed over and absorbed without either party being aware of the nature of the transaction. For instance, an apparently ordinary word like "clean" is value-laden in our schools. It has connotations both of approval and prescriptivity. Implicit in the way the word is used are both "It is good to be clean" and "One ought to do things which lead to cleanliness." The phrase that comes almost automatically to the lips is *"nice* and clean"; and never *"nasty* and clean." That the latter seems a contradiction in terms illustrates how much being clean is, for us, something to be praised. By contrast, in various other cultures and times cleanliness has been a matter of comparative indifference.

It is because we have such a value that when parents, leaving school at open house, remark, "Such a clean school!" no one supposes them to be finding fault. Nor are building principals unaware of this important criterion of judgment as to how well the school is fulfilling its task.


## ROCK-BOTTOM VALUES

I am not advocating that we should stop putting cleanliness next to godliness, but simply asking you to imagine the enormous changes in routine and ways of talking which would be needed to foster an opposing or indifferent attitude towards cleanliness. That it seems absurd even to want to make such a change testifies to the strength of our attachment to whatever values we happen to hold. It would take quite an overhauling to become neutral enough about cleanliness to leave it to the pupils to decide for themselves whether to be clean or not. Similarly, what would it be like to run a school that was neutral in such values as learning, truth-telling, or friendliness? And how can we do without generally shared rules for the protection of life, health, and property?

It would be very difficult indeed, for these values are so much part of our thinking. We would need to be able to say sincerely things like "So what, it was only a lie" as readily as "Never mind, she didn't really mean to hurt your feelings" comes to our lips now. The fabric of the school is woven with the thread of many values, some so basic that we are completely unaware that they are there and that they are values which are continuously being transmitted.

When people get worried about the moral situation, they often talk as if the younger generation were questioning the whole foundation of our life, but in fact there is a substratum of accepted moral standards which are so taken for granted that they are not even noticed. Next time someone starts talking about the crisis in values, ask him *which* values he is talking about. It's very likely that it isn't truth-telling as such, but rather cheating or sex behavior—and this narrow range of questioned values delimits the problem considerably. It's not that all of our values are going out of fashion at the same time, but that specific problems are arising for specific reasons. It isn't as if we're confronted with an abyss in the face of which we have to construct a complete value system; we have a foundation upon which we can't help but build, and these values which we already have *preclude* certain answers to the problems; e.g., to approve wholeheartedly of cheating, we would have to modify the value we place on truthfulness and to abandon the use of exams for grading and diagnosis. Those who justify cheating do so on the basis of certain other overriding values, such as loyalty to a friend who needs help, the desire to be successful, etc. None of these values is *prima facie* despicable. All of them were learned or strengthened at school.

## UNPLANNED VALUE SABOTAGE

In cases such as truth-telling, cleanliness, honesty, etc., our habitual uses of language are working on our side, in that the values imbedded in these words and usages are ones we want the young to have anyway. But there are also cases in which language is working against our interests and where, therefore, it is important to become aware of what we are saying and doing in order to prevent damage. I shall lead into this topic by means of the little word "may." Although the meaning of "may" is unambiguous, it is unnecessarily made ambiguous by the way it is used in the schoolroom—with undesirable consequences. Our language has few words to express the notion that one is being given a choice, and "may" is one of the most natural and simple ways of doing it. On the other hand, the means of politely telling someone to act in a specific manner are infinitely varied and do not require the use of "may."

I choose this little word deliberately. Although we are all aware of the importance of such educational objectives as "enlarging the scope of individual freedom" and "teaching to make good choices," we are apt to forget that in ordinary everyday life these high-sounding concepts are expressed by such humble phrases as "you may," "I invite you to," and "would you like to"; and negated by actions whose appropriate verbal expressions are, "you must," "it is necessary to," "this is the rule," and "I want you to." All too often, teachers use the expressions of freedom for eliciting nonchoice responses, and follow them up by actions which belie the true meaning of their words. They thus violate the big concepts of freedom, choice, and responsibility which they suppose are the organizing principles for their classroom practices.


## "MAY" AND "MUST"

When the teacher says "You may line up, children," she means "You *must* line up." If Robbie takes "may" as meaning *may* and goes on painting, he will soon find out that he is not doing the right thing. The teacher will tell him to line up, or she may even rebuke him for not having listened! We are so accustomed to swaddling commands in the soft garments of requests that it may be forgotten that "You may" does not even make a request. It offers a choice; it gives an option to do otherwise.

An objection may be made that "You may" does not offer a choice; rather, that it is a giving of permission. The children are being permitted to line up. But giving permission entails giving the right not to perform the act in question. If I am given permission to do something but am not allowed to refrain from doing it, then I am not being *permitted* at all; I am being *compelled*. I have no choice but to do it.

Or you may say that this usage is all right because the pupils *want* to line up; they want to go out to play. The children are being given permission to do something they already want to do; their teacher is responding to a request as yet unuttered; there's no question of their being compelled to do something that they don't want to do. This is a questionable assumption. Does "You may take out your arithmetic books" signal your pupils that they are now being allowed to do something which they have been just dying to do all morning? But whether they actually do or don't want to take out their books is immaterial; your use of "may" is unjustified unless you intend your pupils to be equally free not to take them out.


## SOWING SEEDS OF CONFORMITY

Now, contrast telling the same children who were told that they might line up, "You may play on the jungle gym today." Does this mean "Play on the jungle gym and nowhere else," or, alternatively, "One of the places you may play at is the jungle gym"? It could mean either. In the case of lining up, the children soon learn that "may" *means* "must." In cases like that of the jungle gym the teacher's intent in using "may" is unclear.

How is Robbie to handle this troublesome state of affairs? He can respond by looking around to see what everybody else is doing. This, of course, sows a seed of "other-directedness." Or, he can play it safe by going to the jungle gym. Or perhaps he will continue taking "may" as indicating an option to refuse—earning the reputation of being anti-social, stubborn, or not-quite-bright.


## THE BANISHMENT OF "OBEDIENCE"

Observe, however, that he is not likely to be called "disobedient." That term and "obedience," its counterpart on the report card, went out with the coming in of the mythology surrounding the democratic classroom. The same conceptual framework which has led to the use of "may" for "must"—a fallacious identification of giving orders with being authoritarian, and the ensuing masquerading of orders into something less reprehensible—also disguises the use of obedience as a behavior criterion. "Disobeying" implies the existence of a rule, command, or order. One is not disobedient if there is nothing to disobey. Within a frame of reference where teacher-made rules and teacher orders are thought to be undemocratic, and democracy is highly valued, a disobedient child is an implicit reflection on the teacher. She has not been "democratic." Far better to shift the onus on the pupil by calling him "uncooperative." His offense thus is against the group and not against an "authoritarian" teacher, guilty by virtue of the nature of the child's crime.

Using "may" for "must" helps to perpetuate a widespread and pervasive myth among American teachers that they don't give orders and that doing so is undemocratic. Such beliefs are unwarranted. They are relics from an unrealistic and misconceived educational theory which envisaged the teacher as a sort of grown-up peer member rather than as the person in charge. Giving orders is an integral part of almost any leadership function. We may disguise the essential nature of the orders, serving them up as polite requests or indirectly expressed desires for certain responses, and this is a separate, although relevant problem. But when we clothe what are actually commands in the vocabulary of choice, we violate truth just as much as if we were to tell our pupils that the earth is flat. Both of these verbal acts are deceptions about reality, about what is the case.

There are times when "may" does mean "must," and they should be mentioned for the sake of completeness. These are when "may" is used ironically. Irony often assumes its unique character by the inverted use of a word, by putting it in invisible quotation marks, so to speak. With unmistakeable coldness and emphasis a mother will tell her naughty child that he "'may' go to bed." If teachers took that tone when using "may" for "must," there would be no need for this discussion. But, alas, their musting "mays" are as unstressed and dulcet as their permissive "mays."

## THE MANDATORY AND THE PERMISSIVE

In order to do any kind of moral thinking, one needs to be able to distinguish between mandatory rules and permissive rules. "One ought to do such-and-such" and "It is wrong to do so-and-so" take the form of mandatory rules. These require obedience. "It is not wrong to do so-and-so," "It is all right to do so-and-so," and "One may do such-and-such" take the form of permissive rules. These permit choice. One is free to do x or not to do it as one wishes. If adults use "may" to mean both "may" and "must" when they direct children, they thereby make it that much more difficult for the children to learn the all-important distinction between the two concepts, between what they are allowed to choose to do or not do, and what is not being left up to them to decide.

Of course, those children who understand what the teacher has in mind by "You may" know that they *must*. The damage is not *per se* in being told what to do (although this can be overdone), but in having the *telling* disguised. Pupils are not so much deceived by the teacher stratagem as enlightened in respect to the real authoritarianism lurking beneath the sweetness and light.

I have explored the use of "may" in some depth but other examples are available; some may have occurred to the reader. For example, teachers often say, "Would you *like* to come in now?"

when they mean "Playtime is over. Come in!" Although their utterance seems to ask the wishes of the class, seems to be giving the pupils a choice, it is actually an order. Just the other day a nine-year-old pupil told me of her substitute primary teacher, who "invited us to do everything. She'd say 'I invite you to be quiet; I invite you to go to recess; I invite you to sit down.' She was sure mean. The kids called her 'Mrs. Invite' behind her back."

The connection between the misuse of "may" for "must," etc., and the mystique which has grown up around the democratic classroom underlines how an apparently insignificant verbal matter has ramifications which lead to a systematic misrepresentation of the classroom situation. In other words, our *practice* has been confused and misdirected—not just our talk; it's not a matter of words alone, but of actions going astray *because* of confusion in thinking and speaking, which, after all, are done with words. A realistic moral education should sharpen and not blur the distinction between "may" and "must," between the permissive and the mandatory, and thus prepare the pupil for a world in which he will find both positive laws enjoining or forbidding certain courses of action and areas in which he is expected to exercise a responsible choice for himself. This is the area of moral freedom.


## THE AREA OF MORAL FREEDOM

We want pupils to develop into autonomous moral agents, but we should keep in mind that the areas in which we can permit them to exercise their judgment without restriction are circumscribed by values which are too basic to relax, just as in society at large moral autonomy is only permitted within an area circumscribed by law. The teacher's role as the mentor of children and young persons is not unlike the role of law itself in setting up the prohibitions and permissions regulating conduct. If this seems to conflict with our democratic presuppositions, it is because we confuse authoritarianism with authority—misconstrue as authoritarianism the authority of leadership which inevitably goes with positions of responsibility. It is not rules as such which constitute authoritarianism with authority—misconstrue as authoritarianism the authority of leadership which inevitably goes with positions of responsibility. It is not rules as such which constitute authoritarianism, but rules arbitrarily and unjustly formulated and enforced. The teacher who says "Clean up because I tell you to" is being overtly authoritarian, just as the teacher who says "You may clean up

ence between arbitrary and rational leadership, between good and bad ways of exercising control over others.

In routine cases such as cleaning up, it isn't necessary to add one's reasons to the telling. That would be boring to the pupils and a waste of time. The pupils already know the reasons. However, teachers must be *prepared* to give reasons justifying their orders, rules, or requests, as well as to volunteer them at the relevant times. The reasons must be sound, and, ideally, the persons to whom they are addressed should be given every practicable opportunity to offer counterarguments. But the nature of even the most democratically administered authority is such that when neither party is persuaded of the rightness of the other's view, the decision of the one in authority prevails, for that is what it means to be "in authority." This is not authoritarianism, but rather a nonauthoritarian exercise of authority. Often, the authority resides in the vote of the majority—but not in the schoolroom, except in certain specified areas. Only thus can teachers, administrators, parents, and managers exercise the kind of leadership indigenous to their role without abdicating from its crucial characteristic—that of making decisions affecting their charges when there are basic disagreements as to what is right.

The reason why it is important to be aware of what values are being inculcated through our use of language is that we can then decide which of these values we hold to be basic and mandatory. These can be explained to our pupils, and the enforcement of them justified, in rational terms. Within the limits of the mandatory we can extend as much as possible the area in which we invite the pupil to use his own judgment and decide on a course for himself. In this way we can avoid the familiar paradox of moral education by combining both the teaching of positive values and the teaching of independent critical reflection.


VENTRILOQUISM

Moral reflection in the classroom is just a shadow of the real thing unless it leads up to actions in which the pupil has a genuine free choice. If the answer which pupils are to give to the question of what the standards of classroom behavior should be is predetermined by the teacher, the pupils can't help but catch on to the strategy and feed back the expected answer. This isn't a sample of real moral reflection; it isn't education for the burden of real moral choice and for the responsibility of choosing and justifying one's own actions. I have reference to the practice of asking elementary school pupils to volunteer the specific rules by which they want to live in the classroom and then rigging the answers by means of teacher comments on unwanted suggestions, so that what is given back by the pupils are the very rules the teacher would herself have made. I have yet to see among the "pupil-made" rules displayed on chart-racks such a rule as, "If someone hits first, it is all right to hit back." No sensible teacher would include such a rule—and quite rightly—because we can't have schools where pupils are allowed to fight each other, just as we can't allow persons within society itself to settle their disputes by physical force.

The fault lies in pretending that the teacher has not used the pupil as a ventriloquist's dummy to give voice to her own intended rules and to con her pupils into thinking that they ought to obey these rules because they made them up themselves. And this in the name of antiauthoritarianism! This is no preparation for autonomous rule making. Teacher-made rules against physical aggression can be explained without authoritarian overtones and without intellectual dishonesty. There is much scope for pupil-made rules, even with young children, e.g., on the playground, within a system of free choice game areas open to all, led by eight-and nine-year-old play-leaders. And the wider the scope the better. But we should not ask pupils to make up rules in any domain unless we are prepared to accept whatever they come up with. We can avoid the onset of a *Lord of the Flies* situation by clearly circumscribing with mandatory rules the children's area of freedom.

Morality can be made operational by teachers who understand clearly what their basic values are, so that they can teach them deliberately and rationally instead of unconsciously. The next move is to encourage the pupil to make his own rules and choices, within the area of freedom—but these must be genuine, and not induced by manipulation. The blurring of the distinction between the mandatory and the permissive can only have the effect of shielding the pupil from the full meaning of moral responsibility and giving the teacher a disguise for restricting the scope of the pupils' own decisions. The point of being clear about the distinction is to widen the area of pupil responsibility as much as possible, while giving pupils those basic values in the light of which they can make their own decisions.

When the teacher says to Robbie that he should obey the rules listed on the chart-rack because he and his friends made them up, it isn't only that the teacher is being dishonest but that this isn't a good enough reason for Robbie. They aren't his rules, and in one way or another he knows it. If she had said, "Do it because I say so," he *would* have a good enough reason, even though she was being authoritarian, because *she is the teacher.* If she had said, "Do it because we will have a much better time if we obey the rules, and the rules are good ones, the result of much thought and experience on my part," Robbie would have a reason for obeying them twice over, once because a recognized authority says he has to and then again because a recognized authority says there's happiness ahead in following good rules.

## MORAL ARGUMENT

As pupils grow older they may come to question society's basic values. This is the time when rational explanation by teachers becomes even more crucial, for it is unlikely that pupils will challenge all of the values at once. They will have internalized most of them, even as you and I. Pupil-teacher arguments—or discussions, if you like—will be conducted in terms of other values, and pupils will learn how moral differences arise within a framework of general standards accepted by both sides.

It is the outcome of such moral argument that is productive of innovation and progress, stability and sanity in an ever-changing world. Education for such a world must be education for the exercise of genuine moral responsibility in conditions of genuine moral freedom. Such is the task and the obligation of the school, and the moral responsibility of its teachers. "Morality" need not be a nasty word. But it needs to be made operational for the here and now, and for all of us who live in it.

# PART 4
# ALTERNATIVES TO EXTREMISM

Radical humanists are right about the need to conduct education in a manner that preserves and enhances individuality, thereby tending to counter the mass culture values threatening to homogenize America. In this volume a case has been made against the extreme prescriptions of the radicals, although some increase in freedom, with its corresponding obligations and duties, is essential in our times.

American intellectuals inform us that our society is sick. Let us grant that this is not idle speculation. The symptoms of malaise and moral confusion are everywhere, despite our vast GNP and unprecedented dispersion of material wealth. The list of our ailments is almost endless, but some of the more significant are the staggering growth of crime, the epidemic of juvenile delinquency, vandalism (between 1971 and 1972 the damage to school property amounted to $4.5 million in Los Angeles County alone), venereal disease, drug abuse, pornography, television and movie violence, and political and business corruption. A new counter-culture and many militant minorities insist that they participate in political conventions, universities, and employment on a quota system. The vociferous, violent conduct of some groups has brought them victories, despite the fallacious arguments upon which a quota system is based.

While we are a people divided in our beliefs and values as

never before, we are simultaneously suffering from the numbing uniformity of our mass culture. It is no contradiction to say that we are confused and hostile at one level of values and dangerously homogeneous at another level. Most of us at one time or another feel as though we are being processed. Our advertising and entertainment debauch us daily. Few Americans can discriminate between good and bad literature, films, paintings, people, and education. Despite high levels of educational attainment, we see Disneyland, horse racing, rock and roll, and baseball winning out over museums, theater, classical music, and classical literature.

Ironically, Americans have become a youth-worshipping society at the very time they are becoming isolated from their own children. There is probably a close psychological relationship in this interesting but tragic orientation. Youth worship is abstract, allowing room for fantasizing and imitating hair and clothing styles, music and dance. There is no real commitment and responsibility to it—it is the essence of narcissism. Mature adults, in contrast, demonstrate their love for their children precisely by complete commitment, physical contact and related expressions of intimacy, and above all by a recognition that there are natural stages of growth and that modern society has not abolished the distinctions between childhood, adolescence, and maturity.

Let us recall Urie Bronfenbrenner's study of Russian and American child-rearing practices. Bronfenbrenner found that American parents neglect their children, creating a morass of freedom which many philosophers would contend is no freedom at all. Not only is there neglect and permissiveness of an irresponsible kind, there is a nearly complete absence of love. The psychologist James Prescott, of the National Institute of Child Health and Human Development, has documented this pathology of the home. He contends that many of today's youth desperately seek love through early sexual encounters, rebellious behavior, vandalism, and various forms of violence. They are overcompensating for the lack of early physical contact and affection psychologists claim are necessary for normal emotional and psychological development.

The Golden Mean is the only course that can preserve the integrity of our system of public education. The system will not survive the devaluation or destruction of teacher and administrator authority, the abolition of standards of excellence, the refusal to be responsible for the development of moral habits in young children, and the refusal to use curricula which are reasonably well organized. The degree of autonomy allowed senior high students will obviously be greater than that provided younger children, using the developmental approach mentioned earlier, but deep difficulty will arise from an early laissez-faire environment relatively free of teacher judgment and advice.

The Golden Mean can be attained by attempting to integrate a reasonable amount of affective education into otherwise cognitively oriented reforms and traditional programs. Role playing, socio-drama, humanistic games, Glasser sessions, Gestalt therapy techniques, and related forms can well be integrated into more conventional programs. The warnings in this book still hold, however, and excesses by excited neophytes will produce the results discussed herein.

In the first article in Part 4, Bruce Joyce offers a futuristic scenario for humanistic education. He beautifully integrates affective and cognitive elements into his scheme. Surely no educational reform is worthwhile that does not pay attention to all aspects of human nature. We can no more afford a purely affective education than we can a highly intellectual type deficient in moral, aesthetic, and emotional elements.

The second article, by George Issac Brown, will give some idea of the techniques used in the Human Potential Movement. These techniques will encourage discussion and expression of a range of feelings and attitudes. Teachers using these techniques should be warned against unprofessional efforts at psychotherapy. They are unqualified for this and the consequences could be injurious. Books like *Freedom to Learn* and *Learning to Feel—Feeling to Learn* are helpful in assisting teachers in this approach, but again I would warn the teacher to remember the weakness and danger in moral relativism of a subjective kind, the need for better critical thinking and problem-solving in our complex world, and the need to develop in this land a sense of community based upon responsible personal relationships. Some environments, like rural schools and schools in authoritarian communities, need Human Potential techniques far more than, for instance, liberal middle-class communities. They are also needed where widespread racial prejudice exists.

The final article, by Urie Bronfenbrenner, is a step in the direction of saving our youth from themselves, for they are indeed their own captives. Bringing community adults into the educationl process may prove to be a blessing, although we must notice the importance of strong modeling behavior versus soft, fatuous permissiveness. A highly permissive model is worse than no model at all, as Jonathan Kozol pointed out early in this volume.

The time is ripe for the institution of public education to engage in a civilizing process that is rational, aesthetically sensitive, and full of affection and mutal respect. Through the cultivation of knowing, believing, judging, learning, explaining, wondering, and feeling, we will learn how to deal more effectively with problems in the personal, social, political, and economic spheres.

BRUCE R. JOYCE

# CURRICULUM AND HUMANISTIC EDUCATION: "MONOLISM" VS. "PLURALISM"

## HUMANIZATION OF CURRICULAR TECHNOLOGY

The task of the humanist in curriculum is to free himself from the confines of the bureaucratic school and the sorting functions it performs for the status system, and develop instead the capacity to design and actualize a pluralistic education—the educational aspects of a pluralistic society.

The task is to move from educational routes which are largely characterized by bureaucratic procedures that sort students into the channels of the technical-industrial system into an educational panorama providing many avenues toward many kinds of personal and social development and which, through its pluralism, leads the other aspects of the society toward a world of alternatives and commitment to social improvement. . . .

Because we have worked so long within the confines of the school as an institution and the teacher role as usually defined, this task will not be easy, for most existing curriculum theory and subtheories are straitjacketed by the existing structure of the school and that ubiquitous teacher role. What we need to erect are sets of engineering propositions which can be used to bring about a wide variety of educational environments, including the institutional forms which can nurture them.

From Bruce Joyce, "Curriculum and Humanistic Education: 'Monolism' vs. 'Pluralism,'" from *Humanistic Foundations of Education,* Carl Weinberg, Editor, © 1972. Reprinted by permission of Prentice-Hall, Inc., Englewood Cliffs, N.J.

# THE SPECTRUM OF EDUCATIONAL MISSIONS[1]

The pluralistic world of education will be composed of many kinds of educational programs designed to further a large number of educational missions. The missions of the present school are tied to ascendency and survival in the technical-economic system. In place of this, a vast variety of missions must emerge. . . .

*The mission of an educational program can be defined in terms of the domains through which it (the program) enters into the life of the student. Since education is an attempt to enter one's life and change it or assist one in changing oneself, the product of education can be described as a developed capacity to respond to reality in new ways. The primary task in selecting an educational mission is to identify the domains through which the program will enter the life of the learner in order to change his responses to living in the world.* The pluralistic education should represent many domains of possible development.

The possible domains of missions can be divided into three, with the caution that the categories overlap somewhat:

1. We can attempt to improve the capacity of the learner through direct intervention in the personal domain (as through a direct attempt to improve his intelligence or to give him greater control over directing his own destiny);

2. We can attempt to enter the social domain, to assist him at a point where he is in interaction with his fellow man (as when we attempt to teach him social or economic skills); or

3. We can attempt to reach him through an academic domain, by teaching him academic skills and ways of dealing intellectually with complexity (as when we attempt to teach him the social sciences).

We can use these three categories—the personal, the social and the academic—to sort out some of the possible directions of education. Then, for each type of mission we can learn what kinds of environments are likely to promote development in that domain. To assist us, we can turn to those educators who have specialized in creating environments appropriate to specific domains. For example, Rogers,[2] Maslow,[3] and others have developed approaches for achieving missions in the personal domain. The National Training Laboratory [4] among others, has developed principles to apply to the interpersonal domain. Psychologists like Ausubel,[5] Piaget,[6] and others have developed theoretical structures from which engineering propositions in the academic domain can be developed and developers like Schwab,[7] Taba,[8] and Suchman,[9] have developed engineering propositions with which academic missions can be approached.

The result of this work is an array of potiential curriculum theories which can be applied to the creation of alternative educational environments. The figure below displays the theoretical model of such an enterprise:

MEANS

| | 1 | 2 | 3 | 4 | ETC. |
|---|---|---|---|---|---|
| **1** | | | | | |
| **2** | | | | | |
| **3** | | | | | |
| **4** | | | | | |
| **ETC.** | | | | | |

MISSIONS (row label, left side)

Missions-Means Matrix

Just as missions can be categorized into the personal, the social and the academic, so it is with approaches to the creation of educational environments. Approaches vary according to which view of reality is emphasized. The *personalists* view reality from an individual perspective, and concentrate on environments which *help* the individual create his reality and his world view. The *interaction-oriented* emphasize the social negotiation of reality and focus on environments which facilitate social processes. A third category is that of the *information-oriented,* who emphasize the symbolization of knowledge and concentrate on environments which improve our symbolic capacity to process information. A fourth approach focuses on how culture shapes behavior, and concentrates on the manipulation of the social environment to shape external behavior.

Hence, four types of approaches to the creation of educational environments can be related to three categories of educational mission.

The family of "personalists" includes those theoreticians and practitioners who focus primarily on the individual's construction of his own reality. Thus they focus on the development of the individual, and speculate on the environments which might affect his personality or his general ways of relating to the world. Therapists especially tend to share a concern with the distinctive ways each person constructs his world; they see human nature in terms of individuals.

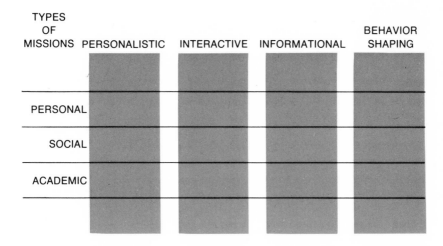

| TYPES OF MISSIONS | PERSONALISTIC | INTERACTIVE | INFORMATIONAL | BEHAVIOR SHAPING |
|---|---|---|---|---|
| PERSONAL | | | | |
| SOCIAL | | | | |
| ACADEMIC | | | | |

Types of Environments

The second family, those educational theorists and practitioners who focus on the processes by which groups and societies negotiate rules and construct social reality, see education as a process of improving the society. Many in this group have suggested an ideal model for society and procedures for creating an education which can help bring that model to a wider audience.

Others who emphasize social behavior concentrate on interpersonal relations and the dynamics of improving them. The approaches to education in either case have a distinctly social character.

The *information-processing* category consists of educational theoreticians and practitioners who are concerned with affecting the information processing system of the student. It includes those who have developed educational procedures designed to increase general thinking capacity (that is, the capacity to think abstractly or to think inductively). It also includes those who focus on ways of teaching students to process information about specific aspects of life. For example, many educational theorists believe that a major mission of education is to develop approaches to the teaching of the academic disciplines, so that the student learns to process information the way the academic scholar processes it and thereby achieve the intellectual power of scholarship.

TABLE 1. A list of educational approaches, grouped by orientation and domain of mission

| Approach | Major Theorist | Orientation (Person, Social Interaction, Information-Processing, or Behavior-Modification) | Missions for Which Applicable |
|---|---|---|---|
| Non-Directive | Carl Rogers[11] | Person | Development into "fully-functioning" individual (however, broad applicability is suggested, for personal development includes all aspects of growth). |
| Awareness Training | Shutz,[12] Perls[13] | Person | Increasing personal capacity. Much emphasis on interpersonal development. |
| Group Investigation | Dewey,[14] Thelen[15] | Social-Interests | Social relations are permanent, but personal development and academic rigor are included. |
| Reflective Thinking and Social Inquiry | Hullfish and Smith,[16] Massialas and Cox[17] | Social Interaction | Improvement of democratic process is central, with more effective thinking the primary route. |
| Inductive Reasoning | Taba,[18] Suchman[19] and others | Information-Processing | Primarily designed to teach academic reasoning, but used for social and personal goals as well. |
| Logical Reasoning | Extrapolations from Piaget (See Sigel, Sullivan)[20] | Information-Processing | Programs are designed to increase thinking, but also are applied to moral development and other areas. (See Koblberg.) |

TABLE 1. (Cont.)

| Approach | Major Theorist | Orientation (Person, Social Interaction, Information-Processing, or Behavior-Modification) | Missions for Which Applicable |
|---|---|---|---|
| Psychoanylistic | See L. Tyler[21] and others | Person | Personal emotional development is primary and would take precedence. |
| Creative Reasoning | Torrance,[22] Gordon | Person | Personal development of creativity in problem-solving has priority, but creative problem-solving in social and academic domains is also emphasized. |
| Academic Modes | Much of the Curriculum Reform Movement (See especially Schwab and Bruner for rationales) | Information-Processing | Designed to teach the research system of the disciplines, but also expected to have effect in other domains (e.g., sociological methods may be taught in order to increase social understanding and problem-solving. |
| Programmed Instruction | Skinner[23] | Behavior Modification & Theory | General applicability; domains of objectives. |
| Conceptual Systems Matching Model | D. E. Hunt[24] | Person | An approach designed to increase personal complexity and flexibility. |

The fourth group focuses on the processes by which human behavior is externally shaped and reinforced. Their major efforts have been devoted to understanding the shaping of human behavior and how education can be built on an understanding of processes. The major theorist in this area is B. F. Skinner.[10]

It is to these four families that curriculum workers can turn for ideas about educational missions and means. The following is a list of some educational theorists and approaches from each of the four categories, grouped according to the domain of mission that each one favors.

BRUCE R. JOYCE     255

*The purpose of the curriculum field is to develop general know-ledge about how to bring educational missions and means together in the real world. It is the creation of pluralistic educational envi-ronments that is our business. We need the ability to specify alter-native missions, to create the environments that will accomplish those missions, and to carry out the engineering necessary to create the material, the social systems, and the instructional systems that will actuate them.* The result will be an array of environments, each serving students in a particular kind of way.

In practice, students will create their own school by selecting from a wide offering of planned educational programs. To see how this might work, let us look at several modes of education—cur-ricular modes, we shall call them—and see how they might be brought together in a student's life. (They represent only a few of the possibilities.)

THREE CURRICULUM MODES

One kind of curriculum mode that we will learn to engineer can be called the individualized self-teaching school or the cybernetic system mode. It is characterized by preplanned, largely automated materials, utilizing self-instruction by individuals or groups for whom instructional activities have been prescribed, again by an automatic assessment system that also feeds back progress reports to the learner. The cybernetic mode will present to the student a large array of self-administering courses or programs in many areas. He will put together much of his education by selecting from this bank of alternatives.

A second curricular mode centers around individual counseling to help the learner structure his own educational goals and activi-ties. The learner might be led to encounter some kinds of prese-lected problem situations, but learning is seen as personal. Conti-nuity comes through the action of the student as he generates purposes and activities. We can call this the tutorial mode.

A third curricular mode involves group inquiry. Groups ana-lyze problems, try on ideas from the various disciplines, and ex-plore social values. The scholarly endeavor of the group and its in-terpersonal processes are included as subjects for study. The disciplines are learned by practicing them. Democratic process is valued. Feedback is collective and emergent. Content may be partly preselected and partly produced by active inquiry and dialogue on the nature of society.

Each of these curricular modes can be adapted to perform unique and important functions in education. Blended, they can offer a common general education, the development of personal talent, and the humanizing effects of cooperative inquiry into critical issues. Let us examine them individually and then see how they can be used together.

## The Cybernetic Systems Mode

We are more certain of some educational objectives than others. The cybernetic mode is appropriate in areas of curriculum where:

1. we have relatively stable agreement about cognitive or skill objectives. That is, we are relatively sure that we want to accomplish the objectives and will want to accomplish them for some time to come. A good example is skill in the four fundamental arithmetic operations with integers and rational numbers. For the next few years (not forever!) it seems safe to say that we want most, possibly all, children to develop reasonable proficiency in this area. Skill in reading is another area of which we are sure that in the forseeable future all possible learners should be brought to a high level of competence. It is not necessary for elementary school facilities or individual teachers to decide annually that the arithmetic operations or reading skills will be taught. We can stabilize these and certain other areas for a long period so far as general objectives are concerned.

2. we can construct adequate self-instructional devices for the vast majority of students. "Self-instructional" should be broadly defined here. One can learn many things by reading about them. Books are self-instructional devices. *Programmed instruction* should be included. Units using films, tapes, and other media have been developed. Computerized games can teach many things. Simulation techniques will expand self-instructional possibilities greatly.

3. we can develop automated feedback systems for keeping the learners and responsible adults informed of progress. Programmed instruction has an edge here, because of the precision with which objectives are specified and ordered and the easy amenability of the process to "embedded" tests. However, precise automated evaluation is possible nearly any time that objectives are clear and self-instruction is possible.

4. the area can be learned as well alone as in a group. Many aspects of social dancing might be acquired in response to films and

computer-controlled instructions, but much of its appeal would be gone. On a more serious side, controversial issues, drama, and improving social and sociointellectual skills require group activity for a good bit (rarely all) of the instruction. Learning map skills, on the other hand, does not *require* group interaction or very much didactic presentation by a teacher.

5. pacing of instruction is important. For example, in any curricular mode, many arithmetic and reading skills are achieved at enormously different rates. In fact, teachers working alone with traditional materials and normal pupil-teacher ratios have been unable to achieve adequate individualization of instruction in most skill areas.

With respect to the social atmosphere in this mode, the norms would stress independence and industriousness. Students would need to learn to judge their own progress and "reward themselves" for progress. An air of calm support and mutual help would be important, as well as openness about progress. Teachers would function as facilitators and troubleshooters.

To summarize: where we have curricular objectives that are very stable, but are achieved effectively by self-instruction that can be monitored by automated feedback systems, we can apply cybernetic principles to create instructional programs. *Such programs would not work for all students* (no curricular mode does), but they could work effectively for many. Effective diagnosis would result in placing some children with tutors, remedial specialists, and teachers in groups. Subprofessional technicians can be trained to work with the children and the feedback can be scrutinized constantly by a specialist who would sound the alarm for students for whom the program wasn't working.

Because of the negative reaction of so many educators to automation, we must stress again that the cybernetic curriculum need not be a deadly array of sequenced "programs." It can be a rich multi-media program, diversely using film games, books, programs, and other devices.[25] Also, it would not be appropriate for all parts of any curricular area. For example, while much science instruction might be automated, instruction requiring a cooperative attack on original problems could not be accomplished this way.

The cybernetic mode would undergo constant revision as objectives change and technology improves. At any given time it would represent a bank of programs which students could dip into the construct part of their education. (High schools, for example, might offer an array of short courses in each curriculum area. By selecting a combination of programs in a subject, a student could create his own layered program in required and elective areas.)

To create this bank of possibilities, systems planning procedures would be employed.


## The Tutorial Mode: The Idiosyncratic Curriculum

The creation of tutorial modes challenges the curriculum worker in different ways. The old story about Mark Hopkins and the log has long been the symbol for a delightful and wise teacher, the idea of having one's personal teacher. We are always trying to find ways to give students personal attention, whether by individualizing reading programs, providing guidance counselors, or offering the opportunity to learn the French horn. The ratio of pupils to teachers has been against us, however, and so has the idea that the "curriculum" must be "covered."

The cybernetic curriculum mode puts books and machines to work, freeing manpower for the development of curriculums devoted not to the individualization of common learning but to the development of personal talents and interests. The idiosyncratic curriculum is appropriate for those ends that:

1. are defined by the learner in his personal quest for understanding and self-development.

2. need personal counseling to assure definition and availability of any special resources and advice which the learner needs.

3. while they might be achieved in group activity, are accomplished socially only through interest groups (in the generic sense of the term). In other words, where personal interests are sufficiently congruent enough, group inquiry serves idiosyncrasy.

An idiosyncratic curriculum might be achieved by assigning students to a kind of tutor whom we could name—an academic counselor—who meets with each student regularly and helps him define personal educational goals and the means for achieving them. In some cases he might serve as a more traditional tutor. In other cases he might help the student to locate a special teacher, resource person, or community resource, for help on a particular problem. If a student were studying justice, the counselor might help him find a court where he could watch cases. If the child were interested in the French horn, the counselor would help arrange for a music teacher.

The counselor would help the child develop a program of wide personal reading (we don't want him stopping with what we provide in the cybernetic curriculum). Also, the counselor would help him get together with others of similar interests (it's not much fun putting on plays or learning modern dance by yourself).

Our academic counselor could have overall charge of ensuring that the child's life in school is a good one and that he receives help with out-of-school problems. If he shows talent or creativity, the counselor would see that it receives nourishment. If things aren't going well for the child in the cybernetic or group inquiry portions of the educational program, the counselor would be able to intervene drastically if necessary, and help change the child's program.

We might envision some teachers who would function solely as academic counselors, each with an assigned quota of students. Available to them would be subject specialists of many kinds. Developing the functions of the academic counselor for the six- and seven-year-old should provide some interesting research, since relatively few people have tried this sort of relationship with the younger child. It should be evident that such a mode would emphasize rewarding initiative and exploration. Seeking, probing, questioning would be highly valued. The technical support systems would need to be responsive to the demands of a great many students seeking a great many ends.

The curricular worker will have to face an enormous variety of tasks in order to depict and engineer tutorial modes. The possible tutorial roles, possible support systems, and alternative ways of bringing students together with tutors and resources provide a dizzying matrix of important engineering questions to be resolved.

The personal discovery curriculum belongs to the student. It can exist because of energy saved by the cybernetic curriculum. Both of these modes emphasize the learner as an individual. That is not all he is, however, so we need another curricular mode.

The Group Inquiry Curricular Mode

The inquiring group was at the core of the progressive movement's approach to education. The group of students, with their teachers, would learn democratic skills and scientific method simultaneously while they explored their world and developed commitment to the ideals of democracy. Until the academic curriculum projects began in the 1950s the chief thrust for social reform was provided by the legatees of the progressives. An overwhelming proportion of curriculum supervisors in the schools of today was influenced by this tradition.

Its Achilles heel has always been its dependence on teachers with extraordinary skills. Given the supply of talent available to education, the demands made were simply too great for the average teacher. He could not know about enough domains of knowledge and handle groups well enough to cope with the range of educational objectives.

However, group inquiry as a mode is extremely useful when:

1. group skills and interdependence are to be acquired. The democratic way must be learned *in situ*.

2. the learner should test himself against the ideas of others. Controversial issues and contemporary social movements, for example, need the interplay of diverse reactions to events. Many kinds of thinking can be learned if we have to balance our ideas against those of others.

3. group dynamics is an important learning agent. The power of the reference group, for example, can accomplish many things. The intellectual and social climate of the school is a consequence of the group process. Students can teach each other a good deal about social life. Drama, debate, sciencing are social and dependent on social feedback as well. International games require groups.

4. individual differences are advantageous. A homogeneous group studying its society would probably develop much less vigor and heat than a heterogeneous one.

As in the case of the other model, the curriculum worker has to face a large number of tasks in order to engineer the setting for academic inquiry. Teaching strategies have to be developed, studied, modified. The kinds of teachers who can employ them need to be identified. Academic inquiry in the various disciplines needs to be compared and contrasted. Ways of combining or separating them have to be clarified. Alternative technical support systems can be studied. The creation of each mode requires the use of systematic planning techniques and a range of instructional technologies.

A SPINNING OF DREAMS

As if the task of creating and studying curriculum modes were not enough, the curriculum worker needs to develop plans for constructing well-balanced educational programs which can be orchestrated to serve (or be served by) a wide variety of students.

To illustrate this task hypothetically, let us construct a design for a school (remembering that "school" means "pattern of education," not a specific building) whose basic organization consists of four teams of teachers and clusters of support systems built around each of the three curricular modes. One team will use the cybernetic mode, one the tutorial mode, and two will employ group inquiry.

## The Basic Education Layer

In the first case, let us build a self-instructional mode, using cybernetic principles and consisting of self-instructional units of many kinds which give the learner the option of developing himself in a number of areas. First of all, for reading skills, then for arithmetic, then for world history, let us build a highly sequenced course within this mode. Let us also make available courses in several foreign languages, in art history, music history, and literature. The staff of this team will need to learn how to build alternative routes for students who are unable to teach themselves by this mode. They will need to be experts in diagnosis and in the training of aides who will do much of the work in these realms. The support systems clearly will have to be massive self-instructional systems employing many media, including television, tape, programmed instruction, conventional books, workbooks, language laboratories, activities packets that instruct people on projects to be carried out, and many other things.

## The Personal Layer

Second, let us build a tutorial mode of the kind that we described earlier. The team administering this mode will be skilled in training people to counsel with children and to facilitate their personal inquiry. Each youngster will need to contact his tutor several times a week and the tutors will need to call in consultants as the students develop interests in problem areas beyond their particular competencies. The support systems for this mode will need to include an enormous library, to utilize many media (television, tape, contact films, motion picture films, filmstrips, slides), to develop books of many sorts, and to make arrangements so that the students can reach out beyond the walls of the school for instruction and for information.

## The Sciencing Layer

Let us also include a scientific inquiry system. In this mode, skilled group leaders will lead groups of children to inquire into significant problems and, in the course of that inquiry, will teach them the modes of inquiry and the structures of the academic disciplines. Each child should be engaged in several groups during each year. The support systems for this layer need to include the products of the academic reform movement, the systems for teaching the discipline to the children. Since many of these teachers will be expert in their discipline, it is probably more important to provide laboratory facilities, excellent libraries, and aides who can construct needed materials and help the youngsters get the necessary data and ideas. In this mode, each group will identify problems and attack them at its relative leisure. Scientific inquiry should not be hurried, and it is through dialogue and debate that the structures of the disciplines become clear and the modes of inquiry become explicated.

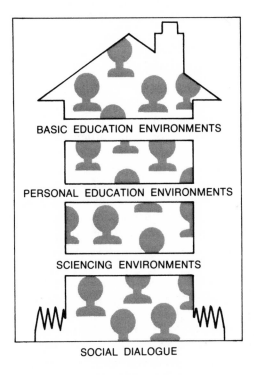

BASIC EDUCATION ENVIRONMENTS

PERSONAL EDUCATION ENVIRONMENTS

SCIENCING ENVIRONMENTS

SOCIAL DIALOGUE

The Four Layer School

The Dialogue Layer

The fourth layer of this school will be devoted to a dialogue on the nature of the society and on its future. In this mode, again, skilled group leaders will help children identify study serious social problems. Also television programs will bring to the youngsters information and analysis about contemporary events on a weekly basis. At present, activities in such a mode would deal with the problems of the cities, poverty, building an international community, and the like. The teachers need to be skilled in group inquiry and to be backed up by support systems and materials which include not only magnificent library facilities of the kind described for the preceding layer, but also by people who can help construct materials when these are needed. Some aspects of this layer can be accomplished through the mass media, as indicated before. Television programs can bring to the students of an entire city information and opinion about certain events, and this should be done regularly. Other activities should be done at the group level where clusters of youngsters attack and try to solve problems that seem worthwhile to them.

## The Balance in a Multilayer Education

In such a school teachers would work in teams. As a result the student is not exposed simply to the personality and opinions of one person at a time, but is a constant participant in a dialogue about what to do next and how to do it. If one teacher cannot help him learn the skill he needs then he can turn to others. If one teacher has strong opinions about some segment of academic inquiry, or about society, then that person's opinions can be balanced by those of the other members of the team. Furthermore, such a school balances the possibilities in the life of the learner. He is not dominated by skills, nor by the dialogue on society. He has the opportunity to participate in all of these. Also, because each teacher does not have to be responsible for all kinds of learnings, it is possible for the teachers to become experts and to teach each other the skills needed to operate in their particular mode.

In today's schools, too many teachers perform too many functions and students are clustered together in such a way that enormous effort has to be expended to treat them as individuals. In the multilayered school, some activities would be organized for individualization, others for group inquiry, and there need be no conflict between the two. Furthermore, the mass media, instead of being argued about as an alternative to the classroom teacher, can be utilized to perform its most effective functions.

The political organization of such a school should provide

places for students to share in steering committees that operate the support systems, create materials, and shape the ways that students select curriculum alternatives. For example, the library should be operated by a faculty, student, and teacher aide committee that keeps in continuous touch with the needs of the students, the needs of the faculty, and the demands that are made on the staff. All the other support systems, too, should have steering committees of this kind so that the governance of the daily life of the school is a cooperation among all the members of the community.

Furthermore, the "school" should link students throughout the nation and even the world to engage in the social dialogue necessary to bring about pluralism in all aspects of life. Film, television, and print media now enable us to study with others far removed from us in space—an essential if we are to face social problems beyond the scope of our village or urban neighborhood.

As an example, let us look at a brief description of a curriculum plan designed to capitalize on television's capacity to link students all over the country in a study of a serious problem that faces them all—the problem of alienation.

## A COMPREHENSIVE CURRICULUM APPROACH TO THE PROBLEM OF ALIENATION

This curriculum is part of the fourth layer of the school: the social dialogue.

> *THE MISSION: A WAR AGAINST ALIENATION.* Our mission is to bring together the young people of America in a war against alienation that divides men in a mass society.
>
> Since the term "alienation" has been rather loosely used in the popular press—although generally it refers to the sense of aloneness and disaffiliation among men in a mass technological society—we should take some pains with its definition; but to avoid a long digression from the substance of this paper, we will eschew a dissertation on its nature and assume that the reader of this paper is familiar with Durkheim, Weber, Keniston, and the other analysts of the phenomenon.
>
> Kenneth Keniston has become a spokesman for the factors which compound youth's dilemma against this general background of cultural alienation. He has pointed out that American society makes extraordinary demands on its members. In the first place they are asked to adapt to chronic social change. America is never still. Ideas come in and out of fashion at a

dizzying rate. The insatiable media search continuously for new sensations and ideas and fads and transmit these as fast as they are discovered. Second, American society is extremely fragmented. At present, particularly, it seems like a collection of minority groups. Caste and class combine with ethnic stratification. The matrix we have been describing above in which there is a great sense of social separation in general, provides a condition in which individuals have to attempt to achieve a sense of personal wholeness in an extremely fragmented situation. In the third case, there is an extraordinary discontinuity between childhood and adulthood in a situation of extreme competitiveness (which itself increases alienation) and great uncertainty. The adolescent is required to make decisions affecting his entire life during a period in which he is very young and while faced with an almost impossibly complex economic and social matrix through which he must find his way.

The purpose of the comprehensive curriculum which we propose will be to reduce the sense of alienation and to decrease the fact of alienation by enabling young people to make life more personal and more filled with the dialogue in which they and their elders examine this aspect of society and attempt to do something about it.

## The General Behavioral Objectives for the Curriculum

It is not possible in a document of reasonable length to provide the detailed behavioral objectives necessary to develop a complete curricular approach. However, it is necessary to provide enough behavioral objectives to give the reader a clear idea of the direction which we are recommending.

1. The student can apply Keniston's conceptual framework for analyzing alienation between contemporary society. The achievement of this objective would be demonstrated by the student's ability to use Keniston's concepts to describe behavior in the contemporary society, including exemplars from his own behavior and those of his associates, and the ability to point out or demonstrate exemplars of alienated and nonalienated behavior.

2. The student can apply conceptual systems for analyzing bureaucratic behavior in contemporary society.

3. The student can engage in a dialogue with peers and elders over the problem of alienation and affiliation in the society.

4. The student can formulate a plan for reducing alienation in a situation in which the student has involvement. This includes working together with others in the school situation to create a less alienated and more authentic and affiliated mode of behavior within that institution.

These are really very general objectives which are only designed to give the flavor of the specificity with which our mission should be approached.

*The teaching strategy* Our strategy is designed to capitalize on the unique advantages of television to enable people all over the country to engage in a simultaneous study of matters of concern to all. It will use television to apply democratic process principles to the problem area. The strategy is engineered from the principles of the Group Investigation model articulated by Thelen. The strategy hinges on the possibility of using open-circuit television plus television tapes to induce the students from all over the area to which the curriculum is directed (we will speak of the nation for illustrative purposes) to engage in the simultaneous study of alienation. This nationwide student body would develop ways of attacking and defeating alienation and replacing bureaucratic contact with authentic personal contact and meaningful interpersonal relationships. The key idea is the radical one of trying to induce a national cooperative inquiry into the problem area—to apply democratic process to what would result in cooperative groups all over the nation being related to each other by means of television, working in the same area. Let's see how this cooperative study on a nationwide scale might work.

*Phase one* The strategy begins with televised confrontations with the problem situation. These confrontations can be in the form of dramatizations of puzzling incidents related to alienation. An example would be the Kitty Genovese incident in which apartment dwellers in New York heard and, at times, watched a young woman being stabbed to death in the courtyard of an apartment house but declined to get involved even to the extent of calling the police. But alienation comes in many forms less dramatic, and a good many of the confrontations should deal with the less dramatic but equally important incidents of human behavior which exemplify the alienated condition. Alienation is so widespread in the contemporary human scene that the task of generating the dramatization should be discouragingly easy. Driver behavior, for example, or commuter behavior in subways, behavior in large organizations, competitive situations, all abound to provide dramatic material.

Our suggestion is that the curriculum sequence begin with the presentation of a number of dramatizations in which various types of alienated behavior are illustrated. These should include routine behavior toward others, the failure to respond or get involved in social situations, withdrawal, criminal behavior of various kinds, interpersonal situations in which individuals do not respond to one another with warmth and authenticity, and others.

*Phase two*  In the second stage, students should begin to make clear their reactions to the situations. For this purpose classes of youngsters in high schools and junior high schools throughout the country could react to the incidents and groups of them could be brought together to make television tapes or to have discussions which would be broadcast live in which they would share their various reactions. A dramatization should stimulate a wide variety of reactions and the variety itself should be puzzling to the student. Some students will not see the alienating effects of competition, or cliques, etc., whereas others will feel it keenly.

Ideally, classrooms all over the country would discuss their reactions to the confrontation dramatizations and then representatives from various regions of the country would appear on television to describe their reactions. This would set the stage for the next phase of the work—planning inquiry into the problem area.

*Phase three*  At this point, using a nationwide hookup, social scientists could meet with the students in the studio and help them to formulate inquiry into their reactions to the situations they had observed. Some of the scholars could introduce them to frameworks for analyzing various phenomena in the alienation complex. Television tapes could be prepared also and distributed to local classrooms to provide suggestions for lines of study into the phenomena.

This phase could be shaped so as to induce groups of local students in classrooms all over the country to study not only the confrontation dramatizations and the questions they raise, but also to expand their range of study into their community life. They could then begin to study the same phenomena in daily life that they are studying by means of their analysis of the confrontation dramatization.

As the study proceeded, classrooms could communicate problems and progress by television. Again the nationwide hookup could be used to provide consultation with social scientists over the study problems as they developed. For example, if a group of students in New York, Los Angeles, and New Orleans were studying bureaucratic behavior in large organizations, the social scientist might appear on the television hookup and present to them ways to go about their study. Simultaneously television tapes could be made and distributed to the local schools providing further and perhaps more detailed advice.

As the studies proceeded, students could begin to share their findings with students in other parts of the United States. Other students could comment on the findings and the social scientists could have their commentary as well. The results of the students' study could be compared with the results of the scholarly study. Keniston, for example, could compare the findings of his analysis with those that are being turned up by students in various parts of the United States.

As soon as the studies were considerably developed and had been discussed and analyzed thoroughly, it would be time for the next phase.

*Phase four* In phase four, the television medium would be used to challenge the students to two kinds of efforts. One would be to formulate plans to reduce alienation in some aspects of their lives. A second would be to formulate plans which could be applied on a nationwide scale to reduce alienation.

Over the nationwide network students and experts could present their plans as they were formulated, criticize the plans, and discuss their implementation. Groups in various parts of the United States that were formulating similar plans could be addressed over the nationwide network or through specially prepared television tapes to provide consultation from experts. (During all the phases up to this point, quite a number of programs would continue to introduce theoretical and student-generated ways of looking at the alienation problem so that in the course of the phases a rather complete coverage of the area would be ensured.) Considerable time would be taken with this phase so that alternative approaches to the reduction of alienation could be well aired and analyzed.

*Phase five* In this phase local groups would begin to put into effect their plans for alleviating some aspect of alienation within the orbit of their competence. As the plans were put into action, they would be reported over the nationwide network and particular local groups would prepare television tapes which would be sent to other local groups reporting their progress and problems. As the progress and problems were reported, experts would address the local groups over the nationwide network and, also, would use the medium of video tape.

Simultaneous with the local activity, a nationwide organization of children would be started using the nationwide network and representatives of the local groups throughout the country would be put together to select some aspect of alienation for a nationwide frontal attack.

*Phase six*  In this phase the local efforts would continue and the nationwide effort would be inaugurated. The nationwide network would be used to coordinate the efforts, to keep the students from various areas of the country in contact with one another, and to develop and refine further plans. Using the nationwide network, aspects of the plan could be put into effect simultaneously all over the country. For example, let us suppose that one aspect of the plan was to increase warmth in hitherto impersonal relations such as the way that one relates to restaurants, waiters, and waitresses. Over the nationwide network, ways of doing this could be discussed and the students could set a target date for implementing the new form of behavior. Then, simultaneously, all over the United States, restaurant employees would find that young people were acting differently toward them. The students would know the plan was being implemented throughout the United States, they would have the reinforcement of the nationwide community and the obligation of holding up their end of the game.

*Phase seven*  Phase seven would consist of reports from local activities and the preparation for further national action. In addition, students would be taught how to evaluate their efforts; that is, how to determine whether or not they would be becoming less alienated in interpersonal relations and in inducing less alienation in other people.

*Curriculum mode*  The combination of nationwide television with the cooperative inquiry strategy would result in an educational mode never before seen: that is, a cooperative inquiry which would have local and national aspects and which would involve all the young people of the country in the simultaneous study of problems that affect them very deeply. If this mode were successful, the students utilizing the nationwide network might select other areas for examination and study. Problems of urbanization, international understanding and relations, developing careers, learning to relate with others, sex and marriage, could be selected. The television-mediated co-operative inquiry mode, enabling a dialogue among representatives of all the children of the nation and permitting them to interact with experts and their elders, might generate a national dialogue on problems of personal and social significance, in which the strength and optimism of the young could be combined with the technological knowhow of the old to produce what really could be a significant effect on the American society.

Curriculum engineering plans of this sort differ from the usual in that they begin with education (missions and means) and create the institutional form from the specification of the environment. If we confine ourselves to those environments which "fit" the format of the present school, then no pluralism will result—we simply will embellish the technical monolithism of the past. On the contrary, our efforts should be to increase on a continual basis the options that are available to the population and the flexibility with which they can be made available. As more options are developed, making more and more kinds of education commonplace, and giving students the power to educate themselves in increasingly humane ways, then the curriculum worker will be making his contribution to the search for an increasingly humanistic education. He will be helping people to clarify alternative educational missions or purposes and to select from among them; he will develop alternative curricular strategies for achieving those missions; and he will develop the means of institutionalizing a very wide range of missions and means in an increasing variety of institutional forms.

Hence, the curriculum worker will have an array of technologies which he can bring to bear on educational problems so that the society and students will have a layer range of options. Presently, schools present very limited alternatives to children and these alternatives are focused to help them to technical proficiency. The wider range envisioned here will enable students to create much of their own education and a large proportion of its remainder to be devoted to a dialogue on the humanization of their society.

# HUMAN TEACHING
# FOR HUMAN LEARNING

SHORT INTEGRATED CONCEPTUAL UNIT
IN DRIVER EDUCATION

*(Ninth-grade social studies, all levels. By Robin D. Montz)*

I. The concept of the machine.
  1. Cognitive context: The study of internal-combustion engines and other moving parts of the automobile.
  2. Affective exercises.
      a. The machine: One person starts an action accompanied by a sound. Other members of the group, as they see where something might fit in, join the machine with their own action and accompanying sound. The objective is to show the structure and function of parts making up the whole and how each part functions for the whole. After doing the machine, have the students express how they felt being part of a machine. Some may like it; others may be frustrated if they get in touch with their individual anonymity as part of a mechanistic system.
      b. Have the students draw a machine. Make up a Rube Goldberg type of "crazy" machine in which all parts have a function for "something."
II. Anger, frustration, and behavior change in driving.
  1. Cognitive concept: What do the extreme emotions of anger and frustration do to your driving behavior?
  2. Affective exercises:
      a. Improvisational theater: "You want to go somewhere, and I won't let you."
      b. Gibberish games ending with "You've got it, I want it."
  3. Cognitive evaluation: How did your behavior change when you were angry? Frustrated? What would that do to your driving? How can you release these inner tensions and revert to normal behavior naturally?

---

III. The concept of courtesy.
   1. Cognitive definition: Courtesy is stepping into the other guy's shoes, understanding, and allowing him to "do his thing."
   2. Affective exercises:
      a. Getting communication going.
         (1) Dyad work.
         (2) Encounter groups.
      b. Getting rid of resentment: Gestalt work with the person you most resent.
      c. Role reversal with resented person.
   3. Cognitive evaluation:
      a. Discussion of courtesy.
      b. Simulation of driving situations involving the need for courteous behavior.

On the following pages are individual lessons and short series of lessons which were used as parts of other units.

The following lessons were developed by Aaron Hillman for so-called "slow learners" in tenth-grade English.

Experiencing Life

*Aim*  Experiencing, illustrating, knowing, and enjoying other parts of life. Providing models and experiences to show other ways of living.

*Format*  Five male students, sophomores in high school (fifteen to seventeen years old), so-called "slow learners," culturally and economically handicapped, had a formal dinner with the teacher at the Madonna Inn in San Luis Obispo, California.

*Events*  Preparations by the boys were extensive. Consideration about what to wear was paramount. The idea of ties (and not having any in three cases) was a problem. On the night of the dinner one did not have a tie, three wore ties and nylon zipper jackets, and one wore a suit and tie. At the inn we were seated in the middle of the room with luxury around us. We were surrounded by other diners and had a good view of the stage. We discussed napkins (What do you do with them?) and which eating utensils to use. We had drinks (Tom Collinses without gin) and discussed the menu. Four opted for filet mignon (after learning what it was and how to pronounce it) and one had fried chicken. During the meal we talked and discussed many things, mostly their feelings about school, school personnel, and relatives. They discussed what they could do with this room at a party. One boy thought the pink satin tufted chair covers would be great for seat covers in an automobile. After dessert and listening to the band, we toured the restaurant. All the staff from bus boys on up were extremely courteous and helpful; they went out of their way to assist us and to show us the place. Before departing, we toured the rest of the complex.

*Conclusions* This was an extremely informative and vibrant experience for the teacher as well as the boys. We got to know one another better, and we exchanged viewpoints on life without the necessity of their bowing to peer pressure or my bowing to social pressure. It was a frank exchange. The boys participated in and enjoyed a segment of living that they had not seen or experienced. From our conversations and their frank expressions of gratitude at the conclusion, I believe the funds were more than well spent. As a side issue, I think we gave the people at the restaurant something to remember. Some asked who we were and talked with the boys, and we received many appreciative glances from other people. As another side event, the relationships between the boys and learning, the boys and their classmates, the boys and the teacher, improved; and they settled into a subtle acceptance of one another and readiness for work in the classroom. The necessity for discipline dwindled, and more work was done by the boys during class time. In all, this was an extremely profitable venture for society, the boys, and the teacher.

*Origin* Funds were provided for this dinner under the Cultural Enrichment section of the Elementary and Secondary Education Act of the federal government.

## Decision by Consensus

*Aim* Experiencing how group decisions are made and how groups can work together to solve a common problem. Experiencing and illustrating the novel. Understanding the characters in a novel. Becoming aware of group interaction and how to function better in a group situation.

*Format* NASA—Decision by Consensus: 1. (To be taken by individuals). Instructions: You are a member of a space crew originally scheduled to rendezvous with a mother ship on the lighted surface of the moon. Because of mechanical difficulties, however, your ship was forced to land at a spot some two hundred miles from the rendezvous point. During the landing much of the ship and the equipment aboard were damaged, and since survival depends on reaching the mother ship, the most critical items still available must be chosen for the two-hundred-mile trip. Below are listed the fifteen items left intact and undamaged after landing. Your task is to rank them in order of their importance in allowing your crew to reach the rendezvous point. Place the number 1 by the most important item, the number 2 by the second most important, and so on through number 15, the least important.

_____ Box of matches
_____ Food concentrate
_____ 50 feet of nylon rope
_____ Parachute silk
_____ Portable heating unit
_____ Two .45 caliber pistols
_____ One case of dehydrated milk
_____ Two 100-pound tanks of oxygen
_____ Map of the stars as seen from the moon
_____ Life raft
_____ Magnetic compass
_____ 5 gallons of water
_____ Signal flares
_____ First-aid kit containing injection needles
_____ Solar powered FM receiver-transmitter

2. (Group consensus.) This is an exercise in group decision-making. Your group is to employ the method of group consensus in reaching its decision. This means that the predicition for each of the fifteen survival items *must* be agreed upon by each group member before it becomes a part of the group decision. Consensus is difficult to reach. Therefore, not every ranking will meet with everyone's complete approval. Try, as a group, to make each ranking one with which *all* group members can at least partially agree. Here are some guides to use in reaching consensus:

1. Avoid arguing for your own individual judgements. Approach the task on the basis of logic.
2. Avoid changing your mind only in order to reach agreement and eliminate conflict. Support only solutions with which you are able to agree to some extent, at least.
3. Avoid conflict-reducing techniques such as majority vote, averaging, or trading in reaching decisions.
4. View differences of opinion as helpful rather than as a hindrance in decision-making.

On the group Summary Sheet place the individual rankings made earlier by each group member. Take as much time as you need in reaching your group decision.

Take the difference between your ranking and the ranking on the key. Add the differences. The lower the score the better. These answers are based on the best judgments that are now available to you. They are not absolute answers.

| | | |
|---|---|---|
| 15 | Box of matches | Little or no use on moon. |
| 4 | Food concentrate | Supply daily food required. |
| 6 | 50 feet of nylon rope | Useful in tying injured together; helpful in climbing. |
| 8 | Parachute silk | Shelter against sun's rays. |
| 13 | Portable heating unit | Useful only if party landed on dark side of moon. |
| 11 | Two .45-caliber pistols | Self-propulsion devices could be made from them. |
| 12 | One case of dehydrated milk | Food; mixed with water for drinking. |
| 1 | Two 100-pound tanks of oxygen | Fills respiration requirements. |
| 3 | Map of the stars as seen from the moon | One of the principal means of finding directions. |
| 9 | Life raft | $CO_2$ bottles for self-propulsion across chasms, etc. |
| 14 | Magnetic compass | Probably no magnetized poles; thus useless. |
| 2 | 5 gallons of water | Replenishes loss by sweating, etc. |
| 10 | Signal flares | Distress call when line of sight possible. |
| 7 | First-aid kit containing injection needles | Oral pills of injection valuable. |
| 5 | Solar-powered FM receiver-transmitter | Distress-signal transmitter—possible communication with mother ship. |

3. (Critique.) Following the exercise, discuss the sources of the problem-solving techniques. How often did individuals use the affective domain in working out the problem? How often did the

cognitive domain dominate? What kind of balance existed? How did their knowledge of the extensional world allow them to work with the unknowns? What did they learn about their own learning styles? Did they work better in groups or alone? Did they score higher as a group or was the individual score better? How did the scores compare with the group average? Did they enjoy the individual work more than the group work?

4. (Applicability.) Compare with the group problems experienced by the boys in the novel *Lord of the Flies.*

*Events* Extremely productive. There was much concentration and thought given to the answers in the individual phase of the exercise. Some went through the items quickly, while others took considerable time and thought out each answer. There was a lot of interest in the work. During the group phase also, some groups finished quickly with little interaction, while some fought long and hard to establish the consensus. In a few cases the decisions were the result of the rest of the group's deferring to one member of that group. The boys were particularly impressed by knowing that they were working on an exercise that was part of NASA's training program. In the writing phase at the end of the exercise these were some of the evaluations:

Nothing happened except we all came to a decision."

"Well, we kept on narrowing down the answers until we got the answer."

"We finally talked it over because we were getting out of hand; some felt like punching me in the mouth."

"We would get excited and start to explain, and everybody would stare at the one who disagreed."

There seemed to be general agreement at the end that if the boys in the novel had practiced what they had learned in the exercise, then they might have been able to solve their problems before the trouble started.

*Conclusions* A perfect vehicle for working with this particular portion of the novel and an excellent way for students to experience the problems inherent in working with groups. In addition, they were able to experience and to work out the emotions that were aroused and felt during both the individual phase and the group phase.

*Addenda*  In William Golding's novel, *Lord of the Flies,* a group of boys isolated on an otherwise uninhabited island attempt to set up a provisional government to solve their problems. The attempt fails and anarchy results because of their inability to mesh their emotions, goals, and ideals. This exercise was used to show what the boys might have done.

*Origin*  National Aeronautics and Space Administration training exercise.


## Personal Communication and Listening

*Aim*  Implementing the point of view about human relations that each person is aware and responsible and direct in his own communications and listens as fully as possible to the other person as an equal.

*Format*  As fully and as quickly as possible the instructor asks that in all interactions that take place in the group people speak directly to each other without the use of the third person. Throughout the exercise he should discourage questions and keep a steady, gentle pressure on the direct and responsible "I-thou" relationship.

*Events*  As occurring.

*Conclusions*  Staying in the Here and Now and directly communicating and listening.

*Addenda*  Relate to training in personal communication and listening, as well as to training in the art of conversation.

*Origin*  Unpublished paper entitled "An Introduction to Gestalt Therapy," by John B. Enright, Ph.D., Langley Porter Neuropsychiatric Institute, 401 Parnassus Avenue, San Francisco, California.


## LSD Brings Out the Real You

*Aim*  Inductive. Use of drugs and knowledge of self.

*Format*  Began as a short talk by the teacher about doors that prevent people from seeing people and doors we hide behind. Two individuals (a boy and a girl, both Mexican American) of a Group 4 (remedial) class took sides and argued their points. Discussion by the teacher was used as a summing up.

*Events*  It began with the boy saying that only under LSD could one show his real self. He was very tense, emotional, and deep as he argued the points. He knew he was right. "Why, if one felt like it, under LSD he could go out and kiss a donkey." The girl was equally intense, deep, and moving. Her main point was that drugs or whiskey weren't necessary to life. Besides, one shouldn't show all that's behind one's cover because everyone needs some secret. Other students listened intently and talked and worked on what was being said.

*Conclusions*  Tremendously moving experience for the teacher as well as the students. A tenth-grade boy who could hardly read or write thought deeply and spoke eloquently. A girl, conscious of her background and her way of expression, found satisfaction in defending her significance. Students saw and heard a valid, moving argument on the drug problem. There is no question to me that inductive learning took place.

*Addenda*  Used in connection with Stephen Crane's *The Red Badge of Courage* and Henry Fleming's feelings and emotions as portrayed in the writing.

*Origin*  Spontaneous. The class began a discussion of the hero of the novel, Henry Fleming, and the doors that had to be opened by him in order for him to take his place in the world, as well as the doors that prevented him from being his real self. When the boy stated that "LSD would open those doors," then the class interaction and the intense argument between the boy and the girl began.

The Sights of Sound

*Aim*  Inductive. Inner imagery; imagery of music. Creativity training. Finding meaning in and feeling the essence of a novel.

*Format*  Students assumed comfortable positions and closed their eyes. The lights were turned off and the blinds drawn. Smetana's *The Moldau* was placed on the phonograph. "While at rest and alert with the mind, close your eyes and listen to this rich, evocative piece of music. Let yourself go into it and absorb it. When the music is finished, stay with your impressions. Ask yourself what images were produced." Afterwards the students were given a copy of Longfellow's poem, "The Sound of the Sea." They were asked to record (1) their impressions while they listened to *The Moldau* and (2) how Longfellow's poem expressed the sound of the music.

*Events* After the usual preliminaries of closing the eyes or resting the head on the desk, the students were picked up and put on by the music. They became absorbed in the sound and the sight. There were many movements of body and feet and hands in response to the audio stimulation. Subsequent to the music, the writing period produced excellent results. The following are selected samples.

"It shows how fast our emotions can change and they always do, just like the record."

"The ocean can be like humans, sometimes there's peace, and sometimes a hard tide washes all the beauty away."

"Made me think of a man standing in front of an audience playing his violence."

"I heard the sound of music in my mind and I see a sea of red blood which is pumped from my heart and will flow right into the hearts of others."

"I saw during the music at first in a big, very large room. The room looked as if it belonged in a mansion in France. Then it got very loud and it reminded me of sailors or fishermen at sea, then I thought about Moby Dick and men struggling to capture it. It was real wild and noisy. The poem, 'The Sound of the Sea,' now that I think about it, matched the music just right."

"I saw a stream of water that flowed into a river then into the sea. Then it flowed into another stream where there was a dam and the sea didn't want to stop following so the sea broke the dam with waves, waves of power almost like a hand hitting a person. Then the stream came to rest in a small valley where it stayed."

*Conclusions* Music by itself in creative exercises seems to me to be of unquestionable value. Combining the music with poetry seems appropriate for understanding both the music and the poem, as well as the person himself. Combining the two further and relating them to the work we are studying enhances the knowledge of the work and possibly helps in retention of its concepts. This particular exercise is valuable also as a simple writing exercise.

*Addenda*   Used in connection with Herman Melville's novel *Moby Dick,* and the feeling of the characters in the novel about the ocean of which they were a part.


Imagine a Cave

*Aim*   Creativity and writing exercise illustrating how a novel may be read and enjoyed. Inductive. Personal insight; inner imagery.

*Format*   Close your eyes and relax. Imagine a countryside in a foothill setting. Large oak trees soar out of the earth as large, immobile sculptures. The sun is about to set, and long shadows are boldly clothing many of the ravines. The shadows of trees seem to be spirit partners of their parent forms. Fog patterns are rising up wraithlike from lowlands to shroud the grasses and trees in moving shapes fantastically human in form. You are walking up a ravine in the last light of day amid the swirling fog. Soon you find a cave. When you enter it, experience whatever occurs. Let yourself continue until the fantasy stops. When it does, write down or draw parts of it.

*Events*   This was soul-satisfying to the students and myself. There was considerable reluctance on the part of the students to close their eyes, and it was extremely difficult for many to keep them closed. As long as they were quiet, I didn't press the point. The picture was presented slowly, distinctly, and softly. Some of the inner lines (i.e., the trees as sculpture) were repeated or embellished. At the conclusion we sat silently for at least three full minutes, and then I asked them to record their experiences. A few wrote very little; most wrote furiously for five to ten minutes. Some found the cave lighted; others found it dark and long. A "dinner for two" was set in one. Some examples: "I was alone in a dark and weary place." "There came shadows walking slow through a crowd." In general, every aim cited above was accomplished. In addition, and this I find the most gratifying, they enjoyed the experience and writing very much.

*Conclusion*   The students were intrigued by the exercise and enjoyed the imagining and the subsequent writing. The massive amount of work done by all was impressive. For stimulating creativity in the use of the imagination and getting students with writing problems to write a lot and to express their feelings, it is an exceptional device. The next time I use this exercise, I plan to try the idea of a trip across a desert on a cold night with subsequent entry into a warm and well-lit house; then I will compare the cave and the house as to what was experienced, what was felt, and which makes the better exercise.

*Addenda* The class is reading and experiencing *Moby Dick*. One main character, Captain Ahab, is said to be surrounded by phantoms. After this exercise, the "cave" was likened to the world of Ahab's brain. A class discussion period followed.

Where Am I Now?

*Aim* Inductive and deductive. Experiencing ourselves as we are; being aware of ourselves. Preparation for creativity and understanding.

*Format* Mary Whitehouse exercise. Students sit where they please. "Let us try an experiment. At this moment you are sitting and listening to me in a particular physical way; let's find out what it is. Please close your eyes. You may feel slightly embarrassed or self-conscious; but once everybody has his eyes closed, the embarrassment is not located on the outside. It is not because someone else is looking, but because you are. The looking is an act of *attention*. Do not move or change your position; just be where you are. Now begin with your feet. Where *are* they? Are they touching the floor; and, if so, what part of the foot is pressing on the floor? Are they touching each other? Are they alike or quite separate and different? Wiggle your toes inside your shoes. Can you feel them? Now travel up to your knees and do the same thing. Are they crossed over each other? Is the back of either one or both touching the chair seat? If not, at what point do the backs of the legs rest on the chair? Travel along underneath and behind yourself. How much of you is touching the chair? What are you sitting on? Go on to your back. Is it rounded or straight? Are you leaning back? Where? Are you sitting more on one side than the other? What are your arms doing? Where is each one? Finally, how does your head feel? Can you feel it, or do you just know it is there? Now try to be aware of yourself all at once, of all of these things at once so you can recognize: I am sitting *this way*. Now open your eyes." Discussion and feedback period follows.

*Events* My preconceptions had been that the students would resist and that much difficulty, snickering, laughter, and inability to close the eyes would result. These happened, but to a minimal degree. The room was darkened, which could have assisted in quieting embarrassment or feelings of unease. During the exercise, a majority of the students could be seen trying to sit and to move and to feel what the instructions were asking. They became absorbed in the exercise. During the discussion and feedback the comments ranged from "I didn't feel nothing" to the expressive "I discovered all of me!" When the teacher tied in this feeling to the lesson we were studying, the students seemed genuinely intrigued both by themselves and the novel.

*Conclusions* All aims were satisfactorily achieved. Students became more aware of themselves and that we don't just happen to be, we *are*. They became more interested in themselves and in our lesson. It seemed to me that the exercise was also useful in overcoming embarrassment, in relaxing with the group, trusting the group, and enjoying the simple pleasures of life. I can also see this exercise as leading into a productive reading and writing exercise.

*Addenda* Related to *Moby Dick*. In today's lesson the novel's narrator, Ishmael, says, "The problems of the universe revolve in me." This exercise and experiment was an attempt to have the students know and experience that feeling. The "problems of the universe" revolve in every one of us. However, we actively seek to avoid this fact in our daily lives.


Isolation

*Aim* Experiencing, illustrating, knowing the feeling of isolation.

*Format* Students were arbitrarily set in groups of six. Sexes and races were deliberately mixed. Two students from each group were asked to step outside for a moment. The remaining four were told to accept one student when they returned and to direct their conversation and questions to that person. The other person was to be ignored entirely and was not to be talked to under any circumstances. Then two students from each group, each one alone, were sent out to walk about the campus and to return in twenty minutes. At the conclusion, each individual and group was told the circumstances and reasoning for the exercise. A critique was held. The teacher reviewed the novel and the concept of isolation.

*Events* The students sent out on their own were very apprehensive at the idea of leaving. In two cases the students returned in a few minutes saying that there wasn't anything out there. In another two cases they came back and requested someone to accompany them. They were, as they said, "lonely and wanted someone with them."

The two students sent out from each group were also apprehensive. The students "in the know" liked the idea and entered freely into the exercise. The students who received all the attention became very animated and delighted with the attention. In two cases, where the student was normally shy or withdrawn, he was brought out of his shell to some degree. The students who were rejected were very much concerned. They tried all sorts of ruses to speak to others and in three cases became abusive because no one would listen to them. Some rejected the whole group and wouldn't speak to them.

In the critique they stated that they felt happy, alone, sad, rejected, mad, uneasy, and in the case of those who were sent out to walk the campus alone, that their friends "didn't want to be with them." It was stated that they had experienced this isolation many times but hadn't paid much attention to it. In one case a boy stated that he wished we could do something like this often, because he got to talk to more students than he had in the classroom all year.

The teacher related to them the circumstances of isolation in the novel and spoke briefly on how groups are formed, how we often isolate people from our groups, and how we often isolate people even within the group.

*Conclusions* The sense of isolation was forcefully presented. The students themselves experienced both exhilaration and isolation, and gained an understanding of how it feels and of how we consciously and unconsciously accept and reject other persons.

*Addenda* The group was reading Herman Melville's novel *Moby Dick*. The sense of isolation felt by the hero, Ishmael, was more clearly understood.

*Source* Unknown.

The following lessons and lesson elements were developed by

Robin Montz for use in junior-high social studies and English, all ability levels.

I. Human-rights concept. Use of improvisational theater to get deeper understanding of the concept.
1. Began with warmup:
   a. Divided into groups of three.
   b. "Talked" to each other in gibberish.
   c. Told them, "Now without gestures or anything, begin slowly to exclude one of the three from the conversation. The one being excluded should concentrate on how it feels."
   d. Found out by repeating this and rotating the exclusion which ones felt it most deeply.
2. Set up the scene: "You have it, he wants it." Worked in gibberish, then English, then gibberish, etc., moving in and out of these two.
3. Got to the basic situation: When there are "in"s and "out"s in a society, the "out"s get angry because they can't have what the "in"s have, and the "in"s get angry because the "out"s try to take it away from them.
4. Students really felt the anger and were able to express it well. They expressed later that they felt that they really understood for the first time how minority groups must feel.

II. *Julius Caesar.* Affective techniques:
1. Attempt to make the play more contemporary by relating it to the assassination of Kennedy.
2. Use of improvisational theater in a contemporary setting to bring out the meaning of some of the scenes. For example: "You are grieving over a friend who has just been killed. You walk out of the funeral to see all the people having a party celebrating your friend's death. They're glad he's dead! Improvise the scene. Go." (Act I, Scene 1.)
3. Use of Frederick Perls' "stage-fright techniques" to overcome reluctance of students to act out scenes. Lots of work with "top dog–underdog."
4. Ritual assassination of a dummy filled with students' gripes. Used a shaman group and chants to work group to a high emotional pitch. Dummy torn to shreds. Then worked with feelings of elation and guilt, love and hate, through use of the play's funeral oration and by evaluation.
5. Creative projects: Students took one emotion either exhibited in the play or felt while reading the play and expressed that

emotion through any medium—dance, music, poetry, art, etc. Many outstanding projects resulted.

All these were extremely successful both in getting across the subject content and in getting the students in touch with their feelings.

III. Simulation games. Used simulations of the electoral process (model American government, which also serves as the class governmental structure) and of a crisis involving six African nations and two major powers (a variation of the "Crisis" game, by Western Behavioral Sciences Institute).
   1. Cognitive content:
      a. Experience of decision-making process.
      b. Firsthand experience of electoral process and international relations and related material.
   2. Affective emphases:
      a. Feeling of responsibility for decisions.
      b. Emphasis on resentments toward major powers.
      c. Feelings of winning or losing.
      d. Feelings of being occasionally lost in complexity.

IV. Remedial work with two groups of "problem-causers."
   1. Began with the "blaming" game. Discovered in both cases that they felt left out of the mainstream of school life, that they had ideas and contributions to offer but that the other students and teachers wouldn't accept them.
   2. Used the Gestalt game "Resentment, Demand, Appreciation" around the group to great success. Students opened up when confronted with resentments against them and developed a real sense of communication and love through the series of appreciations.
   3. At another session we worked through some basic encounter situations, both verbal and nonverbal, which resulted in a heightened awareness of other students and in one girl to break through a sense of self-depreciation and an inability to express aggression. She finally began to fight back.
   4. Used some very simple and basic Gestalt methods with an empty chair and "top dog-underdog" confrontations and worked with "telling secrets."

V. Result thus far (as of April 1968).
   1. General improvement in behavior, contributions, and attitudes of all but one of the students.

2. Greater acceptance of the students by other students.
3. "Smiles" and real creativity from all the students.
4. This is still a somewhat unfinished situation, as the students still feel a real need for more work. They pressure me every day for "the group," and so we meet as often as possible.

By the end of the year all but two of the students in the two groups seemed to have reached a period of adjustment to school and an awareness of their own strength and their position and contribution to themselves, each other, the class, and the school. This was a truly successful remedial situation.

The following is a partial list of ideas and suggestions that came out of our meetings which were not used in the project and still remain to be tested in the classroom.

1. When difficulties arise in getting students to talk to each other, use nonsense talking or gibberish to try to get them involved.
2. Get people to be the parts of a sentence and actually experience the relationships between parts of speech. Devise sentences that can be used with body expressions.
3. Build a box that a student can put his head into and yell—one that muffles the sound.
4. Write gripes on a ball or something. At the end of the week kick the ball around, chanting the gripe. (Modified quite a bit and used by Robin, Aaron, and others.)
5. Use a volleyball, foam-rubber practice golf balls, or cushions as aggression-releasing devices.
6. "Brainstorm" some nonsense syllables to substitute for dirty words, swearing, etc.
7. Training program for *teachers* in using the "Now" game.
8. Have students act out the parts of speech.
9. Have students become a math problem. "What if someone added you up wrong? How would you feel?"
10. In foreign-language classes, if a student doesn't know the word for something, don't let him ask for it in English but have him show the teacher the word he needs by acting it out or doing something.
11. Institute a course combining all the languages. How does each language express the same thing?
12. (After the description of Aaron's ritual murder of the pig in *Lord of the Flies*.) Have students experience being a *victim* as well as a hunter.
13. Other universes: An exercise of moving into paintings and

describing how you feel in there. Feelings can be described through body movement.

14. Have the students who are involved in some kind of encounter switch over and "move into the other guy's skin." If you were Tom, how would you feel? Be Tom; and, Tom, you be Jack.

15. Synectics: Concentration on an object. Three stages: (1) Direct analogy: What is it like? (2) Symbolic analogy: What is its essence—its symbolic meaning? (3) Personal analogy: Become the object and merge with another object.

16. Experience objects physically (rocks, jungle gym, etc.); then paint what you feel (taste, smell, etc.) instead of painting what you see.

17. Have students do some fantasy work with dying. Try to experience dying peacefully and dying violently.

18. Write secrets on a piece of paper, put them in a hat, draw, and tell the secret you draw as if it were your own, *or*

Two or three people working on two or three secrets respond individually to the same secret.

19. Divide the group into dyads. Each person is to write four or five things about the other that he wishes the other person would change. Then the other guesses what the first wrote. They then exchange lists. Do the same with appreciations.

20. Have students act out pictures in magazines or paintings, etc.

21. Develop a really neutral place to go in fantasies (as opposed to a cave, which is not neutral).

22. Build a fantasy dream house.

23. Synesthesia (mixing of sense modalities) used in writing a play: Write a play built around synesthesia.

24. Before taking tests, studying, etc., have students use the body-awakening exercises (toning up the system) and see if learning doesn't increase.

25. Encourage the use of synesthesia in writing poetry. (How does the blue sky smell?) Set up experiences for the students. (Taste the sky; smell red.) Have students describe how they felt as they moved through the experiences.

26. Define and develop statements about the intuitive process.

URIE BRONFENBRENNER
# FROM SCIENCE
# TO SOCIAL ACTION

We now consider how the principles we have derived from research can be applied within the framework of the major American institutions involved in the process of socialization. Clearly the institution which stands at the core of the process in our own culture is the family. And it is the withdrawal of the family from its child-rearing functions that we have identified as a major factor threatening the breakdown of the socialization process in America. Yet, it is not with the family that we propose to begin our discussion of how the needs of children can be most effectively served. Instead we consider first innovations in our educational institutions—specifically classrooms and schools.

The reason for this reversal springs from our social psychological perspective and the picture it reveals of the sources of resistance and change in a social system. In particular, our analysis points to a paradoxical situation. Even though the lack of parental involvement lies at the heart of our present malaise, parents by themselves can do little to bring about the needed change. For, as we have seen, it is not primarily the family, but other institutions in our society that determine how and with whom children spend their time, and it is these institutions that have created and perpetuate the age-segregated, and thereby often amoral or antisocial, world in which our children live and grow. Central among the institutions which, by their structure and limited concern, have encouraged these socially disruptive developments have been our schools. Accordingly, it is with these that we begin our exploration of possibilities for innovation.

In all, we shall consider changes in five major contexts affecting the lives of children: the Classroom, the School, the Family, the Neighborhood, and the Larger Community.

Excerpted from Chapter 6 of *Two Worlds of Childhood—USA and USSR* by Urie Brofenbrenner.© 1970 by The Russell Sage Foundation, New York.

# THE CLASSROOM

In terms of human potential, the classroom contains two major sources for influencing behavior and development: the teacher, and the children themselves.

## Potentialities in the Teacher's Role

In keeping with the traditional emphasis of American schools on conveying subject matter, the teacher has been perceived and has functioned primarily in the role of resource person and giver of information. It is this emphasis which is reflected in Western research on teaching, as documented by N. L. Gage. Only recently has the work of Rosenthal called attention to the powerful impact of the teacher as a reinforcer (often unrecognized by herself), whereas her potency as a model is yet to be examined through systematic research.

But social processes do not wait in the wings for their appearance to be ratified by the data of behavioral science. They function notwithstanding, and their unintended consequences can often be counterproductive. A case in point is provided by the vicious circle set in motion by a teacher's labeling of a child as "disadvantaged" or her tendency to give problem pupils individualized attention— that is, reinforcement—primarily when they display disruptive behavior.

The greatest promise for constructive change, however, lies not with errors of commission but of omission—the failure to provide and reinforce models of desired behavior. We have in mind here not so much the failure of the teacher to set a good example (although, as we shall indicate, much more can be accomplished along these lines), but rather the absence in the classroom and its activities of other models besides the teacher and the children themselves. We view the introduction of such models as desirable, feasible, and central to the teacher's task.

In other words, our discussion implies a broadened conception of the teacher's role. Not only must she herself function as a motivating model, but *it becomes her responsibility to seek out, organize, develop, and coordinate the activities of other appropriate models and reinforcing agents both within the classroom and outside.* How this might be done will become apparent as we proceed.

For the teacher herself to function as an effective model and reinforcer, she must possess the characteristics which we have identified as enhancing inductive power; that is, she must be perceived by the pupils as a person of status who has control over resources. In our view, it is to the advantage of the educational process, and thus to the entire society, to insure that this is, in fact, the case. Teachers who are poorly paid, treated as subordinates, and given little freedom and autonomy by the school administration cannot help but reflect their true position and reduce their influence in the pupil's eyes. A person must have a measure of self-respect and status before he can expect others to admire these traits in him. The occasional teacher who would exploit such power is less of a risk than the devastating loss of good teachers whose functioning is impaired due to the constraints in the present system. When teachers have a true stake in the development of the children under their care, when they have the responsibility and autonomy so often admired and seldom granted, then they themselves can be expected to bring social pressure on the occasional deviant colleague who might abuse this freedom, or, more importantly, on those who fail to use their freedom to act as the agents of society in the forming of the next generation. Moreover, in that task, the teacher must reflect not the preferences and prejudices of a particular class, but the interests of all segments of the society in their quest for a better world.

Finally, if the above considerations are accepted as valid, they call for radical changes in our current practices of teacher selection and training. Specifically, they argue for the recruitment of persons on other than purely academic qualifications, with at least as much emphasis placed on social as on intellectual qualities and skills. For example, the research evidence indicates that learning is facilitated when the teacher is similar to the child in cultural background, race, and, especially in the case of boys, sex. Such findings argue for the recruitment of many more persons from disadvantaged and minority groups—especially males—into the teaching profession and other occupations involving work with young children. But it is in the realm of teacher training that the most far-reaching innovations are required. In addition to knowing his subject, the teacher of tomorrow must acquire both understanding and skill in the use of modeling, social reinforcement, and group processes in work with children. But beyond that, he must know how to discover, recruit, and utilize individuals and groups from outside the school as major adjuncts to the educational process. This implies a far better acquaintance and articulation with the local community—its people, problems, and resources—than has ever been required or expected of teachers in the past.

But before we examine the extension of the teaching process outside the school, we need to consider further potentials for innovation within the classroom itself.


## Potentialities of the Classroom Group

This is one of the most promising and least exploited areas for effecting behavioral change. Although modifications of classroom composition in terms of social class and race can have salutary effects, they by no means represent the most powerful resources at our disposal. Indeed, their potential is realized only to the extent that they facilitate development of the motivating processes (modeling, reinforcement, group commitment, involvement in superordinate goals, etc.) we have outlined. Such development need not be left to chance. It can be directly fostered through setting up within the classroom the kinds of social and situational structures in which these processes thrive. This includes such devices as teams, cooperative group competition, organized patterns of mutual help, etc., including the incorporation into such social units of different mixes of race, social class, sex, achievement level, and the like. In short, we must learn to make more effective use of group forces in fostering human development. As we have seen, the power of the group, including the children's group, in motivating goal-directed activity in its members is well established in American social science, but the practical implications of this knowledge for education have thus far remained unexploited in this country. Where practical applications have been made on a broad scale, as in the Soviet Union, the programs have not yet been subjected to systematic empirical analysis and evaluation. It remains for American educators and social scientists to apply the findings of research in the design of educational experiments susceptible to rigorous test and to the improvements which such evaluation makes possible. For example, one might start by examining the effectiveness of two-pupil teams composed of children of heterogeneous ability designated as partners or playmates, and compare their progress with unpaired individuals or members of homogeneous pairs. Another possibility draws on the potency of group reinforcement by introducing such "customs" as group applause for correct answers, selection and honoring by classmates of members showing greatest individual progress, etc. *But, surely, the most needed innovation in the American classroom is the involvement of pupils in responsible tasks on behalf of others within the classroom, the school, the neighborhood, and the community*. The full potential of the motivational processes here discussed will remain unplumbed and seriously underestimated so long as the social setting in which these processes can take place is limited to the conventional classroom with its homogeneous grouping, by age, and, often, by ability and social class as well. To realize these possibilities requires moving beyond the classroom into the larger contexts of school and neighborhood.


## THE SCHOOL

Perhaps the most promising possibility which the total school offers in furthering the development of the child is the active involvement of older and, subsequently, younger children in the process. For the preschooler or primary-grader, an older child, particularly of the same sex, can be a very influential figure, especially if he is willing to spend time with his younger companion. Except for the occasional anachronism of a one room school, this potential resource remains almost entirely unexploited in American education and, for that matter, in the process of socialization generally as it takes place in our country. Opportunities for experimentation are therefore legion. One might begin with an Americanized adaptation of the Soviet system of *"shevstvo"* in which a preschool or primary class is "adopted" by an older class, with each younger child having an older "brother" or "sister" from the more advanced class. It becomes the responsibility of the older pupil to get to know his younger "sib" and his family, to escort him to and from school, play with him and his friends, teach him games, and, last but not least, become acquainted with his progress and problems in school, reading with and to him, helping and encouraging him to learn. In the meantime the parent class as a whole organizes activities for their "ward class," including trips to athletic events, nature walks, camp-outs, museum visits, etc.

The foregoing examples illustrate how an enduring social situation can be created that simultaneously exploits all of the motivating processes and social structures outlined earlier, for here the effects of modeling and reinforcement are enhanced in the context of intensive relationships, group membership, and common commitment to a superordinate goal.

An extension of this same principle points to a potential contribution of the school as a whole to the development of the individual child. Within the formal educational context, the school is the social unit with which the child, and those concerned for his welfare, can most readily identify. If the school as a total community becomes visibly involved in activities focused on the child and his needs, if older children, school organizations, other teachers, school administrators, PTAs—if all these persons and groups in some way participate in the program and publicly support those most actively engaged in the effort, the reinforcing effect increases by geometric proportions. Conversely, if a special program is confined to an isolated classroom, it is not only deprived of powerful reinforcing influences but also risks the danger that the rest of the school, especially children in other classes, will perceive the "special class" in invidious terms (e.g., "dummies, queers") and treat its members accordingly. When this occurs, the powerful influences of modeling, negative reinforcement, and group pressure serve only to undermine the already unfavorable self-image of a "problem child."

But it is not primarily the needs of problem children or the disadvantaged that call for change in American schools. If the radical innovations that are required are not introduced, it will be *all* children who will be culturally deprived—not of cognitive stimulation, but of their humanity. For their own full development, the young need to be exposed not only to factual knowledge but also to the standards and modes of behavior requisite for living in a cooperative society. As we have seen, in Communist schools, a deliberate effort is made—through appropriate models, reinforcements, and group experiences—to teach the child the values and *behaviors* consistent with Communist ideals. In American schools, training for action consistent with social responsibility and human dignity is at best an extracurricular activity. The belated recognition of our full educational obligations to the nation's children—the so-called advantaged no less than the deprived—offers us a chance to redress this weakness and to make democratic education not only a principle but a practice.


THE FAMILY


Just as a chain breaks first in its weakest link, so the problems of a society become most pressing and visible in the social strata that are under greatest stress. Thus, it is not surprising that we should first recognize the disruption of the process of socialization in American society among the families of the poor. And it is in this same context that we have begun the attempt to develop countermeasures, ways to revitalize the socialization process through the establishment of institutions like Head Start, which re-involve parents and other community members in the lives of their children in a setting that points the way to more constructive patterns of activity and interaction.

Accordingly, in discussing new patterns of family involvement, we draw heavily on the experience of the author as a member of the committee that originally designed and gave professional direction to the Head Start program. Although most of our examples refer to the disadvantaged family, they are readily translatable into the middle-class world, as evidenced by the increasing demand for—and inception of—Head Start-type programs in well-to-do neighborhoods.

Today's Head Start programs typically profess strong commitment to the principle of family involvement, but in practice implementation is limited to two rather restricted forms: the first is the inclusion of some parents on the program's advisory board; the second involves meetings for parents at which staff members make presentations about some aspect of the program. Both of these measures have the effect of bypassing the most important aspect of family involvement—engaging parents and older children in new and more mutually rewarding patterns of interaction with the young.

An essential first step in bringing about such changed patterns of interaction is exposure of the parents and other family members to them. This can be done at one of two places, at a preschool or neighborhood center, or in the home. The basic approach is one of demonstration: showing the family the kinds of things that are done in a preschool program, which also happen to be things that family members can themselves do with the child; e.g., games to play, books to read, pictures to look at and talk about. Particularly valuable in this connection are activities that involve and require more than one person in patterns of interaction with the child; that is, not just the teacher and/or the mother, but also other adults and older children (i.e., father, grandma, brother, sister, next-door neighbor). A useful technique is to ask the visiting or visited family members to help in carrying out particular activities with the child. It is important that the process not be seen as a lesson in which the child must learn something and deserves punishment for failure, but instead simply as an engaging activity in which learning is incidental to a total gratifying experience.

To facilitate the involvement of parents in such nonschoollike educational activities, it is desirable to provide a library consisting not only of books but also of toys and games which require the verbal participation of adults and older children, and which can be borrowed for extended periods of time for home use.

The involvement of family members in the educational program of course poses a difficult dilemma to professional staff. On the one hand, there is the need to expose parents and other family members to new or different ways of dealing with their children. On the other hand, this must be done in such a way as to enhance, rather than lower, the power and prestige of these persons in the eyes of the child. The second requirement arises from the evidence that the inductive and reinforcing capacity of a model varies directly with the model's status, command over resources, and control of the social environment. An ingenious demonstration of how this dilemma can be resolved was observed at an all-Negro Head Start program in the rural South. Since the local, white-dominated school administration had refused to have anything to do with the program, it was organized by Negro church groups under the leadership of an eighty-six-year-old minister. Several days before classes were to begin, this man invited all the parents and teenagers to an orientation meeting, a pass-the-dish picnic in a nearby forest area (a forest which he himself had planted years ago with seeds obtained free from the United States Department of Agriculture). After the picnic, the minister offered to take the whole group on a tour of the forest. During the walk he would ask adults and teen-agers to show him interesting plant and animal life which they observed, give names of flowers, trees, and birds, explain how plants grow, what animals feed on, etc. While drawing out much information from the group, he also added considerable material from his own experience. At the end of the walk, he turned to the group with a request: "On Saturday we start our Head Start program. In the afternoon the children need some recreation and the teachers need a rest. Could you folks bring the children here and tell them all the things *you know* that *they don't know* about the forest?"

The turnout on Saturday was impressive, and so was the performance of the "instant experts."

THE NEIGHBORHOOD

The foregoing example illustrates also the reinforcing potential of the other people with whom the child frequently associates and identifies—his neighbors. These persons, particularly the adults and older children who are looked up to and admired by the young, probably stand second only to parents in terms of their power to influence the child's behavior. For this reason it would be important for educational programs to try to exploit this potential in a systematic way. The most direct approach would be to discover from the families and neighborhoods themselves who are the popular and admired individuals and groups, and then to involve them as aides in the program. It may often be the case that the activities in which such individuals or groups normally engage, indeed, the activities for which they are popular, are not those which one would want children to learn or adopt. This fact should receive consideration, but it should hardly be the determining factor, since the behaviors that matter are those that the model exhibits in the presence of the child. It follows that the activities in which such persons engage as aides, volunteers, and the like must be constructive in nature and reinforce other aspects of the program. They may take a variety of forms: supervising and playing games, exhibiting or teaching a hobby or skill (whittling, playing a musical instrument, magic tricks). The significant factor is that the activity be seen by the child as part of and supporting all of the things the child is doing "in school."

A second important use of neighborhood resources involves exposing the child to successful models in his own locality—persons coming from his own background who are productive members of society: skilled or semiskilled workers, teachers, or government employees. Providing opportunities for such persons to associate with the children (e.g., as escorts, recreation supervisors, parttime aides, or tutors), tell something about their work, and perhaps have the children visit the person at work can help provide a repertoire of possible occupational goals unknown to many children of poverty today. In view of the frequency of father absence among disadvantaged families and the predominance of female personnel in educational programs generally, the involvement of male adults and teenagers is highly desirable, especially for boys.

If people from the neighborhood are to be drawn into the program, it is obvious that many desirable activities cannot be carried out effectively if they are to be conducted only during school hours or solely in a school classroom. To begin with, if the program is to have enduring impact, it must influence the child's behavior outside of school as much as in school. Second, a school classroom does not lend itself to many of the kinds of informal activities involving parents, other adults, and older children which have been described above.

Accordingly, some kind of *neighborhood center* becomes a highly desirable feature of any comprehensive educational program. Such a center would have to be open after school, on weekends, and during vacations and have some staff members on duty at all times. The center should be represented to the community not merely as a place where children go but rather where all members of the community go in the joint interest of themselves and their children. The neighborhood center might be housed in a school building, but, if so, facilities available should include other than traditional classrooms with fixed seats.

## THE LARGER COMMUNITY

The contribution of the total community to educational programs is analogous to that of the neighborhood but now with representatives and resources drawn from the larger context. Use can be made both of older children and adults from middleclass backgrounds provided they are not the only "competent" models on the scene, for without the example and support of "his own people" the child's receptivity to what may then be seen as an alien influence is much reduced. It follows that activities by persons or in settings from outside the child's subculture must be heavily interlaced with representatives from his own world who manifestly cooperate in the total effect. This in turn implies close working relationships of mutual respect between workers from within and outside the child's own milieu. Mutual respect is essential in these relationships, not merely for the purpose of maintaining a viable learning atmosphere, but, more importantly, to further the constructive development of the child's own sense of identity and worth as a person and as a member of society.

However, it is not only what the community does for the child that contributes to his development. Of equal if not greater importance is what he does for that community—quite modestly at first, but gradually at increasing levels of responsibility. As we have noted, it is in part the enforced inutility of children in our society that works to produce feelings of alienation, indifference, and antagonism. Learning early in life the skills and rewards of service to one's community brings with it the benefits of a more stable and gratifying self-identity. Indeed, in the last analysis, the child—so long as he remains a child—must receive more from the community than he can give.

From this point of view, the greatest significance of the total community, especially for the disadvantaged child, lies in the fact that many of the problems he faces, and the possibilities for their solution, are rooted in the community as a whole and are therefore beyond the reach of segmental efforts at the level of the neighborhood, the school, or the home. We have in mind such problems as housing, welfare services, medical care, community recreation programs, sanitation, police services, and television programming.

Given this state of affairs, it is a sobering fact that, neither in our communities nor in the nation as a whole, is there a single agency that is charged with the responsibility of assessing and improving the situation of the child in his total environment. As it stands, the needs of children are parcelled out among a hopeless confusion of agencies with diverse objectives, conflicting jurisdictions, and imperfect channels of communication. The school, the health department, the churches, welfare services, youth organizations, the medical profession, libraries, the police, recreation programs—all of these see the children of the community at one time or another, but no one of them is concerned with the total pattern of life for children in the community: where, how, and with whom they spend their waking hours and what may be the impact of these experiences on the development of the child as an individual and as a member of society. An inquiry of this nature would, we believe, reveal some troubling facts which in themselves could generate concerted action. Accordingly, an important aspect of any program at the level of the total community would be the establishment of a "Commission on Children," which would have as its initial charge finding out how, where, and with whom the children of all ages in the community spend their time. The Commission would include among its members representatives of the major institutions in the community that deal with children, but should also draw in businessmen, parents from all social-class levels, as well as the young themselves, teenagers from diverse segments of the community who can speak from recent experience. The Commission would be expected to report its findings and recommendations to appropriate executive bodies and to the public at large.

Any report of such a Commission is likely to underscore the inescapable fact that many of the problems which beset the lives of children, and the courses of action necessary to combat these problems, lie beyond the power of the local community to control. The design of housing developments, the determination of working hours for industry, the programming policies of television networks, the training of teachers and the new types of personnel needed to work with the young and, above all, the priorities of state and federal spending—all of these factors which, in the last analysis, determine how a society treats its children, are superimposed on the community from without and require understanding and action at higher levels.

Yet, our emphasis here is on *local initiative and concern.*We believe this is the place to start, for that is where the children are. For only a hard look at the world in which they live—a world we adults have created for them in large part by default—can convince us of the urgency of their plight and the consequences of our inaction. Then perhaps it will come to pass that, in the words of Isaiah, "A little child shall lead them."

We have come a long way in our comparative study of socialization in the Soviet Union and the United States. We began with descriptive facts, considered their implications in the light of data and theory from the social sciences, and ultimately ended with a blueprint for change within our own society. In doing so we take cognizance of a new, as yet unfamiliar, and surely presumptuous role for the scientist dealing with problems of human development. Yet it is a role we believe the social scientist must take. As his colleagues in the physical sciences have learned to do long ago, he must go beyond natural history to recognize and probe as yet unexploited theoretical possibilities and their practical applications. The present volume represents a beginning effort toward this broader objective. We have sought to demonstrate that the behavioral sciences, though admittedly limited in knowledge and theoretical grasp, can, nevertheless, illuminate both the problems of a society and possible directions for their solution. Specifically, we have used a comparative approach to expose similarities and differences in the process of human socialization as it takes place in the two most powerful nations of our time, the Soviet Union and the United States. We believe that the results of this inquiry indicate that the rather different Soviet approach to the upbringing of the young is not without significance for our own problems. If the Russians have gone too far in subjecting the child and his peer group to conformity to a single set of values imposed by the adult society, perhaps we have reached the point of diminishing returns in allowing excessive autonomy and in failing to utilize the constructive potential of the peer group in developing social responsibility and consideration for others. Moving to counteract this tendency does not mean subscribing to Soviet insistence on the primacy of the collective over the individual or adopting their practice of shifting major responsibility for upbringing from the family to public institutions. On the contrary, what is called for is greater involvement of parents, and other adults, in the lives of children, and—conversely—greater involvement of children in responsibility on behalf of their own family, community, and society at large. Given the fragmented character of modern American life—its growing separatism and violence—such an injunction may appear to some as a pipe dream, but it need not be. For just as autonomy and aggression have their roots in the American tradition, so have neighborliness, civic concern, and devotion to the young. It is to these that we must look if we are to rediscover our moral identity as a society and as a nation.

# ADDITIONAL READINGS

Blackham, G., and Silberman, A. *Modification of Child Behavior.* Belmont, Calif.: Wadsworth, 1971.

Broudy, H. *The Real World of the Public Schools.* New York: Harcourt Brace Jovanovich, 1972.

Ennis, R. H. *Logic in Teaching.* Englewood Cliffs, N.J.: Prentice-Hall, 1969.

Golding, W. *Lord of the Flies.* New York: G. P. Putnam's Sons, Capricorn Books, 1954.

Hook, Sidney. *Education for Modern Man.* New York: Alfred A. Knopf, 1963.

Muller, H. J. *In Pursuit of Relevance.* Bloomington, Ind.: Indiana University Press, 1971.

Rich, J. M. *Education and Human Values.* Reading, Mass.: Addison-Wesley, 1968.

Shaver, J. P., and Larkins, A. G. *Decision-Making in a Democracy.* Boston: Houghton Mifflin, 1973.

Vredevoe, L. *Discipline.* Dubuque, Iowa: Kendall-Hunt, 1971.

# NOTES

## Introduction

[1]See James P. Jewett, "The Fight Against Corporal Punishment in American Schools," *History of Education Journal* 5 (Autumn, 1958): 1-10.

[2]Lawrence A. Cremin, *The Transformation of the Schools* (New York: A. A. Knopf, 1962).

## Part 1

### Samuel McCracken, *Quackery in the Classroom*

[1]Gross, R., and Gross, B., eds. *Radical School Reform*. New York: Simon and Schuster, 1969, pp. 350.

[2]Holt, John. *How Children Fail* (1964) and *How Children Learn* (1967). New York: Pitman.

[3]Holt, John. *The Underachieving School*. New York: Pitman, 1969.

[4]*New York Review of Books*, October 9, 1969.

[5]Postman, N., and Weingartner, C. *Teaching as a Subversive Activity*. New York: Delacorte Press, 1969.

[6]*Ibid.*, pp. 62-65.

[7]*Ibid.*, p. 206.

[8]Leonard, George. *Education and Ecstasy*. New York: Delacorte Press, 1969.

[9]Dennison, G. *The Lives of Children*. New York: Random House.

### Amitai Etzioni, *A Review of "Crisis in the Classroom"*

[1]I prefer the term *societal guidance* over that of social *engineering*. I use the archaic term "societal" to stress that we are dealing with change in societies and not with changes of a few social relations. The processes involved in societal *guidance* cannot be ordered or streamlined as is implied by the concept of *engineering* nor can solutions be found on the basis of expert or elite decisions, which the concept of engineering implies.

Social systems do change constantly as a result of forces which the members do not understand nor control. The concept of guidance points to those changes which society brings about deliberately. For additional discussion see my *The Active Society* (New York: The Free Press, 1968).

[2]For the most recent document see *Toward Balanced Growth: Quantity with Quality*. Report of the National Goals Research Staff (Washington, D. C.: Government Printing Office, 1970).

[3](Summer, 1970) p. 1.

[4]To cite a journalistic source, William K. Stevens' report (*New York Times*, October 19, 1970, p. 29) about "Oregon High School's Experiment in Free Study" that

> A survey of students indicated that they considered Adams a "humanized" school. "At least you feel like a person here," said one student. But the same survey found that many students felt the intellectual content of the curriculum should be strengthened.

For discussion of the informal school as being more effective as a source of joy than of achievements, in the traditional sense, see Silberman, pp. 231-32.

[5]It may be suggested, at this point, that we fall short by the same criteria we apply to Silberman, of not spelling out and documenting our propositions. It seems, though, proper in a review to cue and indicate, while a $300,000 study report, which stakes claims for policy guidance, may have to go beyond the specificity and empirical validity provided by a review essay.

## Sidney Hook, *Illich's De-Schooled Utopia*

[1]Illich, Ivan. *De-Schooling Society*. New York: Harper & Row, 1970.

## Part 2

## Introduction

[1]For a comprehensive treatment of this subject, see William D. Rohwer, Jr., "Cognitive Development and Education," *Carmichael's Manual of Child Psychology*, ed. Paul Mussen (New York: John Wiley, 1970), pp. 1379-1445.

## Paul H. Hirst, *Liberal Education and the Nature of Knowledge*

[1]*General Education in a Free Society:* Report of the Harvard Committee (London: Oxford University Press, 1946).

[2]*Ibid.*, p. 58.

[3]*Ibid.*, pp. 64-65.

[4]*Ibid.*, pp. 65-73.

[5]*Ibid.*, p. 67.

[6]*Arts and Science Sides in the Sixth Form:* Gulbenkian Foundation Report (Oxford University Department of Education, 1960), p. 15.

[7]Michael Oakeshott, *Rationalism in Politics and Other Essays* (London: Methuen, 1962), pp. 198-199.

## David P. Ausubel, *Learning by Discovery*

[1]Ausubel, D. P., *The Psychology of Meaningful Verbal Learning*. New York: Grune and Stratton, July 1963.

[2]*Living and Learning: A Repeat of the Provincial Committee on Aims and Objectives of Education in the Schools of Ontario*. Toronto: Newton Publishing Company, 1968. One half of the overriding recommendation of this report is that it is "the responsibility of every school authority to provide a child-centered learning continuum that invites learning by individual discovery and inquiry."

[3]Sullivan, E. V., *Piaget and the school curriculum: A critical appraisal*. Toronto, Ontario., The Ontario Institute for Studies in Education, 1967(b).

[4]Ausubel, D. P., *Educational psychology: A cognitive view*. New York: Holt, Rinehart and Winston, Inc., 1968, and *op. cit.*

[5]Hendrix, Gertrude. "Learning by discovery." *Math Teach.*, 1961, 54: 290-299.

[6]Hendrix, Gertrude. "A new clue to transfer of training." *Elem. Sch. J.*, 1947, 48: 197-208.

[7]Hull, C. L. "Qualitative aspects of the evolution of concepts." *Psychol. Monogr.*, 1920, 28 (Whole No. 123). Luchins, A. S., and Edith H. Luchins. "A structural approach to the teaching of the concept of area in intuitive geometry." *J. educ. Res.*, 1947, 40: 528-533.

[8]Direct evidence that verbalized insights are more transferable than subverbal insights comes from experiments on the ability to solve transposition and discrimination problems [Spiker, C. C., and G. Terrell. "Factors associated with transposition behavior of preschool children." J. genet. Psychol., 1955, 23, 278. Weir, M. W., and H. W. Stevenson. "The effect of verbalization in children's learning as a function of chronological age." *Child Develpm.*, 1959, 30: 143-149].

Indirect evidence comes from studies in which verbalization during attempts to discover underlying principles [Gagne, R. M., and E. C. Smith. "A study of the effects of verbalization on problem solving." *J. exp. Psychol.*, 1962, 63: 12-16]. or the knowledge of underlying verbal principles [Ewert, P. H., and J. F. Lambert. "Part II: The effect of verbal instructions upon the formation of a concept." *J. gen. Psychol.*, 1932, 6: 400-413.] facilitated problem solving.

[9]Easley, J. A. "Is the teaching of scientific method a significant educational objective?" *Philosophy and education* (I. Scheffler, ed.). Boston: Allyn and Bacon, Inc., 1958. Easley, J. A. "Is the teaching of scientific method a significant educational objective?" *Harvard educ. Rev.*, 1959, 29: 4-11.

[10]Atkin, J. M., and R. Karplus. *Discovery or invention?* Urbana, Ill.: College of Education, University of Illinois, 1962.

[11]Inhelder, Bärbel, and J. Piaget. *The growth of logical thinking from childhood to adolescence*. New York: Basic Books, Inc., 1958. Karplus, R. "The science-

curriculum—one approach." *Elem. Sch. J.*, 1962, 62: 243-252. Piaget, J. *The child's conception of physical causality.* New York: Harcourt, Brace & World, Inc., 1932.

[12]Bruner, J. S. "After Dewey what?" *Sat. Rev.*, June 17, 1961, 58-59; 76-78(b). Easley, *op. cit.*, 1958. Hibbs, A. R. "Science for elementary students." *Teachers Coll. Rec.*, 1961, 63: 136-142. Suchman, J. R. "Inquiry training: Building skills for autonomous discovery." *Merrill-Palmer Quart*, 1961, 7: 148-169.

[13]Bruner, J. S. "The act of discovery." *Harvard educ. Rev.*, 1961, 31: 21-32(a).

[14]Bruner, J. S. *The process of education.* Cambridge, Mass.: Harvard University Press, 1960. Bruner, "After Dewey what?" *op. cit.*; Bruner, "The act of discovery," *op. cit.*; Hendrix, *op. cit.*; Suchman, *op. cit.*

[15]Other speculations include that of Cronbach. ["The logic of experiments on discovery." *Learning by discovery: A critical appraisal* (L. S. Shulman and E. R. Keisler, eds.) Skokie, Ill.: Rand McNally & Company, 1967], who suggests that "pupils who are negativistic may blossom under discovery training, whereas pupils who are anxiously dependent may be paralyzed by demands for self-reliance." In an empirical study, Carlow ["A study of variables within the method of individually guided discovery in secondary school mathematics: The experimental comparison of conceptual structures, consolidation and learner personality with learning retention, and transfer by ninthgrade college preparatory males" (unpublished doctoral thesis). Syracuse, New York: Syracuse University, 1967] found that students who are submissive and have low conceptual level scores do poorly under discovery approaches.

[16]McConnell, T. R. "Discovery versus authoritative identification in the learning of children." *Univer. Iowa Stud. Educ.*, 1934, 9: No. 5.

[17]Thiele, C. L. *The contribution of generalization to the learning of addition facts.* Contributions to Education, No. 863. New York: Teachers College Press, Columbia University, 1938.

[18]Swenson, E. J. "Organization and generalization as factors in learning, transfer, and retroactive inhibition." *Learning theory in school situations.* Univer. Minn. Stud. Educ. Minneapolis, Minn.: University of Minnesota Press, 1949, pp. 9-39.

[19]Anderson, G. L. "Quantitative thinking as developed under connectionist and field theories of learning." *Learning theory in school situations.* Univer. Minn. Stud. Educ. Minneapolis: University of Minnesota Press, 1949, pp. 40-73.

[20]Kohler, W. *The mentality of apes.* New York: Harcourt, Brace & World, Inc., 1925.

[21]Wertheimer, M. *Productive thinking* (enlarged ed., Michael Wertheimer, ed.). New York: Harper & Row, Publishers, 1959.

[22]Duncker, K. "On problem-solving." *Psychol. Monogr.*, 1945, 58: (Whole No. 270).

[23]Katona, G. *Organizing and memorizing.* New York: Columbia University Press, 1940.

[24]This study is reminiscent of Hendrix's (1947) investigation, whose conclusions were discussed earlier in some detail.

[25]Stacey, C. L. "The law of effect in retained situations with meaningful material." *Learning theory in school situations.* University of Minnesota Studies in Education. Minneapolis, Minn.: University of Minnesota Press, 1949, pp. 74-103.

[26]Craig, R. C. "Directed versus independent discovery of established relations." *J. educ. Psychol.*, 1956, 47: 223-234.

[27]Kittell, J. E. "An experimental study of the effect of external direction during learning on transfer and retention of principles." *J. educ. Psychol.*, 1957, 48: 391-405.

[28]Haselrud, G. M., and Shirley Meyers. "The transfer value of given and individually derived principles." *J. educ. Psychol.*, 1958, 49: 293-298.

[29]Kersh, B. Y. "The adequacy of 'meaning' as an explanation for the superiority of learning by independent discovery." *J. educ. Psychol.*, 1958, 49: 282-292.

[30]Larson, G. L. Comparison of acquisition, retention, and transfer among three styles of learning (unpublished Ph.D. dissertation). Urbana, Illinois: University of Illinois, 1963.

[31]Craig, R. C. "Discovery, task completion, and the assignment as factors in motivation." *Amer. educ. Res. J.*, 1965, 2: 217-222.

[32]Moss, J. An experimental study of the relative effectiveness of the direct-detailed and the directed discovery methods of teaching letter-press imposition (unpublished Ed.D. dissertation). Urbana, Ill.: University of Illinois, 1960.

[33]Maltzman, I., E. Eisman, and L. O. Brooks. "Some relationships between methods of instruction, personality variables, and problem-solving behavior." *J. educ. Psychol.*, 1950, 47: 71-78.

[34]Tomlinson, R. M. A comparison of four presentation methods for teaching complex technical material (unpublished Ed.D. dissertation). Urbana, Ill.: University of Illinois, 1962.

[35]Forgus, R. H. and R. J. Schwartz. "Efficient retention and transfer as affected by learning method." *J. Psychol.*, 1957, 43: 135-139.

[36]A relatively complete, explicit, step-by-step type of guidance.

[37]Ray, W. E. An experimental comparison of direct-detailed and directed discovery methods of teaching micrometer principles and skills (unpublished Ed.D. dissertation). Urbana, Ill.: University of Illinois, 1957.

[38]Rowlett, J. D. An experimental comparison of direct-detailed and directed discovery methods of teaching orthographic projection principles and skills (unpublished Ed.D. dissertation). Urbana, Ill.: University of Illinois, 1960.

[39]Gagné, R. M., and L. T. Brown. "Some factors in the programing of conceptual material." *J. exp. Psychol.*, 1961, 62: 313-321.

[40]Corman, B. R. "The effect of varying amounts and kinds of information as guidance in problem solving." *Psychol. Monogr.*, 1957, 71: No. 2 (Whole No. 431).

[41]Grote, C. N. A comparison of the relative effectiveness of direct-detailed and directed discovery methods of teaching selected principles of mechanics in the

area of physics (unpublished Ed.D. dissertation). Urbana, Ill.: University of Illinois, 1960.

[42]A unit of such duration would seem useful when the teacher is first accommodating himself to less directed classroom activities, and will need time to work out effective classroom arrangements. In addition, a fairly lengthy discovery experience will provide the teacher with some basis for evaluating the learning which takes place.

[43]Sweeney, J. R. "An experimental study comparing the Cuisenaire method with traditional methods in Grade 1 mathematics." *Canadian experience with the Cuisenaire method.* Ottawa, Ont.: Canadian Council for Research in Education, 1964.

## G. H. Bantock, *"Emile" Reconsidered*

[1]Some of the most interesting elucidations are to be found among Arthur Lovejoy's articles in *Essays in the History of Ideas.* Cf. also, Professor Basil Willey's *Eighteenth Century Background.* An admirable chapter in Professor C. D. Hardie's *Truth and Fallacy in Educational Theory,* "Education according to Nature," analyses a number of propositions which are implicit in Rousseau's work, and should be consulted. Cf. also, J. Maritain, *Trois Reformateurs,* which contains an essay on Rousseau.

[2]In an extremely interesting article on *Robinson Crusoe as a Myth* (*Essays in Criticism,* Vol. i, No. 2, April 1951), Mr. Ian Watt seems to pay too little attention to this ambiguity of attitude in Rousseau's approach to "wild nature." Thus, he contrasts Defoe's use of nature, in *Robinson Crusoe,* as matter for exploitation, self-help, purposive possession and colonial development with Rousseau's interpretation of the book in *Emile* as an example of solitary pastoral retreat for self-communion. In actual fact, it is the self-help aspect of *Robinson Crusoe,* which appeals to Rousseau for, as I have pointed out, his attitude to "nature" in this sense involves at times a background for self-indulgence and at times material for "exploitation"; and it is the latter which his use of Defoe's book is intended to advocate. There is a great deal of Defoe's ethos, which Mr. Watt interestingly defines, in Rousseau's educational ideas: his "negative" education is largely a means not to idleness but precisely to self-help and discovery on the part of the pupil; and the virtue which he finds in the savage is not that of blissful peace but the necessity "to reason at every step he takes. He can neither move nor walk without considering the consequences" (*Emile,* p. 83). Cf. Rousseau's comments on *Robinson Crusoe* (*Emile,* pp. 147-8—particularly: "This novel, stripped of irrelevant matter, begins with Robinson's shipwreck on his island and ends with the coming of the ship which bears him from it, and it will furnish Emile with material, both for work and play, during the whole period we are considering. His head should be full of it, he should always be busy with his castle, his goats, his plantations. Let him learn in detail, not from books but from things, all that is necessary in such a case. Let him think he is Robinson himself; . . . he should anxiously consider what steps to take; will this or that be wanting. He should examine his hero's conduct. . . ." Indeed, the passage that Mr. Watt quotes from *Robinson Crusoe* sets out admirably that conception of rational invention which Rousseau permits to the child: "By making and acquiring everything by reason and by making the most rational judgments of things, every man may be in time master of every mechanic art. I had never handled a tool in my life, and yet in time by labour, application, and contrivance I found at least that I wanted nothing but I could have made it; especially if I had had the tools."

Mr. Watt interestingly reveals the fallacy of the desert island existence, how, in fact, those who really suffered such exposure to "nature" reverted to an almost animal state of existence or went mad.

[3]Cf. *Emile*, p. 151: ". . . the art which is most generally useful and necessary, is undoubtedly that which most deserves esteem, and that art which requires the least help from others, is more worthy of honour than those which are dependent on other arts, since it is freer and more nearly independent. These are the true laws of value in the arts; all others are arbitrary and dependent on popular prejudice."

[4]Arthur Lovejoy, "The Supposed Primitivism of Rousseau's Discourse on Inequality," reprinted in *Essays in the History of Ideas*. By "perfectibility" Lovejoy refers to social conceptions of perfection. Rousseau, of course, as is implied, has his own perfectionism.

[5]*Emile*, p. 288.

[6]Cf. *Emile*, p. 56: "Let us lay it down as an incontrovertible rule that the first impulses of nature are always right; there is no original sin in the human heart, the how and why of the entrance of every vice can be traced."

[7]"Progressive" educationists, following Rousseau's abstraction of responsibility from the child, often make extremely naive assessments of child nature.

[8]It is the precise assessment in concrete situations of what a child needs—a problem which, once the child has grown beyond the predominantly biological stage, in most contexts, raises fundamental philosophical issues concerning the ends of human existence, and which educationalists show too little willingness to tackle—which constitutes the value of thinking, educationally, in terms of such "needs." Psychological assessments of these "needs" all too frequently draw attention to the mental presuppositions—and limitations—of the psychologists. And a pervasive stress on physical activity has followed too frequently the Rousseauesque assumption: "let him be a man in strength and he will soon be one in reason" (p. 111).

[9]Rousseau deserves credit, at least, for his perception that such reactions on his part were not the best way of making his pupils "learned and well-disposed." At the same time, his belief that contact with things will never arouse the child's egotism and that the child will accept the discipline of things without resentment shows a surprising lack of observation. Cf. "It looks as if there was a universal tendency to include physical things in the society of living things and to respond to them as such" (W. J. H. Sprott, *Social Psychology*). Certainly, young children make no clear distinction between animate and inanimate objects.

[10]Cf. J. L. Talmon, *Totalitarian Democracy*.

[11]Cf. Reinhold Niebuhr, *The Nature of Man*, particularly Chapter IV, entitled "The Easy Conscience of Modern Man." Very relevant is Rousseau's extraordinary account of how he settled the matter of his own salvation by throwing a stone at a tree, cf. *Confessions*, i, p. 223.

[12]The position is perhaps best summed up in a brief introduction to the study of mental measurement, published in *An Introduction to Modern Psychology* by O. L. Zangwill. Professor Zangwill is there drawing on the researches of Gesell and others: "In 'learning to walk' maturation is far more important than practice; in 'learning to talk,' on the other hand, practice is everything—provided

that the requisite stage of developmental readiness has been reached" (p. 147). We cannot be reminded of this simple truth too often.

[13]*Emile*, p. 140.

[14]Cf. Niebuhr, op. cit.: ". . . the great achievement of modern culture, the understanding of nature, is also the cause of the great confusion of modern man: the misunderstanding of human nature" (p. 101).

[15]*Emile*, p. 49.

[16]Sir Isaiah Berlin has called Rousseau the "first militant lowbrow in history" during a Third Programme broadcast.


## Part 3

### Sidney Hook, *The Teaching of Values*

[1]Cf. Chapter vii, "Standards, Ends and Means," of my book, *John Dewey: An Intellectual Portrait* (New York: John Day Co., 1939).

[2]Morris R. Cohen, "What I Believe," *The Nation*, Vol. 133, No. 3448 (August 5, 1931), p. 130.


### Thomas F. Green, *Judging*

[1]Singer, G. M., William Hay, and Arthur Murphy (eds.), *Reason and the Common Good*, Prentice-Hall, Inc., Englewood Cliffs, N. J., 1963, introduction, p. xi.


## Part 4

### Bruce R. Joyce, *Curriculum and Humanistic Education:* *"Monolism" vs. "Pluralism"*

[1]This description of educational missions has been amplified in Bruce R. Joyce, *Alternative Models for Elementary Education* (Waltham, Mass.: Blaisdell, 1969).

[2]Carl Rogers, *Client Centered Therapy* (Boston: Houghton Mifflin, 1951).

[3]Abraham Maslow, *Toward a Psychology of Being* (Princeton, N. J.: Van Nostrand, 1962).

[4]Leland R. Bradford; Jack Gibb; and Kenneth Benne, eds., *T-Group Theory and Laboratory Method* (New York: John Wiley, 1964).

[5]David Ausubel, *The Psychology of Meaningful Verbal Learning* (New York: Grune and Stratton, 1963).

[6]For curriculum strategies built on Piaget's work see:
(a) Edmund Sullivan, "Piaget and the School Curriculum: A Critical Apprais-

al," Bulletin no. 2 of the Ontario Institute for Studies in Education, 1967.
(b) Irving Siegel, "The Piagetian System and the World of Education," in David Elkind and John Flavell, eds., *Studies in Cognitive Development: Essays in Honor of Jean Piaget* (New York: Oxford University Press, 1969).
(c) Hanne Sonquist, Constance Kamii, and Louise Derman, "A Piaget-Derived Preschool Curriculum," to be published in *Educational Implications of Piaget's Theory: A Book of Readings,* ed. J. J. Athey and D. O. Rubadeau (Waltham, Mass.: Blaisdell, in press).

[7]Joseph Schwab, ed., *The Biology Teachers Handbook* (New York: John Wiley, 1965).

[8]Hilda Taba, *Teaching Strategies and Cognitive Functioning in Elementary School Children,* Cooperative Research Project no. 2404 (San Francisco: San Francisco State College, 1961).

[9]J. Richard Suchman. *The Elementary School Training Program in Scientific Inquiry,* Report of U.S. Office of Education Project Title VIII, Project no. 216 (Urbana: University of Illinois, 1962).

[10]Individually Prescribed Instruction, Learning Research and Development Center, University of Pittsburgh, Pittsburgh, Pa.

[11]Rogers, *Client Centered Therapy.*

[12]See William Schutz, *Joy: Expanding Human Awareness* (New York: Grove Press, 1967).

[13]Fritz Perls, *Gestalt Therapy: Excitement and Growth in Human Personality* (New York: Dell Publishing, 1965).

[14]Dewey, *Democracy and Education.*

[15]Herbert Thelen, *Education and the Human Quest* (New York: Harper & Row, 1960).

[16]H. Gordon Hullfish and Phillip Smith, *Reflective Thinking: The Method of Education* (New York: Dodd, Mead, 1961).

[17]Cox and Massialas, "The Inquiry Potential of the Social Studies."

[18]Taba, *Teaching Strategies and Cognitive Functioning.*

[19]Suchman, *The Elementary School Training Program.*

[20]Siegel, "The Piagetian System. . ." and Sullivan, "Piaget and the School Curriculum."

[21]Louise Tyler, "A Case History: Formulation of Objectives from a Psychoanalytic Framework," *Instructional Objectives,* AERA Monograph no. 3 (Washington, D.C.: National Education Association, 1969).

[22]E. Paul Torrance, *Guiding Creative Behavior* (Englewood Cliffs, N. J.: Prentice-Hall, 1962).

[23]B. F. Skinner, *Verbal Behavior* (New York: Appleton-Century-Crofts, 1957).

[24]David E. Hunt, "A Conceptual Level Matching Model for Coordinating Learner Characteristics with Educational Approaches," *Interchange* 1, no. 2 (June 1970).

[25]The distinction between computer-assisted instruction and computer-monitored instruction is instructive in this regard. Computer-assisted instruction uses computer-controlled devices as the interface between the program and the student and is appropriate only within the cybernetic mode. Computer-monitored instruction orchestrates a wide range of devices, including books, films, etc. The combination—CAI plus CMI—enables the student to employ many learning devices within a program and can be employed in many curricular modes.

Notes